For Mom and Dad

– TD

For Mom and Dad

– RM

Contents

Figures

Contributors

Reuven S. Avi-Yonah, Irwin I. Cohn Professor of Law, Director, International Tax LLM Program at the University of Michigan School of Law

Yariv Brauner, Hugh Culverhouse Eminent Scholar of Law, University of Florida Levin College of Law

Richard Collier, Associate Fellow, University of Oxford, Centre for Business Taxation. Recently a senior tax adviser to the Organization of Economic Cooperation and Development (OECD) to manage the work on taxation of the digitalized economy

Tsilly Dagan, Professor of Taxation Law and co-director of the MSc (in Taxation) at the University of Oxford, Faculty of Law

Steven A. Dean, Professor of Law and Paul Siskind Research Scholar, Boston University School of Law

Mitchell A. Kane, Gerald L. Wallace Professor of Taxation, New York University School of Law, and Editor-in-Chief, Tax Law Review

Ruth Mason, Edwin S. Cohen Distinguished Professor of Law and Taxation and Director of the Virginia Center for Tax Law at the University of Virginia School of Law; Max Planck Law Fellow

Daisy Ogembo, Assistant Professor in Law, University of Birmingham School of Law

Diane M. Ring, Professor of Law and Dr. Thomas F. Carney Distinguished Scholar, Boston College School of Law

Wolfgang Schön, Director and Scientific Member, Max Planck Institute for Tax Law and Public Finance

Daniel Shaviro, Wayne Perry Professor of Taxation, New York University School of Law

Miranda Stewart, Visiting Professor of Tax Law, New York University School of Law; Professor, Melbourne Law School

Afton Titus, Associate Professor in the Commercial Law Department, University of Cape Town

Preface

The modern international tax regime is an intricate web of national laws, bilateral treaties, and multilateral accords aimed at coordinating the entitlement of states to tax individuals. Coordinating state taxes is an old problem. In a 1923 League of Nations report often cited as ushering in the modern international tax system, tax experts observed the decline of political allegiance as an accepted basis for taxing people and the emergence of new – often conflicting – claims by states of entitlements to tax people. More than they ever have before, people operate their lives and livelihoods across national borders, raising difficult questions about which states ought to tax them, and how such taxation can be enforced. Legal, technological, and economic changes have led to fragmentation of the social contract, dissociating the receipt of economic opportunities and public goods and services from the obligation to pay taxes for redistribution. Such fragmentation makes it more difficult for states to promote the collective choices of their constituents and to reconcile states' sometimes-conflicting duties to liberty and justice. Although contributing to individual liberty and economic growth, the fragmentation of aspects of individuals' personal, economic, and political lives across multiple countries has stretched the international consensus to its breaking point, uncovering deep divisions between states over tax entitlements.

Confronted with the most dramatic changes in international tax policy in the past century, scholars across the globe have devoted time and energy to advancing our understanding of the impacts of globalization and digitalization on taxation, carefully studying and criticizing emerging cooperative accords and proposing alternatives. But most of this scholarship has focused on business taxation, and in particular on the multilateral efforts to reform corporate taxation that have been led by the Organization on Economic Cooperation and Development (OECD). These reform efforts have included the Base Erosion and Profit Shifting (BEPS) Project and the more recent so-called two-pillar solution relating to the taxation of the digital economy and a global corporate minimum tax.

This book reflects that the future of international taxation – the next 100 years – will also require rethinking the taxation of people. We must go back to basics to reconsider the complex bonds linking individuals and their states. Increased globalization demands that we rethink taxing people for practical as well as for normative reasons. First, as measured by revenue, taxes on natural persons are typically the largest source of revenue for developed countries, far surpassing business taxes. As such, they are essential for providing public goods and services, supporting state institutions, and promoting justice; and they are therefore essential in legitimizing the power of the state to tax. Just as importantly, individual taxes generate incentives that affect behavior, wealth, and overall wellbeing. Globalization has granted mobility to people and resources, but it has also precipitously increased tax competition and made it more difficult for states to collect taxes. These phenomena not only erode states' ability to provide public goods and services and to promote justice, they also raise major normative questions: the belonging of people to one state or another, the parameters of domestic justice, and questions of global justice all demand re-consideration.

To analyze the next century of taxing people, we assembled an impressive team of tax academics. Our authors hail from four continents and from countries facing widely different tax challenges, all brought on by the same global forces. Rising to the challenges posed by overwhelming social, economic, and technological shifts, our authors consider how the twenty-first century will alter the goals and methods of individual taxation, and they make predictions on what roles governments and international institutions will play in designing taxes for the next century. Each chapter puts people at its core. Part I examines the interaction between people and their states in the new economy. Part II explores new options for global tax governance. Part III takes a closer look at evolving social issues such as remote work and aging, and considers how individual taxation should tackle them.

PEOPLE AND STATES

The rallying cry "no taxation without representation" stresses the close connection between taxation and political representation. Globalization, however, has attenuated this connection. Increased mobility has both severed people's ties with their countries of nationality and caused them to form new ties with other countries. These changes raise deep questions about who should count as a member of the national community, including for the purposes of distributing the benefits and burdens of fiscal policy. Old tax concepts and systems must be rethought and adapted to the new ways that people live.

In Chapter 1, *Must Everybody Pay Tax Somewhere?*, Wolfgang Schön observes that most academics view states as moral actors and argue that states have a moral duty to arrange their tax systems to promote what commentators have referred to as "global tax justice." Schön, however, tackles the question at the level of the individual and asks whether every individual is morally obliged to pay progressive taxes that account for income and wealth. He explains that the notion of social justice requires "the identification of a 'collective,' which provides the framework to produce public goods and to arrange for redistribution." This collective may be statist, cosmopolitan, or something in between, but Schön explains that, because there exists no "truly global tax authority," the only functioning tax systems to which a person could owe a moral duty to pay tax exist at the state level. In Schön's view, even if a moral duty to pay redistributive taxes to support a global community exists, because the apparatus to collect and distribute that tax does not exist, no person can be morally condemned for not paying. According to Schön, "if states fail at implementing supranational structures to establish a worldwide tax order or to coordinate in a fashion that ensures a 'single-tax principle' for individuals or to organize global modes of redistribution, it is not the obligation of the individual to compensate for this deficiency, if indeed it is a deficiency." On the state level, too, Schön claims that no one can morally criticize a particular individual for failing to pay taxes if the state does not impose any. Thus, whereas Schön starts by turning the focus from states to the moral duties of individuals, he ends up concluding that individuals' moral duty to pay tax is conditional upon the government's imposition of a demand to pay tax. Put differently, no person is obliged to impose a tax upon themselves.

In Chapter 2, *Comfortably Numb: Should the Reign of Residence over the International Tax Regime Continue in the Twenty-First Century?*, Yariv Brauner argues against the traditional source-and-residence paradigm for international tax. Current consensus practices acknowledge the entitlement of two states – the source state and the residence state – to tax cross-border income. Source jurisdiction reflects a nexus between the taxing state and income produced within the state. Residence jurisdiction reflects a link between the taxing state and the owner of income. Brauner argues that human mobility in the twenty-first century has caused source and residence to diverge for individuals (especially the wealthiest among them). Brauner calls for a radical reexamination of how we tax individuals, and, in particular, he recommends abandoning residence taxation in favor of exclusive source taxation. Returning to basics, Brauner argues that residence-based taxation of individuals never had a strong justification. Acknowledging that source taxation is only justified to the extent that the rules for sourcing income are themselves justified, Brauner demurs on the precise content of the source rules after his proposed reform. He emphasizes, however, the importance of "a universal unified system of accounting and sourcing income," and he prefers a formulary approach to determining source.

In Chapter 3, *Taxing Nomads: Reviving Citizenship-based Taxation for the Twenty-First Century*, Reuven S. Avi-Yonah draws on the same factors recounted by Brauner – the rise of remote work, digital nomads, and state regimes that employ accommodating tax policies to attract the high income and wealthy – to draw nearly opposite conclusions from Brauner's. Instead of ditching residence tax and reforming source tax, Avi-Yonah would solve the perceived problem of tax dodging by the mobile rich via the widespread adoption of citizenship taxation, including the taxation of citizens permanently residing abroad. Pointing out that most academics – himself included – have criticized the US citizenship tax as anachronistic at best and unfair and impossible to administer at worst, Avi-Yonah argues that the rise of remote work justifies a second look at citizenship taxation. On his account, citizenship taxation can be justified on ability-to-pay grounds. Asserting that nonresident US citizens are members of the same "political community" as resident US citizens, Avi-Yonah reasons that nonresident citizens should "share in the tax burden imposed on that community." He therefore concludes that "all (and only) adults entitled to vote" should be taxable on a citizenship basis. Though diametrically opposed to Brauner's proposal, Avi-Yonah's is no less radical. Whereas Brauner would eliminate residence taxation entirely in favor of robust and exclusive source taxation on the basis of ability to pay, Avi-Yonah would lodge entitlement to tax on the basis of ability to pay – at least in the first instance – in the citizenship state, which is usually, but not always, the residence state. Avi-Yonah recognizes, however, that ending ability-to-pay taxation at source could inspire tax-avoidance behavior, so he suggests several measures for when citizenship tax is infeasible in a particular case; these measures include exit taxation and backup ability-to-pay taxation at source. These measures should also apply, in Avi-Yonah's view, where the citizenship state is not a democracy.

Chapter 4, *Reconsidering Citizenship Taxation*, is our own contribution. We examine citizenship taxation as a potential solution to the challenges of globalization and migration. Although we agree with Avi-Yonah and others that taxing citizens no matter where they live or work might enable states to overcome tax competition and tax-motivated migration, we argue that citizenship alone is too crude a basis for imposing the obligation to contribute taxes on the basis of ability to pay. We analyze both practical and theoretical challenges, including the struggles of the United States (one of the only countries with a citizenship tax) to effectively enforce its citizenship tax regime, the fairness implications of using citizenship as a tax nexus, and the particular difficulties faced by poorer countries in implementing such systems. We conclude that a combination of citizenship and residence factors might better reflect genuine community membership and the moral obligations to contribute to taxes for redistribution than would citizenship alone. We also explore the possibilities and limitations of multilateral cooperation in implementing citizenship taxation, warning that such cooperation might disproportionately benefit stronger states at the expense of weaker ones. Ultimately, we conclude that, while citizenship taxation might work for powerful nations like the United States, it may remain impractical for most countries, leaving unresolved the fundamental challenge of how states can maintain their tax base and pursue distributive justice in an increasingly globalized world.

INTERNATIONAL GOVERNANCE CHALLENGES AND SOLUTIONS

Globalization has already led to major developments in corporate taxation, and adaptations will likewise be necessary for the taxation of people. While global governance can help resolve some of the challenges of individual taxation under competition, such governance raises concerns for democratic accountability and justice within and between nations. Part II considers significant challenges and some radical solutions for international tax governance. Together, the contributions in Part II help us rethink old convictions and broaden our imagination when it comes to global governance.

In Chapter 5, *Exit, Voice, and Electivity: Confronting the Rise of Private Money and Private Taxation*, Mitchell A. Kane explores four trends that will fundamentally alter identity formation and the relationship between individuals and the state, potentially challenging the state's monopoly on taxation – the proliferation of powerful nonstate actors, climate change, the erosion of democratic norms, and the growth of cryptocurrency and blockchain technologies. Instead of religion, nationality, or politics, Kane argues that, in the digital age, group-based identities are increasingly based on nonstate associations, including firms, political or ideological organizations that lack formal recognition as states, social media networks, and online peer-to-peer communities. Kane explains that, at present, we largely associate the power to create money (and crucially, the power to tax it) with the sovereign state. In this way, identity, money, and tax come together. But what happens when they come apart? One possibility he envisions is a future where large corporations or consortiums could issue their own stable cryptocurrencies that rival state-issued fiat currencies. This could enable these private actors to also impose "private taxation" that functions similarly to state taxation, and he explains how people might come to feel compelled to use the private currency and pay the associated levies, which come to function like taxes. Rejecting such private taxation, Kane proposes that individual taxpayers could elect to allocate some fraction of their domestic tax liability to jurisdictions of their choice, in satisfaction of their domestic tax liability. Such a mechanism would allow taxpayers to "vote" directly with their tax dollars. Though Kane admits his proposal is radical, he argues it could have wide appeal. For those distrustful of centralized state power, the mechanisms may reward or punish various policies based on a market-like mechanism. For those who take a more cosmopolitan approach to global distributive justice, the proposal would allow one to direct funds to places in the world that may seem more in need.

In Chapter 6, *Fear of a Black Planet: Africa's Decolonisation and the Transformation of the International Tax Regime*, Steven A. Dean questions received wisdom about the history of tax policymaking. He describes that, in the early 1950s, the United Nations (UN) welcomed recently independent African members. However, notwithstanding the existence and vibrancy of tax policy debates in this newly inclusive forum, Dean explains that a small set of wealthy countries preferred to conduct international tax policy at the Organization for Economic Cooperation and Development (OECD) because it "offered a reassuring, all-white alternative" to the UN. Instead of considering ongoing policy debates at the UN, Dean explains that the OECD "reached back to the work of the League of Nations from the 1920s."

It was this move that cemented the now-familiar treaty framework "capable of preserving the substance of empire in a post-imperial age." Instead of "nurtur[ing] the fiscal economy of poor countries," the League's double tax treaties, upon which the OECD relied, made poor countries poorer. Despite liberated African nations' dire need for revenue to fund education and other social programs long denied under imperialism, tax treaties were not designed to serve those needs. Dean likens tax policymaking at the OECD, which he argues is controlled by the United States, to the aftermath of the US Civil War when white schools were far better funded than were black schools, and many other policies, both official and unofficial, including poll taxes and violence, undermined freedom and equality. In addition to seeing historical parallels between the failure of Reconstruction in the American South and the outcomes of international tax policymaking in the last century, Dean also sees lessons. He presents insights from Reconstruction as to how the OECD could secure meaningful participation in global tax governance for OECD nonmember states. Additionally, using his analogy to Reconstruction, Dean poses vital questions about tax policymaking in our own time, namely, *how inclusive is the Inclusive Framework?* and *does the Inclusive Framework's much-celebrated consensus on the Pillars represent the outcome of "a truly free and fair decision making process"?*

In Chapter 7, *Embracing the African Union and the African Tax Administration Forum in Tax Governance*, Afton Titus reviews the literature explicating and criticizing the failure of current forums – especially the OECD – to reflect, much less serve, the interests of developing countries. Recounting efforts to improve inclusivity, Titus observes that inclusivity is needed not only at the implementation stage, but also at the agenda-setting stage of international tax policymaking. Titus points out that the African Tax Administration Forum (ATAF) has already been working closely with the African Union (AU) to address the work stemming from the OECD's Pillars. But the ambitious proposal that Titus puts forward goes beyond the ATAF. She envisions building upon Africa's eight pre-existing regional economic communities (RECs) – through which 80 percent of intra-African trade flows – to develop tax policy positions and proposals. She explains that, among other benefits, such a policy structure would help countries meet national tax policy objectives, promote economic integration that would improve people's lives, and increase political accountability. Concluding that African countries must "seize the opportunity to make their own decisions for their own people rather than wait for an invitation to do so," Titus proposes an African tax policy structure that would be "completely devoted" to the concerns of its own people.

SOCIAL TRANSFORMATION AND TAXATION

The beginning of the twenty-first century witnessed significant social changes in the labor market, demographics, the distribution of wealth, and political communities. Part III considers how tax policy can be used as a tool to respond to them.

In Chapter 8, *Transformative Constitutionalism: The Role of Citizens in (Tax) State-Building: The Case of Kenya*, Daisy Ogembo explains that the colonial government of Kenya cultivated ethnic divisions and involved "no consent, consultation or participation by the native communities." Because colonial taxation was designed to "force[] more Africans into wage employment," no meaningful sense of citizenship, national identity, or representation was associated with taxation under colonialism. Although the term "citizen" at last applied to Kenyans after independence, authoritarianism prevented nation building, and one-party rule led to dissatisfaction, which in turn was reflected in politically motivated tax evasion. By contrast, Ogembo explains that today, the mandate for "public participation" in the 2010 Kenyan Constitution informs all aspects of tax policymaking. Ogembo sees the public participation mandate as an element of transformative constitutionalism and as an auspicious tool of "tax state-building" due to its potential to "provide significant opportunities to empower citizens, enhance sentiments of belonging, unity, and nationhood, provide the National Assembly with diverse and innovative views, improve the relationship between citizens and the state, and all these benefits contribute to state-building, responsiveness, and accountability." Despite identifying certain risks associated with public deliberation, Ogembo sees public deliberation not only as "shap[ing] the taxation of citizens well into the next century" but also as providing a "crucial opportunity for citizens to play a role in state-building through their participation in tax policy, administration, and legislative processes."

In Chapter 9, *A Century of Labor and Taxation*, Diane M. Ring examines how technological changes and the COVID-19 pandemic have fundamentally transformed the nature of work and its implications for tax policy. She argues that these shifts – particularly the rise of remote work, platform-based employment, and changing worker classifications – are creating significant challenges for traditional tax systems. Ring identifies several key areas requiring reform: the treatment of home office and commuting expenses, worker classification between employees and independent contractors, and jurisdictional issues in taxing remote workers across borders. Ring warns against treating workers more like businesses and less like people, and she emphasizes the importance of maintaining robust tax administration infrastructure to support social safety nets during crises. Looking forward, Ring explains that emerging trends like artificial intelligence and climate change will further complicate workforce taxation, suggesting that tax systems must evolve to address these challenges while ensuring the fair treatment of workers and maintaining stable government revenues.

In Chapter 10, *The Individual, Mobility, and the Corporate*, Richard Collier explores the complex relationship between individual mobility, particularly within multinational enterprises (MNEs), and corporate taxation. Collier argues that existing income-allocation and permanent-establishment (PE) rules – designed to anchor taxable profits to physical locations and decision-making activities – are poorly suited to a world where high-level employees are increasingly mobile.

Mobility can inadvertently trigger taxable presences or permanent establishments, raising thorny issues in profit attribution under transfer-pricing principles and exacerbating disputes between tax authorities. These challenges are particularly acute for senior employees whose decision-making contributes significantly to corporate value, magnifying both tax exposures and administrative complexity. Collier concludes that the tax system, developed with assumptions of immobility, is ill-equipped to handle the realities of modern work patterns and, without substantial reform, disputes and ambiguities will likely continue to escalate.

In Chapter 11, *Time Is, Time Was: Evaluating the Use of the Life-Cycle Model as a Fiscal Tool,* Daniel Shaviro evaluates the use of the life-cycle model as a tool for fiscal policy analysis. He argues that, although the life-cycle model makes a compelling case for evaluating individuals on a lifetime basis rather than annually, there are significant practical and philosophical challenges with the approach. These include borrowing constraints, changes in information over time, and deviations from the assumption of equal marginal utility of consumption across periods. Shaviro argues that the value of the life-cycle model lies as much in showing us where to look for falsifying conditions as in its actual empirical accuracy. Shaviro considers several assumptions of the standard economic model, and he argues for a more nuanced, more complex depiction of reality that could better capture differences between different people and differences within a single individual over time. Taking a deeper look, Shaviro concludes that "there is no simple answer to the question of how lifetime, as opposed to shorter periods (themselves requiring further definition) should be used in measuring economic inequality, fiscal progressivity or the question of why (and how much) inequality matters." But he convincingly argues that it may be more important to practice "methodological humility and agnosticism in how we think about these issues."

In Chapter 12, *Living Long and Living Well: Tax Systems and Population Ageing,* Miranda Stewart discusses the effect of recent changes in economic and demographic conditions on tax and welfare states. She describes the development project of the twentieth century, which relied on economic growth and – importantly – on a gendered care economy. Care focused on children's needs, and women bore much of its costs. In the twenty-first century, aging populations increase the need for care giving. At the same time, aging slows down economic growth and contributes to higher wealth inequality, creating tensions in the gendered distribution of work, care, and wealth. Stewart reviews the demographic trends of ageing and dependency in society, and she emphasizes the gender inequality of care, as well as its resulting wealth inequality. Analyzing these phenomena, Stewart concludes that tax and welfare policies must adjust to these changing conditions to enable a more equal distribution of the cost of care and economic returns, so that we can live long and well in the next 100 years.

Acknowledgments

Over a beautiful two days in June 2023, the authors of the chapters in this book met with international tax experts from around the world, who generously offered comments on all of the draft papers. These comments enormously improved this book, and we thank: Eduardo Baistrocchi (London School of Economics), Philip Baker (Field Court Tax Chambers and University of Oxford), Douglas Bamford (University of Oxford), Anzhela Cédelle (OECD), Michael Devereux (University of Oxford), Ana Paula Dourado (University of Lisbon), Judith Freedman (University of Oxford), Andrew Hayashi (University of Virginia), Martin Hearson (International Centre for Tax and Development and Institute of Development Studies), Michael Lennard (United Nations), Giorgia Maffini (PwC), Susan Morse (University of Texas), Ann Mumford (Kings College London), Victoria Perry (International Monetary Fund, retired, and Georgetown University), Linda Sugin (Fordham University), Alice Pirlot (Geneva Graduate Institute), John Vella (University of Oxford), and Madelline Woker (University of Sheffield).

We owe enormous thanks to Agata Dybisz for her tireless and excellent organization of the conference; no better manager exists. We are also grateful to our research assistants: Matthew Freeman, Jenny Ho, Peter Lernyei, Dominick Luczak, Matthew Turk, and Yvette Wakabi. We are particularly grateful to Katherine Kenny for leading the team of research assistants, and to Shreya Rao, Amedeo Rizzo, and Louis Triggs for their conference notes. We are grateful to the University of Oxford, Oxford Faculty of Law, and the University of Virginia School of Law for generously funding the event, and, finally, we owe deepest thanks to Matthew Gallaway, of Cambridge University Press, for making the publication process such an enjoyable one.

PART I

People and States

1

Must Everybody Pay Tax Somewhere?

Wolfgang Schön

It may further be urged that a man owes certain duties to humanity, and if he fails to discharge the offices of citizenship at home, it is ethically allowable for a foreign government which can lay its hands on him, to force him to do his part towards the support of government.

Richard Theodore Ely (1854–1943), Taxation in American states and cities, 1888, p.9, Fn.2 (discussing the justification to tax foreign citizens)

INTRODUCTION: A 'FAIR SHARE' IN A DECENTRALISED WORLD

In the international tax debate, it is claimed that everybody should pay their 'fair share' of taxes. While this call has been raised in the first place to denounce a perceived lack of tax compliance by (multinational) businesses,[1] the concept of the 'fair share' has evolved into a general societal expectation towards individuals as well.[2] People – it is said – should not be in the position to avoid shouldering a tax burden commensurate with their ability to pay. This proposition is accompanied by large-scale empirical research meant to show the extent to which well-heeled and well-advised individuals are able to reduce their personal tax burden.[3] Today, the public movement for fair taxation to address (ever-growing) public needs seems to be omnipresent.

I would like to thank Johanna Stark for helpful discussions on this matter, Tsilly Dagan and Ruth Mason for their thoughtful editing of this chapter, Michael Devereux for his comment, and the other participants of the workshop 'Taxing People: The Next 100 Years' at Worcester College, Oxford, in June 2023, for further inspiration.

[1] See Maarten Floris de Wilde, Sharing the Pie: Taxing Multinationals in a Global Market 51 (IBFD 2017) (analysing fairness).

[2] Allison Christians, *Buying In: Residence and Citizenship by Investment*, 62 St. Louis U. L.J. 51, 52 (2017).

[3] See Gabriel Zucman, *Taxing across Borders: Tracking Personal Wealth and Corporate Profits*, 28 J. Econ. Perspect. 121 (2014); Henrik Kleven et al., *Taxation and Migration: Evidence and Policy Implications*, 34 J. Econ. Perspect. 119 (2020).

While it is relatively simple to express moral disdain towards those who avoid paying despite their high levels of wealth, income, and consumption, it is much more difficult to answer the fundamental question of where those people should pay their 'fair share'. This issue has become even more complex in recent years as we observe an enormous increase in personal mobility on a global scale. With the rise of mobile high net-worth individuals, transient digital nomads, Olympic citizens,[4] itinerant workers, and more, it becomes increasingly difficult to determine which tax authority should prescribe and enforce tax claims against humans who have no substantial allegiance with a specific country. Which government can rightfully claim to tap a person's financial capacity when it comes to the provision of public goods enjoyed in that country's territory? And, when we talk about solidarity and redistribution as a primary goal of taxation, we must know more. Specifically, we must know to whom the presumed taxpayer should offer support.

Taxation does not exist outside the context of a specific state (or other public entity) that is responsible for both the implementation of distributive justice and the production of public goods. *Robinson Crusoe* on his island is not subject to a tax at all. We need an identifiable and organised community to establish taxation along different dimensions: public or 'common' goods require the delineation of the 'public' or the 'community' enjoying those goods, and redistribution requires a defined group of individuals of which the potential taxpayer is a 'member', thus enabling and justifying financial transfers within that community. How can we put into practice Richard Theodore Ely's impressive and touching admonition that every person's obligation to pay taxes is grounded in 'duties to humanity'? His claim that everybody should 'do his part towards support of government' provides no guidance on the question of *which government* should impose that duty. To this day, there exists no 'world government' steering the whole of humanity, creating global public goods, and organising redistribution across all mankind.[5]

But the problem runs deeper than the technical questions of which tax administration should levy a tax, and who should decide for what purpose the ensuing revenue should be spent. The global debate about tax justice is not only a debate about individuals (and businesses) trying to avoid financial sacrifice. The debate also concerns the right of states to abstain from taxation, i.e. the willingness of many states to use their fiscal autonomy to create a beneficial tax environment for mobile

[4] Ayelet Shachar, *Picking Winners: Olympic Citizens and the Global Race for Talent*, 120 Yale L.J. 2088 (2011).

[5] Tsilly Dagan, International Tax Policy between Competition and Cooperation 205 (Cambridge University Press, 2018) (the proposal by Peters that global interventions by non-governmental organisations (NGO) can somehow substitute for a world government clashes with deficiencies arising from the lack of democratic legitimacy of those institutions); see also, Cees Peters, *Global Tax Justice: Who's Involved?*, *in* Ethics and Taxation 165 (Robert F. van Brederode ed., 2020).

individuals, offering preferential treatment going as far as providing zero-taxation.[6] These policies are an important element of 'tax competition', a concept analysed in the past mainly in business taxation but which has emerged in recent years as a major factor shaping taxation of individuals as well.[7]

Due to their fiscal autonomy and protected by general principles and treaties under international law, jurisdictions engaging in tax competition are to some extent able to prevent other countries from interfering with the beneficial treatment they award to these much sought-after individuals.[8] Critics[9] complain about a lack of coordination between governments when it comes to ensuring the payment of the 'fair share' – but whose fault is this? Can we blame taxpayers for accepting offers from sovereign states to reduce or even wipe out their personal tax burden?

'EVERYBODY' AND THEIR DEFINING FEATURES

As we begin the analysis, it seems necessary to define what is meant by the term 'everybody'. One should exclude legal persons from this analysis and start from the assumption that 'everybody' in the context of this chapter means a human being, that is physically present somewhere on land and sea at all times, engages in consumption at his or her place of physical presence (and possibly in other places as well), and finances consumption by owning assets or deriving income.[10]

6 Mitchell Kane, *Tax and Human Rights: The Moral Valence of Entitlements to Tax, Sovereignty, and Collectives, in* TAX, INEQUALITY, AND HUMAN RIGHTS 99, 103 (Philip Alston & Nikki Reisch ed. 2019).

7 Sarah Godar et al., *New Forms of Tax Competition*, EU Tax Observatory, Report No.3, 9–18 (2021); David Gstrein et al., *Harmful Tax Practices and Competition in the Area of Personal Income and Wealth Taxation, In-Depth Analysis Requested by the FISC Committee of the European Parliament* (Jan. 2022), www.europarl.europa.eu/RegData/etudes/IDAN/2022/703343/IPOL_IDA(2022)703343_EN.pdf.

8 On the different dimensions of the 'jurisdiction not to tax', see Aitor Navarro, *Jurisdiction Not to Tax, Tax Sparing Clauses, and the OECD Minimum Taxation (GloBE) Proposal*, 1 NORDIC TAX J. 6, 6–19 (2021); Belisa Ferreira Liotti, *Limits of International Cooperation: The Concept of 'Jurisdiction not to Tax' from the BEPS Project to GloBE*, 76 BULLETIN FOR INT'L TAXATION 63, 63–81 (2022).

9 Giorgio Beretta, *Cross-Border Mobility of Individuals and the Lack of Fiscal Policy Coordination among Jurisdictions (Even) after the BEPS Project*, 47 INTERTAX 91, 104–107 (2019).

10 In this context it seems sensible to exempt children and other dependents from this analysis as they regularly only consume without acquiring or owning the necessary financial means themselves. Rather one can safely assume that the owner of the wealth or the recipient of the income will – on the basis of family ties – feel emotionally or morally or even legally incentivised to provide means of consumption to his or her family members. In the language of economics they form one 'household' acting like an individual. Thus, one can regard consumption by dependents as an extended mode of consumption by the owner of the relevant assets and/or the recipient of the underlying income. It does not change the nature or the outcome of the analysis.

WHAT DOES IT MEAN TO 'PAY A TAX'?

Before we can go into the details of our research question, one additional clarification is in order: what does it mean to 'pay a tax'? From the legal perspective, this notion is related to the legal obligation to transfer financial means to the state authorities as required by that state's fiscal legislation.[11] Going beyond this legal approach, which is mainly focused on direct taxes (income tax, net wealth tax, inheritance tax, etc.), the notion of 'paying a tax' has to be applied in the context of indirect taxes. These are taxes which are legally owed and formally paid by a taxable person (e.g., a seller or a service provider) but which are according to the intention of the legislator – meant to be borne by their counterparty. This is where nobody can fully escape the impact of taxation. One can even say that a country that tries to attract foreign individuals to migrate to that country will do so with the aim of incentivising the immigrants to spend money in that territory, to consume goods and services and to enable their counterparties – employees, independent contractors, and so on – to pay taxes.[12]

Is this kind of factual taxation the answer to the 'fair share' debate? While it is true that the mechanics of tax incidence will prevent tax-exempt individuals from being completely 'tax free', one can imagine that this outcome will not satisfy those who plead for the 'fair share' being paid by highly mobile individuals. Any incidence-based tax burden inflicted on the migrant will not work on a 'progressive' basis as indirect taxes are typically levied at a flat standard rate and even the incidence of direct taxes paid by the tax-exempt person's counterparties (e.g., taxes paid by service providers) will not consider the comprehensive income or all assets of a person.

Taking a closer look, it is fair to say that the underlying theme of the fairness debate is not the lack of any tax burden (legally and factually) on mobile individuals. It is rather the lack of a progressive direct tax system, which takes full account of income and wealth.[13]

A LEGAL OBLIGATION TO PAY TAXES?

Example

D is a Dutch citizen, who attended school and university in the Netherlands. He left his home country thirty years ago and worked for an international organisation

[11] This definition of a 'tax' is borrowed from OECD, Revenue Statistics, Interpretative Guide; see *Revenue Statetives, Interpretative Guide*, OECD 1 (2021) www.oecd.org/tax/tax-policy/oecd-classification-taxes-interpretative-guide.pdf.

[12] Christians, *supra* note 2, at 51–53.

[13] Allison Christians & Laurens van Apeldoorn, Tax Cooperation in an Unjust World 26 (Oxford University Press, 2021); the demise of progressive taxation under the auspices of international mobility of individuals is described by Henry Ordower. See Henry Ordower, *Immigration, Emigration, Fungible Labour and Progressive Taxation, in* Tax Justice and Tax Law: Understanding Unfairness in Tax Systems 133, 133–152 (Dominic de Cogan & Peter Harris ed., 2020).

located in the United States, and in different developing countries after that. After retirement, he moved to Portugal, planning to grow wine grapes.

D's pension will be taxed nowhere. The Netherlands will not tax it as D is neither a resident of the Netherlands nor does he derive income from Dutch sources. The United States will not tax him as the Double Tax Convention between the United States and Portugal allocates the right to tax pensions to Portugal. Portugal will not tax him as the Portuguese government has decided to attract foreigners by offering a scheme under which foreign income is tax exempt for 'non-habitual residents'.[14]

Home Country and Source Country

The Traditional Layout

In the world of direct taxation (income tax, net wealth tax, inheritance tax) a tax can be levied both in the home country of a person and in the source country, that is, the country where income is derived and assets are held.

Nevertheless, the very concept of the 'home country' is not unambiguous as the prerequisites of unlimited tax liability differ from country to country.[15] Unlimited tax liability can be imposed based on citizenship, a traditional concept stressing the 'personal allegiance' of a human being to a state that is wedded to the nineteenth century evolution of the nation-state but went out of fashion as the defining element for worldwide taxation in the twentieth century. Today, taxation according to citizenship is applied by the United States[16] and a few more countries, in particular Eritrea, which levies a 2 per cent 'diaspora tax' to fund a war,[17] and Hungary.[18] By contrast, most countries prescribe worldwide taxation on the basis of 'residence' which is by nature a fuzzy notion as it mingles a territorial element (residence) with a personal element (unlimited tax liability).[19]

14 In 2020, Portugal introduced a 10 percent tax on pension income received by foreign residents, accompanied by a tax exemption for foreign-source income; in late 2023, the Portuguese Government decided to phase out these benefits over ten years.

15 Hugh J. Ault et al., Comparative Income Taxation 563, 563–567 (4th ed., WoltersKluwer 2020).

16 Michael S. Kirsch, *Taxing Citizens in a Global Economy*, 82 N. Y. U. L. Rev. 443 (2006); Ruth Mason, *Citizenship Taxation*, 89 S. Cal. L. Rev. 169 (2016); Allison Christians, A *Global Perspective on Citizenship-Based Taxation*, 38 Michi. J. Int'l L. 193 (2017); Chapter 3, by Reuven Avi-Yonah.

17 DSP-groep Amsterdam, Tilburg School of Humanities, Department of Culture Studies, *The 2% Tax for Eritreans in the Diaspora* (2020), www.tweedekamer.nl/kamerstukken/detail/detail?id = 2017D25761&did = 2017D25761.

18 *Taxation of International Executives: Hungary*, KPMG at 6 (Jan. 2023), https://assets.kpmg.com/content/dam/kpmg/xx/pdf/2023/01/TIES-Hungary.pdf.

19 Wolfgang Schön, *Persons and Territories; on the International Allocation of Taxing Rights*, 6 Brit. Tax Rev. 554. 555–562 (2010); for a broadening of the concept of tax citizenship, see Yvette Lind, A *Critical Analysis of How Formal and Informal Citizenship Influence Justice between Mobile Taxpayers, in* Tax Justice and Tax Law: Understanding Unfairness in Tax Systems 117, 117–132 (Dominic de Cogan & Peter Harris ed., 2020).

Moreover, the legal concept of home country affiliation is not necessarily a binary 'black or white' concept as some jurisdictions use a sliding scale that increases the tax as a person's personal or economic attachments to the jurisdiction increase. A major example is the United Kingdom, under whose laws mere 'residence' has to be distinguished from 'domicile', which requires not only ongoing physical presence but also a willingness to make the United Kingdom one's home country in the long run – without necessarily aiming at full citizenship.[20] As a result, under UK tax law, 'resident' taxpayers are treated more benevolently than 'domiciled' taxpayers with regard to their foreign income, which for resident taxpayers is only taxed on a 'remittance basis' for up to 15 years after taking residence.[21]

The concept of 'source' – meaning the territorial attachment of income or assets as a basis for limited tax liability – is even more amorphous than the concept of 'residence', as it is meant to identify a specific link between a fiscal territory and an item of income or an asset.[22]

The Impact of Tax Competition on Source Country Taxation and Home Country Taxation

It is a well-known fact that downward pressure on the level of income taxation, wealth taxation, and inheritance taxation is largely due to the rise of international tax competition. Tax competition has been widely examined in the context of business taxation or taxation of capital (income), which can both be conceptualised as taxation at source. But the demise of source country taxation cannot on its own fuel the current debate about individuals paying their 'fair share'. This outcome requires not only a reduction in source taxation but also a waiver of residence taxation. One must fully realize that a defining feature of the current international tax order is the simultaneous erosion of home country taxation and source country taxation.[23] Non-taxation will result if neither the home nor the source country use their fiscal powers to tax a certain item of income or a certain asset. To the extent mobile individuals can benefit from this effect, international taxpayers may face less tax than domestic taxpayers or even no tax at all.

A Non-Binary Status for Mobile Taxpayers?

The combined effect of tax competition at the level of source countries and home countries can result in 'double non-taxation'. One can see this as problematic and

[20] Jonathan Schwarz, Booth & Schwarz Residence, Domicile and UK Taxation 9.01 (21st ed., Bloomsbury 2022).

[21] Id., at 1.15, pp. 12–13.

[22] Hugh J. Ault & David F. Bradford, *Taxing International Income: An Analysis of the U.S. System and Its Economic Premises* 26 (NBER Working Paper No.3056 1989); Ruth Mason, *The Transformation of International Tax*, 114 Am. J. Int'l L. 353, 385–393 (2020).

[23] Christians & van Apeldoorn, *supra* note 13, at 42.

call upon governments to refrain from such policies and to coordinate a 'single-tax principle' for individuals. But it would be overly simplistic to say that the governments of the involved countries are not behaving rationally. For the source country, attracting inbound investment might be worth giving up direct taxation of foreign investors; why should they – in particular 'poor countries' – care about meaningful taxation in the home country?[24] For the home country, attracting inbound migration of special groups might be worth the (same) sacrifice without having regard to a lack of fiscal burden in the source country. To give one example: An industrialised country, such as Italy, offers the most attractive tax waivers to people willing to relocate to small towns in Southern Italy and in 'seismic areas'[25] – obviously a desperate move to stop the depopulation of large areas of the country.

This seems to lead to a paradigm shift in international taxation of individuals. The old principle that the home state will automatically make up for any deficiency in source taxation doesn't hold any more. Home states now tend to create a new status for mobile individuals between mere source taxation (which is applicable to non-resident taxpayers) and unlimited tax liability (which is applicable to immobile residents). They allow mobile resident individuals to be taxed on a territorial basis or to pay a lump-sum tax on foreign income at least for a limited amount of time. In any case, these mobile individuals are not subject to comprehensive taxation of income and assets at the regular progressive tax rate applied to other resident taxpayers.

A new non-binary status of taxpayers thus has been created, who are (from a fiscal point of view) not yet full members of the local community of taxpayers.[26] But most states are not willing to maintain migrant taxpayers in this privileged 'intermediate' status in the long run. Under current legislative practice, these tax benefits are not only time-limited, they also only apply to foreign citizens and not to the jurisdiction's own nationals or to persons who had spent a substantial amount of time in the country. The privileged treatment reflects the perception that these persons, while being (newly) fully resident in a country, do not (yet) fully belong to the local community of regular taxpayers.

A MORAL OBLIGATION TO PAY TAXES?

States and Individuals and Moral Responsibility

Non-taxation of individuals requires interaction between two partners: states that offer tax exemptions and individuals willing to shape their behaviour to benefit from

[24] David C. Elkins, *The Merits of Tax Competition in a Globalized Economy*, 91 IND. L.J. 905, 950 (2016).

[25] *7 Percent Flat Tax for Pensioners Coming to Live in the South of Italy*, ITALIAN TAX (2020), https://taxing.it/7-per-cent-flat-tax-for-pensioners-coming-to-live-in-the-of-south-italy/.

[26] David C. Elkins, A *Scalar Conception of Tax Residence for Individuals*, 41 VA. TAX REV. 149, 172–178 (2021).

these exemptions. Thus, the question of whether non-taxation of an individual infringes on certain moral obligations can be addressed both to states and to individuals.

Most of the academic writing in this area looks to the states as moral actors. They are perceived as the mainstays of 'social justice', and the bone of contention is to what extent they are obliged to establish social justice only within their borders or whether they are obliged to contribute to an international tax order striving for 'global' tax justice. This issue of mutual obligations of justice between fiscal states has been raised under the heading of 'inter-nation equity'.[27] Today there are two strands of the academic debate which focus on possible moral duties between states:

- The debate on 'tax competition' which examines the morally acceptable ways and means available for countries to attract capital (including human capital) and to increase revenue. This debate also includes an assessment of the position of 'tax havens' as these jurisdictions undermine other states' ability to apply 'just' tax systems involving a substantial amount of redistribution.[28]
- The debate on the allocation of taxing rights between developed and developing countries which examines the necessity to shift revenue towards developing countries to reach a 'fair' participation in the global benefits of international trade.[29]

This chapter points in a different direction. It tries to answer the question of whether individuals have a moral obligation to pay a substantial amount of taxes,

[27] Kim Brooks, *Inter-Nation Equity: The Development of an Important but Underappreciated International Tax Value*, *in* Tax Reform in the 21st Century: A Volume in Memory of Richard Musgrave 471 (John G. Head & Richard Krever ed., Kluwer Law, 2008); Dirk Broekhuijsen & Henk Vording, *What May We Expect of a Theory of International Tax Justice*, *in* Tax Justice and Tax Law: Understanding Unfairness in Tax Systems 155, 158–168 (Dominic de Cogan & Peter Harris ed., 2020); Allison Christians, *Sovereignty, Taxation, and the Social Contract*, 18 Minn. J. Int'l L. 99, 144–149 (2009).

[28] Reuven Avi-Yonah, *Globalization, Tax Competition, and the Crisis of the Welfare State*, 113 Harv. L. Rev. 1573 (2000); Wolfgang Schön, *General Report*, *in* Tax Competition in Europe 1, 4–6 (Wolfgang Schön ed., 2003); Dagan, *supra* note 5, at 185; Tsilly Dagan, *Re-Imagining Tax Justice in a Globalised World*, *in* Tax Justice and Tax Law: Understanding Unfairness in Tax Systems 169 (Dominic de Cogan & Peter Harris ed., 2020); Peter Hongler, Justice in International Tax Law 371 (2019); Mathias Risse & Marco Meyer, *Tax Competition and Global Independence*, 27 J. Pol. Phil. 480, 480 (2019); Peter Dietsch & Thomas Rixen, *Tax Competition and Global Background Justice*, 22 J. Pol. Phil. 150, 150 (2014); Peter Dietsch & Thomas Rixen, *Debate: In Defence of Fiscal Autonomy: A Reply to Risse and Meyer*, 27 J. Pol. Phil. 499, 506 (2019); Peter Dietsch, *The State and Tax Competition: A Normative Perspective*, Taxation: Philosophical Perspectives 203 (Martin O'Neill & Shepley Orr ed., 2018); Christians, *supra* note 27.

[29] Miranda Stewart, *Redistribution between Rich and Poor Countries*, 72 Bull. Int'l Taxation 297, 297 (2018); Tarcisio Diniz Magalhaes, *What Is Really Wrong with Global Tax Governance and How to Properly Fix It*, 10 World Tax J. 499 (2018); Christians & van Apeldoorn, *supra* note 13, at 63.

that is, a moral obligation to contribute to 'social justice' and reject available options to minimise individual tax payments – options that are offered to them by existing jurisdictions in a perfectly legal manner. This examination, which looks to individuals and their moral choices, takes the current international tax system for granted, which allows governments to act strategically and to shape their respective tax system in a manner that attracts mobile individuals. Must individuals refrain from playing the games to which the states invite them?

Social Justice and Taxation

Reciprocity and Solidarity

When we talk about 'fairness' in a legal context – and this includes fiscal law – we focus on demands of 'justice'.[30] Concepts like fairness or justice can be applied in a small setting (e.g., between two people contracting with each other) or within the framework of a larger social entity. As taxation does not exist outside the context of a society and of governments, the question of whether and where a person is morally obliged to pay taxes must be discussed not in isolation but in the larger context of 'social justice', which is a major building block of the moral fabric of a society.

Building on a traditional dichotomy, which can be traced back to *Aristotle*, one can distinguish between two major dimensions to social justice playing a role in taxation.[31]

- The notion of reciprocity (*iustitia commutativa*): under this notion, taxes can be justified as payments in consideration of public goods enjoyed. This line of thinking is strongly linked to the benefit principle as a foundation for direct taxation.[32]
- The notion of solidarity (*iustitia distributiva*): under this notion taxes can be justified as an unrequited contribution to public goods and as a means

[30] See, generally, John Rawls, Justice as Fairness: A Restatement (Harvard University Press, 2001).

[31] For a historical account, see Klaus Vogel, *The Justification of Taxation: A Forgotten Question*, 33 Am. J. Juris. 19, 24–59 (1988); Alison Pavlovich, *The Economic Participation Principle as a Justification for Taxation*, 2 Brit. Tax Rev. 156, 157–171 (2022); the necessity to distinguish between the provision of public goods (transferring resources to the public sector) and the redistributive effect of taxation (transferring resources between individuals) is highlighted from the point of view of political philosophy by Liam Murphy & Thomas Nagel, *Taxes, Redistribution, and Public Provision*, 30 Phil. & Pub. Aff. 53 (2001).

[32] Richard A. Musgrave & Peggy B. Musgrave, *Inter-nation Equity*, *in* Modern Fiscal Issues: Essays in Honor of Carl S. Shoup, Toronto 63, 70–85 (Richard M. Bird & John G. Head ed., 1972); Eva Escribano, Jurisdiction to Tax Corporate Income Pursuant to the Presumptive Benefits Principle 31–47 (Wolters Kluwer ed., 2019); for a critical view, see Wolfgang Schön, *International Tax Coordination for a Second-Best World*, 1 World Trade J. 67, 75–77 (2009); Adam Kern, *Illusions of Justice in International Taxation*, 48 Phil. and Pol. Aff. 151, 155 (2020); Michael P. Devereux et al., Taxing Profit in a Global Economy 38–30 (Oxford University Press, 2021).

of redistribution. This line of thinking is strongly related to the idea that a tax is a sacrifice for the benefit of a community to which the taxpayer belongs. This implies in particular that taxes are levied on the basis of ability to pay, as the ability-to-pay principle tries to establish horizontal and vertical equity within a given community of taxpayers.[33]

Statist or Cosmopolitan View?

Both dimensions of social justice require the identification of a 'collective', which provides the framework to produce public goods and to arrange for redistribution. 'Social justice' goes beyond general humanitarian obligations and expectations which we all owe towards all human beings. One needs a 'special relationship' between a person and a state or society to justify moral demands vis-à-vis that person to transfer financial means to the 'collective'.[34]

Two major approaches inform the philosophical debate on social justice.[35] While the traditional 'statist view' applies the concept of social justice only in the context of a given state or society,[36] the 'cosmopolitan view' regards the whole world as home to one 'global community', which in turn justifies (financial) demands of worldwide solidarity.[37] An intermediate position is occupied by 'internationalists' who extend the concept of social justice beyond national borders – not unconditionally but in line with the unfolding development of international commercial relationships and international institutions.[38]

In this chapter, the focus is on the relevance of these views for whether 'everybody is morally obliged to pay taxes somewhere'. On closer inspection, each of those

[33] Dagan, *supra* note 28, at 171–175.

[34] Charles Garavan, *The Membership Theory of Taxation*, 51 INTERTAX 290, 303–307 (2023); Dietsch & Rixen, *supra* note 28, at 157–177; Dietsch & Rixen, *supra* note 28, at 506; Risse & Meyer, *supra* note 28, at 488.

[35] SIMON CANEY, *Global Distributive Justice: Seven Theses about Facts and Empirical Research*, *in* THE OXFORD HANDBOOK OF INTERNATIONAL POLITICAL THEORY 103, 104–117 (Chris Brown & Robyn Eckersley ed., Oxford University Press, 2018).

[36] JOHN RAWLS, THE LAW OF PEOPLES 115 (Harvard University Press 1999); David Miller, *Against Global Egalitarianism*, 9 J. ETHICS 55 (2005); Thomas Nagel, *The Problem of Social Justice*, 33 PHIL. PUB. AFF. 112 (2005); for a critique of 'strong statism', see Joshua Cohen & Charles Sabel, *Extra Rempublicam Nulla Justitia?*, 34 PHIL. PUB. AFF. 147 (2006).

[37] Thomas Pogge, *Cosmopolitanism*, *in* A COMPANION TO CONTEMPORARY POLITICAL PHILOSOPHY 316 (Robert E. Goodin ed., 2007); For an overview, *see*: Roland Pierik & Wouter Werner, *Cosmopolitanism in Context: An Introduction*, *in* COSMOPOLITANISM IN CONTEXT: PERSPECTIVES FROM INTERNATIONAL LAW AND POLITICAL THEORY 15 (Roland Pierik & Wouter Weber ed., 2010).

[38] Ilan Benshalom, *The New Poor at Our Gates: Global Justice Implications for International Trade and Tax Law*, 85 N. Y. U. L. REV. 1, 12–18 (2010); Simon Caney, *International Distributive Justice*, 49 POL. STUD. 974, 974–997 (2001); Miriam Ronzoni & Laura Valentini, *Global Justice and the Role of the State: A Critical Survey*, *in* THE OXFORD HANDBOOK OF GLOBAL JUSTICE 15–35 (Thom Brooks ed., 2020).

approaches suffers from a major disadvantage when it comes to its application in the field of taxation.

- From the cosmopolitan perspective, the main deficiency of the current international tax order is the lack of a truly global tax authority entrusted with prescribing and enforcing ubiquitous tax obligations irrespective of where people are.[39]
- From the statist perspective, the missing element of the current international tax order is the lack of any 'natural' prerogative by any of the involved states to lay hands on the financial means of an individual, not to mention the lack of any obligation for a state to levy taxes from all persons, assets, or events under its jurisdiction.

Both issues deserve a closer look.

Global Tax Justice?

Cosmopolitan View

From the 'cosmopolitan' perspective, the notion of social justice requires the creation of global common goods and the redistribution of financial means across the whole of humankind. It is evident that this does not happen in real life. There is no worldwide tax legislation, no worldwide tax authority, and no worldwide budget, not to mention the lack of a 'world government', that would appropriate global tax revenue to certain global public goods or measures of global redistribution.[40] One might even – after giving the matter some thought – conclude that the creation of such a 'world government' would be a nightmare.[41]

Does it make sense then to assume that – as long as there is no global government – each person should pay a meaningful amount of taxes to one of the existing countries to contribute indirectly to those global arrangements. The argument would be that, by financing one individual government, one contributes to the public sector in general,[42] thus enabling states around the world to pursue common goals together and to distribute financial means beyond territorial boundaries.

[39] This refers to the role of the state as an *agent*. *See* Ronzoni & Valentini, *supra* note 38).

[40] A review of academic proposals for a 'World Tax Organization' is presented by Sieb Kingma, *Inclusive Tax Governance in the Post-BEPS Era*, IBFD 415, 415–436 (2020); see also Vito Tanzi, *Lakes, Oceans, and Taxes: Why the World Needs a World Tax Organization*, *in* GLOBAL TAX FAIRNESS 251–264 (Thomas Pogge & Krishen Mehta ed., 2016).

[41] Michael J. Graetz, *The David R. Tillinghast Lecture: Taxing International Income: Inadequate Principles, Outdated Concepts, and Unsatisfactory Policies*, 54 TAX L. REV. 261, 278 (2001); Miriam Ronzoni, *Global Tax Governance: The Bullets Internationalists Must Bite: And Those They Must Not*, 1 MORAL PHIL. POL. 37, 50–59 (2014); Wolfgang Schön, *Do We Need a World Government?*, *in* NEW GLOBAL ALLIANCES: INSTITUTIONS, ALIGNMENTS AND LEGITIMACY IN THE CONTEMPORARY WORLD, MUNICH 139–148 (Corinne Michaela Flick ed., 2021).

[42] This point is made by: Christians, *supra* note 27, at 146; for a powerful account of 'Sovereigns as Trustees of Humanity: On the Accountability of States to Foreign Stakeholders', see Eyal

Taking a closer look, this calculation doesn't add up.[43] First, demands of worldwide social justice would go beyond and may run opposite to demands of social justice as currently applied in the respective local setting. To give an example regarding the clash between global and domestic measures of redistribution, most countries show hugely different standards of living across all levels of society. A 'poor' national or resident of Germany or the United States may be much better off (in terms of nutrition, housing, education, cultural amenities, working opportunities, public security, etc.) than a relatively 'rich' person in Chad or Mali. Implementing global social justice according to the people's needs would therefore require 'poor Germans' or 'poor Americans' to transfer financial means to relatively 'rich' citizens of the Chad or Mali. But, as things stand today, simply paying more taxes in Germany or the United States will mainly lead to more public goods for those better off anyway (i.e., the inhabitants of Germany and the United States) and to the implementation of some redistribution policies in Germany or the United States, but not beyond.[44] Moreover, the aim to use tax revenue for local expenditure comes naturally with democratic decision-making within the respective communities which cannot easily be ignored under the heading of global justice.[45]

Against this background, Ayelet Shachar has proposed to introduce a special levy on citizenship that is meant to compensate for the enormous advantages a person derives from being born into a wealthy and civilised society. The winners of the 'birthright lottery' – this is her claim[46] – should share these undeserved benefits with those people who grew up in a poor environment, as the place of birth was allocated to them by chance, which is not a morally acceptable justification.

While Shachar's proposal carries clear arguments from the perspective of global social justice, it runs contrary to the traditional role of the state as an institution to look after the needs of its citizens, and it is also inconsistent with current international tax practice. Following traditional rules of international tax law, citizens and residents of a country are legally obliged to pay taxes only in their state of citizenship or residence or in source countries where they own assets that generate income. Against this background, traditional residence and source countries might find it 'somewhat objectionable'[47] if the tax revenue goes to citizens of a developing

Benvenisti, *Sovereigns as Trustees of Humanity: On the Accountability of States to Foreign Stakeholders*, 107 Am. J. Int'l L. 295 (2013); see also Robert E. Goodin, *What Is So Special about Our Fellow Countrymen?*, 98 Ethics 663, 678–686 (1988).

43 Benshalom, *supra* note 38, at 6.

44 Alexander W. Cappelen, *The Moral Rationale for International Fiscal Law*, 15 Ethics Int'l Aff. 97, 107–110 (2001); Stewart, *supra* note 29, at 297; Ivan Ozai, *Inter-Nation Equity Revisited*, 12 Columbia J. Tax L. 58, 66 (2020); Nancy Kaufman, *Fairness and the Taxation of International Income*, 29 Law and Policy in International Business 145, 188 (1998); Benshalom, *supra* note 38, at 20–81; Kane, *supra* note 6, at 109.

45 Risse & Meyer, *supra* note 28, at 494.

46 Ayelet Shachar, The Birthright Lottery: Citizenship and Global Inequality 70–108 (2009).

47 Kern, *supra* note 32, at 159.

country that is not involved in the creation of the taxable income or wealth. Thus, to establish a system that would implement a truly global mode of redistribution, one needs a completely new institutional framework. And this leads us back to the moral position of the individual. If there does not exist an institutional framework linking tax payments effected in 'rich' countries directly to subsidies for the 'poor' in developing countries, what can a single person do? It is not possible for an individual to implement global social justice in the tax area without the necessary legislative and institutional framework.

If there is any moral obligation here, one might – irrespective of taking sides in the controversy between statists and cosmopolitans – appeal to the general humanitarian duties of all (rich) people to make voluntary donations directly supporting the most deserving poor, for example, via non-governmental organisations.[48] But this is a different avenue outside the context of social justice and should not distract from the fact that there cannot be a moral obligation to pay new taxes, which could be justified under the 'birthright lottery' scheme but have not yet come into existence.

There is a second argument rejecting the view that the individual should contribute 'somewhere' to global public goods and global redistribution: tax payments never reach 'the poor' directly. There are at least two intermediate players: the government of the 'rich' state where a person pays their taxes and the government of the 'poor' state where the deserving poor should benefit from those tax payments. The question of if and to what extent tax payments arising in industrialised countries can and will reach the world's poorest human beings by way of development aid very much depends on choices made by the respective governments.[49] Inter-nation equity does not result mechanically in inter-individual equity.[50] Therefore, as Johanna Stark has emphasised in a recent article,[51] the allocation of taxing rights and revenues at the 'collective level' of states does not automatically translate into distributive measures between rich people and poor people. It only re-arranges the fiscal powers of the respective governments with respect to their relative shares in the global 'tax pie'.[52] But this does not tell us anything about the way the money will be spent by the local governments. It might even be – and this happens frequently – that (non-democratic) governments of 'poor' countries spend additional revenue on that country's elite, for example, by corrupt practices or targeted subsidies for a limited group of large businesses.[53]

[48] As to the humanitarian core of cross-border redistribution, see Charles R. Beitz, *Does Global Inequality Matter?*, 32 Metaphilosophy 95 (2001).

[49] Ilan Benshalom, *How to Redistribute? A Critical Examination of Mechanisms to Promote Global Wealth Redistribution*, 64 U. T. L. J. 317, 327–331 (2014).

[50] Peter Hongler, *Justice in International Tax Law*, IBFD 410 (2019).

[51] Johanna Stark, *Tax Justice Beyond Nationals Borders: International or Interpersonal*, 42 Oxf. J. Leg. Stud. 133, 143–160 (2022).

[52] Stewart, *supra* note 29, at 307; Ozai, *supra* note 44, at 58, 86–88; Ivan Ozai, *Two Accounts of International Tax Justice*, 33 Can. J. L. Juris. 317, 332–339 (2020).

[53] Elkins, *supra* note 24, at 950–954; Benshalom, *supra* note 38, at 65; Dagan, *supra* note 5, at 206.

The first step to achieve international social justice should therefore be to support democratic and equitable decision-making in the respective 'poor' states.[54] The attempt to rearrange the international tax order can only bring about – as Dietsch and Rixen call it – a limited degree of 'background justice'[55] which enables sovereign states to implement social justice within their respective jurisdiction. If this cannot be achieved at state level, it is not the task of individuals to establish their private channels of social justice.

From this we can draw the interim conclusion that the current international tax system is not in the position to provide a framework under which tax payments – in whatever state – can be morally required to contribute to global common goods or to global redistribution. For the time being we must live in a world where states apply local tax regimes and taxpayers mainly finance local public goods and distributive measures. If states fail in implementing supranational structures to establish a worldwide tax order or to coordinate in a fashion that ensures a 'single-tax-principle' for individuals or to organise global modes of redistribution, it is not the obligation of the individual to compensate for this deficiency, if indeed it is a deficiency.[56] Thus, even those cosmopolitans who would regard a general moral obligation to pay taxes to be part of everybody's moral framework would have to concede that the lack of implementation and infrastructure renders this obligation meaningless.

In a widely cited paper, Ilan Ben-Shalom has proposed a middle 'internationalist' path. Rejecting an outright cosmopolitan view, he nevertheless emphasises the benefits taxpayers draw from international trade, which in his view results in transnational 'relational duties' between private economic actors in different countries. Yet he rejects the theoretical option to organise direct social transfers between individuals cross-border and supports the view that the respective home state must act 'as an aggregate of its citizens' relational duties'.[57] For the individual, the main result lies in their duty to 'help establish just institutions' at the domestic level.[58] But this does not immediately result in paying a 'fair share' of taxes. Rather, this approach aims at collective decision-making in the respective country and the individual's democratic involvement in how to allocate public revenue. A similar result is reached by Christians and van Apeldoorn,[59] who emphasise mutual 'duties of assistance' between states. They propose to secure minimal subsistence rights for the poor to be funded by a new approach to source taxation. But also, in their view, it is the states and not the individual whose behaviour is regarded as 'just' or 'unjust'.

[54] Mathias Risse, *What We Owe to the Global Poor*, 9 J. Ethics 81 (2005).

[55] Dietsch & Rixen, *supra* note 28, at 175–177; Benshalom, *supra* note 49, at 339–343; the concept of 'background justice' is further explored by Miriam Ronzoni, *The Global Order: A Case of Background Injustice? A Practice-dependent Account*, 37 Phil. Pub. Aff. 229 (2009).

[56] Kane, *supra* note 6, at 104–114.

[57] Benshalom, *supra* note 38, at 56–81; see also Benshalom, *supra* note 49, at 321–326.

[58] Benshalom, *supra* note 38, at 61.

[59] Christians & van Apeldoorn, *supra* note 13, at 63.

Statist View

The statist view does not start from the assumption that social justice aims at the creation of global public goods or the implementation of global redistribution.[60] This perspective assumes that social justice can and must only be achieved in the context of a given state and its society. Within that state, it is up to democratically elected legislatures to decide on the size of the public sector, the choice of which public goods to provide and the level of redistributive efforts.[61] For the resident individual, this does not result in moral obligations going beyond their legal obligations as they will be told by law how much and who to pay.

Looking a bit closer, also note that if social justice can only be applied and social behaviour required within certain well-defined communities, the individual's choice of which community to belong to is not in itself an issue that can be morally judged.[62] There are – in principle – no 'good' or 'bad' communities as such. This is important for our considerations as it means that mobile individuals have a right to choose which community to join, that is, where to live and where to earn and spend money and where to be taxed – if at all. The concept of social justice, in particular the notion of solidarity, only enters the picture under the statist view once a person has joined a certain community (or is just born into that community). But this choice is – morally speaking – neutral. It cannot be criticised as being 'unfair' or 'immoral'. It might even be an infringement on their liberty to make them part of a certain community against their will.

State of Origin and State of Destination

State of Origin

The first candidate for a morally grounded entitlement to receive tax payments from an individual is the 'state of origin', meaning the state where a person was raised, went to school, enjoyed public services, and benefitted from redistribution. One might therefore argue that this state can – based on the notion of reciprocity – expect a person to contribute in the future to those public goods which that person previously enjoyed.[63] One might also claim – based on the notion of solidarity –

[60] Graetz, *supra* note 41, at 277–334; Peter Hongler, *Justice in International Tax Law*, IBFD 346, 371 (2019).

[61] Christians & van Apeldoorn, *supra* note 13, at 63; For the issue of 'tax fairness' within a supranational organization such as the EU, see Alice Pirlot, *The Vagueness of Tax Fairness: A Discursive Analysis of the Commission's 'Fair Tax Agenda'*, 48 INTERTAX 402, 402–415 (2020).

[62] Risse & Meyer, *supra* note 28, at 483–498.

[63] Dietsch & Rixen, *supra* note 28, at 160–177 posit a moral obligation for each resident to contribute to current revenue according to the benefit principle while residing in the respective state. But this statement doesn't tell us anything about the moral assessment of tax-driven emigration.

that having citizenship or residence in the country of origin constitutes membership in a community, which requires financial solidarity in the long run.[64]

But is it 'unfair' if a person who grew up under benevolent circumstances, benefitted from redistributive measures, was well educated and well prepared for economic success, leaves the country to earn their living or to spend their wealth in a low-tax environment? Would we morally require that person to 'stay put' to contribute to public revenue? One can extend this question to those states where the individual spent their working life. Is it immoral to leave a country on the date of retirement after many successful years of participation in that country's economy?

The answer is 'no'. First, the right to leave a country is a deep expression of personal freedom and as such morally not only acceptable but fully justified.[65] The concept that a person 'belongs' to a state and must work for that state all their life was part of (enlightened) absolutism in the eighteenth century and has been abandoned since.[66] In 1815, as part of the Final Act of the Vienna Congress, the full right of emigration was established as a general principle (and has remained a human right ever since).[67]

Second, countries are not powerless when it comes to setting and enforcing 'prices' for emigration.[68] There can be an 'exit tax' on latent gains when it comes to a person moving out who owns appreciated assets.[69] Some countries apply a 'trailing tax' on emigrating citizens for a limited number of years after emigration.[70] There can even be a 'brain drain tax' on human capital as has been proposed by theorists of development economics.[71] But if a country does not apply one of these devices to emigrating people, the person should not be obliged to stay put and to show solidarity in the home state just because there would be no other way to

64 Avi-Yonah, *supra* note 16.

65 Dagan, *supra* note 28, at 183–185.

66 Wolfgang Schön, *Taxation and Democracy*, 72 TAX L. REV. 235, 299 (2019).

67 See *Article XVIII lit.b of the 'Bundesakte'* (1815), www.verfassungen.de/de06-66/bundesakte15-i.htm.

68 Kirsch, *supra* note 16, at 443–445.; Beretta, *supra* note 9, at 99–102; Ordower, *supra* note 13, at 138–152.

69 Wolfgang Schön, *Steuerstaat und Freizügigkeit*, *in* STEUER- UND SOZIALSTAAT IM EUROPÄISCHEN SYSTEMWETTBEWERB, TÜBINGEN 41, 60–74 (Ulrich Becker & Wolfgang Schön ed., 2006).

70 MIRANDA STEWART, TAX & GOVERNMENT IN THE 21ST CENTURY 262 (2022); Christians, *supra* note 2, at 63.

71 Jagdish Bhagwati, *International Migration of the Highly Skilled*, 1 THIRD WORLD Q. 17 (1979); Yariv Brauner, *Brain Drain Taxation as Development Policy*, 55 SAINT LOUIS UNIVERSITY LAW JOURNAL 221 (2010–2011); Mihir A. Desai et al., *Sharing the Spoils: Taxing International Human Capital Flows*, 11 INT'L TAX PUB. FIN. 663 (2004); Kern, *supra* note 32, at 179–185; Stewart, *supra* note 29, at 308; Stewart, *supra* note 70, at 267; Svetislav Kostic, *International Taxation and Migration*, *in* RESEARCH HANDBOOK ON INTERNATIONAL TAXATION 353, 364–366 (Yariv Brauner ed., 2020); the special case of remitted income is addressed by Ariel Stevenson, *Recovering Lost Tax Revenue through Taxation of Transnational Households*, 34 BERKELEY J. INT'L L. 100 (2016).

implement social justice. Rather, if countries have decided against those fiscal schemes, these countries and their voters have shown that they value the personal or economic benefits of international mobility higher than the fiscal benefits of an exit tax or a trailing tax or a similar device.

In the European Union, higher-ranking law constrains the power of national tax legislators to erect substantial tax obstacles to intra-EU migration.[72] This is part and parcel of the joint decision of the EU Member States to give precedence to the Internal Market and its features over territorial fiscal goals. Given this unanimous political commitment expressed by the Member States, the freedom of emigration – including tax-driven emigration – cannot be set aside by general moral considerations.

In this context it may be somewhat surprising that most countries have abandoned worldwide income and wealth taxation based on citizenship and replaced it with unlimited taxation of residents. The argument in favour of taxation based on residence is that resident foreigners (like resident citizens) have a closer relationship with the local community than citizens living abroad. Nevertheless, citizenship taxation is admissible under international law as it is true that citizenship as such is a valuable good – given that it provides diplomatic protection by the home state and the right to return on a continuing basis. Moreover, it may serve as community membership.[73] Therefore, ongoing taxation of foreign-based nationals based on citizenship is a valid policy choice for each country.[74] It also prevents taxpayers from cherry-picking or enjoying beneficial fiscal rules abroad while still having a 'lifeline' to their country of citizenship if the situation in the host state becomes uncomfortable. But if a state decides not to apply unlimited tax liability to its citizens living abroad, people are free to move to other countries and to become part of the host country's fiscal collective without having to renounce citizenship in their home country.

State of Destination

What about the state of destination, that is, the future host state of the taxpayer? As this is the state where the individual will establish himself or herself, the fact that they are invited to enjoy a tax-exempt or preferential status compared to domestic residents or citizens creates the specific moral problem. The question therefore seems to be whether it is 'immoral' for the immigrants to enjoy tax benefits which are not available to their (future) local neighbours.[75]

72 Servaas van Thiel, *Exit Taxes*, 1 Eur. Tax L. 829 (Peter Wattel et al. eds. 2019); Johanna Hey, *Taxation of Business in the EU. Special Problems of Crossborder Losses and Exit Taxation, in* Research Handbook on European Union Tax Law 194, 212–223 (Christiana H. J. I. Panayi et al. eds., 2020).

73 Mason, *supra* note 16, at 197–208.

74 Beretta, *supra* note 9, 440–442; Giorgio Beretta, *Citizenship and Tax*, 11 World Tax J. 227 (2019); Avi-Yonah, *supra* note 16.

75 Kern, *supra* note 32, at 162–185.

In this respect, we must start from the fact that these inbound individuals are – given the mandatory nature of tax law – not allowed to pay higher taxes if the local tax code requires beneficial taxation (e.g., taxation on a purely territorial basis or a lump-sum basis) for specific groups of mobile individuals. There seems to be no 'choice' at all to be made by the individual that is subject to a moral assessment. But even if this beneficial treatment is dependent on the taxpayer making a deliberate election (e.g., by 'checking a box' on the tax declaration form to benefit from tax breaks offered to inbound individuals), it is not easy to claim that this is an immoral act vis-à-vis other taxpayers who do not benefit from that treatment.

When it comes to the moral assessment of inbound tax-driven migration, one should not overlook that the relevant tax benefits have in most cases been introduced by a democratically elected legislature. This means that the electorate of that country – which represents the majority of taxpayers – has (indirectly) agreed to the introduction of this kind of 'split' tax regime, which distinguishes between regular domestic taxpayers and a privileged group of immigrants. Again, the valid background consideration on the side of the government can be the expectation of positive spill overs arising from the attraction of high-net worth individuals or economically useful specialists.[76] If local taxpayers do not agree with this legislation, in many countries they have the right to challenge any tax privilege for foreign migrants in a local constitutional court.[77] This is where the issue of equal treatment under the relevant provisions of the respective constitution can be raised. But if the tax privilege is legitimate in terms of democratic input and in line with the framework provided by the respective constitution, why then should an individual be morally criticised for accepting this offer? This does not mean that one should not plead in the political arena for a different tax policy agenda – namely abolishing any 'price discrimination' between mobile and immobile taxpayers. But this is a decision which the relevant collective must make along the lines provided by the domestic constitution.[78]

This outcome is confirmed when we take a closer look at the two dimensions of social justice relevant in this context:

- When we look to *iustitia commutativa* in a superficial manner, the benefit principle seems to go against granting access to the amenities

[76] Christians, *supra* note 2, at 54; yet this requires a delicate policy balance with regard to the effects of capital inflows on the real economy, the financial markets, and the fiscal framework (see Xin Xu et al., *Too Much of a Good Thing? Prudent Management of Inflows under Economic Citizenship Programs*, IMF Working Paper WP/15/93, 3–4 (2015)).

[77] Schön, *supra* note 66, at 296–298.

[78] It has been said that rich countries will prevail when it comes to competing with poor countries regarding high net-worth individuals (Christians, *supra* note 2, at 68); but it seems that wealthy countries tend to engage less strongly in tax competition for individuals while some poor countries regard this as a budgetary and economic necessity. It seems more convincing to draw a line between small and large countries, as small countries can draw larger benefits from immigration programmes (Xin Xu, *supra* note 76, at 3).

of living in the host country to foreign migrants without them having to pay the same price as other inhabitants. But is this the right description of what's happening here? One can also say that the government has simply realised that 'on the margin' the extra expenditure by the government to finance another bit of public goods provided to the mobile individual is lower than the welfare benefit for society at large that can be captured once the mobile individual enters the country, bringing along consumption power and maybe even valuable human capital.[79] Thus, the outcome of the preferential tax scheme can still be a bargain for the taxing state.[80] The benefit principle is simply not sufficiently granular when it comes to these 'marginal' effects of adding new residents to a jurisdiction.[81]

- When we look to *iustitia distributiva*, the ability-to-pay principle seems to demand that any person living in a country must contribute to the public coffers according to their financial means, which would require full inclusion of income and wealth without any exemptions for foreign income or assets.[82] But this conclusion also fails. One must take into consideration that the mobile individual, when he or she makes the decision to enter the country, is not yet a member of the local society and as such is not obliged to any sacrifice under the auspices of 'membership' in the local community. There is no bond of solidarity at this decisive point in time between the individual and the country's existing residents and therefore the mobile individual is free to accept the offer of the local government to enter the country at a 'lower price'.[83] But the relevant social bond can evolve in the course of time and therefore it is fully justified that those countries who create tax breaks for immigrants regularly set an expiration date for those benefits to account for the ongoing integration of the respective taxpayers into the local community. But again – it is up to the democratically elected government of that country to decide on the limitations governing the relevant tax exemptions.

79 Dagan, *supra* note 28, at 175–179; Tsilly Dagan, *Competition vs. Cooperation in International Taxation*, Research Handbook on International Taxation 141 (Yariv Brauner ed., 2020).

80 Risse & Meyer, *supra* note 28, at 492–498; Dagan, *supra* note 5, at 199, 208; Ronzoni, *supra* note 41, at 44–59.

81 Wolfgang Schön, *Value Creation, the Benefits Principle and Efficiency-Related Allocation of Taxing Rights*, *in* Taxation and Value Creation 155, 163–164 (Werner Haslehner & Marie Lamensch eds., 2021).

82 Richard A. Musgrave & Peggy B. Musgrave, *Inter-nation Equity*, *in* Modern Fiscal Issues: Essays in Honor of Carl S. Shoup, Toronto 63, 68 (Richard M. Bird & John G. Head eds., 1972); critically, see, Nancy Kaufman, *Fairness and the Taxation of International Income*, 29 Law and Policy Int'l Business 145, 153, 172–203 (1998).

83 Schön, *supra* note 66, at 298–302.

CONCLUSION

The outcome of our analysis can be summarised as follows.

- Is there a legal obligation to pay taxes somewhere? No, there are more and more cross-border situations where mobile individuals neither pay tax in the source country nor in the home country (as described in the Preface to this book). This is due to a paradigm shift at the level of international taxation, as both source countries and home countries reduce the scope of taxation to attract investment or individuals.
- Is there a factual obligation to pay taxes somewhere? Yes, everybody does factually pay some taxes. Being exempt from direct taxes does not liberate people from the economic effects of taxation as other taxpayers will be in the position to shift their (indirect or direct) tax burden towards the tax-exempt individuals whenever these persons consume or generate income or assets. But this does not mean that tax-exempt individuals are burdened in the same manner as taxpayers who are personally subject to mainstream income tax, wealth tax or inheritance tax. These mobile individuals are not subject to a progressive tax burden on their comprehensive income or wealth, a feature which is regarded by many to be the core of any truly 'fair' tax system.
- Is there a moral obligation to pay taxes somewhere? Again, this answer is no. At the global level there exists no mechanism to finance global public goods or to organise worldwide redistribution which requires all people living on the earth to contribute. Taxation exists only at the level of individual states. But if neither the country of origin nor the country of destination nor the relevant source countries activate their taxing rights towards a certain group of mobile individuals, it is not up to these individuals to make up for or to reject policy choices legitimately made by local governments.

Where does this leave us? Whoever complains about the rise of double non-taxation in the case of individuals should in principle not go after the persons accepting attractive tax packages from governments around the world. Rather, one should take a critical look at those governments who design tax packages and undercut offers made by other jurisdictions. But again, one should think twice and always ask whether countries have good reasons for their policy choices, for example, to incentivise local investment and local consumption, to improve the workforce or to create a market for local suppliers of goods and services. Any measures countering this kind of competition for mobile individuals would require international coordination comparable to the BEPS Project initiated more than 10 years ago which made the 'single tax principle' of business profits front and centre. Thus, BEPS Project 2.0 for individuals may be on the horizon, but it should be handled with care given the large impact on states' policy choices and individuals' personal lives.

2

Comfortably Numb

Should the Reign of Residence over the International Tax Regime Continue in the Twenty-First Century?

Yariv Brauner

INTRODUCTION

The notion of residence controls the most fundamental jurisdictional norms of the international tax regime. No other factor impacts the taxation of cross-border transactions more than the determination of residence. Essentially, all states comprehensively tax residents on their worldwide income, while non-residents are taxed with limits.[1] This schema worked rather well over the first century of the regime,[2] primarily due to the relatively low mobility of individuals.[3] It worked well, yet it was not without challenges. Some states expanded the scope of worldwide taxation to non-resident citizens, for example.[4] Mobility of individuals has been low but not insignificant. Most notably, the migration of skilled workers has caused what some call a *brain drain*, shifting (unjustly, some argue) revenue from developing to developed states.[5] However, the scope of the challenges to residence taxation remained limited, and, hence, residence taxation of individuals became an increasingly universal norm.

I thank the participants in the Oxford 'Taxing People: The Next 100 Years' conference, Tsilly Dagan and Ruth Mason, the editors of this volume, and especially John Vella, my commentator at that conference, for their useful comments and suggestions. All mistakes and inaccuracies are mine.

1 See, e.g., Reuven S. Avi-Yonah, International Tax as International Law (2007).

2 Especially when compared to corporate residence.

3 The International Organization on Migration (IOM) has been tracking the data and publishing publicly available reports on the magnitude and trends of world migration. See, e.g., *World Migration Report 2022*, IOM (based on 2020 data compiled in IOM) (Dec. 2021), https://worldmigrationreport.iom.int/wmr-2022-interactive/.

4 The United States being the most notable among them. See, e.g., Chapter 3, by Reuven S. Avi-Yonah.

5 See, e.g., Yariv Brauner, *Brain Drain Taxation as Development Policy*, 55 St. Louis U. L. J. 221 (2010); and Svetislav V. Kostic, *International Taxation and Migrations*, *in* Research Handbook on International Taxation 353 (Yariv Brauner ed., 2020).

This is changing. Globalisation and the ascent of digitalisation have contributed to an increasing and distinct mobility of individuals. Remote work (and investment) have become normal,[6] and a new type of mobility, namely that of the *digital nomads*,[7] has raised renewed questions regarding residence taxation of individuals in the twenty-first century.[8] This chapter assesses the fit of this universal residence taxation norm to the new reality by examining the traditional argument for residence taxation of individuals and the viability of alternative schemes.

This chapter specifically examines the feasibility of taxation based only on source. Source taxation is, of course, prevalent in the existing rules of the regime, together with residence-based taxation, and therefore exclusive reliance on source would not be completely unfamiliar. This chapter argues that a single basis for taxing individuals rather than two competing bases could remove much of the complexity of the regime. Source taxation also has the potential to relieve many of the above-mentioned challenges related to increasing digitalisation and mobility, and it is likely to be perceived as more just and consequently more legitimate, a perception which may assist the international tax regime in adapting to the twenty-first century.

The discussion of residence and its role in international taxation is relevant for both individual and corporate taxpayers. This chapter focuses only on the former.[9] Corporate residence has been widely discussed in legal scholarship. It involves a legal fiction, the separate personality of corporations, a fiction that is unnecessary for individual taxation and that has its distinct complexity that does not bear on the more fundamental analysis of the desirability of individual (tax) residence. Nonetheless, the developments that challenge individual income taxation are equally problematic for corporate taxation, and the impact of these developments on business models and operations is not limited to any one tax. This chapter argues that compatibility between norms that apply to taxing individuals and corporations further supports the desirability of reform along the lines examined.

The chapter proceeds as follows: (1) it concisely reviews the origins of residence taxation; (2) it assesses its most common justifications; (3) it reviews the challenges, new and old, that residence taxation faces at present; and (4) it examines the viability of exclusive reliance on source taxation; and (5) it concludes.

6 See, e.g., Andrea Loubier, *How Remote Work Has Spiked Since the COVID Crisis*, Forbes, Mar. 9, 2021, www.forbes.com/sites/andrealoubier/2021/03/09/how-remote-work-has-spiked-since-the-covid-crisis/?sh=75a0a99f2386.

7 See, e.g., Kyle Chayka, *When You're a 'Digital Nomad', the World Is Your Office*, N.Y. Times Mag., Feb. 8, 2018, www.nytimes.com/2018/02/08/magazine/when-youre-a-digital-nomad-the-world-is-your-office.html.

8 See, e.g., Avi-Yonah, *supra* note 4.

9 This is done for simplicity purposes. This author acknowledges and has lamented elsewhere the artificiality of separate discussions of corporate and individual income taxation, both of which impact only individuals. Yet, tax policy is practically devised separately for each tax system, which should be acknowledged and accommodated if one wishes to engage in a pragmatic analysis. A good example for the interdependence of these rules can be found in Chapter 10, by Richard Collier.

THE ORIGINS OF RESIDENCE

The use of a personal connection – some nexus – between a state and an individual is natural in the income tax context, the tax being a personal tax. The taxpayer, rather than a transaction or property, is the subject and the centre of the discussion. The need for nexus arises primarily in the context of income tax jurisdiction, where the implicit question is: *whom may a state tax and in what manner?* The (modern) international income tax laws of all states are, however, allocation rather than conflicts (of laws) norms, although they include a few traditional jurisdiction rules, particularly related to enforcement jurisdiction. Nonetheless, the need for such allocation norms arose with globalisation (beginning with the beginning of the twentieth century) and intuitively attracted analogies to traditional conflicts rules.[10] Given the limited mobility of individuals and the evolutionary way the international tax regime was established, it is understandable that the precise purpose of the tax jurisdiction norms was not extensively explored. Traditional personal connections of nationality and domicile therefore primarily informed the development of the concept of tax jurisdiction.

Domicile, Nationality, and Residence

Traditional personal connections included domicile, nationality, and habitual abode, alternatively and interchangeably with residence.[11] The choice from the start of the tax treaties project to rely upon residence as the basis for taxation influenced domestic laws and led to a global convergence on residence as a primary connecting factor for taxation. This convergence still leaves room for interpretation, and, indeed, the concept of residence has lacked a clear meaning; it also lacks the history and jurisprudence that helped interpret the other mentioned criteria, such as domicile and nationality. This led to wide differences in interpretation of the term residence under domestic laws and ubiquitous overlap with the traditional conflicts laws' criteria. Tax treaty law tried to address divergence among states in the meaning of tax residence by two methods: first, with an independent interpretation of the term, and, second, by accepting the reality of dual residence, while resolving, for the

[10] Both sets of rules introduce priorities among competing jurisdictional norms, yet, whereas conflicts laws determine which courts or which state's laws apply (one or the other), allocation norms accept the laws of both states but limit their reach in terms of potential for taxation. They do so simultaneously, purporting to reach the same outcomes regardless of which court or state implement them.

[11] For a discussion of the private international law origins of the different personal connections used for jurisdiction determining purposes, see, e.g., James J. Fawcett, *Residence and Domicile of Individuals in Private International Law*, *in* RESIDENCE OF INDIVIDUALS UNDER TAX TREATIES AND EC LAW 3 (Guglielmo Maisto ed., 2010).

most part, dual residence cases by a set of tie-breaking rules.[12] The focus of this chapter is, however, on the preliminary stage: the determination of residence and imposition of worldwide taxation by domestic law.

Although taxation based on nationality was not rare, and still exists in a few cases, the more common basis for taxation during the early twentieth century was the concept of domicile. The concept of domicile was especially attractive for income tax purposes. Individuals always have a domicile, and they have only one domicile that may be changed only when a new one is established. Domicile is established based on a person's physical presence *and* intent to make the relevant location their home. There is a long history and jurisprudence about domicile and domicile conflicts in common law, which tax laws could draw on even when states transitioned to personal taxes.[13] Unlike nationality, domicile presented a more direct, perhaps less formalistic and more meaningful, manifestation of an economic allegiance of an individual to a state.

From Domicile to Different Residence Notions

Residence as a basis for income taxation likely arose from the concept of domicile. The term 'domicile' is centuries old[14] and has been used for purposes of determining jurisdiction throughout the western world. In many states, residence, or more accurately various notions of residence, served as mere indications of domicile. Residence as it is used in international tax law at the present should be distinguished therefore from terms such as 'habitual residence' or 'ordinary residence' that also served as indicators for domicile determination purposes.[15]

The concept of domicile implies stability and certainty, which may be more important for legal disciplines other than tax. Yet, annual taxation is first and foremost about calculation of specific and necessarily accurate income, and, therefore, requires a more dynamic reflection of the connection of a person to a state. Residence seemed, to the 'founding fathers' of the international tax regime, more appropriate than domicile, even though the differences and the choice among the two were quite uncertain during its initial decades.

Modern Personal Tax Jurisdiction

The launch of the international tax regime is attributed to the tax treaties work at the League of Nations. The work produced various reports and draft model conventions,

[12] Model Tax Convention on Income and on Capital, art. 4(2), OECD (2017) [hereinafter OECD Model].

[13] See, e.g., Franz Martin Joseph, *Domicile and Residence of Individuals for American Tax Purposes*, 29 Taxes 916 (1951).

[14] See, e.g., www.etymonline.com/word/domicile.

[15] See, e.g., Fawcett, *supra* note 11, 17–29.

most notably the 1928 Draft Model Treaty.[16] The various versions of the League of Nations' work include references to both residence and domicile as bases for taxation and, interestingly, an explicit mention that the treaty would apply regardless of the nationality of the taxpayer.[17]

In any event, domicile or residence are mentioned as decisive in respect to the imposition of personal taxes.[18] The initial follow-up by the OECD, in its 1963 Draft Model Convention, includes Article 4, entitled 'Fiscal Domicile', that defines residence. The title of Article 4 changed to 'Resident' only in the 1977 OECD Model Convention,[19] at which time the earlier reference to domicile was removed, leaving residence as the single acceptable criterion for domestic law in constituting liability to tax throughout the remaining lifetime of the regime.[20]

The shift from domicile to residence in international taxation was a shift from a more static (durable in relation to the person) basis to a more flexible one that presumably corresponded to tax law's dynamic nature and (typically) annual assessment. Similarly, the shift was also from the more law-based concept of domicile to the more factual residence.[21] One should not forget also that the initial phases of the regime were dictated by the wealthier states in the world. National interests were front and centre despite the initial academic aura of the League of Nations tax work. This became obvious in the 1940s when the gap between developed and developing states stalled that work. The next phase, in the 1950s, belonged to an OECD that, at the time, did not pretend to represent any interests other than its most-developed-state members. And, in that environment, residence taxation won the day.

A CRITICAL REVIEW OF JUSTIFICATIONS FOR RESIDENCE-BASED TAXATION

The origins of residence as a basis for taxation of individuals are in pragmatic considerations and legal dogma. Yet, over the years the norm has been set and has become more resilient and universal.[22] This section examines various justifications

16 See, e.g., SUNITA JOGARAJAN, DOUBLE TAXATION AND THE LEAGUE OF NATIONS (Cambridge University Press, 2018), appendices. Notable developments after this Draft were published in 1942 and 1946, known as the Mexico and London Drafts, separately produced by developing and developed states. See, e.g., THE LEAGUE OF NATIONS, LONDON AND MEXICO MODEL TAX CONVENTIONS: COMMENTARY AND TEXT (The League 1946). See also Jacques Sasseville, *History and Interpretation of the Tiebreaking Rule in Art. 4(2) of the OECD Model Convention*, *in* RESIDENCE OF INDIVIDUALS UNDER TAX TREATIES AND EC LAW 153 (Guglielmo Maisto ed., 2010).

17 League of Nations Model, supra.

18 Id., art. 10.

19 Today in OECD Model, art. 4 (2017).

20 Id.

21 See, e.g., Sasseville, *supra* note 16.

22 Nonetheless, one cannot argue that it is harmonised: different criteria, including nationality, permanent home, etc., are used to determine residence, although substantial presence, usually

for the norm, explaining its stability. Doing so requires, first, a clear view of the norm's impact. As already mentioned, both source and residence bases are found in modern income tax rules pertaining to individuals. The primary basis is source, while residence taxation as such serves two residual purposes: taxing income that cannot be or is hard to source[23] and residually taxing income that is taxed too lightly (from the perspective of the residence state).[24] The core question discussed in this chapter is why the residence state should tax these incomes.

Dogma

The most straightforward justification of residence taxation is that it is the natural implication of the personal connection between an individual and their state of residence. This justification is not very different from the justification for taxation based on nationality. It relies mainly on benefits-theory justifications, namely, the assumption that a resident will benefit from the various expenditures and protections available to them in the residence state.[25] It further assumes that the more income one earns, the more benefits they enjoy. The other dogmatic theory of income taxation, the ability-to-pay theory, may similarly be used to support residence taxation. This theory is based on the idea that only the residence state can tax one's worldwide income in a manner that reflects their ability to pay.[26] But, even if this is beneficial for the state of residence, it does not justify the state of residence's taxing rights' claim. Other states have their own interests in taxing the individual. Moreover, it is not necessarily the case that residence taxation is necessary to preserve progressivity in domestic income tax systems.

Another argument for residence taxation stems from the weakness of the existing source rules. These rules are interesting in that they are both almost universal and quite difficult to justify.[27] For the purposes of this chapter, however, the first

(but not always) counted as 183 days within a fiscal year, seems to be the most ubiquitous determining test. For a comparative review of residence rules see, e.g., Angel Schindel & Adolfo Atchabahian, *General Report*, *in* SOURCE AND RESIDENCE: NEW CONFIGURATION OF THEIR PRINCIPLES 58–60 (IFA ed., 2005). Much of the standardisation can be attributed to the OECD Model, yet the need for and the utility of the tie breaking rules in tax treaties (OECD Model, art. 4(2) (2017)) demonstrate that the rules are not harmonised. Id.

23 This may be homeless or stateless income or other income that is difficult to source.

24 Such residual taxation may arise not only when the source state taxes the relevant income at its regular low rate but also when, according to an applicable tax treaty, the source state is limited to a low rate of taxation (leaving the residual taxing right to the residence state).

25 See, e.g., Angelo Nikolakakis, *Civil Law and Common Law Perspectives: A View from the Left*, *in* RESIDENCE OF INDIVIDUALS UNDER TAX TREATIES AND EC LAW 75, 83 (Guglielmo Maisto, ed., IBFD 2010).

26 See, e.g., 1923 Economist Report to the League of Nations; Robert A. Green, *The Future of Source-Based Taxation of Income of Multinational Enterprises*, 79 CORNELL L. REV. 18, 29 (1993).

27 But see, e.g., Mitchell A. Kane, A *Defense of Source Rules in International Taxation*, 32 YALE J. REG. 311 (2015).

question must be whether exclusive source taxation (rather than the current mixed rules) is justified. It would not be justifiable to advocate source taxation if the content of the source rules cannot be justified. Yet, it would not be preferable to keep a deficient existing regime, including the allegedly deficient source rules. Similarly, one may argue for residence taxation based on the difficulty to source some income.[28] But, as already mentioned, such an argument cannot, by itself, justify granting the residence state the taxing rights of such income.[29]

Finally, a common argument for residence taxation is that it is simpler and provides more certainty than source taxation.[30] Often, one would include such arguments under the administrability criterion for good tax policy. The idea here is that the residence of individuals (usually when contrasted with corporations) is simple to determine, and therefore the administration of residence taxation is simpler than that of source taxation where interpretation and classification conflicts may more often arise. This too is not a very convincing argument, as the fact that a tax is simpler does not mean that it is more desirable, especially where international taxation is concerned. The fairness of the regime and its legitimacy, which leads to longevity, cannot be compromised (too much) for the sake of its administrability.

Efficiency

The business taxation debate overshadows the traditional policy discussion of international taxation of individuals. The basic principles, however, are similar. Residence taxation was associated with what is commonly called *capital export neutrality* (CEN),[31] the traditional US policy. CEN was often contrasted with *capital import neutrality* (CIN),[32] which was associated with source taxation. Much of the economic literature expressed a preference for CEN because it resulted in less distortion of investment location decisions and hence a more efficient allocation of global resources (a larger 'pie').[33]

[28] See, e.g., the United States' position in the context of the taxation of electronic commerce, discussed in Dale Pinto, *Exclusive Source or Residence-based Taxation – Is a New and Simpler World Tax Order Possible?*, 61 Bull. Int'l Tax'n 277, 278 (2007).

[29] For a similar conclusion, see John K. Sweet, *Formulating International Tax Laws in the Age of Electronic Commerce: The Possible Ascendancy of Residence-based Taxation in an Era of Eroding Traditional Income Tax Principles*, 146 U. Pa. L. Rev. 1949, 1991 (1998).

[30] See, e.g., Reuven S. Avi-Yonah, *The Structure of International Taxation: A Proposal for Simplification*, 74 Tex. L. Rev. 1301, 1311–1313 (1996).

[31] CEN aims to make the decision where to locate one's investment unimpacted by taxation, leading to similar taxation of investment at home or abroad. For the classic exposition of this concept, see Peggy Richman, Taxation of Foreign Investment Income: An Economic Analysis (1963).

[32] In contrast to CEN, CIN focuses on the tax neutrality of the investment's host state, aiming to similarly tax foreign and domestic investors. See, e.g., id.

[33] See, e.g., Charles E. McLure, Jr., *US Tax Laws and Capital Flight from Latin America*, 20 U. Mia. Inter-Am. L. Rev. 321, 325 (1989).

There are many problems with this argument, which have been extensively explored in scholarship. First, global efficiency is essentially irrelevant when states come together in a system that is not fully cooperative. Global redistribution certainly does not take place, and, therefore, states care about their slice, not the entire proverbial 'pie'. Second, even after so many years of CEN rhetoric, no state actually implements CEN; even the United States employs multiple exemption mechanisms and imposes limitations on foreign tax credits. Third, the traditional CEN and CIN discourse did not consider globalisation, the opening of economies, and the ascent of technology.[34] Fourth, a more recent discourse of investment neutralities demonstrates that the preference for residence taxation is far from obvious.[35]

Politics

States view tax policy as the last bastion of sovereignty when all other economic policy avenues are restricted by international agreements and market conditions. By the same token, states view their subjects automatically as taxpayers, as if residence is coupled with an automatic duty of taxation, almost a mirror image of the 'no taxation without representation' slogan. In a way, this view is a broader, rougher version of the benefits theory (without commitment to benefits). This idea is, however, weak when applied to residents rather than nationals, who typically are the voters in a state. A political perspective of the benefits theory is perhaps more convincing but also cannot justify worldwide taxation of income clearly earned in a different jurisdiction, especially in cases of non-nationals. This is particularly true in a world where states increasingly 'compete' for citizens and residents. Various recent developments, such as the rise of 'digital nomads', demonstrate the decreasing persuasiveness of benefits theories as justification for taxation.[36]

A Technical Argument

Shay, Fleming, and Peroni[37] argued that the net income basis of the income tax mandates taxation of the taxpayer as a single unit, on a worldwide basis. This is a valid argument in support of taxing individuals in a system where a single state

[34] See, e.g., Daniel J. Frisch, *The Economics of International Tax Policy: Some Old and New Approaches*, 47 TAX NOTES 581 (1990).

[35] See, e.g., Mihir A. Desai & James R. Hines Jr., *Evaluating International Tax Reform*, 56 NAT'L TAX J. 487 (2003).

[36] See, e.g., Giorgio Beretta, *Cross-Border Mobility of Individuals and the Lack of Fiscal Policy Coordination among Jurisdictions (Even) after the BEPS Project*, 47 INTERTAX 91, 96–99, 102–104 (2019) (reviewing citizenship by investment programs and immigration tax incentives for pensioners).

[37] See Stephen E. Shay, J. Clifton Fleming Jr. & Robert J. Peroni, *What's Source Got to Do with It? Source Rules and US International Taxation*, 56 TAX LAW REV. 81 (2002).

determines the net tax base and makes sure that the income tax applies to all such taxpayer's income (regardless of other tax systems). It is similar to the CEN justification, yet it is not based on efficiency. Rather, a state that wishes to employ a legitimate redistributive tax system must begin with assessing its taxpayers' worldwide income.

There are, however, important counterarguments. First, the existing income tax is only an approximation of a net income tax, of the ideal Haig-Simon-von Schanz variety.[38] Secondly, such a second-best system must be evaluated against other arrangements that could achieve other values, including the important fairness interests that support source taxation. Thirdly, and most relevant, net taxation could be achieved by methods other than residence taxation, and recent examples in the corporate tax context have manifestly demonstrated that.

OLD AND NEW PROBLEMS WITH RESIDENCE TAXATION

Corporate taxation has been the focus of recent tax reform discourse. Less attention has been paid to the taxation of individuals.[39] This section examines both old and new problems with individual taxation in the global context.

Old Problems

Perhaps the most notable long-standing grievance with residence taxation is the migration of high-skilled workers. High-skilled migration from less developed states to the most developed, often labelled as 'brain drain', has been continuous and concerning for many states.[40] The idea that a high-skilled immigrant automatically becomes a resident of its host state due to their work and continuous physical presence in such state, albeit simple and straightforward, may be considered unfair by the home state that 'prepared' the migrant to become the taxpayer they are, yet sees no revenue in return. The balance of costs and benefits from high-skilled migration is, however, much more complex than the term brain drain implies,[41] and the fact that most of such migration occurs in one direction (certain developing

38 See, e.g., James Alm, *Is the Haig–Simons Standard Dead? The Uneasy Case for a Comprehensive Income Tax*, 71 NAT'L TAX J. 379 (2018).

39 See also María T. Soler Roch, *Individuals: The Forgotten Taxpayers in a BEPS Scenario, in* BUILDING GLOBAL INTERNATIONAL TAX LAW: ESSAYS IN HONOUR OF GUGLIELMO MAISTO 197 (Pasquale Pistone ed., 2022).

40 See, e.g., Kostic, *supra* note 5.

41 See, e.g., Kostic, *supra* note 5; Simon Commander, Mari Kangasniemi & L. Alan Winters, *The Brain Drain: Curse or Boon? A Survey of the Literature, in* CHALLENGES TO GLOBALIZATION (R. Baldwin & L. Winters eds., 2004); PIERPAOLO GIANNOCCOLO, THE BRAIN DRAIN: A SURVEY OF THE LITERATURE (Università degli Studi di Milano-Bicocca, Dep't Stat., Working Paper No. 2006-03-02, April 7, 2009), http://ssrn.com/abstract=1374329; Michel Beine, Frederic Docquier & Hillel Rapoport, *Brain Drain and Human Capital Formation in Developing Countries: Winners and Losers*, 118 ECON. J. 631 (2008); AnnaLee Saxenian, *From Brain*

states to a few most developed states) makes a policy response to the phenomenon challenging.

A comprehensive review of the complex tax implications of high-skilled migration is beyond the scope of this chapter. Yet, it is clear that this migration challenges the dogmatic justifications of residence taxation, increasingly so in the twenty-first century.[42] This challenge, although not decisive in the past, probably due to the limited political and economic power of the developing states involved, may raise its head due to recent geo-political changes and the new challenges to residence taxation.

A similar, albeit less contentious, problem involves transitory workers. This group is diverse. It includes border workers, whose taxation has long been resolved on bilateral bases or even pursuant to domestic laws, yet not without complications.[43] Once cross-border work involves residents of states beyond the immediate borders, tax problems related to cross-border work become harder to resolve.[44] Increased displacements, working migrants beyond the highly skilled, and the case of the EU further challenge the existing rules in a manner not conceptually different, even if less visible, than in the case of brain drain.

New Problems: Increasing Mobility of Individuals

Globalisation opened unique opportunities for wealthy individuals to change their tax residence. The increased competition among states for capital and human talent contributed to the mobility of high earners.[45] The mobility of wealthy individuals was accompanied by convenient tax planning and evasion techniques that could not be deterred by weak anti-avoidance rules designed to target corporate, rather than individual, abuse. A diametrically opposite phenomenon, but one that presents similar challenges, is increasing displacement of individuals in many regions of the world.[46]

The twenty-first century has seen an ongoing increase in the mobility of individuals, continuing the trends set in prior years,[47] but some aspects of this greater mobility, even if not dramatic, have serious tax policy consequences.

Drain to Brain Circulation: Transnational Communities and Regional Upgrading in India and China, 40 Stud. Compar. Int'l Dev. 35 (2005).

42 See, e.g., Ognjen Radonjić & Mirjana Bobić, *Brain Drain Losses: A Case Study of Serbia*, 59 Int'l Migration 5 (2021).

43 Even within the EU, issues regarding the appropriate calculation of income taxes arose. See, most notably Case C-279/93, Finanzamt Köln Altstadt v Schumacker, 1995 ECLI:EU:C:1995:31.

44 Border arrangements are often backed by domestic legislation, and the specific issues and relations are known and long-term.

45 Soler Roch, *supra* note 39, at 204–205.

46 *World Migration Report 2022*, *supra* note 3. See also Rita de la Feria & Giorgia Maffini, *The Impact of Digitalisation on Personal Income Taxes*, 2 Brit. Tax Rev. 154 (2021).

47 See, e.g., *World Migration Report 2022*, *supra* note 3.

Remote Work

Working remotely is not an entirely new phenomenon; it obviously dramatically increased during the COVID-19 pandemic and promises to continue and remain important as the pandemic winds down.[48] Remote work does not directly challenge residence taxation, but it does raise questions about its justification. Before the rise of remote work, the paradigmatic worker was physically present in their workplace, in direct contact with their customers, and typically all their work occurred in their state of residence. For most, the state where services were performed and the worker's state of residence were one and the same. Moreover, an almost universal rule in tax treaties prevents source taxation when an individual works for their residence–state employer in the source state for up to 183 days.[49]

Remote work interferes with this narrative. Most directly, the service provider and the service recipient are not located in the same location. The intuitive source rule that tracks income from services to the place of performance now requires interpretation as it is not clear whether the place of performance is where the service provider or recipient is located. The OECD Model Commentary expressed a preference for the location of the service provider,[50] yet this is far from a consensus interpretation. This interpretation converts a destination spirited source rule into de facto residence taxation (the location of the service provider is likely their residence). This problem is similar to other incomes generated by the digital economy, such as data-related advertising fees and offshore (e-commerce) portals. The growing acknowledgement that the source state, often called the market economy in this context, should be granted taxing rights, as exemplified by the Pillar One work, reduces residence taxation of this income.

Another aspect of remote work – the future magnitude of which is unclear yet unlikely to decrease even compared to pandemic numbers – is that it allows people to choose their location. This may also mean a residence change. Changes in residency may not be similar to the experiences with brain drain, and they may

48 See, e.g., Alicia Adamczyk, *A Government Report Says WFH Is Dying Out. A Remote Work Guru Says That's False*, Fortune, Mar. 28, 2023, 10:57 AM EDT, https://fortune.com/2023/03/28/remote-work-dying-out-bls-data-nick-bloom/; Emma Goldberg, *Do We Know How Many People Are Working From Home?* N. Y. Times (Mar. 30, 2023), www.nytimes.com/2023/03/30/business/economy/remote-work-measure-surveys.html. Most remote workers (of both groups) come from developed and emerging economies, with more than half originating from the United States. Around 50 per cent according to www.statista.com/statistics/1298849/digital-nomads-by-nationality-worldwide/ (last visited Apr. 21, 2024).The number of remote workers tripled during the pandemic, with the US originating nomads' number estimated at over 15 million, which implies a global number of over 30 million individuals. See, e.g., www.statista.com/statistics/1298313/number-digital-nomads-united-states/ (last visited June 7, 2023). This magnitude requires policy attention of a different kind in comparison to pre-pandemic numbers. See also de la Feria & Maffini, *supra* note 46, at 158–160.

49 OECD Model, art. 15(2) (2017).

50 *Commentaries on the Articles of the Model Tax Convention*, art. 15 para. 1 (2017).

not be tax driven, but they raise similar questions about allegiances of individuals to taxing jurisdictions.

Changes of location are likely to be even more significant within states.[51] We have all heard about workers who have left cities for suburbs or even more remote locations without changing employment. Although such moves do not impact international tax policy directly, they definitely impact employment patterns and growth within states, especially in states with multiple tax jurisdictions.[52] Such changes impact redistribution patterns within states, as well as the progressivity of their tax regimes, which in turn may impact their international tax policy stances and the legitimacy of residence taxations.

The New Nomads

A subset of workers that lacks a specific or fixed base (country) can be distinguished from the larger group of remote workers. Although not a perfectly discreet or identifiable group, such 'digital nomads' present different challenges to tax law than do other remote workers, who are not really nomads but rather workers who changed their base from their home country to another for a prolonged or indefinite period due to the opportunity for remote work.

The number of true digital nomads among remote workers is still quite small. If one uses the number of countries visited by these individuals (using five per year as a threshold), less than one sixth of remote workers qualify as such.[53] Surveys estimate that the overwhelming majority of remote workers (of both groups) are highly educated and well-paid, and therefore it is reasonable to view the groups as highly skilled overall.[54] They are generally affluent as well, and therefore they overlap with the group of immigrants who change residence or nationality for tax or other incentives.[55] Most notably, in the context of the digital nomads, states have begun offering targeted so-called e-residence programs, which further muddy the analysis of individual tax residence, especially when some of these states have a wide network of tax treaties that may potentially accommodate this practice.[56]

An interesting feature of the rise of *digital nomads* is that their movement is generally in the opposite direction to traditional migration by the highly skilled. In a

[51] See, e.g., Lukas Althoff, Fabian Eckert, Sharat Ganapati & Conor Walsh, *The Geography of Remote Work*, 93 REG'L SCI. & URB. ECON. (2022).

[52] From a US perspective, intra-country *nomadness* may have spillovers into cross-border movements and already present challenges to state taxation. See, e.g., MBO PARTNERS, www.mbopartners.com/state-of-independence/SOI-2021/ (last visited June 7, 2023). *See also* David R. Agrawal & Kirk J. Stark, *Will the Remote Work Revolution Undermine Progressive State Income Taxes?* 42 VA. TAX REV. 47 (2022); Hayes R. Holderness, *Individual Home-Work Assignments for State Taxes*, 98 WASH. L. REV 1 (2023).

[53] See, e.g., www.projectuntethered.com/digital-nomad-statistics/ (last visited June 7, 2023).

[54] See, e.g., www.nomadlist.com/digital-nomad-statistics (last visited June 7, 2023).

[55] See further, e.g., Tsilly Dagan & Talia Fischer, *State Inc.*, 27 CORNELL J. LAW & PUB. POL'Y 661 (2018).

[56] See, e.g., Republic of Estonia E-residency, https://e-resident.gov.ee/ (last visited Apr. 21, 2024).

reversal of the 'brain drain' pattern, digital nomads migrate from the most developed countries to some developing countries. Naturally, due to the nature of temporary stays, it is difficult to produce reliable and useful data about the precise directionality and magnitude of this phenomenon. Nonetheless, this is perhaps the best example of one having strong economic and even personal, political or historical ties to one state while having none to their resident state under the current residency rules. This also best demonstrates the urgency for an international tax policy discussion of the existing rules' viability. Some states have responded to this challenge with a variety of extensions of their tax jurisdiction, and scholars have outlined different proposals to do the same based on existing mechanisms.[57] This chapter does not dispute the logic of these unilateral actions. Yet, like what happens in the corporate tax world, these unilateral actions lead to further incoherence of the tax regime. A principled multilateral discourse is therefore inevitable.

A New Work Environment and New Business

Although it is beyond the immediate scope of this chapter, one must acknowledge the impact of the new work environment on business and, eventually, on corporate tax policy. The disconnect between the physical presence of employees and that of their employer puts further pressure on business taxation in general and the corporate income tax in particular. The most obvious example of this is the potential trigger of permanent establishment by employees present in states where they perform the same functions as they did when residing in the same state as their employer.[58] This may expose the employer to taxation in the employee's new state of residence. These pressures naturally lead corporations to change their investments and rearrange employment and other business schemes, all without any real change to their business or the specific functions filled by their employees.

The Increasingly Weaker Case for Residence Taxation

The challenges arising from increased mobility reinforce the arguments against residence taxation. The most obvious of these is the reliance of the regime on the legal definition of residence.[59] As discussed, residence is a purely legal concept and, for the most part, one that developed under tax law with little interaction with other disciplines. Like similar definitions, it is sensitive to different interpretations and inconsistent policy perspectives. This is obvious in the case of tax residence since even tax treaties do not simply accept it, instead relying on supporting interpretative

[57] See, e.g., Avi-Yonah, *supra* note 4, which proposes to tax nomads based on citizenship, rejects the 'benefits theory' of taxation, applies ability-to-pay principles based on the belonging to a political community, and applies anti-abuse rules.

[58] See Collier, *supra* note 9 (explaining these phenomena).

[59] See also Pinto, *supra* note 28, at 281–282.

mechanisms. The lack of a normative justification for the use of tax residence beyond administrative convenience makes it even weaker.

The lack of normative support for residence taxation, the perception that source taxation aligns with benefits intuitions, and the reality that residence is fluid for the wealthiest exacerbates the view that residence taxation is unjust. Put simply, source states or traditional capital importers find it difficult to accept that the fruits of business activities within their jurisdiction are primarily or exclusively taxed elsewhere. However, traditional residence jurisdictions are similarly concerned about the fluidity of residence. Although they enjoyed the outcome of residence taxation in a world with less mobility, the developments mentioned put traditional residence jurisdictions in a strange alliance with traditional source jurisdictions. At present, these states prefer to address these concerns with anti-base erosion rules. Yet, as has become apparent during the BEPS Project, reaching consensus over these rules is very difficult.

A Comment on Citizenship-based Taxation

Finally, an evaluation of residence taxation would not be complete without a note about citizenship taxation. The discussion of citizenship taxation, especially the academic discourse of the US policy, the sole state to truly implement it, has been going on for many years. The changes in individual mobility in the twenty-first century have made the debate even more intense. But the bottom line of this discourse is that citizenship taxation can be supported either on the grounds of the special value of citizenship[60] or administrability.[61] The former argument is realistically unique to the United States, while the latter is weak to begin with, as evidenced by the original and persistent choice of states to use domicile and residence rather than nationality as the bases for taxation.

The weakness of citizenship taxation becomes even more evident when considering its unfairness and potential waste.[62] The most basic support for citizenship taxation relies on the connection between the taxpayer and their political community and the right to vote, which is typically associated with citizenship. One cannot avoid thinking about the slogan of no taxation without representation in this context. The slogan is, in my view, irrelevant for the purposes of this chapter, since its origins are in colonialism and have nothing to do with our increasingly mobile and liberal world. It is difficult to find the connection between the right to vote and the obligation to pay tax on a worldwide basis. Voters decide the taxation framework

60 See, e.g., Michael S. Kirsch, *Taxing Citizens in a Global Economy*, 82 N. Y. U. L. REV. 443 (2007).

61 See, e.g., Edward A. Zelinsky, *Citizenship and Worldwide Taxation: Citizenship as an Administrable Proxy for Domicile*, 96 IOWA L. REV. 1289 (2011). But see Ruth Mason, *Citizenship Taxation*, 89 S. CAL. L. REV. 169 (2015).

62 See, e.g., Mason, *supra* note 61.

within their state, including their own taxation, subject to the constraints of global competition for resources. Arguing that they are somehow confined to taxing themselves on a worldwide basis is essentially undemocratic and can be justified only by some natural law basis that this chapter rejects as a basis for taxation. Moreover, no state will concede taxation of income clearly generated within its jurisdiction regardless of the voting status of the income earner, and, therefore, the voting argument is weak at best in this context. The same logic applies, albeit with lesser force to residence taxation more generally. Furthermore, there are clear cases where states will not concede taxation yet at the same time will also not give voting rights; the cases of immigrants, and of course refugees, immediately come to mind. The political community argument is, therefore, not persuasive.

Interim Conclusion

The discussion in this section demonstrates that there is weak normative support for residence taxation. Therefore, only administrative convenience and ability-to-pay may justify the existing rules. The next section ponders whether residence taxation is necessary to achieve these modest goals, demonstrating that redistribution and administrability could be equally preserved with exclusive source taxation of individuals.

SOURCE-BASED INCOME TAXATION OF INDIVIDUALS

This section describes the idea of taxing individuals solely on the basis of source, elaborates the merits of such a reform, and describes the conditions for its success.

A Preliminary Proposal

The core proposal is straightforward: award exclusive taxing rights of income earned by all individuals to the source states of such income. This means, first, that each item of income will be allocated to a source jurisdiction.[63] That implies that individual taxpayers will not have residual non-sourced income or, put differently, there will not be income that is homeless or stateless. Further, the potential for double taxation (or double non-taxation) will vanish, making all matters related to relief from double taxation irrelevant. Secondly, income earned by individuals will potentially be taxed by multiple jurisdictions, independently, when each jurisdiction determines its tax rates and administration according to its own political process. Finally, a universal unified system of accounting and sourcing income will make the

[63] Fully or partly. As explained next, some items of income may be apportioned among two or more jurisdictions.

reform smoother, especially if it is encoded in a multilateral agreement. Yet, the reform could also be implemented (at least initially) bilaterally or even unilaterally.

Universal Sourcing

Most obviously, the proposal will depend on a wide acceptance of a universal sourcing system. Existing source rules are anachronistic, and their coverage is incomplete. Still, for most (and most ubiquitous) items of income, common sourcing rules are already in place. Therefore, existing sourcing rules may serve as a useful basis for the construction of the new system.[64]

The Inevitability of a Formulary Solution

The key problem of source rules is that they purport to provide a normative connection between income and jurisdiction. Yet, they often do not. The existing source rules have been useful as acceptable and perceivably fair approximations of normative connections. Yet, globalisation and the other challenges discussed call the legitimacy of the existing source rules into question. It is clear that income taxation by nation states requires political, rather than normative or economic, arrangement among states. Formulary apportionment allows for this division, using proxies for acceptable connections between income and jurisdictions, without the pretension of normativity. Therefore, formulary taxation may be the only way to preserve international income taxation and the legitimacy of the international tax regime.

Conditions and Advantages

The key advantage of a regime based only on source income taxation of individuals is the elimination of complexity involved with multiple bases for taxation and the focus on a single basis that can gain legitimacy in the twenty-first century. It does not require us to rely on unsatisfactory definitions or criteria nor wasteful incentives for tax competition. One may argue that competition for individuals, capital, and talent will simply be replaced with competition for those things based on their connection to the source rules. This is true, yet the desirability of the change would depend on the source rule or the formula used. It is likely that a basic understanding of territorial demands will govern most income, the BEPS Project 'value creation' being an example, albeit operationally useless.

So, the obvious first step would be that states work on a revised set of source rules that fit the twenty-first century. Fortunately, this is already being done, even if primarily in the corporate income tax context. Moreover, only meaningful competition for investment will take place if a few basic measures are taken, such as adopting

64 Another advantage of building up from the existing rules is that they heavily rely on residence anyway, which may help alleviate potential anxiety of states over losing what they may initially consider as *their* tax bases.

a norm that income cannot be allocated to a jurisdiction where only money is invested, at least not income beyond market bank interest rate.[65]

The second stage requires that all income be apportioned or sourced. To do that, one can think of a parallel mechanism used by the Pillar proposals or by Country-by-Country Reporting (CbCR), that is, that each person will be required to account for their income based on the rules of their country of residence. In complex cases, authorities may use tax treaty tie-breaking rules of the OECD Model Article 4(2) sort. Income not falling into any other category requires a solution. The most appealing solution is to allocate proportionately such income among all other jurisdictions with income. This should create an incentive to ensure that the source rules cover all income.

Third, one may argue that states will engage in tax competition to attract investment in a manner compatible with the source rules adopted. This could be particularly problematic with mobile capital income. Here, meaningful formulary taxation is superior to the traditional source rules, but the latter could work if appropriately revised to prevent elective allocation of income to a jurisdiction.[66] The adoption of a minimum rate by all the countries is another potential solution. This chapter is agnostic about the need for such a rule; yet, since it may remind one of the Pillar Two idea, one should note that the operation of the rate would be different – no Income Inclusion Rule (IRR) or Under-Taxed Payments Rule (UTPR). At most, one can think about allocating under-taxed income to other jurisdictions as an incentive to ensure minimum taxation.

Similar Ideas

This chapter does not provide a prescription for tax reform but only outlines one idea. Further, the author would support other genuine political solutions reached by states to the political challenge of taxing income in the twenty-first century. This chapter merely presents a framework for such negotiations.

Indeed, this chapter relies on many ideas expressed by other proposals to reform individual income taxation. Most notably, Giorgio Beretta made significant contributions to the literature when he comprehensively analysed developments discussed in this chapter, concluding similarly that the existing rules cannot be justified in the twenty-first century.[67] Beretta also promoted a proposal to adopt a single basis for taxation: straightforward physical presence (based on number of days spent in each jurisdiction). His proposal would allocate the income of individuals among jurisdictions based on physical presence. He, like me, was not concerned with the ability-to-

[65] This should not be controversial and has already been agreed on conceptually during the BEPS Project's work on transfer pricing.

[66] See also Wei Cui, *The Mirage of Mobile Capital* (May 7, 2023), https://ssrn.com/abstract=4440596 (challenging the perceived difficulties presented by the mobility of capital income).

[67] See, Beretta, *supra* note 36.

pay argument, referring to an idea raised first by Peter Wattel in the context of the European Court's famous *Schumacker* case to allocate personal allowances and other credits and deductions on fractional bases in the same way income is allocated.[68]

There are many parallels between the proposal examined in this chapter and Beretta's, and the latter has a clear advantage in terms of simplicity and administrability. Yet, as already mentioned, this chapter consistently argues that administrability should not be the primary reason for the adoption of tax policy. Taxation based on days spent in a state include, as admitted by Beretta, non-productive (vacation) days. But it would be costly to monitor which days are productive and which are not, although, on the other hand, failing to take non-productive days into account may undermine legitimacy of the norm. Moreover, adopting Beretta's simple regime would incentivise manipulation, and clearly the people most capable of manipulating these rules would be the same wealthy people who manipulate the existing residence rules. Beretta's regime would also lead to tax competition that resembles the existing competition for the rich and the talented. Finally, Beretta's proposal is completely isolated from the corporate income tax challenge and ignores the tensions that remote work and digital nomads create. It will therefore not be acceptable for many states, in the same way that the current rules are not, and hence it is unlikely to gain widespread support, much less improve the legitimacy of the international tax regime.

Compatibility of the Proposal with the Existing Rules

A key advantage of taxing individuals based only on source is the idea's relative compatibility with existing rules.[69] Of course, this would still be quite a fundamental reform, and it would require revisions of long-standing domestic tax traditions and of tax treaties. Yet, some of these changes must happen regardless, a good example being source rule revisions.

Ending residence taxation would generate the need for certain reforms. These include allocating and apportioning non-sourced income to a jurisdiction or jurisdictions, resolving the treatment of undertaxed income, and enabling states to maintain their preferred levels of redistribution through their income taxes. The first requirement may entail revision of the existing source rules or a more ambitious (though inevitable in the view of this author) formulary apportionment of individual income. The second requirement requires rules to prevent artificial allocation or apportionment of income to a jurisdiction. This may also take the form of a minimal

[68] Peter J. Wattel, *The EC Court's Attempts to Reconcile the Treaty Freedoms with International Tax Law*, 33(2) Common Mkt. L. Rev. 226 (1996).

[69] Again, the assumption of this chapter is that states do not have an appetite for a complete overhaul of the international tax regime, such as replacing income taxation with another tax, perhaps a consumption tax.

rate requirement. Both are familiar to the modern international tax regime. This last requirement may be the most difficult to accept for some states, and is perhaps the least familiar. Yet, the technical solution is not different from any other allocation or apportionment. The most straightforward solution would be proportional apportionment, so that if one earns 50 per cent of their income in a jurisdiction, all relevant tax calculations (exemptions, credits, rate brackets, etc.) will apply at 50 per cent levels. Other calculations are also possible, yet, again, the specifics must be left for the states themselves. The chapter does not discuss at length possible scenarios for adoption of this idea. However, the compatibility with existing rules allows states to adopt it unilaterally or on a bilateral basis, the latter being more appropriate in cases of applicable tax treaties that will need to be revised accordingly.

CONCLUSION

This chapter concludes that eliminating the current mix of residence and source taxation in favour of taxing individuals based solely on source could achieve progress in all the above-mentioned ways. It acknowledges that reform of the existing source rules may be required, but it notes that such reform is needed regardless and independently of the decision to tax individuals based only on source. Additional adaptations are required, but these adaptations are modest.

3

Taxing Nomads

Reviving Citizenship-based Taxation for the Twenty-First Century

Reuven S. Avi-Yonah

If a stranger owns something in the territory of a civitas, no taxes can be imposed on him ... no taxes can be imposed on a person who is not subject to rule[1]

INTRODUCTION: THE NEW NOMADS

On July 20, 2022, Bloomberg published a story entitled "Americans Who Can't Afford Homes Are Moving to Europe Instead."[2] The story explained that "[p]-rohibitive housing prices, a strong dollar and political rancor have contributed to a wave of Americans relocating to Europe." The reporter interviewed several such Americans, who relocated to sunny, relatively quiet locations like Sicily, but continued to work remotely at their previous jobs.

The global mobility of relatively affluent people (as opposed to economic and political migrants, who tend to be less well-off) has been a reality for many years.[3] The ability of the rich to migrate legally has undermined the traditional view that, in the current age of globalization, capital is more mobile than labor, especially in the context of evading taxation. In this century, capital has been increasingly subject to strict reporting methods such as the Foreign Account Tax Compliance Act (FATCA) and the Common Reporting Standard for automatic exchange of tax

I would like to thank Tsilly Dagan, Ana Paula Dourado, Ruth Mason, and the participants of the conference for very helpful comments.

1 Franciscus Lucanus Parmensis, De privilegio fisci, in: Tractatus universi iuris, vol. 12, Venice 1584, quoted in Andreas Thier, Traditionselemente des Finanzföderalismus in der Schweiz: Zur Geschichte des interkantonalen D oppelbesteuerungsverbots (2014) ("ideo si forensis possideret in territorio unius civitatis, non posset imponi collecta ... persona non subdita non potest sibi collecta imponi.")

2 Taegan Goddard, Taegan Goddard's Political Wire, politicalwire.com/2022/07/20/more-americans-are-moving-to-europe/ (last visited Dec. 11, 2023).

3 See Tsilly Dagan and Talia Fischer, *State Inc.*, 27 Cornell J. L. & Pub. Pol'y 661 (2018); Reuven Avi-Yonah, *And Yet It Moves: Taxation and Labor Mobility in the Twenty-First Century*, 67 Tax L. Rev. 169 (2014); Taxation and Migration (Reuven Avi-Yonah and Joel Slemrod eds., 2015).

information (CRS). These regimes and a series of well-publicized leaks have meant that, even though capital is mobile, it is becoming more difficult for individuals to use this mobility to illegally evade taxation in their country of residence. At the same time, the rise of "golden visas" and other schemes intended to attract rich migrants (such as the United Kingdom and other countries' non-domicile or "non-dom" schemes under which rich migrants are subject to tax only on locally derived income) have made it much easier for the rich to immigrate. Typically, these rich migrants do not acquire citizenship in their new country of residence, and instead retain their previous citizenship because, other than the United States, their country of citizenship will not tax nonresident citizens on global income. As a result, their foreign-source income (that is, income derived from locations other than their new country of residence) is not subject to taxation anywhere. Additionally, the OECD has found that such migrants can more easily avoid CRS reporting because it is linked to the migrants' former country of residence, and because they declare to banks that they are resident only in their new country of residence, where they have no income.[4]

The United States is very different from most other countries in taxing its citizens living permanently elsewhere on their global income.[5] By contrast, almost every developed country and most developing countries tax their residents on global income. The question I will address here considers how best to tax the new nomads. Most of the literature (including my previous writing on this topic) criticizes the US approach of taxing citizens living abroad as a historical anachronism and instead accepts the approach of taxing only residents on their global income as the obviously better approach.[6] However, under changing conditions, this question warrants reconsideration, which I undertake in this chapter. I discuss ability to pay as the theoretical basis of the US income tax. I also explain why ability-to-pay taxation was applied to citizens living overseas before I explore the critiques of this rule. I then

4 OECD, Preventing Abuse of Residence by Investment Schemes to Circumvent the CRS (2018), https://web-archive.oecd.org/2018-02-19/473012-consultation-document-preventing-abuse-of-residence-by-investment-schemes.pdf; See also Reuven Avi-Yonah & Gianluca Mazzoni, *Due Diligence in International Tax Law*, *in* Due Diligence in the International Legal Order 302, 302–312 (Heike Krieger et al. eds., 2020).

5 Hungary also taxes nonresident citizens on global income. Eritrea purports to tax citizens living overseas on global income, but it is doubtful that this tax is enforced. The Philippines abolished a similar tax.

6 See Cynthia Blum & Paula N. Singer, *A Coherent Policy Proposal for U.S. Residence-based Taxation of Individuals*, 41 Vand. J. Transnat'l L. 705 (2008); Reuven Avi-Yonah, *The Case against Taxing Citizens*, 58 Tax Notes Int'l 389 (2010) (arguing against citizenship taxation); Michael S. Kirsch, *Taxing Citizens in a Global Economy*, 82 N. Y. U. L. Rev. 443 (2007); Edward A. Zelinsky, *Citizenship and Worldwide Taxation: Citizenship as an Administrable Proxy for Domicile*, 96 Iowa L. Rev. 1289 (2011) (arguing in favor); see also Ruth Mason, *Citizenship Taxation*, S. Cal. Rev. 89 (2016) (arguing that basing global taxation on residence and citizenship would be better than using either criterion alone).

attempt to justify citizenship taxation as applied to the new nomads, and finally I explore the implications of the US approach for taxation of noncitizen residents.

SELIGMAN, ABILITY TO PAY, BENEFITS, AND THE 1923 REPORT

To understand why the United States taxes nonresident citizens, it is helpful to consider the theoretical basis of the income tax.

The United States first taxed income during the Civil War, but this tax (which was upheld by the Supreme Court) was allowed to expire in 1872.[7] In 1894, the Democrats in Congress were able to enact another income tax because they argued that the existing federal taxes (duties and excises on imported and domestic goods) were regressive and unrelated to ability to pay. This tax, however, was struck down by the Supreme Court in 1895 as an unconstitutional "direct tax" that was not apportioned among the states by population.[8] The result was a long struggle to overcome this decision, which culminated in 1913 with the passage of the Sixteenth Amendment authorizing Congress to levy an individual income tax.[9] The personal income tax has since then been the main source of revenue of the federal government.

Before 1913, the main tax on the rich was levied by the states and localities. Before the 1890s, these were primarily property taxes, which mostly applied only to real property. However, most of the wealth of the rich at that time consisted of intangible property, such as stocks and bonds, which were effectively unreachable by the property taxes because the intangible property could easily be moved from state to state. Wisconsin was the pioneer of the state-level income tax, but early income taxes were based on the benefits theory because they were levied in exchange for the benefits provided by the state, such as police protection or the rule of law as applied to contracts, and not based on ability to pay as measured by comparison to fellow citizens of the same state.

Edwin R. A. Seligman, Columbia economics professor (1861–1939), author of Progressive Income Taxation (1894), and the US member of the League of Nations committee of economists (1923), was a major proponent of taxation based on ability to pay. Unlike his colleague Thomas S. Adams (1873–1933), who served on the Wisconsin tax commission (1911–1915), Seligman was never involved in state taxation, and never supported benefits-based taxation. A lifelong progressive (unlike Adams, who was the main tax advisor to the Treasury in both the Wilson administration and in the Republican administrations that followed), Seligman consistently argued in favor of progressive taxation based on ability to pay. Congress's passage of

7 See a fuller discussion of the historical context in the following section.

8 Pollock v. Farmers' Loan & Trust Co., 157 U.S. 429 (1895), *aff'd* 158. U.S. 601 (1895).

9 Steven R. Weisman, The Great Tax Wars (2004).

the Sixteenth Amendment authorizing taxing "all income from whatever source derived," that is, including capital gains (which were exempt in the United Kingdom) and foreign-source income, reflected the ability-to-pay principle advocated by Seligman. As Michael J. Graetz and Michael M. O'Hear have shown, Adams was more in favor of source-based than residence-based taxation, even though he rejected exemption systems in favor of the foreign tax credit (1918). But Adams' position was based on the practical view that the United States should not "leave money on the table" by not taxing income that the source country failed to tax.[10] Seligman, on the other hand, favored residence-based taxation of global income because all income contributed to ability to pay.

When Seligman served on the 1923 committee and drafted its report, he faced a dilemma – ability to pay did not resolve the question of which countries had the right to tax the individual. Seligman responded by developing the concept of economic allegiance, which established that individuals should pay tax to the countries that enabled them to produce the income, which reflects a broad view of benefits-based taxation. But Seligman also insisted that these individuals must be subject to full taxation somewhere, which is why he rejected the common practice of the residence country exempting foreign-source income (because it may not be taxed in the source country, thereby violating the ideal of full taxation based on ability to pay). Instead, the committee developed four methods of preventing double taxation: first, the foreign-tax-credit method, which they rejected as too generous to source jurisdictions; second, the exemption-by-the-source-country method, which they preferred but regarded as unrealistic; third, division of the revenues resulting from full taxation by formula; and fourth, classification of the income into different types and assigning some types (active income) to source countries exclusively and other types (passive income) to residence countries exclusively. As the report states,

> The ideal solution is that the individual's whole faculty should be taxed, but that it should be taxed only once, and that the liability should be divided among the tax districts according to his relative interests in each. The individual has certain economic interests in the place of his permanent residence or domicile, as well as in the place or places where his property is situated or from which his income is derived.[11]

Thus, as early as a century ago, the US income tax was based primarily on ability to pay. But how did this apply to US citizens living abroad? For an answer to this question, I will examine the origins of the unique US system of citizenship-based taxation, which can be traced back to the Civil War income tax.

[10] Michael J. Graetz & Michael M. O'Hear, *The "Original Intent" of U.S. International Taxation*, 46 Duke L.J. 1021 (1997).

[11] Report, 24.

THE ORIGINS AND DEBATE ON US CITIZENSHIP TAXATION

Citizenship-based taxation[12] of Americans living overseas began during the Civil War. The original Civil War income tax from 1861 was only imposed on residents (regardless of citizenship) and on the US-source income of nonresident citizens.[13] The tax on nonresident citizens was imposed at a higher rate and with no exemption amount.[14] In 1864, the tax was amended to apply to the income of "every person residing in the United States, or of any citizen of the United States residing abroad," regardless of whether the income arose "in the United States or elsewhere."[15] The application of the US tax to citizens living overseas continued until the Civil War income tax expired in 1872; it was revived in the aborted income tax of 1894, and finally it was incorporated into the "modern" income tax of 1913.[16]

What was the rationale of taxing citizens living overseas? The original enactors of the provision must have known it would be very difficult to enforce, and in fact negligible tax was collected even from the US-source income of citizens living overseas during the Civil War.[17] The application of tax to citizens living overseas was a symbolic gesture: at a time of severe national crisis, when citizens living in the United States were expected not just to pay tax but also to serve in the military and potentially die for their country (or at least pay for a substitute), the perception of rich citizens living overseas was too much for Congress to bear. As stated by a senator who served as a manager in the conference committee that adopted the 1861 tax law (taxing nonresident citizens at a higher rate):

> We do not desire that our citizens who have incomes in this country ... should go out of the country, reside in Paris or elsewhere, avoiding the risk of being drafted or contributing anything personally to the requirements of the country at this time, and get off with as low a tax as everybody else ... If a man draws his income from our public debt, or from property here, and resides in Paris, skulking away from contributing his personal support to the Government in this day of its extremity, he ought to pay a higher income tax.[18]

The same rhetoric was eventually applied to taxing nonresident citizens on their worldwide income. Senator George Hoar stated in 1894 that:

> There are a great many people, I am sorry to say, who go abroad for that very purpose [of avoiding tax], and some of them went abroad during the late [Civil War]. They

12 This section is based in part on Avi-Yonah, *supra* note 6.

13 Act of Aug. 5, 1861, ch. 45, § 49, 12 Stat. 292, 309.

14 Id.

15 Act of June 30, 1864, ch. 173, § 116, 13 Stat. 223, 281.

16 Act of Aug. 27, 1894, ch. 349, § 27, 28 Stat. 509, 553; Act of Oct. 3, 1913, ch. 16, § II(A)(1), 38 Stat. 114, 166.

17 Kirsch, *supra* note 6 (noting that from 1863 to 1865 US citizens living overseas paid $230,470 of $84,015,918 of income tax collected, or 0.003%).

18 Id., at 451.

lived in luxury, at the same time at less cost, in a foreign capital; they had none of the voluntary obligations which rest upon citizens, of charity, or contributions, or supporting churches, or anything of that sort, and they escaped taxation.[19]

The origin of US taxation of nonresident citizens should thus be understood as stemming from a period in which only the rich paid the income tax. Under this early income tax, which applied to both resident and nonresident citizens, the $800 exemption excluded most resident citizens. Additionally, the tax was introduced against the background of the most severe crisis in the history of the country, at a time when resident citizens could be drafted, and when the likelihood of dying in the service of the country was the highest it has ever been in the history of the United States. In that context, it is understandable that Congress would want to appear to impose an equal tax burden on resident and nonresident citizens, since nonresident citizens were few and likely to be residing overseas for the purpose of avoiding both the draft and the tax. As Senator Hoar implicitly acknowledged, there was in practice no hope of collecting tax from nonresident citizens, and "they escaped taxation" even though the tax nominally applied to them.

In 1924, the Supreme Court upheld the taxation of nonresident citizens in *Cook v. Tait.*[20] The case involved a native citizen of the United States who lived permanently in Mexico and derived his income from real and personal property located in Mexico. The taxpayer argued that the United States lacked jurisdiction to tax because both residence jurisdiction and source jurisdiction were lacking. Nevertheless, the Court upheld the power to tax nonresident citizens because of the benefits provided to them by the US government: "the government, by its very nature, benefits the citizen and his property wherever found and, therefore, has the power to make the benefit complete" by taxing the nonresident citizen.[21]

Cook v. Tait permits Congress to tax nonresident citizens, but it does not require the United States to do so. The history of US taxation of nonresident citizens is a dubious basis from which to argue that the practice should continue.[22] The application of the income tax to nonresident citizens stemmed from a great national crisis in which resident citizens were expected not just to pay tax but also to risk their lives for their country. At the same time, nonresident citizens were likely to be few, rich (or else they would not be subject to tax), and suspected of living overseas to avoid both the draft and the tax. None of these conditions apply today. The United States is not in crisis, there is no draft, and millions of US citizens live permanently overseas for reasons that have nothing to do with taxation.[23] In many cases, they

[19] Id., at 453.
[20] Cook v. Tait, 265 U.S. 47 (1924).
[21] Id.
[22] See Mason, *supra* note 6; but cf. Kirsch, *supra* note 6.
[23] We have no idea how many US citizens live overseas. The GAO conducted an experimental study of expatriate population in three randomly selected countries in 2004 in an attempt to start counting expatriates in the 2010 Census, and concluded that it "would not be cost

are citizens merely because they were born in the United States, even though they left the country when they were young, and may therefore be entirely unaware of their tax obligations. In many other cases, they choose or are assigned to live overseas because of the opportunities presented by globalization.

Under these twenty-first century circumstances, does the United States still have a good reason for taxing citizens living permanently overseas? Michael S. Kirsch argues that the answer is yes because of the benefits afforded to nonresident citizens by virtue of their citizenship.[24] Edward A. Zelinsky rejects these arguments but argues that citizenship is an administrable proxy for domicile, which justifies taxation.[25] In my view, neither of these arguments are persuasive, but, in the following paragraphs, I agree with Kirsch's alternative argument, favoring ability-to-pay taxation of nonresident citizens.[26]

The Benefits Argument for Citizenship Taxation

Kirsch lists the following benefits accorded to nonresident citizens: personal protection, property protection, right to vote, right to enter, and past benefits.[27] As Zelinsky and Mason separately observe, these benefits do not seem sufficient to justify taxation.[28] The protection afforded by the United States to its nonresident citizens and their property is rarely invoked and, when it is invoked, it is frequently ineffective. For example, as shown by the Supreme Court cases involving foreign citizens on death row, the right to consular assistance when a citizen is accused of a crime in a foreign country is frequently not utilized at all or utilized too late to be effective.[29]

The right to vote argument is upside down. It is legitimate to argue that nonresident citizens must be given the right to vote because they are subject to US tax, although even that "no taxation without representation" tradition is sometimes ignored (just ask DC residents and resident aliens). But it does not follow that because nonresident citizens vote they must be taxed. Moreover, many countries do not allow nonresident citizens to vote because they do not fully bear the

effective" to do so; it refers to the Census Bureau's acknowledgment that currently "no accurate estimate exists" on the number of Americans abroad. The several reports to Congress by the Census Bureau and the GAO on this issue do not even attempt to give a range or an estimate of the number of Americans overseas. See U.S. Gov't Accountability Off., GAO-04-898, 2010 Census: Counting Americans Overseas as Part of the Decennial Census Would Not Be Cost Effective (2004); see also Mason, *supra* note 6.

24 Kirsch, *supra* note 6.

25 Zelinsky, *supra* note 6.

26 For my previous view, see Avi-Yonah, *supra* note 6; see also Mason, *supra* note 6.

27 Kirsch, *supra* note 6.

28 Zelinsky, *supra* note 6; see also Mason, *supra* note 6.

29 See Medellín v. Texas, 552 U.S. 491 (2008).

consequences of their votes, and it would be legitimate for the United States to follow that route if it stopped taxing nonresident citizens.[30]

One of the most valuable rights of citizenship is the right to enter, but the right to enter is a tenuous basis for taxation. Having US citizenship overseas does give individuals the peace of mind that they can enter the United States at any time, but before it is exercised this option seems a weak basis for such a heavy price as worldwide taxation. It is true that many nonresident aliens would like to obtain US citizenship, and worldwide taxation can be seen as a "price" to be paid for it, but that is because they want to live and work in the United States, not because of citizenship per se.

Finally, even Kirsch acknowledges that the past benefit argument is weak. Nonresident citizens may or may not have received benefits from the United States while living there; in many cases they left at too young an age to receive significant benefits, and in other cases they resided long enough to pay tax for their benefits.

To see why the benefits argument for taxing nonresident citizens is wrong, one should compare the benefits conferred by citizenship to the benefits conferred by residency to US residents.[31] The latter are much more significant. US residents benefit from first-class government protection, the rule of law, an outstanding educational system, and the many opportunities of a free market economy. These benefits, all paid for by tax dollars, are the reason why the United States is still the top choice of immigrants from other countries. Nonresident citizens do not receive these benefits, or, at best, they receive them in a much weaker form. Finally, the same benefits cited by Kirsch as supporting taxation of nonresident citizens (protection of self and property, right to vote, right to enter, past benefits) are also afforded to nonresident citizens by every other major democracy, and yet no other country taxes its nonresident citizens. It is hard to argue that the protections of US citizenship are significantly more valuable than those of EU or Swiss citizenship – in fact, in many places carrying a US passport is more burdensome (because of visa requirements) and potentially more dangerous than an EU or Swiss passport. If the other democracies do not impose worldwide taxation on their nonresident citizens because of the benefits they provide, it is unclear why the United States should exact such a high price for its benefits.

[30] The United Kingdom, Switzerland, Ireland, Israel, India, Chile, and Greece are among the democratic countries that do not allow most nonresident citizens to vote, while Canada only allows them to do so if their nonresident status has lasted for 5 years or less. http://aceproject.org/epic-en/CDTable?question = VO004. See Wolfgang Schön, *Taxation and Democracy*, 72 Tax L. Rev. 235 (2019) for a normative discussion of whether this is justified (arguing that it is if they are not subject to tax, but not otherwise).

[31] Cf. Mason, *supra* note 6, at 189–196 (comparing benefits received by resident and nonresident US citizens).

The Administrability Argument for Citizenship Taxation

Zelinsky, after acknowledging that the traditional benefit rationale for taxing nonresident citizens is weak, advanced a novel and ingenious argument, that citizenship is an administrable proxy for domicile.[32] It is true that many countries base their worldwide tax on residents in part on fiscal domicile. Domicile is a standard, not a rule, and is embodied in the tax treaties (including US tax treaties) as a tie-breaker in cases of dual residency. As defined in the treaties, domicile requires weighing of several factors, including where the taxpayer's "permanent home" is, their "habitual abode," "center of vital interests," and their "nationality."[33] Except for nationality (citizenship), all of these terms are undefined and tax administrations take different approaches in defining them.

Zelinsky correctly notes that the fiscal domicile standard is hard to administer, and in fact the United States abandoned this standard in its federal law in 1984 and replaced it with a physical presence rule. However, Zelinsky's suggestion that citizenship be used as a proxy for domicile is misplaced, because it is so clearly overbroad. For citizens who are US residents, there is no need to base taxation on citizenship because they would be taxed on worldwide income as residents. For nonresident citizens, citizenship is a very poor proxy for domicile because so many of them live permanently overseas and do not have any of the other indicia of US domicile other than citizenship. At the extreme, citizenship-based taxation applies to someone who was born in the United States but has no other US connections at all and may even be unaware that he is a US citizen. If the United States was looking for an administrable definition of residency, it already has one in the physical presence test. Unlike corporations, individuals cannot be in more than one place at the same time, and therefore the United States and every other country base residency on physical presence, which is easily monitored using entry and exit records. With certain exceptions, any individual who is physically present in the United States for over half a year (183 days) is subject to worldwide taxation regardless of their citizenship. The argument against basing residency solely on physical presence is that it encourages individuals to "count days" and maintain their permanent home in the United States while being absent for enough days to escape worldwide taxation. Therefore, the United States also counts days in previous years, so that it is not possible to be in the United States 182 days in every year and avoid residency status.

Because physical presence is perfectly administrable, administrability is not an argument for taxing nonresident citizens. In fact, administrability is perhaps the strongest argument for not taxing nonresident citizens.[34] Imagine for a moment that

[32] Zelinsky, *supra* note 6.

[33] *See* US Model Tax Treaty (2016), Art. 4; OECD Model Tax Treaty (2021), Art. 4.

[34] See Mason, *supra* note 6, at 212–222 (detailing onerous compliance complexity for taxpayers and the inability of the US government to enforce its citizenship tax abroad, observing that "the

Section 911 is repealed (as many critics have advocated). In that case every US citizen living permanently overseas would in theory be subject to full tax on the first dollar of income and would need to claim the foreign tax credit (if applicable) to prevent dual taxation, but that would not help for cases in which the country of residence taxes the US citizen on US-source income. Even with the current resources of the IRS, the only nonresident citizens the United States is likely to tax in this scenario are temporary expatriates working for US multinationals. In other cases, the only way to administer the tax is to condition the renewal of US passports on reporting the tax ID number to the IRS so they can check if returns have been filed. This system works in many cases today because Section 911 ensures that many nonresident citizens do not owe any US tax and are therefore willing to file returns. If they had to actually pay tax, many of them might simply forego renewing their US passports, since they usually have other passports as well. I seriously doubt the IRS could catch most of them under that scenario. A law that cannot be enforced is a bad law.

As a practical matter, taxing nonresident citizens is possible because (a) some of them work for large US employers who aid the IRS in enforcing the tax, (b) most others do not owe any US tax because of Section 911. I am doubtful that the United States collects much tax from nonresident citizens living permanently overseas.[35] The cost of what the United States does collect is having to administer Section 911, a very complex provision that imposes significant transaction costs on both taxpayers and the IRS. Blum and Singer, writing together at the time of the adoption of Section 911, and Mason more recently, argued that the taxation of nonresident citizens is not administrable.[36] The attempt to tax such individuals imposes a burden on the IRS that it is unable to meet. The result is a statute that is not complied with in many cases, that imposes heavy transaction costs on those taxpayers that do comply, and that is saved from being completely ignored by a complicated provision (Section 911) that could be drastically simplified or abandoned if we did not tax nonresident citizens.

Having said that, I do believe that, today, it is possible to administer the taxation of nonresident US citizens by relying on FATCA. The question is whether we should tax them on ability to pay grounds.

ABILITY TO PAY AND CITIZENSHIP TAXATION IN THE TWENTY-FIRST CENTURY

Historically, progressive taxation has been defended on benefits grounds. The rich, it was said, derive more benefits from e.g., police protection or the sanctity of contracts

assessment of taxes that a country has no means of collecting may itself undermine the perceived fairness of the tax system").

35 See Joint Committee on Taxation, "Review of the Present-law Tax and Immigration Treatment of Relinquishment of Citizenship and Termination of Long-Term Residency," JCS-2-03, p.79 (Feb. 2003).

36 Blum & Singer, *supra* note 6; Mason, *supra* note 6.

than do the poor, and therefore they should pay more in tax. But this argument has been debunked by Walter J. Blum and Harry Jr. Kalven on the basis that it is difficult to show a correlation between the progressive tax and the benefit.[37] Turning to our case of interest – in which a citizen resides outside their nationality state, it is difficult to establish what benefits justify taxing a nonresidents citizen's global income since, as explained in the previous section, the benefits derived by non-resident citizens from the US government are minimal. More recently, progressive taxation has been based on the declining marginal utility of money, but that too has been cogently criticized because of the difficulty in making interpersonal comparisons of utility.[38] For example, it is plausible that Elon Musk, the richest man in the world, derives more utility from having additional money and the power it confers upon him than a relatively poorer person. As Henry Simons observed in 1938, progressivity is ultimately a political decision made by a community of citizens voting on the degree of inequality which they are prepared to tolerate, and on the desirable limits to the power that the rich derive from their wealth.[39]

The ability-to-pay argument for taxing nonresident US citizens is that they are part of a political community with resident US citizens and therefore should share in the tax burden imposed on that community.[40] I define the political community to include all (and only) adults who are entitled to vote. Even though they are nonresident, Americans living permanently abroad continue to be members of the political community and when they vote they share in the decision (that is hotly contested in every US election) of how large the government should be, and consequently what tax burden the community should impose on itself, and on how progressive those taxes should be. As discussed later in this section, the inability of resident noncitizens to vote is a strong argument for not taxing them on an ability-to-pay basis, that is, taxing them on only domestic income.

It could be argued that the United States is not administratively able to tax citizens living overseas on an ability to pay basis. In the case of the poorer citizens, in many instances the IRS is not even aware of their existence, hence the inability to count them in the decennial census. In the case of most of the richer nonresident citizens, their residence states are likely to tax them, and so the United States needs to concede the primary right to tax them to their country of residence and to either exempt their income from taxation or grant a foreign tax credit. Thus, their income

[37] Walter J. Blum & Harry Kalven Jr., *The Uneasy Case for Progressive Taxation*, 19 U. CHI. L. REV. 2 (1952).

[38] Id.; see, generally, Reuven Avi-Yonah, *Why Tax the Rich? Efficiency, Equity, and Progressive Taxation*, 111 YALE L.J. 1391 (2002).

[39] HENRY SIMONS, PERSONAL INCOME TAXATION (1938).

[40] Cf. Mason, *supra* note 6, at 196–200 (characterizing the obligation for nonresident citizens to pay tax as a social obligation arising from their national community membership, but not identifying the national community as consisting solely of voting members).

is not available to be taxed by the United States, because it has already been taxed by another country.[41]

But this argument against citizenship-based taxation (which I have made previously) is less convincing under current conditions, in which an increasing number of US citizens live permanently overseas. It is true that their country of residence gets to tax them first. But that does not mean that the United States should not tax them as well on an ability to pay basis, with a foreign tax credit to avoid double taxation. The point of ability to pay is not that the tax must be paid to the United States. The point is that all members of the US political community pay tax in proportion to their ability to pay. The fact that the United States has to concede the tax revenue to the residence country to prevent double taxation does not mean that nonresident citizens are not taxed based on ability to pay, and it is taxation based on ability to pay and not benefits that was chosen by the US political community as the basis for US income taxation. The idea is to base the tax burden on vertical and horizontal equity, and for equity it does not matter who collects the revenue.

As for administrability, conditions have changed since my 2010 article (and the other articles cited previously).[42] The enactment of FATCA means that it is no longer easy for US citizens living overseas to evade US taxation, and they are also much more aware of their US citizenship.[43] Any US citizen that has tried to open a bank account overseas after 2010 is made aware of their US tax obligations by the bureaucratic hurdles the foreign bank imposes under FATCA and the Intergovernmental Agreements implementing FATCA. Moreover, Section 911 and the foreign tax credit significantly alleviate the US tax burden, so it is only the new nomads that derive US source earned income above $120,000 that are really affected. Even in those cases, a treaty would usually solve the problem by treating them solely as residents of the residence country, unless there is no treaty, and in that case there usually is no double taxation either. As Seligman argued over a

[41] See Avi-Yonah, *supra* note 6.

[42] See Blum & Singer, *supra* note 6; Mason, *supra* note 6 (the same argument applies to most countries that can use CRS to tax nonresident citizens, so a citizenship-based tax has become administrable).

[43] See Joel Slemrod et al., *The Offshore World According to Fatca: New Evidence on the Foreign Wealth of U.S. Households* (Nat'l Bureau of Econ. Rsch., Working Paper No. 31055 2023), www.nber.org/system/files/working_papers/w31055/w31055.pdf ("This paper uses account-level information, reported to the IRS by foreign financial institutions under the Foreign Account Tax Compliance Act (FATCA), to produce new evidence on the foreign financial wealth of US households. We find that US taxpayers hold around $4 trillion in foreign accounts, almost half in jurisdictions usually considered tax havens. Combining the FATCA reports with other administrative tax data and tracing account ownership through partnerships, we document a steep income gradient in the propensity to hold assets in foreign financial institutions. Specifically, more than 60% of the individuals in the top 0.01% of the income distribution own foreign accounts, the vast majority in tax havens and more than half through a partnership. We discuss the likely implications of these findings for the overall impact of FATCA on tax compliance and government revenue." The concentration at the top suggests FATCA is very effective even for the super-rich.)

century ago, progressive taxation based on ability to pay is a political decision, made by a political community of citizens that vote to tax themselves.[44]

US citizens living permanently overseas are part of the US political community and should share the burden of taxation to finance the government even if they choose to derive fewer benefits from its services. However, this analysis also means that the United States and every other country is wrong in taxing noncitizen residents on global income, because global taxation is based on ability to pay, and the taxation of noncitizen residents must be based not on ability to pay (since noncitizen residents are not members of the political community) but on benefits, and benefits-based taxation is inherently local.

BENEFITS TAXATION OF RESIDENTS: SOLVING THE "NON-DOM" PROBLEM

If membership in a political community (citizenship) is the basis for taxation based on ability to pay (global taxation), then it follows that resident noncitizens who cannot vote and are not members of the political community in which they live should not be taxed based on ability to pay.[45] Instead, taxation of residents is based on the benefits principle, that is, it is justified by the benefits provided to residents by the country in which they reside. These benefits are local, that is, confined to the territory of the state of residence: the relatively tenuous benefits provided to nonresident citizens (diplomatic protection and the right to abode) do not apply to noncitizen residents who cannot invoke the diplomatic protection of the state of residency and who cannot be assured of being able to return if they leave.[46] The proposed rule creates a motivation for them not to become citizens, but there are other reasons to become citizens that may outweigh this. Under the current regime, they have a motivation to leave and not be subject to global taxation. US citizens have a motivation to expatriate, but that carries a price, both symbolically (they are denounced as traitors and their names are published) and financially under the exit tax.

Taxing citizens on global income and residents on only local (domestic) income is also more consistent with the traditional bases of jurisdiction in international law, namely nationality and territoriality. A state has jurisdiction over its nationals regardless of where they live, but it only has jurisdiction over non-nationals within its territorial borders (although this has been construed to justify global taxation of residents). The reason tax has always been applied differently by being based on residence and (except in the US) not on citizenship is because it is easy for the rich to acquire a foreign passport and give up their citizenship of the country in which

44 See Reuven Avi-Yonah & Yoseph M. Edrey, *Constitutional Review of Federal Tax Legislation*, U. Ill. L. Rev. 1 (2023).

45 Id.

46 And any benefits conferred by the state of residency on foreign source income are outweighed by the benefits conferred by the source country, as the 1923 committee argued.

they live but continue living there and enjoying its benefits. If these rich individuals are not taxed on a global basis and their new country of citizenship does not tax them either, then their foreign-source income escapes tax altogether.

Such a result used to be considered acceptable in territorial states before globalization because there were limits on the ability of individuals to earn foreign-source income without migrating, but in the age of globalization in which such limits (e.g., exchange controls) have mostly disappeared, most countries tax residents on a global basis. The exception is those countries, such as the United Kingdom and many others, that have "non-dom" regimes. Under "non-dom" regimes, a resident who is not a citizen can legally avoid tax on foreign-source income even if their country of citizenship does not tax them.

The "non-dom" problem is difficult because it is unlikely that sovereign countries would succumb to outside pressure to give up on "non-dom" regimes to attract the rich. Taxation of individuals is closely linked to sovereignty because individuals' residency in a sovereign state is meaningful, unlike the residence of multinational corporations, which is not meaningful because companies can be in many places simultaneously. That is why the kind of agreement for a global minimum tax on corporations that was reached recently to limit tax competition is less likely in the individual context. However, this does not mean that the "non-dom" problem cannot be solved. The basic point is that "non-dom" regimes in democratic countries are unpopular because resident citizens are unhappy that rich "non-doms" avoid taxes while they must pay. For example, Rishi Sunak had difficulties justifying the previous "non-dom" status of his wife during the recent UK prime ministerial campaign. UK citizens are understandably unhappy with a regime that allows rich foreigners living amongst them and enjoying the benefits of living in the United Kingdom to avoid global taxation. "Non-dom" regimes are especially likely to generate resentment when, because the non-domiciliary has no income in the residence state, he or she escapes tax entirely in the residence state. Because of this unpopularity, it is plausible that the United Kingdom and other countries would abolish "non-dom" regimes aimed at the rich. In place of "non-dom" regimes, countries could adopt the regime advocated here, in which all noncitizen residents are taxed only on domestic-source income. For poorer residents, this will not make a difference because typically they will not have foreign source income.

But will this not lead to massive under-taxation? Not if the country of citizenship taxes these noncitizen residents. For example, US-citizen residents of Italy are subject to US tax on a global basis, with a credit for Italian taxes. There would, of course, be a risk that people would transfer their citizenship from countries with citizenship taxation to countries that do not tax citizens. Because of this, I would suggest four limits to be adopted by the country of residence.

First, as is the case today in some countries (e.g., Canada), there should be an exit tax on residents that leave the country permanently to address the problem of unrealized gains accrued while being a resident.

Secondly, if the country of citizenship does not tax nonresident citizens at all (e.g., if it is a tax haven with no income tax, or if it simply does not tax nonresident citizens like most countries under the current rule), the country of residence should be able to tax them on a global basis. This rule should not apply to countries of citizenship that have merely low taxes, because members of a sovereign and democratic political community should be able to establish the rates at which they tax themselves.

Thirdly, if it can be established that the noncitizen residents do not have a genuine link to their country of citizenship because they only acquired citizenship to avoid worldwide taxation, then the country of residence should be able to tax them on a global basis. For example, if they have never lived in the country of citizenship, even if it taxes them on a global basis at low rates, they could be taxed globally in the country of residence. This rule can be administered using the criteria established by the ICJ in the *Nottebohm* case, in which the Court stated that a state need not respect citizenship in another state that was acquired

> with the sole aim of thus coming within (its) protection ... but not of becoming wedded to its traditions, its interests, its way of life or of assuming the obligations – other than fiscal obligations – and exercising the rights pertaining to the status thus acquired.[47]

There are other ways that can be suggested to establish a genuine link. For example, Savvas Kostikidis has proposed to grant the taxing right to the country in which the taxpayer has acquired the knowledge needed to earn the significant income that enabled them to emigrate, which would usually be where they lived before expatriating. This could be an alternative way of resolving cases of multiple citizenship, since it is easier to administer than the standard treaty tie-breakers.[48]

Finally, the country of residence should be able to tax noncitizen residents on a global basis if the country of citizenship is not a democracy (e.g., Russia, the origin of many UK "non-doms") (as evaluated by outside observers), because then they are not truly members of a political community that taxes itself.

Overall, I believe that the "non-dom" problem can be solved, and that the regime advocated herein is feasible without giving rise to massive under-taxation of the rich.

CONCLUSION

Hannah Arendt defined citizenship as "the right to have rights." In today's deglobalizing world, citizenship is more important than it was in the heyday of globalization in the 1990s, when cosmopolitanism was all the rage. One good

[47] Liechtenstein v. Guatemala, I. C. J. 1 (1955).

[48] Savvas Kostikidis, A *Better Way to Establish Tax Treaty Residence for Mobile Individuals*, 110 Tax Notes Int'l 1461 (2023).

example is refugees like the Rohingya, who are citizens of Myanmar but residents of Bangladesh. Their citizenship is worthless because it does not give them either diplomatic protection or the right to abode in Myanmar. They are effectively stateless. Another good example are the non-Chinese residents of Hong Kong after the Chinese takeover in 1997. Under the UK–China agreement of 1984, they had the right of abode in Hong Kong but not citizenship because that was limited to ethnic Chinese. However, this right of abode was not guaranteed, and the United Kingdom refused for a long time to give non-Chinese residents of Hong Kong full UK citizenship with the right of abode in the United Kingdom. For that reason, other countries refused to admit them, because they could not deport them to either Hong Kong or the United Kingdom. Effectively, they were stateless, until public pressure in the United Kingdom forced the government to grant them full UK citizenship.[49] In a world in which citizenship is once again important, but individuals are freer than ever to migrate because they can work remotely, global taxation should be based on membership in a political community and ability to pay, and not on benefits. Noncitizen residents, on the other hand, should only be taxed locally based on the benefits provided by the state of residence, which do not extend beyond its borders. Seligman, I believe, would have approved.

49 Michael Avi-Yonah, *The Nation State that Never Sets*, 46 YALE J. INT'L L., 325 (2022).

4

Reconsidering Citizenship Taxation

Tsilly Dagan & Ruth Mason

INTRODUCTION

As both people and work become less connected to particular states, forms of taxation invented for a less mobile, less digitized world become obsolete. Scholars and policymakers point to citizenship taxation as a solution to the tax challenges of globalization and migration because citizenship taxation would enable states to tax people no matter where they work or migrate. By tying taxation to a more durable jurisdictional hook than residence or source, citizenship taxation directly addresses globalization and migration. Citizenship taxation may, indeed, turn out to be an important tool in combating income-tax base erosion. But we argue that citizenship alone is too crude a basis for imposing worldwide income taxation, and so it demands adjustments. Additionally, pointing to the failure of the United States to effectively enforce its citizenship tax, we address the significant administrative and strategic obstacles posed by the unilateral adoption of citizenship taxation. Finally, although citizenship taxation has been offered as a panacea, we explain why rich countries will find it much easier to implement citizenship tax regimes than poor countries will, and why multilateral cooperation (though potentially helpful in supporting citizenship taxation) might benefit rich countries at the expense of poor ones.

THE IMPERILED SOCIAL CONTRACT

For most of history, people resided, worked, and invested only in the state of their nationality. The coincidence of these factors in a single state for much of the history of income taxation made it easy to enforce tax obligations, and such taxation was perceived as legitimate. Increasingly, however, we cannot assume that these aspects

For helpful comments on earlier drafts, we thank Hanoch Dagan, Diane Ring, and Afton Titus, and seminar participants at the University of Surrey and King's College London.

of a person's life will coincide in a single state that hosts a single community to which that person pays taxes and owes duties of justice, and from which that person receives public goods and services. Hundreds of millions of people have migrated outside their state of birth or citizenship. Regional economic unions further liberalize migration and cross-border work while deemphasizing the importance of nationality.[1] Enhanced by technological and social changes brought on by the pandemic, the labor market increasingly accommodates work-from-home and remote work over long distances.[2] People increasingly work for employers or do business outside the state where they reside.[3]

These phenomena present challenges for a tax system devised in the last century. Consider labor income: our international tax system commonly sources labor income to the place of performance of the services. For a long time, it seemed obvious that the place of performance of services was the place where the service-provider was physically located. But new modes of work have begun to erode this consensus. During the world's massive experiment with working from home during the pandemic, some states changed their source rules to recapture income that they could not tax under their "place of performance" rules. Such amended rules sourced income to the location of the employer or even the *former* place of performance of work.[4] States' readiness to change their source rules to maintain their budgets is not only portentous, but it also suggests that the concept of "source" lacks strong normative grounding.[5] When consensus unravels, radical change to ungrounded rules becomes possible.

Our changing economy also raises the stakes of tax competition. States have long enticed highly skilled and wealthy migrants with alluring tax packages.[6] Some countries offer non-domiciliary or "non-dom" regimes that allow people to enjoy the benefits of living in a modern social welfare state without the obligation to contribute taxes in the same way as the incumbent population. A commonplace way to structure such regimes is for the receiving state to allow wealthy foreign nationals to pay tax only on income they bring into the receiving state, or to pay tax at a special

1 See also Chapter 7, by Afton Titus, discussing economic union in Africa.

2 See Chapter 9, by Diane M. Ring.

3 Jeanne Batalova, Top Statistics on Global Migration and Migrants (Migration Policy Institute, Migration Information Source, July 2022), at 2 ("According to the latest available estimates, there were 280.6 million global migrants in 2020 – representing close to 4 percent of the world's 7.8 billion people").

4 See, e.g., New Hampshire v. Massachusetts, 141 S.Ct. 1262 (2021), cert. denied (challenging a Massachusetts rule that sourced income to pre-pandemic place of performance).

5 But see Mitchell Kane, *A Defense of Source*, 32 Yale J. Reg. 311 (2015).

6 Economists have calculated that the "average net present fiscal value of a (permanent) immigrant [is]...$198,000 for an immigrant with more than a high school education." Mihir A. Desai et al., *Sharing the Spoils: Taxing International Human Capital Flows*, 11 Int'l Tax & Pub. Fin. 663, 669–670 (2004).

rate.[7] If the person's origin state does not tax the person's worldwide income – for example, because the origin state, like nearly all states, taxes only residents on their worldwide income – the person may escape ability-to-pay taxation on their worldwide income in both the receiving state and the origin state. Some countries even offer so-called citizenship-for-sale regimes.[8] Although not entirely free from risk,[9] such regimes allow states and individuals to strike a bargain different from that available to other members of society. The emerging phenomenon of digital nomads – people who work remotely and who may reside in several countries over the course of a year, establishing tax nexus in none[10] – raises concerns similar to those raised by non-dom regimes, namely, that some people can completely avoid ability-to-pay taxation on their worldwide income.

Although they escape tax, the beneficiaries of these regimes nevertheless consume public goods and services in various jurisdictions. These people thus retain (or at least preserve the option to use) substantially all the benefits of the social contract of one or more rich welfare states, without paying for those benefits the way that other taxpayers do. Interstate competition for the most desirable migrants – the rich and high-skilled – thus erodes the ability of states to enforce people's duties to fund not only taxes for redistribution, but even to fund the costs of providing public goods and

7 Under a UK regime set to be repealed, for example, qualified residents could opt for remittance-based taxation which effectively exempted from UK tax any foreign-source income and gains not remitted to the United Kingdom. Whilst other UK residents paid tax to the United Kingdom on their worldwide income and gains, regardless of remittance, those opting for non-dom status would pay only an annual charge of £30,000, and even that charge applied only if the person lived in the United Kingdom for at least seven of the previous nine years (with the charge increasing to £60,000 after at least twelve years of residence out of the previous fourteen years. See Income Tax Act 2007, c. 3, §§ 809B, 809C(1A), 809C(4), and 809H. Other examples for favorable residency regimes include Italy, Malta, Ireland, Israel, and Portugal; *see* Tsilly Dagan, *Tax and Globalization: Toward a New Social Contract*, 44 Oxf. J. Leg. St. 487 (2024).

8 See Ayelet Shachar, *Citizenship*, *in* The Oxford Handbook of Comparative Constitutional Law (Michel Rosenfeld & András Sajó eds., 2012). See also Allison Christians, *Buying In: Residence and Citizenship by Investment*, 62 St. Louis U. L.J. (2017); Emma Agyemanghe, *The Low-tax Countries Wooing the World's Wealthy*, Fin. Times., Aug. 12, 2024 ("it's never been so easy for the super-rich to relocate"). Id. (describing attractive regimes in Switzerland, the UAE, Singapore, and Monaco and the tightening or possible tightening of regimes in France, Italy, Portugal, and the United Kingdom). See also OECD, *Why Do OECD Countries Offer Tax Relief Programs to Attract Foreign Migrants and Returning Nationals?*, Migrant Policy Debate, No. 25 (June 2024) (describing programs ranging from reduced tax rates to full or partial exemptions) [hereinafter OECD, *Why Do OECD Countries*].

9 Recent developments demonstrated that there is also a flip-side to such choices: the risk that one's assets may not be as well protected as those of full members. See, e.g., Foreign, Commonwealth & Development Office, *Press Release: UK Hits Key Russian Oligarchs with Sanctions Worth Up to £10 Billion*, GOV.UK, April 14, 2022, www.gov.uk/government/news/uk-hits-key-russian-oligarchs-with-sanctions-worth-up-to-10bn.

10 For a discussion on whether everyone must pay taxes somewhere, see Chapter 1, by Wolfgang Schön.

services. In this way, the twin pressures of mobility and state competition unbundle the social contract.[11]

If we accept that membership in a political or social community generates a moral obligation to pay taxes for redistribution, then the ability of some, but not all, taxpayers to escape that responsibility is inequitable. Of course, the problems of migration and economic mobility are not new, but globalization, digitalization, and free movement exacerbate the problem by increasing opportunities for people not only to exit but also to splinter their interactions with states by placing various aspects of their life and livelihood in multiple jurisdictions.

An initial, but very important, question is whether states ought to do anything at all to curb tax-motivated migration and other forms of economic mobility. After all, free exit is an important aspect of liberty, and taxpayers choosing to leave a country (whatever the reason) exercise a fundamental right. Likewise, economic mobility enhances people's options and thereby their liberty. Utilitarian arguments may also support competition among states for residents, workers, and investment: such competition checks government spending,[12] and movement in response to taxation represents an alternative and amplifier to voice[13] in helping to reveal preferences for levels of tax and public goods and services.[14] It thereby encourages governments to respond to voter preferences. Thus, one possible response to complaints about revenue lost from tax-motivated migration is that it is a needed and acceptable disciplinary and accountability device. But even if we could agree – and not all would[15] – that tax competition is salutary, tax-motivated migration and other forms of economic mobility raise fairness concerns because not everyone has equal access to them as a means to avoid tax. The ability of domiciliaries to de-link the receipt of a state's publicly funded benefits from the obligation to pay taxes that fund those benefits also undermines the utilitarian arguments for tax competition. If taxpayers can exit the tax part of the bargain, but not the benefit part, then mobility loses its value as a government accountability device. Moreover, because it hampers states from providing redistribution and other public goods and services, it creates new rifts within society.[16]

[11] For more on this *see* Dagan, *supra* note 7.

[12] Wolfram F. Richter, *Delaying Integration of Immigrant Labour for the Purpose of Taxation* 5 (CESifo Working Paper No. 802 2002) ("Taxpayers become exploitable when they cannot avoid home taxes by emigrating").

[13] Jonathan W. Moses, *Exit, Vote and Sovereignty: Migration, States and Globalization*, 12 Rev. Int'l Pol. Econ. 53, 53 (2005) (modeling free international migration and showing that it improves government responsiveness to citizen demands).

[14] See generally, Charles M. Tiebout, A *Pure Theory of Local Expenditures*, 64 J. Pol. Econ. 416 (1956).

[15] Tsilly Dagan, International Tax Policy: Between Competition and Cooperation 120–141 (2017), chapter 4.

[16] Dagan, *supra* note 7.

POSSIBLE POLICY RESPONSES

Recognizing trends in migration and mobility, scholars have considered possible policy responses. The issue with some of these responses is that the pressures of tax competition make it unlikely for receiving states to implement them, even if such states possess both the nexus and enforcement capacity needed to collect tax from their incoming residents and domiciliaries. This is because such states often lack the *desire* to prevent migration and mobility as they perceive themselves as benefitting from it. Put equivalently, they are either the winners in tax competition or they perceive themselves as winning in tax competition.[17] An instructive example is provided by the United Kingdom's non-dom regime, which granted significant tax benefits to many high-net-worth individuals including Akshata Murty, a citizen of India and the spouse of the former UK Chancellor Rishi Sunak. Following popular outrage, the regime was recently announced to be abolished by both the previous Conservative UK government (led by Rishi Sunak himself),[18] and the new Labour government's own reform as part of the 2024 Autumn Budget. Each of these reforms, however, nonetheless maintained significant tax benefits for certain new arrivals to the United Kingdom with respect to their foreign income and gains.[19] This example illustrates that, even where there is public pressure to renounce such a favorable regime, there are limits to what a receiving state is willing to do, making it less likely that *receiving* states will develop effective unilateral responses to tax competition for migrants. Furthermore, voters in democracies may not object to the idea of foregoing tax revenue if the inbound investment, business, and migration of highly skilled and wealthy people generates enough local benefit.[20]

The weight of perceptions that desirable migrants respond to tax incentives in receiving states – even limiting the effect of policy responses such as those set out by the United Kingdom – means that the principal responses to tax-motivated migration (or migration of work) will likely come from sending states. One traditional response has been for sending states to tax residents on a worldwide basis. Under such worldwide tax regimes, the person's residence state taxes all their income, wherever in the world derived, typically with a credit for taxes paid at source. Other

[17] OECD, *Why Do OECD Countries*, *supra* note 8, at 10 (noting evidence that such regimes affect migration).

[18] See HM Treasury, *Spring Budget 2024: Non-UK Domiciled Individuals Policy Summary*, GOV.UK, March 6, 2024, www.gov.uk/government/publications/spring-budget-2024-non-uk-domiciled-individuals-policy-summary/spring-budget-2024-non-uk-domiciled-individuals-policy-summary.

[19] For the Labour government's proposed Foreign Income and Gains (FIG) regime, see HM Treasury, *Autumn Budget 2024*, GOV.UK, Oct. 30, 2024, https://assets.publishing.service.gov.uk/media/672b9695fbd69e1861921c63/Autumn_Budget_2024_Accessible.pdf.

[20] For suggestions for coordinated source responses, see Chapter 2, by Yariv Brauner, advocating formulary source-only taxation and emphasizing that whatever source rules are chosen should be consistent across all states.

proposals have been advanced for how sending states might use their tax systems to respond to human migration. For example, as early as the 1970s, in response to the massive migration of professionals from developing countries to developed countries, economist Jagdish Bhagwati advocated for a 10 percent tax on the disposable incomes of professional emigrants.[21] Such "brain-drain" tax proposals, which have taken various forms, could help migrant-sending states recoup the costs associated with educating and training residents who accept jobs elsewhere.[22] They could also help compensate the sending country for the loss of skills of the migrant. Additionally, Bhagwati claimed, the migrant has "a moral obligation to share their gains with those left behind."[23] A possible reason why such taxes have not proved popular is that migrants benefit their origin states by sending remittances back home; beyond the immediate benefit to the recipients of remittances, both remittances and international migration are regarded as having a positive impact on poverty in developing countries by creating an increased incentive for domestic population to improve their skills and education.[24] Such remittances confer political clout on emigrants and their beneficiaries back home.

It is to such residence-based worldwide tax regimes that human migration of the highly skilled and ultra-wealthy in part responds. To avoid residence-based taxation on worldwide income, people increasingly change their residence state. To be effective, then, solutions to tax-based migration must apply, irrespective of residence. One such response is exit taxation. Whereas states would levy "brain drain" taxes on an ongoing basis, exit taxes typically involve a one-time assessment by the origin state against the wealth of a departing national or resident. Exit taxes typically treat the loss of tax residence as a realization event, and the exiting person pays tax on the appreciation of her assets.[25] The problem with lump-sum exit taxation is that it significantly inhibits human migration, undermining liberty. Thus, exit taxation has proved unpopular in liberal societies that value the free movement of persons. Liberal states that have exit taxes today typically limit them in various ways,

[21] Jagdish Bhagwati, *Taxing the Brain Drain*, 19 CHALLENGE 34 (July/Aug. 1976).

[22] See e.g., Bhagwati, *supra* note 21, at 37 (describing a 10 percent surcharge on the income of professional immigrants from lesser developed countries to developed countries that would apply for a limited period such as ten years, collected by developed host countries, and routed to lesser developed countries for development spending).

[23] Bhagwati, *supra* note 21, at 35.

[24] Whereas remittances may not play a vital role in a large and growing economy like India's, they are a significant source of income for some low-income countries. *See* Batalova, *supra* note 3, at 6. See, also, Bhagwati, *supra* note 21, at 35 (explaining that Pakistan had to suspend its brain drain tax due to unpopularity). *See* Richard H. Adams Jr. & John Page, *Do International Migration and Remittances Reduce Poverty in Developing Countries?*, 33 WORLD DEVELOPMENT 1645 (2005), finding that both remittances and international migration have a significant and positive effect on poverty in developing countries.

[25] Luc de Broe, *General Report: The Tax Treatment of Transfer of Residence by Individuals*, 87 CAHIERS DE DROIT FISCAL INT'L 19, 29 (2002); see also Andrew Appleby, *No Migration without Taxation: State Exit Taxes*, 60 HARV. J. ON LEGIS. 55 (2023).

including with large exemption amounts and opportunities for significant deferral and even waiver.

Another response is citizenship taxation. Citizenship taxation could, in principle, solve the twin problems of economic mobility and tax-motivated migration by taxing the migrant (and her mobile investment, work, and business) on a worldwide basis.[26] Under citizenship taxation, a person would be liable to her citizenship state to pay tax on her worldwide income, no matter where that person resided. Such a regime would treat the migrant and her economic interests as if they never left the citizenship state. Proponents tout citizenship taxation as a solution to both tax-motivated migration and state-level tax competition. The argument is straightforward: because most people will not relinquish their citizenship, taxing people on the basis of citizenship, no matter where they reside, will reduce incentives for people to move to take advantage of lower taxes elsewhere. If people cannot benefit from lower taxes by migrating to other countries, then receiving countries would have no (or less) reason to offer a non-dom regime or other tax incentives to migrants. The broad adoption of citizenship taxation therefore could help avoid a damaging race to to attract high-skilled, high-income, high-net-worth individuals.[27] It would also serve as an effective unilateral response to tax incentives offered by receiving states.

CITIZENSHIP TAXATION AND FAIRNESS

In response to increasing calls for citizenship taxation, particularly as a solution to tax-motivated migration, the rest of this chapter aims to provide a clear-eyed evaluation of citizenship tax as it exists in the world today, as well as evaluating prospects for the wider adoption of citizenship taxation.[28] As we explained, scholars have begun advocating for citizenship taxation mainly as a response to revenue losses already associated with or expected to arise from increased human mobility. But because there are many ways a state can raise revenue, advocacy for citizenship

[26] Other options include extended residence rules; retention of citizenship-based taxation if the migrant retains an abode in the country of origin; and citizenship taxation of a limited subset of citizens, such as military personnel, students, or temporary corporate secondees. See Ruth Mason, *Citizenship Taxation*, 89 S. Cal. L. Rev. 169 (2015) (discussing proposals of coauthors Cynthia Blum and Paula N. Singer and of Bernard Schneider).

[27] OECD, *Why Do OECD Countries*, *supra* note 8, at 14 (reporting "no indication of a 'race to the bottom'").

[28] Much has been written on citizenship taxation. See, e.g., Chapter 3, by Reuven Avi-Yonah; Chapter 1, by Schön. See also David Elkins, *A Scalar Conception of Tax Residence*, 41 Va. Tax Rev. 149 (2022); Shayak Sarkar, *Tax Law's Migration*, 62 B. C. L. Rev. 2209 (2021); Giorgio Beretta, *Citizenship and Tax*, World Tax J. 227 (May 2019); Shu-Yi Oei, *The Offshore Tax Enforcement Dragnet*, 67 Emory L.J. 655 (2018); Young Ran (Christine) Kim, *Considering 'Citizenship Taxation': In Defence of FATCA*, 20 Fla. Tax Rev. 335 (2017); Edward A. Zelinsky, *Citizenship and Worldwide Taxation: Citizenship as an Administrable Proxy for Domicile*, 96 Iowa L. Rev. 1289 (2011); Michael S. Kirsch, *Taxing Citizens in a Global Economy*, 82 N. Y. U. L. Rev. 443 (2007).

taxation as the correct method to raise revenue has to be supported by arguments apart from mere revenue needs. One such argument is fairness. The conventional fairness argument for citizenship taxation has three elements. First, by retaining their citizenship, citizens would tacitly consent to taxation. Second, citizenship taxation represents fair payment for government benefits that citizens receive while abroad. Third, citizens should not be able to escape their social obligation to pay taxes simply because they live abroad.[29] We will not spend significant time on arguments trying to justify citizenship taxation on the basis of taxpayers' consent or benefits received, which we find unconvincing.[30] Besides, no matter to whom one applies it, an argument based on the receipt of benefits supports only limited taxation equal to the value of those benefits.[31]

That leaves arguments about social obligation of citizens to pay taxes as the remaining fairness basis supporting citizenship taxation. What seems to concern advocates of citizenship taxation is the impact of human migration (and economic mobility in general) on the ability of states to maintain the welfare state. Thus, the concern is not merely about how states will fund the provision of government goods and services, but also how states will fund redistribution. Modern welfare states fund many public benefits, as well as redistributive programs, using not only benefits taxation but also ability-to-pay taxation, under which a person's liability to pay tax increases with their income, so income constitutes the measure of the taxpayer's ability to pay. Each society defines both income and ability to pay differently, just as each society defines how much redistribution it wants to accomplish through the fiscal system. Each society also defines who will receive redistributive benefits, as well as who it will require to fund them. The fairness question at the core of citizenship taxation, then, is whether it is fair for a country to ask its citizens to contribute taxes to fund redistribution.

At first glance, the answer to this question seems obvious: if not citizens, who would the state require to fund taxes for redistribution? The answer becomes murkier, however, when we consider that, across the globe, only a small handful of countries – the United States being the most notable among them – use citizenship as the basis for attaching the obligation to pay taxes on worldwide income to fund public benefits and redistribution. Far more commonly – although this choice may be motivated by the legal and practical considerations addressed in the next section – states impose worldwide taxation on residents, not citizens. Since most people reside in their nationality state, the difference in these two nexuses matters only for people who reside outside their citizenship state or who possess multiple citizenships or residences.

[29] See generally Ruth Mason, *Citizenship Taxation*, 89 S. Cal. L. Rev. 169 (2016).
[30] See Mason, *supra* note 29, at 187–196.
[31] Mason, *supra* note 29, at 189–196.

The typical fairness argument for worldwide taxation posits that people's membership in a national community triggers an obligation to pay taxes for redistribution. To the extent that that argument is correct (and we assume for purposes of our discussion that it is), then evaluating the fairness of citizenship taxation in the case that interests us – the one in which a taxpayer resides *outside* their citizenship state – depends on how well citizenship aligns with national community membership for people who reside abroad. The question *who is a member of the national community?* is a complex one that touches on fundamental issues of belonging, morality, and solidarity; it goes to the very foundations of the state, and we cannot do it justice here. Some commentators conclude that political membership or citizenship qua citizenship generates a moral obligation to pay taxes for redistribution (and some even argue that only citizenship *in a democracy* can generate such a moral obligation[32]). But, in our view, citizenship and national community membership are not identical, even though they substantially overlap. Therefore, evaluating the fairness of citizenship taxation relative to states' current systems, which tax on the basis of residence, requires consideration of whether residence or citizenship is a better proxy for national community membership. Although we cannot fully address the arguments here, we think it relatively easy to see that, at least in some cases, nonresident citizens are not members of the national community and, in other cases, nonresident citizens, such as immigrants, *are* members of the national community.[33]

To elaborate, diverse reasons motivate people to reside outside their citizenship state. A refugee driven from the state of her birth by political persecution may justly feel no obligation to contribute to redistribution in the state she fled, although any moral obligation she would have to support the national community of her receiving state would presumably take some time to develop. The lifelong citizenship taxation of so-called Accidental Americans is often cited as unfair. These people are US citizens because they happen to have been born in the United States, rather than because they have any meaningful connection with the country. A person may be born outside the state of nationality of their parents due to tourism, education, temporary employment, deprivation, or war. Permanent resettlers pose particularly challenging questions: they may, after a transition period, become a bona fide member of their receiving state's national community who are morally obliged to contribute to that community even before they naturalize as citizens of the adoptive state (or even if they never naturalize). But a student who lives temporarily abroad for education, for example, is unlikely to become a member of her school's national community; she may nevertheless satisfy that state's tax residence or domicile test in a particular year. Likewise, a temporary corporate transferee may earn significant

32 See Chapter 3, by Avi-Yonah, arguing that, because only citizenship can support ability-to-pay taxation, countries should not tax resident aliens on their worldwide income.

33 See Mason, *supra* note 29, at 196–205.

income from her host state, while remaining outside its national community and owing no greater moral obligation to support members of her host state's national community than her citizenship state's national community. Considering just a few scenarios demonstrates that neither citizenship nor residence/domicile is a perfect proxy for a person's membership in a national community, and therefore for her moral obligation to pay taxes for redistribution.

These few examples suggest that neither citizenship alone nor residence alone represent perfect proxies for national community membership. As a result, using either as the sole basis for imposing the obligation on an individual to pay taxes on their worldwide income to fund redistribution will be unfair in a range of circumstances. By contrast, states could improve the correspondence between the basis for worldwide taxation and national community membership by combining elements of both – that is, by using both citizenship and residence (or other substantive indicia of national community membership). In this way, states could secure a better match between those legally obliged to pay taxes for redistribution and those morally obliged to do so. Substantive connections, such as domicile or residence, could help determine which state takes priority in taxing a person as a member of its community.[34] One way to better reflect people's belonging to a certain community may be to let individuals make specific choices: for example, a citizen moving abroad might even be offered an election to remain subject to worldwide citizenship taxation or to pay an exit tax.[35] This election could help increase the correspondence between national community membership and the set of people subject to worldwide taxation. Such an approach could be particularly important for states that convey citizenship by birth and, as a result, have potentially large populations of accidental citizens residing abroad. Alternatively, a dramatic option would be to simply let an individual choose the state that should benefit from her taxes among the several states to which she is connected.[36]

In our view, citizenship is a good proxy for substantive national community membership most of the time. However, whereas citizenship is binary – you are either a citizen or you are not – membership in the community is not all or nothing. As a result, although citizenship is a good proxy for community membership, it will not always coincide with community membership. Thus, voters and policymakers should think carefully about how they can align the population they subject to worldwide taxation with membership in the national community. Although we fully acknowledge that in tax, as in many other legal areas, we choose bright-line binary classifications for administrability or other reasons, we believe states can and should fine-tune taxation in cases where citizenship and membership diverge. Regardless of

[34] See Mason, *supra* note 29, at 231–233.

[35] See Mason, *supra* note 29, at 235.

[36] For a suggestion along these lines, see Chapter 5, by Mitchell A. Kane. Rules to prevent unintended strategic selections (i.e., the lowest rate) would have to accompany such proposals.

whether countries make dramatic changes, they should consider targeted anti-abuse rules for residents or citizens who move abroad temporarily to avoid tax on the sale of assets.

ENFORCING CITIZENSHIP TAXATION

Notwithstanding that, in our view, citizenship should not be the sole factor for subjecting an individual to worldwide taxation and most policy proposals concern exactly that. This section considers challenges that arise in implementing a citizenship tax. We start by considering the challenges that would arise if a state attempted to impose citizenship taxation unilaterally. At present, the United States is one of two or three states in the world that tax citizens on their worldwide income, no matter where in the world those citizens reside, and no matter how long those citizens reside abroad.[37] The experience of the United States with citizenship taxation is, however, no success story.

Unilateral Enforcement of Citizenship Taxes

The problems with enforcing citizenship taxation begin with administration. As compared to taxing the worldwide income of only resident taxpayers, taxing the worldwide income of citizens residing abroad is considerably harder.[38] The citizenship state cannot employ the same mechanisms – such as wage withholding – in the foreign as in the domestic context. The US citizenship tax, for example, is thought to be characterized by widespread noncompliance but, the truth is, the United States cannot accurately estimate the tax gap related to failure of nonresident Americans to pay the citizenship tax because the United States does not and, by its own admission, cannot keep track of Americans residing abroad.[39] Although some commentators have argued that legislation called the Foreign Account Tax Compliance Act (FATCA) will enable the United States to accurately police nonresident citizens' income, government departments disagree; the US government notes capacity

[37] See I.R.C. §§ 1, 7701(b).

[38] For the argument that citizenship taxation, as compared to residents or domicile taxation, eases the initial question of who is subject to worldwide taxation, see Edward A. Zelinsky, *Citizenship and Worldwide Taxation: Citizenship as an Administrable Proxy for Domicile*, 96 Iowa L. Rev. 1289 (2011).

[39] See National Taxpayer Advocate Serv., 2023 Annual Report to Congress 118 (2023) (the number of noncompliant overseas American taxpayers is "unknown but potentially sizeable") (hereinafter NTA Report 2023). *See also* Patricia A. Dalton, U.S. Gov't Accountability Office, GAO-04-1077T, 2010 Census: Counting Americans Overseas as Part of a Census Would Not Be Feasible (2004), www.gao.gov/assets/120/111231.pdf (a government project to evaluate the feasibility of counting overseas Americans for purposes of congressional apportionment and redistricting concluded that such counting would be infeasible). If the United States cannot even count the number of Americans abroad, it has no realistic prospect of learning the exact amount of their incomes.

issues that prevent the IRS from effectively enforcing citizenship-based taxation.[40] If, by its own estimation, the United States has been unable to effectively enforce its citizenship tax despite its high tax capacity,[41] states with less tax capacity would face even more serious obstacles.

In addition to the enforcement challenges it generates for the government, citizenship taxation also generates significant administrative burdens for overseas taxpayers, who would likely be required to file full residence-based returns twice: once in their residence state and once in their citizenship state. This has proven especially difficult for overseas Americans who, because they earn income abroad, are subject to "the Kafka-esque US international tax regime."[42] This means that Americans abroad operating small businesses in the form of corporations must, for example, comply with Subpart F and GILTI. These taxpayers lack access to affordable, qualified tax preparers abroad, leading the National Taxpayer Advocate to attribute record-breaking US citizenship-renunciation numbers to the compliance burden associated with citizenship tax.[43] For all the complexity, however, the majority of Americans abroad owe no residual tax to the United States because the United States is a low-tax country relative to the states in which Americans reside abroad, and the United States credits taxes paid abroad against the US taxes that

40 The National Taxpayer Advocate concluded in 2012 that, as a result of FATCA, the IRS "will increasingly have to ignore violations that it can detect ...". National Taxpayer Advocate Serv., 2012 Annual Report to Congress: Volume One 134–153, 143 (2012), www.taxpayeradvocate.irs.gov/wp-content/uploads/2020/08/Most-Serious-Problems-IRS-Offshore-Voluntary-Disclosure-Programs.pdf. More recently, the GAO concluded that IRS tax enforcement for Americans abroad was ineffective, in part due to the IRS's own failure to incorporate FATCA data. GAO, Foreign Asset Reporting: Actions Needed to Enhance Compliance Efforts, Eliminate Overlapping Requirements, and Mitigate Burdens on U.S. Persons Abroad, *GAO Highlights* (April 2019), at 16 (observing that "TIGTA's 2018 report concluded that IRS was still unprepared to enforce compliance with FATCA in part because [IRS] took limited or no action" to integrate FATCA data into enforcement efforts); see also Treas. Inspector Gen. Tax Admin, The Internal Revenue Service Needs to Enhance Its International Collection Efforts, Sept. 12, 2014 (detailing the many additional obstacles the IRS faces in enforcement abroad).

41 The Global Forum's peer review of the compliance by the United States of the global standard for information sharing on request noted that "[t]he power of the IRS to obtain information for tax purposes is wide-ranging and is coupled with strong compulsory powers. Such powers are used regularly." OECD Global Forum on Transparency and Exchange of Information for Tax Purposes, Peer Review Report Combined: Phase: United States 8 (2013). It went on to observe that "[p]ersons seeking to obscure their affairs for tax or other reasons wouldn't generally be eager to expose themselves to the authority of the Internal Revenue Service." Id.

42 Taxpayer Advocate Serv., 2011 Annual Report to Congress 151 (2011).

43 NTA Report 2023, *supra* note 40, at 121. A recent empirical study of US citizenship by Americans abroad concluded that recent citizenship-renunciations were motivated by increased compliance costs, not the tax liability associated with citizenship taxation. Paul R. Organ, *Citizenship and Taxes*, 31 Int'l Tax & Pub. Fin. 404 (2024).

nonresident citizens owe.[44] Nevertheless, this experience raises serious questions about the effectiveness of citizenship taxation, even as practiced by one of the highest tax-capacity jurisdictions in the world.

Availability of Unilateral Citizenship Taxation to Poor States

We now move to the question of whether citizenship taxation is even an option for all states. Not every state is in a position to address the same problem in the same way. Tax evasion through the use of secret foreign bank accounts provides a good illustration. For many years, the act of hiding assets in a foreign financial institution and fraudulently omitting to report the income earned on those assets was an effective tax evasion strategy for the simple reason that, because the foreign financial institution had no tax-information-reporting obligation to holders' residence states, those residence states typically would not learn of the foreign income if the owner refused to report it. Bank secrecy jurisdictions – such as Switzerland and Luxembourg – turned a tidy profit on administering the accounts of tax evaders from all over the globe.

But at least some countries could act unilaterally to address such tax evasion. To staunch the loss of an estimated $100 billion in annual tax revenue from the fraudulent underreporting of income in such foreign accounts,[45] and to overcome foreign bank-secrecy legislation, the United States passed the FATCA legislation mentioned in the previous section that requires foreign financial institutions to report directly to the United States on foreign accounts held by US citizens. To ensure compliance with its regime, the United States subjected uncooperative foreign financial institutions to a 30 percent withholding tax on certain US-source payments, including US-source interest, dividends, and gross proceeds from the sale of assets that generate US dividends and interest.[46]

Although other countries experienced similar tax evasion, not every jurisdiction could counter it unilaterally. FATCA worked for the United States because no foreign financial institution could afford to remain invested in the US capital market while paying the penalty for noncompliance. Nor were financial institutions willing to make the business decision to exit the US capital market to avoid the penalty; the United States leveraged its massive capital market to gain regulatory control over foreign banks. Few other countries – maybe no other country – could have adopted

[44] See also NTA Report 2023, *supra* note 40, at 117 (62 percent of Americans abroad reported zero liability between 2015 and 2021). Id., at 122 (in 2021, only 5 percent of international filers had an adjusted gross income of over $400,000). See also Mason, *supra* note 29, at 181–186, explaining the impact of foreign-earned income exclusion and foreign tax credits on residual US liability.

[45] Staff of the Homeland Security and Governmental Affairs Permanent Subcommittee on Investigations, 110th Cong., *Tax Haven Banks and US Tax Compliance*, at 3 (2008).

[46] Joshua D. Blank & Ruth Mason, *Exporting* FATCA, 142 Tax Notes 1245 (2014), explaining US strategy and other countries' responses.

FATCA unilaterally. States with smaller capital markets were, however, able to free-ride on the introduction of FATCA. They adopted their own cross-border account-information-sharing regime, without an enforcement mechanism.[47]

A similar problem arises for citizenship taxation. Although citizenship taxation could help reduce tax-motivated migration, if not all countries adopt citizenship taxation, then countries that hold out can be expected to be even more attractive target states for the most desirable migrants, at least some of whom may desire to naturalize in their receiving state.[48] Worse, the adoption of citizenship taxation by high-tax states could motivate lower-tax states to respond by offering citizenship havens.

More generally, not every state is equally able to tax its citizens abroad. Citizenship is relatively sticky; it is both an important part of personal identity and guarantees free egress, ingress, and entitlement to work in a country. When people value their citizenship highly, their states can demand a tax price that enables those states to pursue domestic distributive justice using mandatory contributions from citizens abroad. Moreover, international law discourages people from becoming stateless.

But states' relaxation of their prohibitions on dual and multiple nationality has conferred upon individuals the opportunity to choose among multiple citizenships. Additionally, some states offer attractive naturalization programs in the hopes of attracting wealthy, high income, and high skilled immigrants.[49] People with dual or multiple nationalities, and those in high demand outside their states of original citizenship (e.g., the talented, wealthy, and young), can jettison their original citizenship if the tax price is too high. People will retain their citizenship only if they regard that citizenship as worth the associated tax costs.

Less attractive states, whose citizens view their citizenship as easier to relinquish, would find it difficult or impossible to raise revenues from the worldwide taxation of nonresident citizens' income and wealth. States may be relatively unattractive for a variety of reasons. A state may be relatively unattractive because it is oppressive or undemocratic, in which case, the threat or pressure of exit by its elites may incentivize needed and welcome changes. But a state may be relatively unattractive because it is poor, subject to climate change or other natural disasters, or simply too small to offer economic opportunities equally attractive to those available in other states. Such states might suffer from increased competition over their strongest members due to the perpetually widening gaps between what they can offer and what stronger states can offer in terms of public goods, and this difference may be due not to any particular mismanagement or malfeasance on the part of the less

[47] See, e.g., Council Directive 2011/16/EU of Feb. 15, 2011 on administrative cooperation in the field of taxation and repealing Directive 77/799/EEC, 2011 O. J. (L. 64) 1. See, generally, Noam Noked, *Should the United States Adopt CRS?*, 118 Mich. L. Rev. Online 118 (2019).

[48] See Mason, *supra* note 29, at 227–231, making this argument in the US context.

[49] See Tsilly Dagan & Talia Fisher, *State Inc.*, 27 Cornell J.L. & Pub. Pol'y 661.

attractive state, but rather due to accidents or crimes of history, geography, climate, and so on. Moreover, unlike with FATCA, with citizenship taxation other states cannot simply follow the leader. The adoption by the United States of citizenship taxation does not make it any easier for other states to adopt similar policies. This is evidenced by the fact that, even though the United States began taxing citizens during its Civil War, other states have not followed suit.[50] In the absence of policy cooperation, as the best-off and most mobile people accept citizenship or residence offers from more attractive states, less attractive states would lose not only valuable citizens but also a part of their tax base, thereby continually worsening their competitive position. This could lead to a vicious circle, as thinner public goods and benefits and less redistribution make membership less attractive to those who remain.

Multilateral Enforcement of Citizenship Taxation

If citizenship tax is a luxury policy that only the richest and strongest states can unilaterally implement, one might ask whether international cooperation could help by restraining competition over migrants and citizens. Multilateral cooperation is often offered as a solution to tax competition, and perhaps it could overcome some of the obstacles to citizenship taxation. If states join forces, the argument goes, they could overcome collective-action problems, enabling them to afford the public goods their constituents prefer and pursue the distributive justice their constituents demand. Multilateral cooperation on citizenship taxation or similar policies could mimic past multilateral efforts to curb state competition for corporate residents and corporate investment. States could agree, for example, to refrain from enacting ring-fenced non-dom regimes or to impose minimum individual taxes. But cooperation is difficult. Negotiating a bargain among states with conflicting interests and getting them to agree on how to allocate the costs and benefits of cooperation is daunting. Sustaining such a deal is even trickier because participants have incentives to defect when some states benefit more from lowering their taxes and attracting (or retaining) non-dom residents or new citizens than do others.

Moreover, a global deal on citizenship taxation would raise significant questions of global justice. A uniform minimum tax imposed on all taxpayers by their country of citizenship, for example, might create a comparative advantage for states that can

[50] Although the risk to states of permanently losing their most mobile and wealthiest members might make US-style worldwide taxation impossible for many states, those states might be able to impose an optimal citizenship-retention fee that is less than full ability-to-pay taxation based on worldwide income. In the absence of policy cooperation, as the best-off and most mobile people accept citizenship or residence offers from more attractive states, less attractive states would lose not only valuable citizens but also a part of their tax base, thereby continually worsening their competitive position. This could lead to a vicious circle, as thinner public goods and benefits and less redistribution make membership less attractive to those who remain.

currently offer superior public goods, services, and institutions to their citizens relative to other states that are not in a position to offer equally good benefits. Would there be a duty for cooperating states to compensate weaker states under such a regime? Questions of global justice are highly disputed even on a theoretical level as cosmopolitans support a *global* duty of distributive justice irrespective of state association, statists argue for duties of distributive justice that stop at the border, and institutionalists take a middle-of-the-road position that transnational duties of distributive justice emerge from cooperation. We cannot settle such debates in this chapter.[51] Politics, however, dictates that, as multilateralism imposes greater duties on strong countries, their interest in multilateralism will wane. We therefore worry that a cooperative accord, even if attainable, might advantage stronger countries at the expense of weaker ones.

Importantly, state consent does not ensure that multilateralism in citizenship taxation will serve the interests of all cooperating parties. Even in the absence of deception or coercion, tax cooperation may provide some actors with excessive power. Such excess power may derive not only from some states' superior bargaining power, but also from the greater expertise and resources that they can afford to invest in negotiations and from their ability to use agenda-setting.[52] This is not theoretical speculation. Seemingly innocuous and undoubtedly consensual cooperative accords, such as bilateral tax treaties, have tended to favor developed countries over developing ones. Because the format of tax treaties requires the source state to forebear tax in favor of the tax entitlement of the residence state, and because poor states tend to be net source states relative to rich states, when negotiated between a rich and a poor state a bilateral tax treaty will tend to shift tax revenue from the poor to the rich state. This effect has been so pronounced that the IMF has advised that developing countries carefully consider whether they ought to enter such treaties.[53] Another example of multilateral cooperation that many have argued will disproportionately benefit strong states relative to weak ones was the 2021 two-pillar accord, which claims to solve a problem – corporate tax competition – that not all states agree even constitutes a problem.[54]

[51] For a full analysis of application of the different approaches in political philosophy to international taxation, see Dagan *supra* note 15, chapter 6.

[52] For some examples, see Dagan *supra* note 15, chapter 5. See also MARTIN HEARSON, IMPOSING STANDARDS (2021).

[53] IMF, Spillovers in International Corporate Taxation 28–29 (2014), www.imf.org/external/np/pp/eng/2014/050914.pdf ("Some would simply advise developing countries not to sign BTTs"). Sebastien Leduc & Geerten Michielse, *Are Tax Treaties Worth It for Developing Economies?*, *in* CORPORATE INCOME TAXES UNDER PRESSURE: WHY REFORM IS NEEDED AND HOW IT COULD BE DESIGNED (Ruud A. de Mooij, Alexander D. Klemm, & Victoria J. Perry, eds., 2021). For more on this, see e.g., Dagan *supra* note 15, 72–119.

[54] See Tsilly Dagan, *Globe: The Potential Costs of Cooperation*, 51 INTERTAX 638 (2023). Leopoldo Parada, *Global Minimum Taxation: A Strategic Approach for Developing Countries*, 15 COLUMBIA J. TAX LAW 188 (2024). Suranjali Tandon, *Policy Note: Assessing the Impact of Pillar Two on Developing Countries*, 50 INTERTAX 923 (2022). Rita de la Feria, *The Perceived*

Given this history, we should not assume that cooperation – should it emerge in order to support citizenship-based taxation – is inherently beneficial to all parties. We also should not assume that consent assures that each participant benefits, particularly when the ultimate outcome of the agreement depends in part on how private parties respond, which may be difficult to predict in advance. Even if we could surmount the global justice problems implicated by multilateral cooperation on citizenship taxation – a big if – such cooperation would raise serious concerns about individual liberty with respect to its potential constraints on human migration. Moreover, as with corporate taxation, cooperation on individual taxation would raise the risk that competition would be shifted to another field, such as competition over definitions of social membership, including citizenship, or competition over the provision of public goods and services.

CONCLUSION

The pressures of globalization undermine the ability of states to collect taxes and pursue distributive justice. Free movement and other opportunities for people to engage with different jurisdictions on a personal and economic level are essential for liberty. But unrestrained market competition between states to provide the world's wealthiest and most skilled a fragment of the social contract in exchange for a reduction in their tax obligations imperils the welfare state.

If, as most scholars argue, the duty to pay taxes for redistribution exists within self-defining communities, then our new world of multiple and partial community allegiances raises fundamental questions. Modern people are increasingly mobile, frequently live outside their state of nationality, and interact with multiple jurisdictions in a variety of ways. In the next century, as in the last, people and their governments will have to answer the question *who* is obliged to contribute taxes for redistribution to *which community*? The answer to that question in the second century of income taxation may be different from the answer in the first. Although what constitutes membership may be decided by each community independently, human mobility and interstate competition erode the ability of a single community, acting alone, to enforce its view of membership. As the community loses the ability to define itself and to bind people it considers members to that choice, the community also loses the material support it needs to sustain itself. In such a world, the very definition of community becomes subject to the rules of supply and demand, under which diverging elasticities and the relative attractiveness of both jurisdictions and taxpayers become paramount.

The strongest states may be able to overcome these challenges unilaterally with the aid of citizenship taxation (although we conclude that a regime that combines

(Un)Fairness of the Global Minimum Corporate Tax Rate, in The Pillar 2 Global Minimum Tax (W. Haslehner et al. eds., 2024).

citizenship and residence would be fairer than using either factor alone). We emphasize, however, that the United States may remain an outlier. Its citizenship has proved extremely sticky, and therefore capable of sustaining a lightly administered form of citizenship taxation characterized by toleration for what is presumed to be widespread noncompliance. But weaker and less attractive states may be unable to sustain even a limited form of citizenship taxation, and they may therefore lose their tax base as they lose residents. This result would undermine domestic justice and increase the gaps between stronger and weaker states on the global level.

A cooperative accord on the global level could tame some interstate competition over migrants. Such a global accord would, however, face difficulties, including setting the desirable balance between personal liberty and community responsibility; determining the duty of justice between states; and defining the procedures that will determine the arrangements. States would also face accountability, legitimacy, and practical difficulties in implementing any such arrangements. These difficulties should not be underestimated, yet overcoming them is one of the challenges of the next 100 years of taxing people.

PART II

International Governance Challenges and Solutions

5

Exit, Voice, and Electivity

Confronting the Rise of Private Money and Private Taxation

Mitchell A. Kane

INTRODUCTION

The circle of legal academics who study international taxation will immediately recognise the occasion for publishing this book at this time. Two years ago marks the 100th anniversary of the 1923 League of Nations Report of the Four Economists – a report which is well-known by all within that circle but likely by very few outside of it.[1] The report is widely understood to have laid the foundation for the architecture underlying national approaches to international taxation for the entire century following its drafting. But few are happy with the current state of affairs in international tax. Indeed, few hold a firm belief that this system, which arose in response to the perceived ill of excessive taxation of international transactions, could possibly provide meaningful guidance today when inadequate, rather than excessive, taxation is a central problem.

How should we begin to think about how to build a more appropriate international architecture? Quite sensibly the prominent efforts currently proceeding within the OECD Inclusive Framework take business taxation (more specifically *large business* taxation) as the most important focal point. This is a sensible approach because the large businesses are where the money is. They are also the legal actors most able to comply with the intense complexity that is likely to accompany any architecture that surfaces to address international taxation in the coming years.

The organisers of this collection, however, have steered us in a different direction. They have asked us to consider people rather than businesses or firms – that is human persons, not legal ones. This too is sensible. Most scholars of international tax policy concern themselves ultimately with people and view firms as having only

I thank Susan Morse for her helpful comments.

[1] Luigi Einaudi et al., *Report on Double Taxation*, League of Nations Doc. E.F.S. 73 F.19 (1923).

instrumental importance.[2] Further, the lived experience of people has changed drastically in the last 100 years and will likely change even more in the next 100. The time therefore seems ripe to ask the question as this collection does: whither the taxation of people in the next 100 years?

The time may be ripe for this question, but our organisers have, nonetheless, charged the authors with a next-to-impossible task. It would seem to require both a retrospective understanding of the last century and a prospective analysis of the next one. At the same time, we have been asked to shift focus from businesses to individuals. This shift seems to require a fairly substantial revision of normative frameworks in a field that is not well-known for having sound normative frameworks even in the domain of business taxation, where it has primarily been of relevance (at least in terms of revenue). One could make the task more tractable by interpreting 'The Next 100 Years' not literally but as a rhetorical framing device. In other words, the charge could be something like: 'what changes to taxation should we make now, to be effective going forward, especially if we think about people rather than businesses?' That is no easy question either. Some of the contributors have taken it head on and have produced provocative analyses and accompanying prescriptions. But I thought it might be fruitful, or at least entertaining, to take the description literally. If we stretch the bounds of our imaginative capacity, what do we actually think the next century might look like? How will this affect the way we think about taxing people?

It is hard to predict the future. That is true in life; so too for tax law. But perhaps the horizon of a 100-year timeframe is helpful here rather than a hindrance. It is true that it is very hard to predict what will happen tomorrow. What is less difficult is to analyse the basic secular trends that we are observing today and to extrapolate from them to make predictions about what is likely to be the case in the indefinite future.

In that spirit, I will focus on four such secular trends in this chapter. The first is the proliferation of what I will refer to generally as non-state actors in terms of size, power, and influence. Much as the nation state came to challenge and displace the authority and power of the Church in the West, we observe at present the continual rise of counterweights to the traditional Westphalian nation state. I mean non-state actor here to be a very broad category – a non-exhaustive list would include firms, political or ideological organisations that lack formal recognition as states, social media networks, and online peer-to-peer communities. My claim about a secular trend is that collectively these sorts of organisations have resources, organisational capacity, and memberships that rival or exceed more traditional states (those that

[2] This position itself could be contested. I would personally contest it. To make that argument would take me too far down the path of a critique of the near ubiquity of consequentialist ethical theories in tax policy. Although I do not have space to make that critique in this chapter, some of what I say here about the evolution of firms in terms of their size, complexity, and power might itself give one pause about ethical theories that would simply write such actors out of the picture as principals.

have been thought of as the exclusive locus of the taxing power). The second is climate change, about which I will make no specific predictions other than that we should expect it to have substantial effects on the movement of people, the allocation of capital, and the need to finance public adaptation measures. All of these effects are global and implicate taxation. The third is the erosion of democratic norms and challenges to democratic governance. I write as a US legal academic, so I am obviously influenced as a citizen of the world's longest-standing democracy having undergone a violent insurrection during the most recent Presidential transition. But the uptick in willingness to dabble with, or outright embrace, autocracy is clearly a trend in evidence in democracies other than the United States. We can hope this is actually not a secular trend, but regrettably that story remains to be told. The fourth is the growth of cryptocurrency and other blockchain technologies. This is perhaps the most controversial of the trends I highlight here. There is no shortage of crypto-critics who see here nothing but a speculative asset bubble, which has largely popped, will continue to deflate, and will never have meaningful relevance alongside fiat currencies. I think that view is short-sighted.

To these trends, one could easily add the continual evolution of AI and machine learning as an obvious fifth. It is difficult to imagine that these technologies will not have a profound impact on taxation in the next century across a range of issues, including enforcement, the practice of law, and the possible shift towards understanding artificial intelligence as an appropriate object of taxation. As fascinating and important as these issues are, I will bracket them because they are less immediately relevant than questions of international taxation in particular. They are, rather, a series of questions that any taxing power would have to face individually, even under conditions of autarky.

Do the four trends I have highlighted paint a happy or a bleak picture? The pessimistic story is not difficult to tell. Climate disruptions will cause mass migrations of individuals, which will in turn provide ever greater fuel for right-wing extremists, with a full-blown resurrection of the deadly nationalistic and fascistic movements of the first half of the twentieth century to follow. Among the non-state actors in a world of closing borders, terrorist organisations that advocate violent means to overthrow the old order and power dynamic will thrive. The currently wealthy countries of the world will face immense fiscal pressures – aging populations with low birth-rates, high costs of climate adaptation, high costs of attempting to hold the line on state borders – whether through first-order costs to administer immigration policy or second-order costs of addressing social unrest arising in the face of tight immigration policy with increasingly unliveable conditions elsewhere.

This may all come to pass; though this scenario will not be my focus. In part, I prefer to think that this is not the world we have built to be inherited by my children. Also, thinking about such a world dampens my enthusiasm for the study of tax policy. Admittedly, there would be acute fiscal pressures in such a world, and there will be better and worse fiscal instruments to respond to those pressures. Yet, it's hard to see the fiscal problems as the most urgent ones in this bleakest of pictures. I could not see myself being content to devote my life to the study of tax law and policy if the world around me were in flames. So, whether out of cowardice or a head-in-the-sand mentality, or maybe just a lack of sufficient imagination to solve seemingly intractable social problems through fiscal policy, I am going to focus on a different way that these four trends could develop over the next century.

My basic thesis – perhaps merely a diluted form of the apocalyptic one just sketched – is that the various forces we currently observe will redefine the way we experience identity formation. I begin with the assumption that identity formation is a core aspect of the human experience. No matter how much we work to stress the commonality of the human condition, people will still feel a deep need to forge their self-identity in relation to group membership. And resulting identity groups will never arise solely from the ascription of positive properties. And they will never be able to do so in a way that arises solely from the ascription of positive properties. Identity formation, that is, will always have an aspect of holding oneself out as different from the other, from those persons not in the group. This phenomenon can, and has, taken on the whole gamut of expressions and perniciousness. At its worst we see mythic depictions of the state which can descend into genocides and ethnic cleansings. At its best we see national allegiances channelled into largely peaceful sporting competitions like the Olympics or the World Cup.

Accordingly, I take the need for identity formation to be a constant. What varies over time is the nature of the identity groups and the degree of harm that insiders wreak upon outsiders. For approximately the last 500 years, the sovereign state has played a crucial role in identity formation. Individuals have often identified crucially with some state of which they are a citizen or subject. They may identify with a small handful of additional states, perhaps states from which they or ancestors emigrated, or they may also identify with any number of groups, many of which have some sort of territorial dimension which bears a high correlation to national boundaries. That is not to say that there have not been crucial movements in tension with this idea – international workers' movements perhaps being the most significant. Even so, much identity formation has continued to operate either at the state level or has been local within a state.

One part of my thesis is that this aspect of identity formation has begun, and will continue, to evolve, which can be expected to weaken state power. The second part of my thesis is that once we pair the evolution of identity formation with another evolution – particularly that of *money* – we can expect to see not just a weakening of state power generally but a weakening of the power to tax. My prediction is that these forces could become so strong that reconceiving the very meaning of taxation may become necessary.

This chapter will proceed in two parts. First, I will elaborate on how I see the evolution of identity formation challenging the ability of the state to tax, possibly to the extent that the very meaning of taxation will have to evolve. I will not have space within this chapter to offer a normative assessment of that phenomenon, though I do believe it to be potentially a very troubling development. Secondly, I will bring the discussion back to the present or near future. Are there ways in which we might restructure the current system as a form of preventative medicine? Can we take account of different ideas of identity formation without core erosion of the state taxing function? I will lightly sketch one possibility – a new mechanism by which individuals would be able to voluntarily settle tax liability via payments to a state of their choosing, with such payment giving rise to a foreign tax credit in the home country to which tax is otherwise due.

THE EVOLUTION OF IDENTITY FORMATION, MONEY, AND THE CONCEPT OF TAXATION

Many commentators have begun to discuss the implications and challenges of cryptocurrencies for tax systems. These discussions tend to grapple with the application of familiar questions regarding tax base, timing, and information to a new medium or asset class. The discussion here is a bit different and is designed to focus not so much on the evolution of the object of taxation but rather on the evolution of the 'taxing' authority itself and the relationship between that authority and the party meant to owe and pay tax.

Evolution of Identity

I have already hinted at how the highlighted secular trends might be expected to affect the formation of identity groups. Proliferation of non-state actors provides a broader range of groups with which one can identify. Mass migrations will complicate state-based identity formation. Erosion of democratic governance will spur disillusionment with the state and searches for other identity groups. These phenomena are all augmented by increasing digitalisation and the ability of individuals to form virtual communities that are entirely divorced from geographical state boundaries. What I have yet to discuss is how the emergence of blockchain assets could also have an important impact here.

Regarding the possible connections between blockchain and identity, one should begin by distinguishing fungible tokens (like Bitcoin) and non-fungible tokens (NFTs). First, consider fungibility. Currency, whether US dollars or crypto (if it is considered to be currency rather than property), aspires to be fungible because fungibility – as a characteristic of money – has highly desirable characteristics. Greater fungibility was one of the great advances with paper money (as contrasted with coined metal which could be shaved down over time). Because the value of paper (and digital) money rests on something conceptual rather than physical, every token can be literally identical. But there is an interesting implication. Unlike nonfungible assets that have traditionally signalled status (land, livestock, physical assets, etc.), the only way to signal status with fungible currency is by quantity: by having a lot of it.

In this sense, there is nothing new going on with respect to blockchain in terms of identity. The way one would signal individual status via Bitcoin (as currency) is the same as the channel for doing so with dollars. One would amass a large quantity of it. To connect identity and blockchain in an interesting, novel way we need to reintroduce nonfungibility or NFTs.

When NFTs burst onto the scene in 2021 and generated substantial monetary gains for investors during a crypto bull market, it was tempting to cast NFTs simply as the latest exemplar of a demand-driven bubble. Once the bubble burst, we would be able to see that the asset class itself had little, or no, fundamental value. But, as the crypto bull market imploded in 2022, NFTs did not disappear. Further, there are interesting explanations of the fundamentals of NFT asset value that are not connected to bubble economics but rather tied back to identity. One can view an NFT not simply as a collectible but rather as evidence of membership in some community. At first blush this this might make an NFT look like little more than a glorified password. The fact that NFTs exist on a blockchain, however, gives them particular power as signals of *temporal* status. Acquiring cultural capital (rather than financial capital) on account of first-mover status is an old story – the avant garde Bohemians who settle in a previously overlooked neighbourhood (before it is ruined by gentrification and unaffordable rents). This is not to say that NFTs are at present the most important way in which individuals form identity through digital communities that are not state-based. That is clearly not the case. At present, individuals are much more likely to form identity through social media groups or basic tech company brand identity. But I am attempting to look forward many years and, in this respect, NFTs have two features that should be acknowledged. First, NFTs provide a novel digital way to signal and credibly authenticate early adoption and entry into a community. Latecomers cannot fake their way into the group (as one might by buying the latest trendy branded tech item and prominently flaunting it at the local café) by buying NFTs on the secondary market down the road. Blockchain can forever record the temporal ordering of who entered which community when. Second, NFTs exist as tokens on a blockchain that can also accommodate fungible tokens. In other words, members in NFT-based communities have at hand the technical ability to issue *fungible* tokens which can function as money. We are not quite yet to taxation, or private taxation, but we are getting closer. To draw that connection, one must say something briefly about the various functions of money and how they relate to state power.

Evolution of Money

What is the relationship between the state and money? It is not difficult to state particular connections. For example, money is commonly considered to serve a range of different functions. It can serve as a unit of account, a means of exchange, or a store of value. All these functions come together in modern state-issued money. Although this state of affairs has come to seem very natural, this is a contingent feature of money – not a necessary one.[3] The various functions of money were once much more disaggregated than they are today. The idea of state-issued money that folds all the various aspects of money into a single medium is a relatively recent phenomenon. The state is not even a ubiquitous actor in causal explanations of the initial adoption or use of money in human cultures. Under typical barter theories, money is assumed to arise as a neutral means to facilitate exchange that would otherwise have to occur only with respect to direct trades of goods or services. One does not need a state to create money in the standard origin story based on barter.

Just as the various functions of money came to rest in the instrument of state-issued money over time, they can come apart again because the relationship is contingent. Indeed, there are many examples of non-state instruments that serve at least some of the functions of money. Consider something like a merchant-based gift card that can be used only for the purchase of items through the merchant but cannot be exchanged into fiat currency. Such an item functions as a means of exchange and a store of value. Such cards do not generally, however, represent money that operates as an independent unit of account and, in that sense, they are generally denominated in fiat currency and are thus derivative of it.

At present, then, some of the functions of money can be accomplished with private instruments. Yet, such instruments are likely to be either directly or indirectly derivative upon fiat currencies, thus preserving the hegemony of fiat currencies for the time being. There is a further important way in which fiat currencies would seem to have a monopoly at present. They are almost uniquely how taxpayers pay taxes with a sovereign.[4] It would seem, then that, although it is possible for private money to take on some of the particular functions of fiat money, before now it has been very difficult to see private money as actually competing to displace state fiat money to any meaningful extent. We can generalise here and ascribe the limits to three interconnected phenomena.

The first is stability. No money is completely stable, but the experience with cryptocurrencies (other than stablecoins, which seek to maintain a peg to some fiat currency) is that their value is highly volatile compared to fiat currencies. This reflects in part that people put at least some faith in central bankers (and the rules or institutions that bind them) in some jurisdictions not to undertake unbounded devaluation of the currency through monetary policy. Again, one should be a realist here. Human institutions are always imperfect. But central banks do at least operate

[3] For an extended, historical illustration of the contingent relationship between the state and the various aspects of money, see, generally, Akinobu Kuroba, A Global History of Money (2020).

[4] Isolated exceptions have begun to crop up. See Samira Sadeque, *Colorado to Become First US State to Accept Cryptocurrency Tax Payments*, Guardian, Mar. 1, 2022.

against the backdrop of charters and governance constraints. It was, of course, part of the initial appeal of Bitcoin that one might peel away monetary policy from the central bankers by making it entirely decentralised. Crypto-evangelists have not, to my mind, really built that case or explained why it would be desirable to live in a world organised along the political lines of nation states, none of which have any control over monetary policy. If no such explanation exists, then the observed volatility of cryptocurrency may not be a mere growing pain of a novel technology but rather an inherent feature. Perhaps decentralised money is necessarily volatile money.

The second phenomenon is acceptability. A natural limit on the ability of cryptocurrency to compete with fiat currency is that holders want to know that their currency will be accepted broadly as a means of exchange for goods and services. Even the most popular cryptocurrencies (in terms of volume) have not approached anything close to the point of broad acceptability as a means of exchange in the market. This is perhaps inseparable from the stability point just mentioned. Merchants or providers of services can be expectedly reluctant to take payment in the form of an instrument with great volatility.

The third phenomenon has already been mentioned and is a subcase of the second. That is, one particularly important form of acceptability is the willingness of a sovereign to accept only its money as payment in satisfaction of its tax liabilities.

We can now see why the world's most influential fiat currency (by aggregate value) would seem to have such a chokehold here. In relation to the first phenomenon, we might say that stability is going to require a large base of currency which generates substantial trust that is sufficient to outweigh market swings driven by speculators. Small fiat currencies may struggle in this respect. Such currencies are themselves prone to volatility driven by speculative currency traders. But for the currencies of the economic powerhouses – say the G7 – it is difficult to see volatility (or predictions of it) rivalling what we have seen in cryptocurrency. Issuing crypto stablecoins is the only way that has been derived so far to address this issue. Interestingly, though not surprisingly, almost all stablecoin is pegged to the US dollar.[5] For now, then, one could at least say that the US dollar seems to be the necessary link to bring stability to non-stable crypto.

The second phenomenon plays out much the same way and for the same reason. One can certainly imagine more and more merchants and service providers accepting cryptocurrencies as payment but likely only to the extent that such crypto

[5] For a listing of leading stablecoins by market capitalisation, see *Stablecoins by Market Capitalisation*, COINGECKO, www.coingecko.com/en/categories/stablecoins. In order to maintain a 1:1 peg to the US dollar, a stablecoin issuer must hold sufficient assets to satisfy demands to convert the stablecoin into dollars. At present there is little to no regulation of the quantity or type of assets that must be held by an issuer. This invites the possibility of conversion requests in a panic that have the same effect as a bank run and can cause the coin to de-peg. See Gary B. Gorton & Jeffrey Y. Zhang, *Taming Wildcat Stablecoins*, 90 U. CHI. L. REV. 909 (2023).

could be readily converted either to dollars or to trustworthy and adequately-backed stablecoin.

Even if, due to their stability and acceptability, the US dollar (and other large fiat currencies) have an effective monopoly, one could see this as a short-term phenomenon only. That is, with very widespread, trustworthy stablecoin, one could see the stability and acceptability concerns gradually overcome, possibly eliminated. Stablecoin at that point would operate in direct and widespread competition with fiat currencies, even though at present stablecoin is not subject to the regulatory constraints of central bank money or commercial bank money. In light of this possibility, it is not at all surprising that various statements and actions arising out of the Biden administration manifest an attempt to silo crypto assets generally, and stablecoin specifically, from the mainstream fiat money-based economy.[6] One tactic to isolate stablecoin is to deny banks federal reserve privileges if they offer deposit accounts to stablecoin issuers.[7] But banks cannot function without being part of the federal reserve system. And stablecoin issuers would have great difficulty securely holding dollars or dollar-tied assets to secure their coin if nobody will bank with them.[8] I am telling a very US-centric story here – which is presently justified given the status of the US dollar as the world's reserve currency and the fact that almost all stablecoin is tied to dollars. But US attempts to isolate crypto assets from the US Federal Reserve system could well fail if the effort simply drives crypto business and stablecoins to rely upon non-dollar fiat currency for stability.

Of course, this just pushes the derivative nature of crypto onto some other fiat currency. If the currency is relatively small, then it may not be able to provide the desired stability. And if it is not relatively small, the issuer of the currency may well opt for a US-style isolation approach. Aside from the issue of separating crypto from the mainstream economy, the third phenomenon (that is, acceptability of currency for tax purposes) would seem directly and completely in the control of the sovereign. If OECD countries are collecting a substantial portion of GDP in taxes and can insist that such amounts be paid in their fiat currency, will not crypto necessarily maintain a derivative status?

Not necessarily. We may need to broaden what we are able to readily imagine. Stability and acceptability seem highly correlated with size or volume. The state's monopolistic demand that its taxes can only be settled in the official currency that it issues is immutable only if we assume that states are the only actors that can function as tax collectors. But what if other powerful non-state actors come to collect amounts

[6] See, e.g., Michael J. Hsu, *Acting Comptroller of the Currency, Remarks Before the Institute of International Economic Law at Georgetown University Law School*, 'Thoughts on the Architecture of Stablecoins' (Apr. 8, 2022).

[7] See Joe Light, Crypto is Being Debanked: What It Means for Bitcoin and the Industry (Barrons Mar. 13, 2023).

[8] This assumes the stablecoin retains its peg in virtue of being backed by some form of reserve as opposed to an algorithmically-backed coin in the nature of TerraUSD.

as levies, payable only in the money created by such actors? Whether we are willing to call such levies 'taxes' or whether we want to make a valiant terminological stand and attempt to tie taxes and states together definitionally may not ultimately matter. What is likely to matter more is whether any such levies come to compete as a functional matter with instruments that we commonly call taxes at present.

Let us consider a thought experiment.[9] My premise is that the hurdles of widespread acceptability and general stability might be surmountable with sufficient size. Scanning the list of the largest companies in the world, Amazon immediately stands out. It is currently fifth in the world in terms of market capitalisation, just shy of 1 trillion dollars. Of the top ten companies (by market capitalisation), it is the only one whose business model involves selling a broad range of consumer goods. The others, by comparison, have valuable, but relatively narrow, portfolios (i.e., software, hardware, natural resources, cars, and investment products). Suppose that Amazon were to issue a dollar-denominated crypto stablecoin: the Bezos. One Bezos would be pegged to one dollar. Amazon has a lot of cash on hand. For the quarter ending 2022, it had approximately $70B cash on hand. Coincidentally, as of this writing, that is about the same amount as the market capitalisation of Tether, which is by far the largest stablecoin by market capitalisation, representing about 75% of the entire market. In effect, then, overnight Amazon could issue the Bezos, promise dollar convertibility based on its cash reserves, and immediately rival the largest stable coin issuer in the world.

Now suppose that Amazon has grand ambitions to compete not with Tether – but with states themselves. If Amazon wanted to achieve a foothold as a competitor to states in the currency-issuance game, it would have a number of options.[10] First, calling upon its tested strategy of taking losses upfront to build market share, it could provide powerful incentives for Amazon customers to use the Bezos. Specifically, Amazon could give some *x* per cent discount for using the Bezos to buy items on Amazon. Second, Amazon could form a consortium with other large, powerful companies who would stand behind convertibility and would also guarantee acceptance of the coin as payment. For example, imagine an Amazon–Apple–Microsoft–Google stablecoin consortium.[11] The market capitalisation of those four companies

[9] This thought experiment is motivated by the failed attempt of Facebook to launch its stablecoin Diem. Although that effort ultimately failed rather spectacularly, there is little reason to think that another mega-firm will not make a similar attempt in the future.

[10] Note that the architecture of the TerraUSD stablecoin, which maintained an algorithmic peg to the US dollar through its connection to the Luna coin, explicitly incorporated a type of seigniorage. The currencies were decentralised, such that the proceeds of seigniorage went to the 'treasury' for fiscal stimulus (essentially financial incentives for parties to mine currency). This seems a short conceptual step away from a powerful actor launching a blockchain-based currency and retaining some central control over seigniorage and 'taxation'.

[11] We can hope the order of adoption would not be Microsoft–Apple–Google–Amazon, with the coin being called the MAGA, thereby validating a particularly spurious claim of the 45th President of the United States. See Steven Nelson, *Trump Says MAGA also Stands for*

is over six trillion dollars. A 10 per cent annual return on market capitalisation would yield $600B, enough money to place the consortium about twentieth in the world in terms of national GDPs.[12]

In this thought experiment, it seems that we have gone a long way to address the issues of stability and acceptability. It is true that the Bezos is still derivative on the dollar. It is using the dollar as the unit of account and holding dollar reserves to secure convertibility. But it is not obvious that existing regulatory tools allow the government to shut the activity down based on that connection between the dollar and the Bezos. Perhaps Amazon is a de facto bank if it stands ready to take dollars and issue Bezos in return. But if this is not the case, then the government would likely need completely new regulatory tools. We could ultimately witness a temporal race to monetary dominance as the derivative aspect of the Bezos would not necessarily be a permanent feature. At one time, people were quite convinced that all faith in state-issued money would be lost if metal convertibility were suspended. We learned this was not the case at least 400 years ago when England suspended convertibility and the pound did not crash.[13] If people were to come to widely use and trust the Bezos, would they stop doing so simply based on the dollar reserves that Amazon happened to hold at any given time?

Evolution of Taxation

Let us take stock. I have so far suggested that the blockchain and crypto may have two crucial effects in time. The first is to have a profound impact on identity formation that may well weaken the ties between individuals and states. The second is to allow non-state actors to issue cryptocurrency that could come to be in genuine competition with state-issued currency. Importantly, these two effects are related to one another. As a social construct the very idea of money requires trust. For money to work one must trust that the tokens you are being paid are authentic and one must trust that downstream recipients of the tokens will likewise have faith in them. Because we are accustomed to functioning in global capital markets where the trust problem has essentially been solved (at least for reserve currencies), modern money can work as between complete strangers – or even complete enemies. But this obscures the problem of generating trust upon the initial creation of some currency. In such cases individuals who share common identity as group members will likely

Microsoft, Apple, Google and Amazon, N. Y. Post, Feb. 11, 2020, https://nypost.com/2020/02/11/trump-says-maga-also-stands-for-microsoft-apple-google-and-amazon/.

12 My knowledge of antitrust law is quite limited. Based on casual conversations with experts, though, I understand that such a consortium is not obviously any sort of antitrust violation because the firms that are coming together do not compete in a market for money issuance or creation.

13 See, generally, Stefan Eich, The Currency of Politics: The Political Theory of Money from Aristotle to Keynes 47–75 (2022).

find it easier to solve the trust problems that arise upon creation of a new currency. Once we consider the identity formation issue and the privately-issued cryptocurrency issue together, then it seems that one might be further forced to fundamentally rethink the very concept of taxation. My confidence in my powers of prognostication grow weaker by the sentence. So, let me resort to history to make two final points here.

The first relates to the origin story of money and the connection between that story and taxation. There are rival explanations for the origin of money, reflecting perhaps the fact that there is no single causal path for the evolution of a social convention that serves the various functions that money is thought to serve. Although it is tempting to derive conceptual, decontextualised evolutionary stories for money, such an approach invites error. This seems to be the basic object lesson of barter explanations of money. Such explanations are highly compelling in the sense that *if* an economy functioned by barter, then surely as the economy became more complex a single medium of exchange (money) would be highly desirable. The problem, though, is that anthropological study has failed to demonstrate the general truth of the conditional part of that proposition.[14] Beyond barter theories, the theory that seems most relevant to the current discussion is chartalism. Unlike barter theory (which is a spontaneous, non-state-based story), the chartalists tied the *value* of money inextricably to the state.[15] Specifically, money obtained value precisely because it could be used to satisfy tax debts owed to the state. Further, once circulating money had such value, the state could use the money it created to pay for services, typically the services of soldiers to wage war and conquest. Chartalism may not explain the rise of money in all cases. Sumeria seems to provide counter-evidence.[16] But it is a compelling story in at least some circumstances, which means that there is something to learn from it.

We might begin with a canonical definition of taxation: '[a] tax is a mandatory payment or charge collected by local, state, and national governments from individuals or businesses to cover the costs of general government services, goods, and activities.'[17] This definition, by its terms, precludes private actors from enacting 'taxes'. This seems to be by convention, however, and not by reasoned argument. Seen from the standpoint of the chartalists, the canonical definition takes on a particular cast. The fact that taxation is limited to governments can be seen as a contingent feature. That is, to date, it has been sensible to think of governments as the only bodies that were capable of issuing money and simultaneously imbuing it with value by requiring parties to pay the money back to the issuer in the form of a mandatory levy. This is an empirical claim, not a conceptual one.

[14] David Orrell & Roman Chlupatý, The Evolution of Money 13–14 (2016).
[15] Eich, *supra* note 13, at 151–152.
[16] Orrell & Chlupatý, *supra* note 14, at 15–17.
[17] See *Definition of Tax*, Tax Foundation, https://taxfoundation.org/tax-basics/tax/.

What if non-state actors also had sufficient power to create money as under the chartalist account. Then, a better canonical definition of a 'tax' might be something like: a tax is a mandatory payment collected by some principal who has the capacity to issue money and require that the mandatory payment be satisfied with such money. This would open the door to private taxation. One can readily see hints of modern monetary theory (an intellectual heir to chartalism) in this conclusion. Under the standard account, the government taxes in order to spend. And we imagine that it is the state that has this unique power to tax in the first place. Modern monetary theory (MMT) flips the account, arguing that states spend in order to tax. But, if that is true, why should we think that taxation is uniquely a state-based phenomenon? The foundational step is spending, which both private and public actors can do. If a private actor can spend and then force recipients of the spending to return spent amounts (without unwinding the transactions that gave rise to the initial expenditure), then it seems like we have space for private taxation under chartalism and MMT.

There remains the issue of whether a private actor could make a payment mandatory. But we must remember here that even the mandatory nature of accepted state-based taxes is not an absolute phenomenon. Payment of tax is required to avoid injurious consequences if the putative taxpayer is within the state's taxing jurisdiction. But it is often possible to exit the taxing jurisdiction. The same set of factors may well arise with private actors. A private actor may have sufficient power or leverage to impose injurious consequences if payment is not made. And avoiding that trade-off may require the putative payor to exit transactional relations to the private imposer of the 'tax'. Note that I am not suggesting a shakedown. The extraction of such 'taxes' could arise out of voluntary contract and private law arrangements.

Some might continue to insist that the domain of private taxation is a null set. Genuine taxation involves the coercive power of a state – coercion which we accept as *legally* justified precisely because it is exercised by the state. Any other sort of coerced payment is not, under this argument, a tax. But this is to fall for a dogmatic conceptualisation of taxation. State-based taxation and the coercive power of the state ultimately depends upon territory – and people need to be physically located *somewhere*. But, increasingly, people need to be located virtually as well. What if one's sole access to the internet depended upon a privately-owned satellite that orbits earth in no state-owned or controlled territory? Suppose the owner of the satellite issues private money and that money has value precisely because the monopolist controller of internet access demands certain payments which can only be satisfied in such money. The sanction for non-payment is termination of internet access – and all of the social, financial, and professional connections that it provides. My claim is not that such a levy is identical to state-based taxation. The claim, rather, is that the levy is a social phenomenon that shares most (perhaps all) of the crucial features of state-based taxation. Just as private money can compete with state money on the margin, so too can private taxation. Moreover, if this still strikes us as unjustified coercion in a way that state-based is not, query whether that intuition might not begin to fade away if we take seriously the evolution of identity formation sketched in the last section. Individuals who identify with the relevant community might well come to see the levy as part of a civic duty to support the community in the same way that many citizens pay their taxes not in order to avoid penalties but because it is the right thing to do.

What I suggest here is not entirely novel. We have some limited precedent for the basic idea. The closest analogy would be a company's payment of workers in scrip and requiring use of such scrip as payment in the company store that functioned as the only plausible seller of merchandise for workers in a company town. In this model, companies would charge above-market (as measured by prevailing wage rates and state-currency retail price levels) prices, effectively taxing back some of the scrip that it had issued. This parallels the basic chartalist account.

This model did not scale, however. Companies could issue and tax back scrip only in isolated company towns with retail monopolies. And, even with that limitation, the practice was condemned and made illegal.[18] The previous thought experiment regarding the Bezos is meant to call into question whether such an account could never scale. Certainly, the idea of private *money* is well understood. But the idea of private *taxation* seems an oxymoron. But if we think it is so, it may just be that historically only state actors have had sufficient concentration of power to issue money and credibly assert that such money would have value into the indefinite future precisely because it would be needed to satisfy an obligation to the state. Might Amazon and the Bezos, or a conglomerate of large powerful firms, be able to do the same?

This is deeply ironic. It was meant to be one of the chief advantages of Bitcoin to break money away from centralised power. But the blockchain simply allows for decentralised creation of tokens that people might come to honour as a means of exchange. It does not necessitate decentralisation because a centralised power can certainly harness blockchain technology to issue money. Indeed, the technology may well make it uniquely possible for centralised, non-state actors to do so because of how generally secure it is. One might contrast the case where Amazon attempted to turn consumer refunds (each designated with some unique, long string of alphanumeric characters stored somewhere on an Amazon server and sent to customers by e-mail) into a form of Amazon-issued money. This could function much like the Bezos – except for the fact that the costs of verification and the potential for fraud would make it completely unworkable.

The second point I wanted to make here is that, by expanding the notion of taxation to include the possibility of private taxation, I do not mean to suggest that

[18] For a discussion of scrips and governmental action to make them illegal in the case of France and the United States, ORRELL & CHLUPATÝ, *supra* note 14, at 8.

state-based taxation is about to disappear. The claim rather is that states could face a new form of competition from private actors in the money issuance-and-taxation game. I cannot elaborate here on the many potential ramifications, but I will highlight one. Such an alternate non-state money-tax would likely lead to the resurrection of long-rejected exchange theories of taxation. At least for now, it is much easier to imagine Amazon requiring payment of the Bezos in exchange for provision of a certain value to the payor. This is the old exchange theory. The idea of an ability-to-pay-based system of private taxation (Amazon demanding payment of some amount of Bezos in order to provide value to other users of the Bezos) would take much longer to evolve.

I suspect there would be robust disagreement about the normative desirability of the various evolutions I have sketched here. I hold a strong personal view that the onset of private taxation at scale would be deeply problematic. It could be expected to pose serious challenges not just to monetary policy (the initial focus of the Bitcoin creator(s)) but to fiscal policy as well because private competition with states over the power of taxation would likely erode the ability to have robust financing of a range of public goods and of social insurance safety nets. What are the alternatives?

A PROPOSAL FOR ELECTIVE ALLOCATION OF STATE-BASED TAXES

One can imagine many state responses to the further evolution and potential dominance of private money. These would most likely be regulatory in nature. Creators of private money systems might be subject to regulation under current, or revised, law regarding banking, general financial regulation, counterfeiting or antitrust. The state might alternatively attempt to outcompete private actors regarding the issuance of digital currency, particularly through the adoption of central bank digital currencies.[19] My focus here is a bit different – mostly because I am interested not just in the potential growth of private money (a possibility that has presented itself for some time) but rather in the connection between private money and private taxation. From within the bounds of the tax system – and the structure of international taxation specifically – might we acknowledge some of the pressures arising from some of the secular trends noted at the beginning of this chapter, specifically breakdowns in democratic governance, climate change induced diasporas, proliferation of powerful actors (who are at present taxpayers rather than tax creators and collectors), and the evolution of cryptocurrency?

In Albert O. Hirschman's classic work *Exit, Voice, and Loyalty*, disgruntled participants in an organisational structure have two basic options: leave the structure (exit) or remain in the structure and try to change it (voice).[20] Hirschman's model is

[19] For a comprehensive argument in favour of central bank digital currencies, see Eswar Prasad, The Future of Money (2021).

[20] Albert O. Hirschman, Exit, Voice and Loyalty (Harvard 1970).

general and was meant to apply to participants in both states and non-state organisations. There is, of course, a logical necessity (following from the law of the excluded middle) to concluding there are only two options: that I either stay (voice) or that I do not stay (exit). But formal logic may not capture everything we care about. The secular trends highlighted at the outset suggest that, for many people, exit may become increasingly difficult (because receptivity in receiving states will be put under stress by climate-induced diasporas) and that voice (understood as meaningful democratic participation in the state) is also under threat. Supposing I cannot leave, and I feel that my political voice has no efficacy – am I out of options? One remaining option that I have discussed is to attempt to forge one's identity with less reliance on the state, opting instead for non-state organisations. If such organisation is virtual, then one can participate in it without moving. If such organisation can gain enough power and prominence it may come to compete with the state in many ways, including, possibly, the power to implement levies that function much like taxes. In short, if there is continued shrinking of the exit and voice avenues, one can expect hydraulic pressure for dissatisfied individuals to simply seek membership or attachment to a different *type* of organisation, rather than a different token of the same type of organisation.

That pressure may well be resisted by state actors who stand to lose power and influence to non-state actors. It may also be resisted by individuals who are not part of the official state apparatus but who doubt the ability of a world with an excessive amount of decentralised power to deal with the host of problems that require coordination (whether it be responses to pandemics, climate, or monetary crises). I will assume, but not defend here, that such resistance to the transfer of power and influence to non-state actors is desirable, at least to some extent.

To that end, I propose a middle ground between exit and voice that does not rely upon members of a state simply seeking out alternate non-state organisations. I refer to it as *electivity* and what I have in mind is allowing individuals to voluntarily associate to some extent with other state actors via the mechanism of elective tax allocations.[21] More specifically, consider the world largely as we experience it today in which individuals are generally tied in a primary way to some state under either some sort of residence standard or citizenship standard. On that basis, individuals calculate a tax liability to the state of which they are resident/citizen. At that point we do not usually think there is much left that is interesting to say about to whom the taxpayer remits tax. The taxpayer, of course, must remit tax to the government under whose laws the taxpayer is resident or citizen and in virtue of which the liability arises. (And payment must be made, almost always, in the currency that is legal tender in that state.) But what if, at this point, we said to taxpayers: you may *choose* to which state some portion of your tax payment will flow. As a technical matter, we can slot such a proposal into existing rules by imagining that such payment would

[21] My thanks to Daniel Hemel for suggesting this framing.

count as a 'tax' for foreign tax credit purposes and would be creditable in the home country.

This approach produces a number of benefits. It would allow for a type of direct democracy that might go some of the way to addressing grievances about breakdowns in governance mechanisms. People would now be tied not to some single set of governance outputs, but instead they could see themselves as directly supporting a range of governmental approaches. Suppose you do not like your country's lackadaisical approach to climate change? Solution: allocate some of your tax dollars to a country that is doing better in your opinion. One can easily imagine similar arguments for other social and economic problems – hunger, extreme poverty, public health – about which governments take widely disparate approaches. It is conceivable this sort of allocation would bolster people's willingness to pay taxes generally and this in turn could bolster the position of states against the rise of non-state actors, who might be tempted to compete in the money/taxation game.

There are also some obvious challenges. How could governments produce budgets and plan long-term expenditures with this potential variability? How could we be certain of payment to a foreign government? Would this not invite fraud? But these strike me as technical problems that could be solved. As a proof of concept, one could begin by allowing taxpayers to allocate just some small fraction of their overall liability in this fashion. Proof and fraud problems can never be removed, but we are familiar with how to approach such issues.

For now, I mean to float the basic idea in the hope that it will lead to further discussion. I will close with an interesting observation. The proposal will likely come across as radical, but, in an era when it is difficult to achieve ideological consensus about the role of the state and the scope of taxation, it is interesting to observe that one can see in my proposal an appeal to people across the ideological spectrum. For those on the right who are distrustful of centralised state power, the proposal creates a sort of global market for tax dollars. States would be rewarded or punished for various policies and may even receive valuable market-based information to inform future governance decisions. For those on the left who take a more cosmopolitan approach to global distributive justice, the proposal allows one to direct funds to places in the world that may seem more in need. Yet, this approach achieves such distribution of global resources without relying on greater centralised global governance and tax collection, which, even if desirable as a means to address global inequalities, seems a long way off indeed.

6

Fear of a Black Planet

Africa's Decolonisation and the Transformation of the International Tax Regime

Steven A. Dean

INTRODUCTION

For the last century, international tax policy has been defined not by consistency but by disparate treatment. A selective cosmopolitanism has denied to some the resources it has offered freely to others. This chapter casts an unflattering light on institutions and technologies at the heart of global tax policy. And it pairs that critique with a call for robust efforts to ensure that the next 100 years delivers the tax sovereignty that fear has long denied to more than a billion Black people.

The United States has long helped guide the evolution of international tax policy. An outsized influence has translated into a disproportionate impact on that policy's trajectory, no different than the story that has played out in countless other contexts. With the 'proliferation of institutions designed to manage, or "govern" global capitalism . . . the United States in particular benefited from these institutions since, as the preeminent power involved in setting up such capitalist infrastructure after 1945, it was able to shape their design, influence staffing, and otherwise exert power.'[1] That US influence has not always been acknowledged.[2] Nor has it been consistently benign, inevitably reflecting America's flaws as well as its strengths.

I am grateful to Tsilly Dagan, Martin Hearson, and Ruth Mason for their very helpful comments, and to Akindele Kitwana for his research assistance. For more on the impact of racism on international tax law, read my book RACIAL CAPITALISM AND INTERNATIONAL TAX LAW: THE STORY OF GLOBAL JIM CROW (2025).

[1] Vanessa Ogle, *Global Capitalist Infrastructure and US Power*, *in* THE CAMBRIDGE HISTORY OF AMERICA AND THE WORLD (David C. Engerman et al. eds., 2022).

[2] The implausible conventional narrative of global inattention and US passivity in a context as impactful as taxation has been upended by new research demonstrating that the rise of the OECD disrupted a vibrant debate within the United Nations about the future of international tax. See Michael J. Graetz, *Taxing International Income: Inadequate Principles, Outdated Concepts, and Unsatisfactory Policies*, 26 BROOK. J. INT'L L. 1357, 1358 (2001) ('Nothing comparable to the thoroughgoing multilateral restructurings of international monetary and trade relationships that followed the Second World War (which themselves have been substantially revised and refined since) has affected the system of international income taxation.'); but

In a world in which racial bias continues to shape policies and to fuel politics, a failure of US leadership helped to create a global tax system defined by separate and unequal treatment, reinscribing a shameful history of disenfranchisement on a far larger scale. The central role of tax revenues in supporting economic development and the elevation of human rights from aspiration into reality makes that failure profoundly impactful. For more than half a century international tax rules have been crafted by an organisation that robbed a continent of its tax sovereignty at a crucial moment.

Fear of a Black planet helped give rise to an institution that over decades has boasted dozens of members, not a single one of which has ever been majority Black. Created as an alternative to increasingly diverse international organisations like the United Nations as the decolonisation of Africa gained momentum, the Organisation for Economic Cooperation and Development (OECD) has built a troubling legacy. In time, it would oversee a global tax regime that left the developing world bound by chains of debt while securing freedom for the wealthy world's multinationals. Its birth, as this chapter explains, stripped Africans of their voice at their independence.

This would not, of course, be the first time that fear had helped disenfranchise Black people. The same prejudices long prevented the United States from realising the promise of Emancipation in the wake of its Civil War. The painful history of Reconstruction – with racial bias legitimising the disenfranchisement of formerly enslaved people – serves as a cautionary tale for efforts to make global tax policy-making more inclusive. Only military intervention by the North provided Black Americans in the South with a meaningful opportunity to influence the policy-making process during Reconstruction. Once the soldiers left, the freedom they briefly enjoyed came to an end.

A successful remaking of the global tax policymaking process – sufficient to overcome entrenched structural obstacles to the participation of states not members of the OECD – would require remedies far more potent than those offered to date. This chapter draws on the lessons of US post-Civil War Reconstruction to suggest what might begin to undo the damage of more than a half-century of exclusion. That history reveals why merely extending an invitation for disenfranchised states to participate in global tax policy discussions will not be enough.

TAX AND DECOLONISATION

In the 1950s, the world faced the prospect of Black governance of a continent. At that time, Reconstruction remained deeply misunderstood. Scholars – labelled the

see Nikki Teo, The United Nations in Global Tax Coordination 2 (2023), describing a long-overlooked post–World War II era featuring 'promising developments of the UN as a forum for double taxation matters and the interested participation of non-European, post-colonial developing countries in the subject'.

Dunning School after the Columbia University professor most closely associated with its ideas – described Reconstruction 'as a time of corruption and misgovernment caused by the enfranchisement of the former slaves'.[3] That misreading of history – which would not be definitively put to rest until the 1980s – would have made Africa's dawning independence the source of grave concern.

Those fears would not have been confined to the United States. Thanks to influential scholars and mainstream books like the 'sensationalist bestseller of the 1920s, *The Tragic Era*, that described Louisiana's Reconstruction legislature as a "zoo"',[4] such views had an opportunity to spread far and wide. As a result, 'the alleged failure of Reconstruction became part of the ideology of the white man's burden, cited all over the world to demonstrate the incapacity of non-white peoples for self-government'.[5]

In the 1950s those fears would have grown acute. Put bluntly, as African independence loomed '[m]any Europeans . . . held deep-seated racist convictions about the absence of business acumen among native populations and simply could not imagine economic life continuing in regular form after independence'.[6] With the Dunning School offering Reconstruction to the world as the epitome of non-white mismanagement, Black sovereignty on such a scale could hardly have sat easily with the public.

That feared misgovernance would have included the possibility of outright nationalisation of foreign-owned ventures.[7] But other changes would have been certain. Given the demands of statehood, 'increased taxation'[8] would have been a foregone conclusion. Before independence, rates remained well below those of the metropoles. Those differences hid even more substantial disparities in actual tax burdens as 'evasion of income taxes in colonies was widespread'.[9]

Public demand for long-neglected public services like education and healthcare promised a swift end to an era of modest colonial taxation. Under direct imperial control, financial pressures ruled out such spending. 'Colonies that struggled to make their budgets balance were particularly wary of public investments that would commit them to future spending. This included building schools and hospitals, which would need to be maintained and staffed in future years.'[10]

3 Eric Foner, Reconstruction: America's Unfinished Revolution 1863–1877, xxxix (2014).
4 Id., at xxxii.
5 Id., at xxxix.
6 See Vanessa Ogle, *Funk Money: The End of Empires, The Expansion of Tax Havens, and Decolonization as an Economic and Financial Event*, 249 Past & Present 213, 214 (2020).
7 Id.
8 Id., 'Distrustful of newly independent governments and non-white rule, fearing resentment, increased taxation or possibly even nationalization, Euro-American businesses active in the colonial world divested from empire.'
9 Id., at 236.
10 Leigh A. Gardner, Taxing Colonial Africa: The Political Economy of British Imperialism 10 (2012).

After independence, new nations promised to remedy those failures. 'With the transfer of power came widespread optimism that independence would allow for the provision of services, particularly education, at a more generous level than colonial authorities had allowed.'[11] But, without tax sovereignty, new governments could not keep those promises. Although newly independent states 'dramatically increased their spending on services like education and healthcare, neglected during the colonial period ... these increases were ultimately unsustainable'.[12]

The impact of that failure – like the unravelling of Reconstruction almost a century before – would be broad and deep. Without tax revenues, new governments proved unable to deliver schools and hospitals. In time, 'the tax systems established by colonial governments were unable to cope with the demands of democracy, and the political systems of many independent African countries descended into single-party autocracy and military rule'.[13] In both the post-Civil War American South and in a newly independent Africa, fear fuelled by anti-Black racism helped young democracies die on the vine.

THE SABOTAGE OF AFRICA'S RECONSTRUCTION

In Africa's Reconstruction, America and Europe perceived a familiar threat. They responded by embracing tools and structures designed to limit Africa's sovereignty. That pattern can be seen clearly in taxation. Until the early 1950s, the United Nations retained jurisdiction over global tax policy.[14] With Africa's decolonisation imminent, that would change.

Formed by adding Canada and the United States to the Organisation for European Economic Cooperation, the OECD offered a reassuring, all-white[15] alternative. This substitute for multiracial democracy took shape at the same time the United Nations prepared to welcome a host of new Black members. Little effort was made to disguise the impetus for such changes. The OECD charter, for

[11] Id., at 245.

[12] Gardner suggests that the failure of African tax systems not only prevented them from providing the hoped-for social services but contributed to the rise of dictatorships. Id.

[13] Id.

[14] Teo details the involvement of the United Nations in global tax policy in the years following World War II, noting that it 'formulated principles on two difficult issues that were indirectly related to revising the model conventions, namely the general allocation principles to apply in relations between developed and undeveloped countries, and the taxation of international air transport'. TEO, *supra* note 2, at 10.

[15] Many might be surprised to find that the US Census includes Turkey in its definition of white. U.S. CENSUS BUREAU, ABOUT THE TOPIC OF RACE (2022), www.census.gov/topics/population/race/about.html ('White. A person having origins in any of the original peoples of Europe, the Middle East, or North Africa. It includes people who indicate their race as "White" or report responses such as German, Irish, English, Italian, Lebanese, and Egyptian.').

example, would be signed on the same day in 1960 as the UN General Assembly adopted its Declaration on Decolonisation.[16]

Vibrant debates over international tax policy flourished in the United Nations through the early 1950s. During World War II, the United States had found it useful to make a show of embracing inclusive global tax governance.[17] Yet, with Africa's decolonisation, US support allowed the OECD to effortlessly take control of global tax policy.

By the 1960s, thanks to that US change of heart, a 'thoroughgoing multilateral restructuring [] of ... the system of international income taxation'[18] occurred. But neither that restructuring nor its devastating impact has ever been acknowledged. Thanks to the rise of the OECD, global tax policy would no longer be part of what economist John Maynard Keynes described in a cable to the British Treasury – paraphrasing, perhaps unintentionally, *The Tragic Era*[19] – not as a zoo but as 'the most monstrous monkey-house assembled for years'.[20]

THE LEAGUE OF NATIONS

In the years to come, the OECD would dominate global tax policymaking. But, at its inception, it possessed neither tax expertise or experience.[21] Despite – or perhaps because of – a need to add heft to its international tax policy efforts, the OECD ignored the work of the United Nations. Instead, it reached back to the work of the League of Nations from the 1920s.

The failure of the League of Nations – and more pointedly its failure to prevent renewed conflict in the wake of World War I – tends to be overshadowed in tax circles by what would prove to be a notable posthumous success. Specifically, the League published a series of model tax treaties in the 1920s. Fittingly described as a 'flawed miracle',[22] the League's treaties came to play a central role in global tax

[16] Both the OECD Charter and the General Assembly's Declaration on the Granting of Independence to Colonial Countries and Peoples (General Assembly resolution 1514 (XV)) were adopted on 14 December 1960.

[17] Teo corrects the story of the fabled Mexico draft of the model tax treaty by showing that it was the product of US efforts to curry favour with Latin America during the war, unnecessary after the war ended. See TEO, *supra* note 2, at 82, expressing skepticism about the 'League's wartime engagement of developing countries into its double taxation work'.

[18] Compare Graetz, *supra* note 2, at 1358, with TEO, *supra* note 2, at 2.

[19] Bowers described the Louisiana Legislature as 'a monkey-house'. CLAUDE G. BOWERS, THE TRAGIC ERA: THE REVOLUTION AFTER LINCOLN 364 (1929).

[20] Letter from John Maynard Keynes to Sir David Walley (1944), *in* THE COLLECTED WRITINGS OF JOHN MAYNARD KEYNES 42 (Elizabeth Johnson & Donald Moggridge, eds. 1972), describing a UN conference that included African and Latin American representatives.

[21] See TEO, *supra* note 2, at 353, noting that because 'the OEEC had no experts in the field' and with 'the UN staff suitably skilled' the UN 'flagged the possibility of seconding an International Tax Section official for a few months to furnish the OEEC Secretariat with technical support'.

[22] Reuven S. Avi-Yonah, *The Structure of International Taxation: A Proposal for Simplification*, 74 TEX. L. REV. 1301, 1303 (1996).

governance well after the League itself had collapsed. Designed in such a way that those treaties subtly constrain the tax sovereignty of poor countries, they reflect a darker aspect of the League's work.

Anticipating precisely the future the world confronted in the 1950s, the League's efforts would be informed both by empire's evident decline and fears of non-white governance. It worked to craft a legal framework capable of preserving the substance of empire in a post-imperial age. What could no longer be accomplished through direct control, the imperial powers hoped to accomplish with treaties and other international legal instruments.

That dynamic can be observed in the fate of Germany's colonies. Most of the war's victors had hoped to annex the imperial possessions of the losing side. But US objections and a growing distaste for imperial control made that impossible. 'Only reluctantly did they bend to American pressure and the wave of internationalist and anti-imperialist sentiment sweeping the globe' by agreeing that Germany's former possessions would instead be nominally sovereign and 'governed under League oversight'.[23]

The League's architects hoped to formally embrace the 'right to self-determination' while 'repurpos[ing] the principle to preserve racial hierarchy in the new international organization'.[24] The League's '"colonial" branch, the Mandate System'[25] reveals how lofty ideals co-existed with racist beliefs. By the time the Permanent Mandates Commission met for the first time in 1921, 'whatever purposes the mandates system had been devised to serve, extending the right of national self-determination was not one of them'.[26]

The League's Mandate System alarmed some observers and dashed the hopes of those that would be governed by it. Armed with the lessons of Reconstruction, W. E. B. Du Bois fruitlessly 'urge[d] that a "man of African descent" be added to the Commission'.[27] Bitterly disappointed that they would not be fully independent, the subjects of the Mandate System 'responded by resisting its imposition almost as strenuously as had the imperial powers'.[28]

There might be no future for empire, but racism and hierarchy tainted the League's vision. Despite their growing distaste for empire its 'architects and officials had intended ... to uphold imperial authority and strengthen the prestige and legitimacy of alien, non-consensual rule'.[29] While insisting that they supported the

[23] Susan Pedersen, The Guardians: The League of Nations and the Crisis of Empire 1 (2015).

[24] Adom Getachew, Worldmaking after Empire: The Rise and Fall of Self-Determination 10 (2019), arguing that 'Woodrow Wilson and Jan Smuts excised the revolutionary implications of the Bolshevik right to self-determination and repurposed the principle to preserve racial hierarchy in the new international organization.'

[25] Ntina Tzouvala, Capitalism as Civilization 89 (2020).

[26] See Pedersen, *supra* note 23, at 3.

[27] Id.

[28] Id.

[29] Id. at 13.

principle of self-determination, US President Woodrow Wilson and others 'argued that racially backward people were not suited for democracy but could partake in minimal forms of consent and were owed some modicum of respect'.[30] The League crafted legal technologies that delivered control with a veneer of legitimacy.

The territory Germany once held in Africa now became Mandates, independent, but subject to the 'tutelage' of European powers. The Mandate System would in theory help 'peoples not yet able to stand by themselves under the strenuous conditions of the modern world'[31] learn the skills necessary to one day graduate to true sovereignty. That notion would be reflected in the Mandate System's racially stratified classification system.

The whitest Mandates – including portions of what had been the Ottoman Empire – would possess A status, providing them with a significant degree of autonomy. Next in the hierarchy came 'B Mandates, which included former German colonies in Central Africa' over which 'Mandatory powers were granted much broader powers'.[32] Finally, 'C Mandates included South West Africa, New Guinea and small Pacific islands like Nauru, Samoa and those under Japan's South Pacific Mandate' which 'were in the peculiar legal position of being "administered under the laws of the Mandatory as integral portions of its territory"'.[33] The League's Mandate System promised former imperial powers the capacity to contain the risks posed by non-white misgovernance.

DOUBLE TAX TREATIES

For tax experts only familiar with its double tax treaties, the League's Mandate System may seem incongruous. But the two share a common purpose. Understanding the origins and operation of its Mandate System offers critical context for the League's tax work. It suggests why the OECD pointedly ignored the United Nations in favour of the League. Those treaties, like the Mandate System, paired formal equality with hierarchy.

Every student of international tax law learns that the League's experts designed its treaties for 'the sole purpose of mitigat[ing] international double taxation so that governments could benefit from international economic liberalization'.[34] That myth,[35] as tenacious as the fiction of Reconstruction's failure because of Black misgovernance, survives despite ample evidence to the contrary. Logically,

[30] *See* GETACHEW, *supra* note 24, at 42.
[31] League of Nations covenant article 22
[32] TZOUVALA, *supra* note 25, at 101.
[33] Id.
[34] Thomas Rixen, *From Double Tax Avoidance to Tax Competition: Explaining the Institutional Trajectory of International Tax Governance*, 18 REV. INT'L. POL. ECONOMY 197 (2011).
[35] Tsilly Dagan, *The Myth of Tax Treaties*, 32 N. Y. U. J. INT'L. L. P. 939 (2000).

unilateral measures could just as easily – and more justly – eliminate the threat of two countries taxing the same cross-border activities or investment.[36]

The League's treaties operate according to the same hierarchical principles as its Mandate System. In contrast to alternatives that might nurture the fiscal autonomy of poor countries, those treaties make such countries poorer. In the waning days of World War I, the United States took a very different approach. It embraced an extraordinarily generous unilateral remedy for double taxation.[37] Unlike that intervention – embraced before the League developed its treaties – double tax treaties resolve tax conflicts in favour of wealthy states.[38]

In contrast to the unilateral measures that preceded them, but like its Mandate System, the League's treaties recreated the substance of empire while maintaining the illusion of self-determination. The permanent establishment concept illustrates that dynamic.[39] A hallmark of the League's treaties, still operative today, permanent establishment applies universally but limits the tax sovereignty of states in lockstep with their dependence on foreign capital. States with a surplus of capital accrue tax sovereignty while those dependent on capital imports sacrifice it under the League's permanent establishment framework.

The League's vision of a world that replicates the logic of imperialism without its formal trappings produced its Mandate System. It also shaped its double tax treaties. As mechanisms for reproducing the constraints of an imperial relationship without empire, both the League's Mandate System and its double tax treaties delivered. In formal terms, those reciprocal double tax treaties appear the inverse of imperial control. They afford the same rights to – and impose the same obligations on – each signatory. But they entrench economic power by shifting tax sovereignty towards wealthier states. Thanks to the League's ingenious design, embraced decades later by the OECD, the richer the state, the more tax sovereignty it enjoys.

FEAR OF A BLACK PLANET

The League was no more when the OECD confronted the reality of decolonisation by reviving its double tax treaties. An extraordinary bounty of post-war growth belies any notion that economic necessity breathed new life into treaties. The impending threat of Africa's decolonisation, by contrast, offers a coherent, if less savoury, explanation for their long-delayed deployment.

36 Id.

37 Edwin Seligman, Double Taxation and International Fiscal Cooperation 135 (1928).

38 Dagan, *supra* note 35.

39 Graetz observes that, by lobbying for the inclusion of the permanent establishment concept in the League's treaties, the 'United States, a major net exporter of goods in the 1920s, thus relieved its businesses of much foreign taxation with the permanent establishment rule, while preserving the spirit of source-based taxation'. Michael J. Graetz & Michael M. O'Hear, *The 'Original Intent' of U.S. International Taxation*, 46 Duke L.J. 1021, 1089 (1997).

Precisely as the League's creators might have hoped, those treaties allowed the OECD to rise to power as an informal World Tax Organisation, displacing Keynes' 'monkey house'. The UN had demonstrated a commitment to international tax policy, embodying precisely the sort of multiracial democracy Reconstruction had taught the world to fear. The United States helped orchestrate a quiet takeover by the OECD. In turn, the OECD acquired much-needed legitimacy by embracing the handiwork of the long-dead League.

The end of formal empire in Africa transformed a dynamic that had oscillated between selflessness and selfishness. Before the League was formed, the United States unilaterally made a 'present' of revenues to a Europe desperate for capital after World War I.[40] Later, in a tentative effort to claw back some of that generosity, the United States and the League would work closely together, with the League 'urging treaty negotiations between governments' while 'sidestepping procedural formalities and collaborating with the US government as well as with US business interests'.[41]

As African colonies neared independence, that ambivalence dissipated. Both the generosity the US had once shown Europe and any scepticism of the League's vision of alien, non-consensual rule yielded to fear. To constrain the tax sovereignty of new African states desperate to fund the schools and hospitals denied them under colonial rule, the United States, Canada, and Europe embraced the League's treaties. In 1963, just three years after the OECD's creation, it issued its first model treaty. All but moribund in the intervening three decades since the League created them, those treaties quickly proliferated, becoming the backbone of an international tax system that persists today.

SEPARATE BUT EQUAL

From a US perspective, Africa's decolonisation posed a familiar threat. It may be true that today global tax policymaking follows a predictable path: 'the United States takes the lead, the OECD and its members reach a compromise, and the rest of the world follows the OECD'.[42] But, before that could be true, the OECD would itself blossom thanks to a widely shared anxiety over Black governance fanned by lies about Reconstruction.

Over the past decade, concern over disenfranchisement of states has prompted a push to shift global tax policymaking back to the United Nations.[43] To many, such a

40 SELIGMAN, *supra note* 37, at 135.

41 TEO, *supra* note 2, at 82.

42 Jinyan Li, *Global Profit Split: An Evolutionary Approach to International Income Allocation*, 50 CAN. TAX J. 823, 867 (2002), discussing transfer pricing.

43 PHILLIP INMAN, *Rich Countries Accused of Foiling Effort to Give Poorer Nations a Voice on Tax*, The Guardian, July 13, 2015, www.theguardian.com/global-development/2015/jul/14/financing-for-development-conference-addis-ababa-rich-countries-accused-poorer-nations-voice-tax, quoting advocates urging that 'the UN should create an international body to oversee global tax matters'.

dramatic transformation may seem excessive. The history of Reconstruction suggests that it may not be nearly enough.

The same fears that stripped the UN of its central role in global tax policy once doomed Reconstruction. Reconstruction represented a concerted effort to remake the legal architecture of the Southern states that once comprised the Confederacy. Having seceded from the United States in order to preserve the right to enslave Blacks people the Confederacy suffered a devastating military loss at the hands of the Northern army. Even in defeat, those Confederate states fiercely resisted granting equal status to millions of formerly enslaved people.

Over time, former Confederate states embraced an approach that provided Black Americans with hollow rights promising equal – but delivering discriminatory – treatment. Forty years after the end of the Civil War, the US Supreme Court delivered one of its most infamous rulings, rejecting a direct challenge to such arrangements. In *Plessy v. Ferguson*, the Court blessed the notion of 'separate but equal' – a term used by the dissent – embedding discrimination into the law of the entire United States.[44] The Louisiana law at issue required Black and white passengers to travel in separate train cars. With the Supreme Court's blessing, segregation kept Americans apart in nearly every aspect of their lives, basking on separate beaches and mourning in separate graveyards.

RECONSTRUCTION

The US path to *Plessy* serves as a stark warning for the current unsettled state of global tax policymaking. With the end of the Civil War, the matter of slavery had been resolved but little else seemed certain. A humiliated Confederacy found its enslaved population free. It would be an understatement to say that Southern whites displayed ambivalence about treating them as equals. In practice, the North's success and the Emancipation it delivered did little to dispel the anti-Black racism that fostered – and was fuelled by – centuries of dehumanising trafficking.

The process of remaking American society to ensure that Black freedom would be more than an empty promise demanded profound changes in US law. The US Constitution itself would be repeatedly altered to deliver fundamental rights to the millions of men, women, and children the legal system had once treated as property.[45] The Fourteenth Amendment prohibited disparate treatment because of a person's race. The Fifteenth 'prohibit[ed] the federal and state governments from depriving any citizen of the vote on racial grounds'.[46]

[44] 163 U.S. 537, 552 (1896) (Harlan, J., dissenting) (using the phrase 'separate but equal').

[45] The Supreme Court ruled that Black Americans were property and could not be citizens. Dred Scott v. Sandford, 60 U.S. 393 (1857).

[46] FONER, *supra* note 3, at 446, critics noted that 'the Amendment did not forbid literacy, property, and educational tests that, while nonracial, might effectively exclude the majority of blacks from the polls'.

The most important lesson of Reconstruction may be that none of those changes proved to be enough. In part, that was because of the laws of the former Confederate states themselves. Those laws would define the contours of the relationship between former slaveholders and formerly enslaved persons.

In a series of state constitutional conventions from 1867–1869, the South deliberated over Black civil and political rights.[47] They weighed the reality of integration in education.[48] They even grappled with the challenges of tax reform.[49] Southern states considered 'the need to provide freedman with land and encourage the breakup of the plantation system'.[50]

These efforts faced fierce opposition. But a surprising coalition assembled in support of change. Alongside Black Freedmen, white Republicans – a combination of Southern-born 'scalawags' and Northern transplants known as 'carpetbaggers' – helped ensure that those revisionist state constitutions succeeded throughout the South, with the exception of Alabama and Mississippi.[51]

Those federal and state reforms aimed to ensure that the end of slavery meant real freedom. But they would not be enough. A swift backlash to Reconstruction came in a variety of forms. The most searing response would be unchecked violence designed to intimidate Black Southerners and their white allies. An extraordinary 'wave of counterrevolutionary terror . . . swept over large parts of the South between 1868 and 1871'.[52] That violence had no 'counterpart either in the American experience or in that of the other Western Hemisphere societies that abolished slavery in the 19th century'.[53]

Such violence severely compromised the capacity of Black Americans to exercise their newfound rights. The Fifteenth Amendment was ratified in 1970, but countless murders of officials and ordinary citizens made exercising the rights it guaranteed exceedingly dangerous. The eventual response to that wave of terror would be dramatic and – all too briefly – effective.

The North interceded, relying on a combination of law enforcement and military intervention to ensure that Black Americans could vote. The 'federal legal offensive of 1871'[54] targeted terror organisations like the Ku Klux Klan. It produced 'nearly 700 indictments'[55] against Klansmen in Mississippi alone.

47 Id., at 320.
48 Id., at 321.
49 Id., at 327.
50 Id., at 329.
51 Id., at 332.
52 Id., 'the Klan was a military force serving the interests of the Democratic party, the planter class, and all those who desired the restoration of white supremacy . . . it sought to affect power relations, both public and private . . . and restore racial subordination in every aspect of Southern life'.
53 Id.
54 Id., at 458.
55 Id., at 457.

But even that would not be enough to protect the rights of Freedmen. Federal and state reforms paired with vigorous law enforcement efforts still left them and their white supporters vulnerable to violence. Keeping the peace and ensuring the integrity of the voting process would ultimately require far more.

The Federal effort to counter white terror in the former Confederacy ultimately required military intervention. The Northern military incursion into the South 'culminat[ed] in the use of troops to root out the South Carolina Klan'.[56] Those interventions by the federal government demonstrated a 'willingness to bring its legal and coercive authority to bear'.[57] By 1872 the combination of criminal prosecutions and troops 'had broken the Klan's back and produced a dramatic decline in violence throughout the South'.[58]

But by 1876 the nation's appetite for such extraordinary measures waned. Without them, the elaborate protections offered by Federal and state law would prove meaningless. Northern indifference would eviscerate the Fourteenth and Fifteenth Amendments and ultimately breathe life into *Plessy*.

Even as 'electoral fraud became the order of the day in counties with black majorities'[59] it became clear 'that the northern public would no longer support federal intervention in southern affairs'.[60] Renewed violence and 'the President's refusal to send federal troops ... thoroughly demoralized'[61] those fighting for Reconstruction. The results would be felt slowly in parts of the south, with Black Americans continuing to vote freely in some states. By contrast, 'in the Deep South, where electoral fraud was widespread and the threat of violence hung most heavily over the black community ... long before their outright disenfranchisement around the turn of the century, blacks saw their political rights progressively eroded'.[62]

THE LESSONS OF RECONSTRUCTION

When history repeats itself, as it has with the rise of the OECD in response to fears of Black misgovernance, the hard-won lessons of the past can offer critical guidance. This chapter draws four insights from Reconstruction for those struggling to secure meaningful participation for non-OECD member states in global tax governance:

(1) Truth matters;
(2) Rights alone are not enough;
(3) Not all rights are created equal; and
(4) Vigilance is essential.

56 Id., at 458.
57 Id., at 458–459.
58 Id.
59 Id., at 490.
60 Id., at 567.
61 Id., at 569.
62 Id., at 590.

Truth Matters

By 1877, violence and fraud had brought Reconstruction to an end. Today, historians agree that the collapse of Reconstruction never served as an indictment of Black governance. Despite the efforts of historians like W. E. B. Du Bois, it came to be seen as precisely that.

Formerly enslaved persons, offered the opportunity to take control of their futures, it would long be thought, demonstrated that they could not be trusted to rule. Well into the mid-twentieth century, scholars openly embraced racist notions of Black incompetence to explain the failure of Reconstruction.[63] They lamented that 'childlike blacks … unprepared for freedom and incapable of properly exercising the political rights' Reconstruction 'thrust upon them'[64] governed with predictably disastrous consequences. Not until the Civil Rights movement of the 1960s would that dominant narrative – falsely ascribing the failure of Reconstruction to the greed of carpetbaggers, the naïveté of scalawags and incompetence of freed Black people – be successfully challenged.

Du Bois published Black Reconstruction in 1935, offering an accurate telling of its rise and fall. But the conventional account – articulated by the Dunning school – steadfastly ignored Du Bois. Historians would later rely on copious evidence that had long gone unexamined to demonstrate that Southern resistance and Northern indifference, not Black incapacity, doomed Reconstruction. Only with the 1988 publication of the definitive history of Reconstruction would the last embers of the Dunning School be snuffed out.[65]

The myth of Reconstruction's failure becomes even more troubling when considered against its initial successes in the years following the North's use of military force to protect Black rights. Black Americans acquired political power in a variety of arenas. States that had made them the legal equivalent of livestock not long before sent Black Senators and Representatives to Washington. In 1870, the South sent Mississippi's Hiram Revels to the Senate. In 1872, Louisiana elected its first Black governor.

The conventional account of global tax policymaking's path pointedly omits any mention of the initial successes of inclusive tax policymaking.[66] The substantive discussions that took place in the United Nations in the years before the OECD took

63 Foner describes a Dunning School book published in 1947. Id., at xviii (quoting E. Merton Coulter, The South During Reconstruction, 1865–1877 (1947)), 'The fact that blacks took part in government wrote E. Merton Coulter in the last full-scale history of Reconstruction written entirely within the Dunning tradition, was a "diabolical" development, "to be remembered, shuddered at, and execrated".'

64 Id., at xviii.

65 Id.

66 Teo, *supra* note 2, at 6 ('Many prominent works that outline international tax history overlook the [UN Fiscal] Commission altogether, citing the OECD's Fiscal Committee as the effective successor to the League's Fiscal Committee.').

control dispel the widespread belief that it merely stepped into the League's empty shoes.[67] Developing states demonstrated both an interest in and a capacity for high-level international tax work.

Ignoring that inconvenient fact continues to legitimise the disenfranchisement that followed. The myth that the OECD and the League's treaties filled a gap rather than displacing a far more democratic form of global tax governance made the lack of representation within the OECD more palatable. Knowing that the OECD silenced an important conversation about global tax justice that had hardly begun amplifies concerns about its capacity to empathise with the needs and concerns of non-members.

Rights Alone Are Not Enough

More than six decades after its creation, the OECD has still never had a Black member. In the tax context, it now insists that membership has become irrelevant. The OECD asserts that – thanks to its Inclusive Framework – all states participate in global tax policymaking 'on an equal footing'.[68]

Research indicates that – despite the OECD's assurances – poor, non-member states have no meaningful opportunity to participate in that policymaking process.[69] To students of Reconstruction, the distance between the OECD's statements and the experience of non-member states comes as no surprise. First the Fourteenth and then the Fifteenth Amendments promised to protect the rights of Black Americans. State reforms attempted to deliver equality in an array of areas.

None of those protections would prevent the emergence of the separate but equal doctrine under *Plessy v. Ferguson*. Thanks to extraordinary legal and

[67] Id., at 2 (noting that the fact that 'the reports and resolutions of the period would never be broached again in successive international taxation efforts' does not erase the promise of its initial efforts).

[68] The OECD uses the phrase to describe participation in its anti-tax avoidance initiative launched in 2013. See *Closing Tax Gaps: OECD Launches Action Plan on Base Erosion and Profit Shifting*, OECD, 19 July 2013, www.oecd.org/tax/closing-tax-gaps-oecd-launches-action-plan-on-base-erosion-and-profit-shifting.htm, applying the phrase to 'all OECD members and G20 countries on an equal footing'. Under pressure from states excluded from that group, the OECD expanded the promise of equal footing to members of what it termed the inclusive framework. See *Developing Countries and the OECD/G20 Inclusive Framework on BEPS: OECD Report for the G20 Finance Ministers and Central Bank Governors*, OCED, Oct. 2021, www.oecd.org/tax/beps/developingcountries-and-the-oecd-g20-inclusive-framework-on-beps.htm, '[t]he Inclusive Framework now includes 140 members, who, on an equal footing, monitor the implementation and contribute to the development of measures to combat Base Erosion and Profit Shifting (BEPS)'.

[69] Rasmus Christensen et al., *At the Table, Off the Menu? Assessing the Participation of Lower-Income Countries in Global Tax Negotiations* (ICTD Working Paper, Paper No. 115, 2020), www.ictd.ac/publication/at-table-off-menu-assessing-participation-lower-income-countries-global-tax-negotiations, concluding that the inclusive framework had only a limited impact.

military interventions Black Americans enjoyed a brief period during which they possessed real freedom to engage in civic life. Intimidation and electoral fraud brought that to an end, forcing them to accept a second-class status masked by a pretence of equality.

Whatever the reality of the OECD's Inclusive Framework, the history of Reconstruction leaves no doubt that rights alone – without robust enforcement – produce unsatisfying results. *Brown v. Board of Education*[70] would ultimately find that separate schools violated the Fourteenth Amendment. Before that landmark decision, Black families and businesses paid taxes that funded schools for whites.[71] Without a meaningful Black voice in structuring tax rules, separate Black schools remained systematically underfunded. Often, they simply closed.[72] When able to operate at all, they lacked the resources white schools enjoyed. Before *Brown*, Black Americans challenging underfunded schools received favourable verdicts from courts again and again, to no effect.[73]

Under decades of OECD leadership, African states have consistently lacked the resources necessary to provide their people with the education and healthcare available to their counterparts within the OECD.[74] Against that backdrop, the Inclusive Framework's absence of any mechanism to ensure that the rights it grants to non-members lend them a voice in global tax policymaking sounds alarm bells. For such reasons, the Inclusive Framework – created in response to criticism of the OECD's exclusive membership – has done little to mollify sceptics.

Because of structural obstacles, participation by non-member states in the Inclusive Framework remains limited.[75] Merely inviting states to participate, without ensuring the conditions exist to allow them to do so freely and fully falls far short of true inclusion. It certainly seems no more likely than the Fourteenth or Fifteenth Amendments to deliver justice to those long denied a voice.

70 347 U.S. 483 (1954).

71 Camille Walsh, Racial Taxation: Schools, Segregation, and Taxpayer Citizenship, 1869–1973 52 (2018), describing the challenge of 'a Kentucky state statute that designated all corporate property taxes for the benefit of white schools only'. Id.

72 Walsh cites a number of cases in which Black schools were closed due to a lack of funding while white schools remained open. See, e.g., id., at 37, describing a challenge arguing that 'a tax benefiting the high school for white girls while the black high school had been closed was an unconstitutional deprivation of their property rights, forcing them to pay in support of a white school they were excluded from utilizing'.

73 Id., at 51 ('lawsuits that succeeded ... challenged the constitutionality of separate taxation or other methods of funding and resource inequality ... [h]owever, many of these seeming victories did very little').

74 Attiya Waris, Financing Africa 27 (2019).

75 Christensen et al., *supra* note 69, 'We find that the explosion in formal membership has not in itself led to the step-change in developing country influence that the raw numbers imply. This is because of a combination of structural obstacles that are not unique to the IF, and some challenging aspects of the OECD's way of working.'

Not All Rights Are Created Equal

Black Codes 'favored by the Southern legislatures'[76] in the years immediately following the Civil War offer an even sterner warning over the perils of false inclusivity. They represented an 'indisputable attempt on the part of the Southern States to make Negroes slaves in everything but name'.[77] Much like the League's C Mandates did for newly liberated colonies, they only offered the appearance of equality.

Black Codes gave Black people both 'the right to hold property' and 'to sue and be sued'.[78] They ensured that their 'family relations for the first time were legally recognized'.[79] But, in the words of Du Bois, the 'the Black Codes were deliberately designed to take advantage of every misfortune of the Negro'.[80]

Du Bois details the extraordinary lengths some states went to in order to recreate the conditions of slavery, Emancipation notwithstanding. 'Mississippi simply re-enacted her slave code' so that the all the laws that once governed enslaved persons applied to Freedmen.[81] A local law in Louisiana provided that any Freedman on the streets after 10pm without written permission from his employer could be compelled to work for five days.[82] North Carolina permitted Black people to testify in court only where the 'rights of persons or property of persons of color shall be put in issue' but made their testimony inadmissible in all other cases.[83]

Those Black Codes may be a more apt comparison for the Inclusive Framework than the Fourteenth and Fifteenth Amendments. The former represented an effort to retain power while the latter constituted a sincere but ineffectual attempt to lend a voice to Black Americans. History will ultimately reveal what the Inclusive Framework was meant to accomplish.

Vigilance Is Essential

For the first half-century of the OECD's dominance of global tax policy, it did not even dignify non-members with the pretence of rights offered by the Black Codes. The results of that complete lack of representation could at times prove awkward for the OECD.[84] The last decade has – in the form of the Inclusive Framework –

[76] W. E. B. Du Bois, Black Reconstruction in America 167 (1935).
[77] Id.
[78] Id.
[79] Id.
[80] Id.
[81] Id., at 177.
[82] Id.
[83] Id., at 176–177.
[84] In 2000, the OECD once produced a blacklist of supposed tax havens that included Liberia but excluded Switzerland. The resulting backlash proved quite damaging to the OECD. See

delivered either a twenty-first century Black Code or an ineffectual attempt at inclusion.

An invitation to engage in the global tax policymaking process made under circumstances certain to prevent meaningful participation, the Inclusive Framework may represent a good faith effort. If so, it remains woefully inadequate. That should come as no great surprise. Even the best of intentions means little without adequate oversight.

Early in Reconstruction, former Confederate states introduced 'modest poll taxes, with the revenue earmarked for the new school systems'.[85] Gradually, those poll taxes would become tools to disenfranchise Black and poor white voters. But when they were introduced 'Blacks generally supported these imposts, convinced that public education financed entirely by property taxes would quickly lose white support.'[86]

Thanks to a lack of vigilance, poll taxes evolved from a tool of inclusiveness into a potent mechanism of disenfranchisement. Undermining the protections offered by the Fifteenth Amendment, for decades poll taxes prevented Black Americans from voting. Ironically, once embraced as a symbol of citizenship, those taxes – alongside 'literacy tests, and property qualifications' – would 'severely restrict black voting'.[87]

During the Civil Rights era, the Federal military would again be deployed to protect Black Americans as they accepted the invitation offered by *Brown*. Along with measures like the 1965 Voting Rights Act, that intervention constituted a Second Reconstruction. Described as 'an act to enforce the Fifteenth Amendment', the Voting Rights Act finally did away with 'the discriminatory voting practices adopted in many southern states after the Civil War'.[88] A full century after the war that ended slavery, Black Americans finally had a meaningful opportunity to participate in shaping their country.

The Voting Rights Act gave substance to the Fifteenth Amendment by eliminating structural barriers to participation. Even if the Inclusive Framework deserves to be compared to the Fifteenth Amendment rather than the Black Codes, it will not be enough on its own to guarantee a meaningful voice for non-members. If the OECD were to take inclusion seriously, far more than a right with no mechanism to ensure beneficiaries have a meaningful opportunity to exercise it would be required.

Steven A. Dean & Attiya Warris, *Ten Truths about Tax Havens: Inclusion and the 'Liberia' Problem*, 70 EMORY L.J. 1659 (2021).

85 FONER, *supra* note 3, at 328.

86 Id. Foner notes that 'black delegates had been misled into believing that a poll tax to support education could not be employed to limit black voting'. Id., at 319.

87 Id., at 590.

88 *Voting Rights Act (1965)*, NATIONAL ARCHIVES, www.archives.gov/milestone-documents/voting-rights-act#, discussing how 'African Americans in the South faced tremendous obstacles to voting, including poll taxes, literacy tests, and other bureaucratic restrictions to deny them the right to vote. They also risked harassment, intimidation, economic reprisals, and physical violence when they tried to register or vote.'

Of course, ensuring that non-OECD members no longer face structural obstacles to participating in the Inclusive Framework would not be enough if it represents a modern-day Black Code, offering a thinly disguised form of bondage.

CONCLUSION

Even if the OECD were to be stripped of its governance role, replaced by a reinvigorated United Nations, vigilance would be essential. Federal and state constitutional reforms failed to provide a meaningful voice to disenfranchised Americans. Poll taxes began as tools of inclusion but became something quite different. That history poses urgent questions for global tax governance.

What does the OECD's announcement that '[o]n 11 July 2023, 138 members of the OECD/G20 Inclusive Framework on BEPS – representing over 90% of global GDP – agreed on an Outcome Statement recognising the significant progress made and allowing countries and jurisdictions to move forward with historic, major reform of the international tax system'[89] mean? It might say little about what those states would say in a truly free and fair decision-making process overseen by a disinterested third party. In a world as sharply divided as today's, that striking uniformity of opinion on such a contentious issue should itself be viewed as a warning.

In recent years, a new kind of tax has emerged. Known as a digital services tax, jurisdictions ranging from France to Kenya have imposed it on global digital giants like Meta. The United States perceived these new taxes as anti-American and sought to prevent them from taking root. The OECD's 2023 announcement purports to represent the near-universal rejection of such taxes.[90] It seemed that, once again, thanks to the intervention of the OECD, the US position had become the world's, 'thus reliev[ing] its businesses of much foreign taxation . . . while preserving the spirit of source-based taxation'.[91]

Its summary rejection of digital services taxes suggests that the Inclusive Framework lies uncomfortably close to the Black Code end of the legitimacy spectrum. Whether the ongoing negotiations at the United Nations might adequately guard against the risks suggested by the history of Reconstruction – or be as ineffective as the Reconstruction-era Constitutional Amendments proved to be – remains to be seen. From the impotence of those Constitutional reforms to the hidden threat posed by poll taxes, the evidence of those risks must not be ignored.

89 *Action 1: Tax Challenges Arising from Digitalization*, OECD, www.oecd.org/tax/beps/beps-actions/action1/.

90 The reform it describes includes a ban on digital services taxes.

91 See *supra* note 39.

7

Embracing the African Union and the African Tax Administration Forum in Tax Governance

Afton Titus

INTRODUCTION

The international tax governance system has been failing developing countries for decades. Some of this is by design, as only a handful of rich countries have set the agenda for international tax affairs and co-operation,[1] and some of it is by circumstance, like the 2008 financial crisis and then the COVID-19 pandemic where immense pressure was (and is) placed on the economies and fiscal systems of governments to recover and function optimally.[2]

International tax governance involves the relations between countries as they determine the taxation of cross-border transactions.[3] To date, this area has been monopolised by the Organisation for Economic Co-operation and Development (OECD), largely to the exclusion of developing countries.[4] Although the OECD has recently attempted to create more inclusive spaces within its governance structure, through the creation of the Inclusive Forum, Country-by-Country reporting, and the multilateral instrument (MLI),[5] these measures have mostly failed to create meaningful inclusion as developing countries were consistently left out of the

This work is based on the research supported partly by the National Research Foundation (NRF) of South Africa (Grant Number: 149057). The author expresses her appreciation to the NRF and also to Professor Eduardo Baistrocchi for his useful comments on an earlier draft of this chapter.

1 See SUNITA JOGARAJAN, DOUBLE TAXATION AND THE LEAGUE OF NATIONS 112 (2018).

2 See Irma J. Mosquera Valderrama, *Legitimacy and the Making of International Tax Law: The Challenges of Multilateralism*, 7 WORLD TAX J. 343 (2015).

3 See Christiana Panayi, *The Globalisation of Tax Good Governance* 2 (Sing. Mgmt. Univ. Sch. of Acct. Paper Series, Vol. 6, No. 1, Paper No: 2018-S-74, 2018).

4 See *Global Tax Governance: What It Is and Why It Matters*, *in* GLOBAL TAX GOVERNANCE: WHAT IS WRONG WITH IT AND HOW TO FIX IT 8 (Peter Dietsch & Thomas Rixen eds., ECPR Press, 2016).

5 See Yariv Brauner, *Serenity Now! The (Not So) Inclusive Framework and the Multilateral Instrument*, 25 FLA. TAX REV. 489 (2022).

agenda-setting stage.[6] In fact, the legitimacy of the OECD has long been questioned.[7] For instance, Christians points to the closed membership of the OECD which includes a small group of developed countries who may participate in the agenda-setting process.[8] Moreover, Mosquera Valderrama writes that the OECD lacks legitimacy in that the solutions it proposes for international tax issues are not tailored for developing countries and are, in fact, suited for the OECD countries who designed them.[9] Additionally, Fung comments that the OECD has been criticised for unelected bureaucrats making far-reaching global tax policy decisions behind closed doors.[10]

The international tax landscape is changing rapidly as governments grapple with the difficulties of taxing the profits of multinational companies and people. Thus, it has become increasingly important for developing countries, especially, to participate in the discussions and negotiations that bring about global measures for the implementation of global tax policies. This is difficult to do if developing countries are not invited to participate in these discussions.

In order to address this, Tarcísio D. Magalhães argues that it is integral to create regional governance structures that can act as a counterbalance to the OECD's concentration of power and expertise.[11] This call is particularly relevant for African countries given that most of the least-developed countries are in Africa.[12] Regionalism has been prevalent in Africa for a long time,[13] and currently Africa has a number of geographically-linked regional economic communities (RECs)

6 See id.; see also Rasmus C. Christensen et al., *At the Table, Off the Menu? Assessing the Participation of Lower-Income Countries in Global Tax Negotiations* 3 (ICTD Working Paper No. 115, 2020); see also Linda Brosens & Jasper Bossuyt, *Legitimacy in International Tax Law-Making: Can the OECD Remain the Guardian of Open Tax Norms?*, 12 World Tax J. 313 (2020); Allison Christians & Laurens van Apeldoorn, *The OECD Inclusive Framework*, 72 Bull. Int'l Tax'n 226 (2018).

7 See Jan Wouters & Katrien Meuwissen, *Global Tax Governance: Work in Progress?* 1, 29 (Working Paper No. 59, 2011); see also Irma J. Mosquera Valderrama, *Output Legitimacy Deficits and the Inclusive Framework of the OECD/G20 Base Erosion and Profit Shifting Initiative*, 72 Bull. Int'l Tax'n 160 (2018); Sissie Fung, *The Questionable Legitimacy of the OECD/G20 BEPS Project*, 10 Erasmus L. Rev. 76 (2017); Mosquera Valderrama, *supra* note 2; Tarcísio D. Magalhães, *What Is Really Wrong with Global Tax Governance and How to Properly Fix It*, 10 World Tax J. 4, 499 (2018); Allison Christians, *Taxation in a Time of Crisis: Policy Leadership from the OECD to the G20*, 5 Nw. J. L. & Soc. Pol'y 1, 23 (2010); Stefanie Geringer, *European Union/OECD/International: Dissemination of Tax Good Governance Standards by the European Union and the OECD: A Comparative Analysis of Changes in Treatment and Tone*, 77 Bull. Int'l Tax'n 148 (2023); Brosens & Bossuyt, *supra* note 6.

8 Christians, *supra* note 7, at 16.

9 Mosquera Valderrama, *supra* note 7, at 169.

10 Fung, *supra* note 7, at 81.

11 Magalhães, *supra* note 7.

12 *UN List of Least Developed Countries*, United Nations Conference on Trade and Development (UNCTAD), https://unctad.org/topic/least-developed-countries/list.

13 See Vusi Gumede, *The African Continental Free Trade Area Agreement and the Future of Regional Economic Communities*, 39 J. Contemp. Afr. Stud. 470, 472 (2021).

recognised by the African Union,[14] as well as other international governance organisations that are not geographically linked, such as BRICS (Brazil, Russia, India, China, and South Africa).[15]

The shifting sands of international tax governance come at an opportune time, as many Africans look forward to realising the vast potential of the recently signed African Continental Free Trade Area Agreement (AfCFTA).[16] This multilateral instrument calls for the creation of a continental-wide free-trade area and eventually a common market. The AfCFTA is the flagship project of the African Union (AU), a continental organisation to which all African countries belong, as part of the AU's strategic framework to create inclusive and sustainable development to accelerate Africa's economic growth.[17] Some of the AU's other flagship projects include an integrated high-speed train network that would connect all of Africa's capital cities and commercial centres; strategies to end all conflicts in Africa; and the establishment of African Financial Institutions, like the African Monetary Fund, Pan African Stock Exchange and African Central Bank, to manage the financial sector across Africa.[18]

As strides are being made to bring about deeper economic integration and the creation of a continental-wide common market,[19] I argue that African countries should harness the enthusiasm for economic integration to consider the possibility of creating an African tax governance structure within the AU. Such a structure could use RECs as building blocks together with the African Tax Administration Forum (ATAF). ATAF is an organisation that provides technical assistance to African countries to improve their tax systems.[20] While ATAF was initially created to assist with tax administration, the organisation has since moved into the tax policy

[14] The following are RECs recognised by the African Union: the Arab Maghreb Union (UMA); the Common Market for Eastern and Southern Africa (COMESA); the Community of Sahel-Saharan States (CEN-SAD); the East African Community (EAC); the Economic Community of Central African States (ECCAS); the Economic Community of West African States (ECOWAS); the Intergovernmental Authority on Development (IGAD); and the Southern African Development Community (SADC). See *Agreement Establishing the African Continental Free Trade Area*, African Union, https://au.int/sites/default/files/treaties/36437-treaty-consolidated_text_on_cfta_-_en.pdf.

[15] See Moorosi Leshoele, *AfCFTA and Regional Integration in Africa: Is African Union Government a Dream or Reality?*, 38 J. Contemp. Afr. Stud. 1, 4 (2020).

[16] *Agreement Establishing the African Continental Free Trade Area*, African Union (Mar. 21, 2018), https://au.int/en/treaties/agreement-establishing-african-continental-free-trade-area.

[17] *Flagship Projects of Agenda 2063*, African Union, https://au.int/en/agenda2063/flagship-projects; see Gerhard Erasmus, Legal Aspects of the Relationship between the AfCFTA and the African Union (Tralac, July 1, 2022), www.tralac.org/blog/article/15670-legal-aspects-of-the-relationship-between-the-afcfta-and-the-african-union.html.

[18] *Flagship Projects of Agenda*, *supra* note 17.

[19] See Kingsley Ighobor, One Year of Free Trading in Africa Calls for Celebration Despite Teething Problems (Africa Renewal, Jan. 5, 2022), www.un.org/africarenewal/magazine/january-2022/one-year-free-trading-africa-calls-celebration-despite-teething-problems.

[20] *Overview*, African Tax Administration Forum, www.ataftax.org/overview.

arena as it serves to communicate the position of African countries on international tax issues.[21] Although the AU is not without its (serious) flaws,[22] it represents an established institutional framework mandated to work towards deeper political and economic integration.[23] Building on the existing structure, it may then be possible for African countries to move beyond colonially imposed borders to regional power hubs demarcated by parameters African countries have defined themselves. This is because 'only collectively can governments recapture what they have lost individually'.[24]

First, the proposed structure would allow African governments to make tax policies that align with their own national objectives, allowing such governments to better serve the needs of their people. ATAF has long called for an international tax policy forum to be formed within Africa.[25] This idea is picking up momentum as several references were made the Fourth High-Level Tax Policy Dialogue organised by ATAF and the AU in 2020 to a 'Continental Platform for Tax Policy' to be created at the AU level with ATAF's able assistance.[26] It would seem that the beginnings of such a platform may be in the works following the announcement of the Memorandum of Understanding signed between ATAF and the AU Commission, in which their association with each other was formalised in 2023.[27] The Memorandum is a good step because the AU and ATAF have already worked closely together as they addressed the OECD's two-pillar proposal.[28] The structure proposed in this chapter speaks directly to these calls and developments.

Secondly, the structure would create the opportunity for the design and implementation of comprehensive tax, trade, development, and integration policies to work together to improve the lives of people within the RECs. In this way,

21 Id.

22 See Rita K. Edozie & Keith Grottschalk, The African Union's Africa: New Pan-African Initiatives in Global Governance 191 (2014); These include, for instance, the AU's reliance on representation by Members State representatives who have other pressing commitments in their home country limiting their time; the AU's overreliance on financial support from its Western donors; and the AU's inability to enforce its own rules.

23 Babatunde Fagbayibo, *Looking Back, Thinking Forward: Understanding the Feasibility of Normative Supranationalism in the African Union*, 20 J. Int'l Aff. 411, 421 (2013).

24 Thomas Rixen, *Tax Competition and Inequality: The Case for Global Tax Governance*, 17 Global Governance: A Review of Multilateralism and International Institutions 447, 462 (2011).

25 See ATAF, *The Place of Africa in the Shift towards Global Tax Governance* 32 (2019).

26 ATAF, 4th High-Level Tax Policy Dialogue 2020 (ATAF, Aug. 26 and 27, 2020), www.ataftax.org/4th-high-level-tax-policy-dialogue-a-collaboration-between-the-african-tax-administration-forum-and-the-african-union-commission#:~:text=The%20High%2DLevel%20Tax%20Policy,Tax%20Policymakers%20and%20Tax%20Administrators%E2%80%9D.

27 See ATAF, ATAF and AUC Strengthen the African Voice in Global Tax Discussion (ATAF, May 31, 2023), www.ataftax.org/ataf-and-auc-strengthen-the-african-voice-in-global-tax-discussion.

28 See Dries Lesage et al., Regional Tax Governance in Handbook of Regional Cooperation and Integration 231 (Phillippe de Lombaerde ed., Edward Elgar Publishing 2024).

integration could occur more naturally and inclusively, as people within a region would be able to move and trade freely across national borders.[29] I argue that this proposed structure would tie in directly with the AU's aim to create a more integrated African continent through its flagship projects, like the AfCFTA and the removal of travel restrictions to enable Africans to move freely across the continent.[30]

Thirdly, the structure would create the opportunity for people within a region to hold their elected officials accountable for acting in the best interest of the people when engaging with other RECs at the AU in respect of tax policies that may benefit or otherwise affect them. I envisage that the proposed structure would allow some degree of transparency into the regionally beneficial tax policies discussed at the AU level along with insight into which RECs have supported these policies and which not. Rosenbloom et al. comment that such collaborative efforts may make it easier for policymakers to withstand lobbying against such policies if it would mean that it would become public that they did not implement the regionally beneficial policies.[31]

This chapter expands on these arguments. The next section describes the current international tax governance context and sketches the problems and proposed solutions to the governance issues of today. I then propose how African countries might create their own international tax governance structure within the AU. Finally, the chapter concludes with a call for African countries to act decisively and relatively quickly, using available circumstances to build a more promising future in international tax governance for themselves and for their people.

THE NEED FOR CHANGE

The international tax governance system is broken.[32] The concentration of decision-making power in an international organisation like the OECD, which struggles to move past its elitist processes,[33] has resulted in an international governance system that fails to consider, or even hear, the voices of developing countries.[34] This has created and perpetuates inequalities within the governance system itself.[35] Although it is widely accepted that the economic needs of developing countries are different from those of developed countries, and thus a governance structure should bring

[29] See Leshoele, *supra* note 15, at 6.

[30] *Flagship Projects of Agenda*, *supra* note 17.

[31] H. David Rosenbloom et al., *The Unruly World of Tax: A Proposal for an International Tax Cooperation Forum*, 15 FLA TAX REV. 2, 57, 85 (2023).

[32] *See* Dietsch & Rixen, *supra* note 4.

[33] See id., at 8.

[34] See Magalhães, *supra* note 7, at 499.

[35] See id., at 522; also see Rixen, *supra* note 24, at 448.

about more tailor-made fiscal responses to suit their context,[36] the OECD has consistently left developing countries out of the agenda-setting process in determining and addressing international tax issues.[37]

While this has been the status quo for decades, a watershed moment seems to have been reached with the OECD's latest Two Pillar proposal.[38] Pillar One proposes a watered-down formulary-apportionment model, which ostensibly gives market states a greater share of the profits of giant multinational companies. Pillar Two proposes the adoption of a global minimum corporate income tax rate. The blatant unfairness of the initial proposals as they applied to developing countries triggered the shift against the OECD.[39] The unfairness was both procedural and substantive. From a procedural perspective, Rita de la Feria comments that a small group of developed countries had designed the rules to benefit themselves.[40] From a substantive perspective, the rules have the effect of limiting tax competition in a way that favours already rich countries, such as the OECD group of countries.[41] Moreover, I argued elsewhere that the proposals would disproportionately affect developing countries as they would force them to eliminate their tax incentive policies, however well-designed and suited they are for such developing countries.[42]

Not only did this awaken an onslaught of criticism internationally[43] but it seems to have created a juggernaut movement across African developing countries to move away from the OECD and towards a new forum for international tax relations within

[36] See Richard Collier & Nadine Riedel, *The OECD/G20 BEPS Initiative and Developing Countries*, 12 BULL. INT'L TX'N 3, 716 (2018).

[37] *See* Christensen et al., *supra* note 6. This can be seen especially in the lack of inclusivity in the OECD's Inclusive Framework in so far as the Inclusive Framework members have no say or participation in the agenda-setting process.

[38] *See* OECD, *Tax Challenges Arising from Digitalisation: Report on Pillar One Blueprint: Inclusive Framework on BEPS, OECD/G20 Base Erosion and Profit Shifting Project* (2020).

[39] See RITA DE LA FERIA, THE PERCEIVED (UN)FAIRNESS OF THE GLOBAL MINIMUM CORPORATE TAX RATE (W. Haslehner et al. eds., 2022); see also Afton Titus, *Global Minimum Corporate Tax: A Death Knell for African Country Tax Policies?*, 50 INTERTAX 414 (2022).

[40] DE LA FERIA, *supra* note 39, at para. 4.4.5.

[41] Id.

[42] Titus, *supra* note 39.

[43] See Annet W. Oguttu, *A Critique from a Developing Country Perspective of the Proposals to Tax the Digital Economy*, 12 WORLD TAX J. 799, 811 (2020); see also Ana P. Dourado, *The OECD Report on Pillar I Blueprint and Article 12B in the UN Report*, 49 INTERTAX 3 (2021); Yariv Brauner, *Editorial: Lost in Construction: What Is the Direction of the Work on the Taxation of the Digital Economy?*, 48 INTERTAX 270 (2020); Ana P. Dourado, *Editorial: The OECD Unified Approach and the New International Tax System: A Half-Way Solution*, 48 INTERTAX 3 (2020); Maarten F. de Wilde, *Guest Editorial: On the OECD's 'Unified Approach' as Frankenstein's Monster and a Dented Shape Shifter*, 48 INTERTAX 9 (2020); Ulrich Schreiber, *Remarks on the Future Prospects of the OECD/G20 Programme of Work: Profit Allocation (Pillar One) and Minimum Taxation (Pillar Two)*, 74 BULL. INT'L TAX'N 338 (2020); MICHAEL P. DEVEREUX ET AL., THE OECD GLOBAL ANTI-BASE EROSION PROPOSAL (Oxford Univ. Ctr. for Bus. Tax'n. 2020).

the United Nations.[44] Such a movement could hold many benefits for African countries.[45]

However, because the right to taxation in cross-border transactions is still tied to the concept of nations/states, the current international tax regime is still based on the tax sovereignty of countries, and this would be the case even if a new forum for international tax negotiations were established in the United Nations in the future.[46] Although this has always been problematic,[47] it has become increasingly so with globalisation's ability to de-link income from its geography.[48] Peter Dietsch and Thomas Rixen note that the current era has emphasised the need for multilateralism; specifically, today's international tax challenges are beyond the scope of domestic policies alone.[49]

While there are some innovative proposals for reforming the international tax governance system to make it more inclusive and effective, some commentators like Sunita Jogarajan are of the view that meaningful change is unlikely, arguing that this is due to the 'lock in' effect and path dependency of existing structures and norms.[50] Rasmus C. Christensen and Martin Hearson, however, take a different view.[51] They note that not only is there room for meaningful change but also such change may be initiated by traditionally marginalised groups.[52] Moreover, their work provides examples where sovereign countries have chosen to work together to address international tax issues rather than rely solely on unilateral actions.[53]

44 Tax Justice Network, *G7 Countries Cost the World $115 Billion in Lost Tax: African Finance Ministers Call for a UN Tax Convention* (May 20, 2022), https://taxjustice.net/press/g7-countries-cost-the-world-115-billion-in-lost-tax-african-finance-ministers-call-for-a-un-tax-convention; United Nations, *General Assembly Resolution on 'Promotion of Inclusive and Effective Tax Cooperation at the United Nations'* (A/RES/77/244) (Jan. 9, 2023).

45 See Afton Titus, *Pillar Two and African Countries: What Should Their Response Be? The Case for a Regional One*, 50 INTERTAX 711 (2022).

46 See Richard Eccleston, *The Dynamics of Global Economic Governance: The Financial Crisis, the OECD and the Politics of International Tax Cooperation*, 33 (2012); Dietsch & Rixen, *supra* note 4, at 3.

47 Thomas Rixen, *From Double Taxation to Tax Competition: Explaining the Institutional Trajectory of International Tax Governance*, 18 REV. INT'L TAX GOVERNANCE 2, 197–198 (2011); JOGARAJAN, *supra* note 1, at 113; Sol Picciotto, *Technocracy in the Era of Twitter: Between Intergovernmentalism and Supranational Technocratic Politics in Global Tax Governance*, 16 REG. & GOVERNANCE 3, 635 (2022).

48 *See* Rasmus C. Christensen & Martin Hearson, *The New Politics of Global Tax Governance: Taking Stock a Decade after the Financial Crisis*, 26 REV. INT'L POL. ECON. 5, 1072 (2019).

49 Rixen, *supra* note 24, at 447; Dietsch & Rixen, *supra* note 4, at 4.

50 See JOGARAJAN, *supra* note 1, at 254.

51 See Christensen & Hearson, *supra* note 48, at 1078.

52 See id.

53 Id., at 1084. The authors cite big data as an enabler of international tax co-operation. FATCA and its OECD multilateral counterpart have brought about the automatic exchange of information across borders, which allows a scale of transparency not seen since the elimination of capital controls.

There is also great enthusiasm for the idea that multilateralism holds the answer to addressing current international tax issues. For instance, Fen O. Hampson and Paul Heinbecker argue that countries are 'rediscovering' the benefits of multilateralism as they try to deal with the aftermath of the global financial crisis.[54] Itai Grinberg echoes this sentiment as he writes that we are now in the age of multilateralism.[55] Moreover, Michael Motala argues that the BEPS Project only served to spotlight the ineffectiveness of individual countries to stop the eroding practices of multinational companies.[56] According to Motala, it is necessary for countries to pool their sovereignty and create a global institution in order to address the international tax challenges of globalisation in a fair and just manner.[57]

Of course, when undertaking such global efforts, it matters not only who is included in them but also when they are included. Okanga Okanga and Lyla Latief argue that it is necessary for all countries to participate not only in the implementation of global decisions but also the agenda-setting and decision-making parts of the process as well.[58] With respect to African countries specifically, they opine that the onus is on African countries to form the alliances necessary to create inclusive global tax structures.[59] Similarly, Frances M. Horner is of the view that a new global institutional governance structure should involve the meaningful inclusion of developing countries and place issues they face at the forefront of discussions.[60]

Building on this, Magalhães argues that developing countries should create regional projects that will counterbalance the dominance of the OECD in international tax governance in order to create meaningful change.[61] Only in this way is it possible for the power relations in international tax to be more evenly distributed.[62] In the creation of such regional bodies, however, Moorosi Leshoele cautions that regional integration plans should also focus on the political and cultural aspects of deeper integration and not just trade and economic integration.[63]

That being said, deeper integration is not without its drawbacks. A country's loss of tax sovereignty, and with it the lost ability to make tax policies best suited for that country, was the crux of the heated litigation between Ireland and the European

[54] Fen O. Hampson & Paul Heinbecker, *The 'New' Multilateralism of the Twenty-First Century*, 17 GLOBAL GOVERNANCE 3, 299 (2011).

[55] Itai Grinberg, *The New International Tax Diplomacy*, 104 GEO. L.J. 1137, 1195 (2016).

[56] Michael Motala, *The New Global Politics of Sovereign International Tax: Space, Time and Why BEPS Is Not the Final Frontier*, 33 BANK & FIN. L. REV. 365 (2018).

[57] Id.

[58] Okanga Okanga & Lyla Latief, *Effective Taxation in Africa: Confronting Systemic Vulnerability through Inclusive Global Tax Governance*, 2 AFR. J. INT'L ECON. L. 100 (2021).

[59] Id., at 108.

[60] Frances M. Horner, *Do We Need an International Tax Organisation?*, 24 TAX NOTES INT'L 179 (2001).

[61] Magalhães, *supra* note 7, at 534.

[62] Id.

[63] Leshoele, *supra* note 15, at 7.

Union's Competition Commission regarding Ireland's tax treatment of certain entities within the Apple Group. Although Ireland and the Apple Group were able to successfully appeal the Competition Commission's 2016 decision that Ireland had granted the Apple Group entities an economic advantage through state aid,[64] the statement of Ireland's Minister of Finance that the Competition Commission's decision is an encroachment of Ireland's tax sovereignty remains true.[65] The Commission has taken this case on appeal.[66] This example illustrates that even when regional integration projects reach advanced stages of integration, such as with the European Union, a country's loss of tax sovereignty may have negative implications.

A further drawback of regional integration is evident in the European Union. Irma Mosquera Valderrama noted that the European Union's decision-making is often driven by strong players: namely Germany and France, sometimes to the exclusion of other smaller countries.[67] This has also played out politically, as many European Union countries refused to support a proposal to end national vetoes in respect of tax matters.[68] One of the reasons for this vote was cited as the need to ensure the participation of all countries in the European Union.[69]

Moreover, the European Union and its institutions is an example of jurisdictional overreach, as it seeks to impose its own standards on other sovereign and non-member countries. Mosquera Valderrama comments that the European Union's attempts to impose its Standard of Good Tax Governance to third party countries has only served to weaken the European Union's claims to legitimacy, both with respect to its own citizens and other countries.[70] The European Union therefore illustrates that a further drawback of regional integration is that the REC itself may pose a threat to other countries in its zeal to ensure harmonisation within the region. In the light of these drawbacks, it is important that regional integration plans strike the right balance between meaningful participation by all member states and the integration effort itself.

In sum, the current international governance institutions, mainly the OECD, are unequal and ineffective in agenda-setting, process, and outcomes. Commentators

[64] *See* Ireland v. European Commission, Case No. T-778/16, European General Court (July 15, 2020).

[65] Joe Brennan, *Getting to the Core of Europe's Case against Apple and Ireland*, The Irish Times (Feb. 3, 2017), www.irishtimes.com/business/economy/getting-to-the-core-of-europe-s-case-against-apple-and-ireland-1.2960870.

[66] See Commission v. Ireland et al., Case C-465/20 P, Opinion of Advocate General Pitruzzella (Nov. 3, 2023).

[67] Irma Mosquera Valderrama, *A New Wind Change in Direct Taxation*, 21 Ger. Law J. 90, 95 (2020).

[68] See Jorge Valero, *Member States Shield National Vetoes on Tax Matters*, Euractiv (Feb. 12, 2019), www.euractiv.com/section/economy-jobs/news/member-states-shield-national-vetoes-on-tax-matters/.

[69] See id.

[70] Mosquera Valderrama, *supra* note 67, 95.

have noted that international tax governance appears to be on the precipice of change.[71] Moreover, some speculate that it is unlikely that the OECD will remain as the dominant forum for international tax negotiations.[72] Amid this shift, commentators have noted that a new order of international tax governance requires an inclusive multilateral governance structure that involves developing countries in all parts of the process – from agenda-setting to implementation – while being sensitive to political and cultural overtones. Once this is in place, the creation of regional projects may then be possible. These would counterbalance the dominance of the OECD in international tax governance in a way that would benefit the most marginalised; namely, developing countries and their people.

PROPOSED TAX GOVERNANCE STRUCTURE

African countries are one of the most marginalised groups of all developing countries. This can be seen in the most basic requirement for a country to exist: national borders. Makau wa Mutua writes that the borders of African countries are artificial and represent random lines drawn by colonial occupiers.[73] It is therefore vital for African countries to use this period of power-shifting in international tax governance to consolidate their political powers and create a meaningful governance structure that allows their voices to be heard and their concerns to be addressed. In so doing, they would be better able to serve their people.

The African continent has just reached an important milestone in the signing of the AfCFTA. The speed with which many African countries ratified this instrument is remarkable.[74] This seems to indicate a willingness on the part of most African countries to surrender some degree of sovereignty for the interest of forming common policies and objectives. I argue that some of this willingness should be carried over to international tax governance concerns.

I further argue that the best way to do this is to create an African international tax governance structure within the AU, because the AU has established a framework for the realisation of deeper and continent-wide integration.[75] Moreover, despite Africa's colonially imposed borders, the concept of nations/states will continue to be important in international relations.[76] The AU offers an established and flexible framework, allowing for the creation of a politically sensitive, inclusive, multilateral, and counterhegemonic African tax governance structure that would serve the

[71] Okanga & Latief, *supra* note 58; Motala, *supra* note 56.

[72] See Christensen & Hearson, *supra* note 48, at 1069.

[73] Makau wa Mutua, *Why Redraw the Map of Africa: A Moral and Legal Inquiry*, 16 Mich. J. Int'l. L. 1113, 1115 (1995).

[74] See *Africa's Ambitious Trade Plan Needs to Speed Up*, The Economist (Mar. 26, 2022), www.economist.com/leaders/2022/03/26/africas-ambitious-trade-plan-needs-to-speed-up.

[75] See Fagbayibo, *supra* note 23, at 416.

[76] See id., at 418.

African people. Artificially drawn borders of African countries, with no sense of the peoples living within those borders, have resulted in conflicts and violence within many African countries as African people were told that they are now encompassed within one country.[77] In contrast, if the AU were empowered to engage in tax policy to find a pan-African position, perhaps it would allow for such borders to matter less. African countries could then focus on creating tax policies that would suit most, if not all, African countries.

I envisage that this could occur both in instances where a regional response and a common continental response is required in international tax relations. A regional response would encompass issues such as whether African regionals should design and implement a digital service tax. A common continental response, on the other hand, would be one where the international tax issue requires countries to either support or oppose a proffered proposal, such as with respect to the OECD's Pillar One proposal.

In terms of eliciting a regional response, it is proposed that the fifty-four African countries be divided into working groups within which they decide on tax policies, based on their similar contexts, that would best represent their approach and response to international tax issues. I propose that ATAF be a member of each working group. In this way, ATAF would have knowledge of all the tax policies across the continent. This would enable ATAF to resolve technical, tax-related incoherencies at the working-group level and at an early stage.

Once these tax policies have been decided, the working groups would then present these policies to the AU Assembly, comprised of the heads of state of the member countries, to enable all the AU member states to participate. The purpose of the AU Assembly's involvement here would not be to grant approval or make decisions about the policies, but rather to ensure that these policies are coherent with other non-tax policies, such as trade, development, or integration policies. Such checks could be performed by the other organs of the AU, such as its specialised technical committees. The idea with this step is to create the opportunity for the Ministers of Finance, Trade, Development and other portfolios to speak to each other about their policies and prevent conflicts between such policies. By providing a forum for Ministers to design their policies together, it could perhaps result in all policies being designed in a way to support each other.

In instances where a common continental response is required, the above proposed structure would also work well. Here, each working group, together with ATAF, would consider the implications for each member state of either supporting or opposing a particular international tax proposal. Such deliberations would include conducting cost-benefit analyses of the proposal to determine the proposal's implications for each member of the REC and also for the region. Once decided,

[77] See Tim Marshall, Prisoners of Geography: Ten Maps That Tell You Everything You Need to Know about Global Politics 126 (Elliott & Thompson 2016).

each working group would present their position to the AU Assembly. Discussions at the AU level would allow for the full spectrum of implications of the presented position or positions to be discussed – that is, the tax, political, social, and other dimensions of the positions could be fully and simultaneously discussed until a common continental position is found. Following this, the AU would be in a position to fulfil one of its objectives, which is to defend an African common position on issues of interest to the continent as a whole and to its people.[78] Having said that, I am aware of the reluctance of African countries to relinquish any aspect of their tax sovereignty to a supranational entity, even one of their own making, as was noted by Agupusi.[79] In such an event, it would be possible for groups of RECs working together to defend their common position on an international tax proposal.

I also propose that African countries approach all aspects of international tax negotiation through this proposed structure. Perhaps through these groupings of concentrated and focused political power, the working groups could enter into more beneficial double taxation agreements with non-African countries or push for the renegotiation of existing double taxation agreements, if all the members of the working group were to act in sync with this demand. Again here, it is envisaged that the AU Assembly could be used to find a broader coherence and some level of uniformity in the proposed negotiations undertaken by the working groups. Given the great disparities between African countries, I am aware of the extreme difficulty there may be in finding such uniformity. However, I am hopeful that some level of homogeneity may be discernible in the formation of a common continental position, which would then be noted at the AU level.

Such homogeneity may already be seen in the strides ATAF is making in communicating Africa's common position on international tax issues. For instance, ATAF was successful in having an African-based example included in the OECD's Transfer Pricing Guidelines.[80] This was the first time in the 22-year history of the OECD Transfer Pricing Guidelines that an Africa-based approach was included in OECD documents.[81] Moreover, following ATAF's lobbying, the OECD's guidelines on the attribution of profits to a permanent establishment now include the recognition that developing countries may use calculation methods other than the Authorised OECD Approach.[82] Also, ATAF successfully introduced an elective binding dispute resolution mechanism for African countries with low levels of

78 See Constitutive Act of the African Unionart. 3(d) (July 11, 2000),

79 Patricia Agupusi, *The African Union and the Path to an African Renaissance*, 39 J. CONTEMP. AFR. STUD. 261, 270 (2021).

80 ATAF, *supra* note 25, at 6.

81 Id.

82 Christensen et al. *supra* note 6, at 27; LESAGE et al. *supra* note 28, at 231.

disputes and met certain criteria.[83] In the light of these developments, it is not inconceivable to imagine that African countries may succeed in having the international tax issues that are most important to them addressed fairly at a global level. I envisage that this proposed governance structure would allow African countries to directly address issues like the creation of new taxing rights and an African-based solution to addressing the imbalance in the allocation of taxing rights between residence and source countries, as alluded to at the Fourth High-Level Tax Policy Dialogue organised by ATAF and the AU Commission in 2020.[84]

Notwithstanding this, disparities continue to exist. This gives rise to the bigger question: how to divide fifty-four African countries into meaningful working groups. For this, I propose that the African countries be divided according to the eight RECs recognised by the AU, as set out in the Appendix.[85] Collectively, these RECs have 106 members, which includes overlapping memberships by some African countries. Bearing in mind capacity constraints, it may be necessary for these African countries to choose one REC to which they feel the most affiliated.

Grouping African countries in this way would acknowledge the achievements the RECs have made over the years and also create the space for further achievements. RECs have been instrumental in improving the levels of intra-Africa trade. Eighty per cent of all intra-Africa trade between 2000 and 2019 occurred through RECs.[86] In particular, five RECs had significantly improved trade flows across Africa: CEN-SAD, EAC, ECOWAS, SADC, and UMA.[87] Such improved trade flows have also seen the start of regional value chains facilitated by RECs.[88] For instance, ECOWAS was instrumental in the creation of the first cross-border special economic zone spanning Burkina Faso, Mali, and Côte d'Ivoire.[89] Moreover, RECs have been successful in motivating business development and investment initiatives in the private sector.[90] According to the United Nations Economic Commission for Africa, major manufacturing and services companies such as Vodacom, MTN,

[83] ATAF, *The Inclusive Framework's Two-Pillar Solution to Address the Tax Challenges Arising from the Digitalisation of the Economy*, 8 Technical Note 5 (Aug. 2021).

[84] ATAF, *supra* note 26.

[85] *Regional Economic Communities (RECs)*, African Union, https://au.int/en/organs/recs. For membership, see the Appendix.

[86] *From Regional Economic Communities to a Continental Free Trade Area: Strategic Tools to Assist Negotiators and Agricultural Policy Design in Africa*, United Nations Conference on Trade and Development 9 (Jan. 2017); *Governing the African Continental Free Trade Area–Regional Economic Communities Interface,* United Nations Commission for Africa (2022) 25.

[87] *From Regional Economic Communities to a Continental Free Trade Area: Strategic Tools to Assist Negotiators and Agricultural Policy Design in Africa*, *supra* note 86, at 34.

[88] Id., at 35.

[89] Id.

[90] Id., at 29.

Illovo Sugar Company, Safaricom, and Bidco Company have benefitted from the COMESA, EAC, and SADC free-trade-area provisions.[91] Furthermore, RECs like the EAC and COMESA have made great strides in removing foreign exchange restrictions, taxes on foreign exchange and the easing of customs formalities.[92] From a person's perspective, the ECOWAS passport and biometric identity cards have significantly facilitated the free movement of persons within the region.[93] Finally, ECOWAS, IGAD, and SADC have done well in their peacekeeping and peacemaking initiatives within their regions.[94]

From a practical perspective, REC grouping holds promise because it allows for the existing REC structures within Africa to coordinate and function alongside AU organs, such as the AU Assembly. It would also make sense logistically because the members of the RECs have already found some level of common interest which brought them together into the REC in the first place, and which has allowed them to function for some time. These pre-existing commonalities should make it easier to identify and agree on tax policies that would work best for the region.

A problem that these REC working groups would bring to light is the need to balance power relations between some of the more powerful African countries that may be members of the same REC. This is a difficult issue to address. One way to address this is to ensure that each African country is given technical support and enough time to prepare for their working group discussions. Such support could come from civil society, for instance. I suggest that each of the working groups be chaired by an independent third party who would be capable of identifying and stopping intimidating negotiation patterns.[95] A final suggestion is that accommodations be made for differences in languages among the members of the working group. This may be done by identifying the common language within the group and using that as the main medium of communication. Interpreters may then be available, as needed.

A further issue that arises is concern about how to make the RECs accountable for when, as they operate now, members of the RECs commit themselves to courses of action that contradict their regional commitments. For instance, Kenya announced on 31 March 2023 that it would scrap its digital service tax in order to obtain favourable trade terms with the United States.[96] Yet, a month earlier, as part of the Fiftieth East Africa Revenue Commissioner General's General Meeting, Kenya

[91] Id., at 29.

[92] Id., at 34.

[93] Id.

[94] See Dawn Nagar & Fritza Nganje, *The AU and Africa's Regional Economic Communities*, Ctr. for Conflict Resol. Rep. 26, 28 (2016).

[95] See Albie M. Davis & Richard A. Salem, *Dealing with Power Imbalances in the Mediation of Interpersonal Disputes*, 6 Mediation Q. 17 (1984).

[96] Kepha Muiruri, *President Ruto Drops Digital Service Tax against Multinationals*, Business Daily (Mar. 31, 2023), www.businessdailyafrica.com/bd/economy/ruto-drops-digital-service-tax-against-multinationals–4179322.

and the other EAC Partner States passed a resolution supporting the adoption of digital service taxes in the region.[97]

In my view, the governance structure proposed here may allow for both a bottom-up and top-down approach to be followed to ensure some level of accountability for RECs and their members. First, bottom-up accountability could be generated through the inclusion and buy-in of the public in the REC member countries. This could come about through encouraging reporting of the adoption of the tax governance structure in the media. Reporting should include the benefits the governance structure and processes are expected to generate for the people within the region and for African people as a whole. Moreover, when a REC does not follow a regionally beneficial AU decision, for instance, this should be brought to the public's attention in the region, again through the media. An informed public would be in a position to apply pressure to their elected officials and demand explanations if not action.

The proposed tax governance structure would also allow for a top-down approach to be adopted in keeping RECs accountable. Placing an issue on the AU agenda makes it visible and would require input from the RECs. While the AU currently faces difficulty in enforcing its rules, and it has been noted that countries often do not carry out AU policies,[98] I argue that this governance structure may bring about accountability through the other RECs. As the bottom-up approach would make the RECs accountable to the public, this may motivate some form of peer accountability as well. The other RECs, for whom the AU agenda item is important, may be motivated to question their peers of the RECs that are delaying the discussion on such an agenda item. Whether or not this would be enough to motivate action on the part of the recalcitrant REC is debatable, but at the very least it would allow the compliant REC to report to its people that it is doing everything it can to move the AU agenda item along.

A further concern this proposed tax governance structure may raise is questions around the differing levels of development of the member countries within the RECs. Not all members would be at the same level of development. This may then make it difficult, if not impossible, to reach the required consensus in respect of either a regional or common continental approach. To my mind, this concern raises two issues – first, how to address a lack of consensus in the short term and, second, how to address the fact that differences in development exist within the REC at all.

As a short-term measure, a lack of consensus could be addressed by allowing countries that agree with the proposed course of action to implement such action together, separate from those who are unable or unwilling to do the same. This could be similar to the 'enhanced cooperation' procedures adopted by the European Union.[99] My recommendation here would be that this procedure be designed as

97 Ambrose Gahene, EAC Revenue Commissioners Roots For Digital Tax Service (CIO Africa Feb. 20, 2023), https://cioafrica.co/eac-revenue-commissioners-roots-for-digital-taxservice/#:~:text=The%2050th%20East%20Africa%20Revenue%20Commissioners'%20General%20Meeting%20sat%20at,cross%2Dborder%20smuggling%20of%20goods.

98 See Edozie & Grottschalk, *supra* note 22, at 191.

99 TFEU arts. 326–84.

though the other non-participating countries are included while also including transitional measures to account for the fact that they are not participating. In this way, it would allow for the participating countries to continue the course of action that would support their tax policies while also creating the possibility for the other non-participating countries to slot in seamlessly once they are in a position to do so. Such a short-term measure could be implemented within the REC and within the AU.

In terms of long-term measures to address disparity in the development stages within the REC, mechanisms outside of a governance structure are required to address the concern. One mechanism could be to use the corporate income tax system to incorporate a redistributive measure from the more developed member countries to the lesser developed member countries of the REC.[100] This could be more easily done once the REC has reached a level of integration that would allow for the corporate income tax system to assume a supranational quality.[101] I have argued elsewhere how such a mechanism could be designed in the context of the EAC.[102] The suggested mechanism could also be used for other taxes, such as value-added tax, for instance.

In my view, the adoption of both short-term and long-term measures should address the concerns regarding disparate development levels hindering consensus within RECs and across the RECs as they participate at the AU level.

In sum, the proposed governance structure would allow African countries to find some level of commonality as they seek to identify tax policies that would benefit their particular working group, while not sacrificing too much of their tax sovereignty in adopting those policies. The proposed governance structure would also allow for the existing AU organ, the AU Assembly, to continue its work as the supreme organ of the AU in determining common policies.[103] Furthermore, the proposed structure allows for accountability measures to be implemented both from a bottom-up perspective by including the people of the REC and from a top-down perspective through peer accountability in respect of the other RECs. Most importantly, the proposed governance structure would allow African countries to create an international tax forum that not only works for them but could also act as counterweight to the OECD's dominance in international tax relations.

CONCLUSION

The current international tax governance system has not been kind to African countries. Many have noted how the current system only serves to deepen existing inequalities and encourage more disparity in economic outcomes. At the same time, Africa has embarked upon a momentous journey with the AfCFTA. Not only does

[100] See Afton L. Titus, The Design of a Corporate Income Tax System and How to Protect It for the East African Federation 41–93 (2020) (PhD Thesis, UvA-Dare); *see also* Afton Titus, *Domestic Revenue Mobilisation through Corporate Income Tax in an East African Developing Country Context*, 44 Dalhousie L.J. 151 (2021).

[101] See id.

[102] See id.

[103] See Christof Heyns et al., *The African Union*, 46 Ger. Y.B. Int'l. L., 252, 265 (2003).

this instrument hold the potential to bring prosperity to Africa and her citizens; it also reflects an uncharacteristic willingness on the part of African leaders to work together to collectively realise a common goal.

I argue that African countries should take advantage of this spirit of cooperation to make some difficult, yet necessary, decisions about the future of their place in international tax relations. Moreover, I propose that African countries form their own international tax governance structure within the framework of the AU.

I propose that African countries be divided into working groups according to the AU-recognised RECs. These REC working groups, working together with ATAF, would be instrumental in ensuring adoption of tax policies that require a regional response or a common continental position. In respect of regional tax policies, the task of the working groups would be to formulate common tax policies and approaches to international tax issues that would best suit the group's development needs. These policies are then to be put to the AU Assembly where they will be checked for coherence with other non-tax policies, such as trade and development. To the extent that incoherence exists, I suggest that these be addressed through the use of the AU organs, such as its specialised technical committees. In so doing, it may be possible to design international tax, trade, development and integration policies that support both international and national objectives.

In terms of tax policies that require a common continental position, the aim of the working groups and ATAF would be to undertake cost-benefit analyses of international tax proposals and determine the policies' implications for each member of the REC and for the region as a whole. Once such a common continental position is found, it would be presented to the AU Assembly following which the AU may be given the opportunity to defend such position in the interest of the continent and its people.

I argue that such a governance structure would allow for the AU to continue to play a prominent role leading the way for deeper African integration, while also allowing for the existing RECs in Africa to continue to play a key role in making such integration a reality on the ground. This proposal would also allow for the existing institutions of the RECs to continue to have relevance as they interface with the AU. But, most importantly, I argue that this structure would allow African countries to not only finally create an international tax forum that would be completely devoted to its concerns, but also to create a counterbalance to the dominance of the OECD in this area. This would allow for more fairness and justice to feature in international tax solutions as power relations become more balanced.

Finally, time is of the essence in international tax, as important global tax policy decisions are being made at the speed of light. In order for African countries to participate in such decision-making, it is vital that they seize the opportunity to make their own decisions for their own people rather than wait for an invitation to do so.

APPENDIX:

AFRICAN REGIONAL ECONOMIC COMMUNITIES

Arab Maghreb Union (UMA)

Algeria
Libya
Mauritania
Morocco
Tunisia

Common Market for Eastern and Southern Africa (COMESA)

Burundi
Comoros
DR Congo
Djibouti
Egypt
Eritrea
Ethiopia
Kenya
Libya
Madagascar
Malawi
Mauritius
Rwanda
Seychelles
Sudan
Swaziland
Uganda
Zambia
Zimbabwe

Community of Sahel–Saharan States (CEN–SAD)

Benin
Burkina Faso
Cabo Verde
Central African Republic
Chad
Comoros
Côte d'Ivoire
Djibouti
Egypt
Eritrea
Gambia
Ghana
Guinea
Guinea Bissau
Kenya
Liberia
Libya
Mali
Mauritania
Morocco
Niger
Nigeria
São Tomé and Príncipe
Senegal
Sierra Leone
Somalia
Sudan
Togo
Tunisia

East African Community (EAC)

Burundi
Democratic Republic of Congo
Kenya
Rwanda
South Sudan
Tanzania
Uganda

Economic Community of Central African States (ECCAS)

Angola
Burundi
Cameroon
Central African Republic
Chad
Congo
DR Congo
Equatorial Guinea
Gabon
São Tomé and Príncipe

Economic Community of West African States (ECOWAS)

Benin
Burkina Faso
Cabo Verde
Côte d'Ivoire
Gambia
Ghana
Guinea
Guinea Bissau
Liberia
Mali
Niger
Nigeria
Senegal
Sierra Leone
Togo

Intergovernmental Authority on Development (IGAD)

Djibouti
Eritrea
Ethiopia
Kenya
Somalia
South Sudan
Sudan
Uganda

Southern African Development Community (SADC)

Angola
Botswana
DR Congo
Lesotho
Madagascar
Malawi
Mauritius
Mozambique
Namibia
Seychelles
South Africa
Swaziland
Tanzania
Zambia
Zimbabwe

PART III

Social Transformation and Taxation

8

Transformative Constitutionalism

The Role of Citizens in (Tax) State-Building: The Case of Kenya

Daisy Ogembo

INTRODUCTION

This chapter considers the role of Kenyan citizens in state-building through participation in government decision-making on tax matters in light of the so-called third wave of democracy marked by the enactment of a transformative constitution. Before that discussion, the chapter begins by tracing the evolution of the role of citizens in tax state-building in colonial and post-colonial Kenya. Against this backdrop, it then explores the extent to which, pursuant to Kenya's 2010 transformative constitution, citizens can and are contributing to state-building through public deliberation in tax matters, and it concludes by considering the potential challenges and opportunities for taxing the citizens of Kenya over the next 100 years.

A study of constitutionalism and the role of the citizen in tax state-building is necessary for various reasons. First, taxation plays a crucial role in the state's formation, growth, and stability, that is, taxation is an essential ingredient in state-building.[1] Because states are not commercial entities with the option of generating adequate income through commercial activities, tax plays a politically significant role by enabling states to raise the revenue that the executive needs to function, maintain critical institutions, and meet its socio-economic obligations to its citizens. Further, taxation cannot be ignored for economic reasons; the executive's ability to increase tax rates can affect citizens in harmful ways, including a reduction in income, or the closure of fledgling businesses, and it is, therefore, necessary to understand how taxation interacts with constitutional rights and principles. Additionally, taxation is administratively important because proper tax administration contributes to

I thank Philip Baker for his useful comments and suggestions and gratefully acknowledge that this research would not have been possible without a generous postdoctoral fellowship grant by the British Academy.

[1] Deborah Brautigam, *Introduction: Taxation and State-Building in Developing Countries, in* TAXATION AND STATE-BUILDING IN DEVELOPING COUNTRIES: CAPACITY AND CONSENT 1 (Odd-Helge Fjeldstad, Mick Moore, & Deborah Brautigam eds., 2008).

administrative justice and the upholding of the rule of law in the state; the decision-making powers of the tax administration have the potential to affect the freedoms of all citizens to varying degrees.

Crucially, revenue raising through taxes also has the potential to contribute to state-building, responsive government, and accountability. A growing body of political science literature shows that bargaining between citizens and governments over tax revenue collection can have significant positive effects on governance because efforts by governments to expand the tax revenue they collect can often result in a push by citizens for reciprocal service provision and expanded accountability.[2] This chapter proceeds from the premise that enabling principles, rules, and values in transformative constitutions, including constitutional supremacy, state reconstruction, redistribution of power, transparency and accountability, good governance, social justice and egalitarianism, substantive equality, and socio-economic revolution, all crucially contribute to citizens' ability to effectively play their role in tax state-building and encouraging responsive government and accountability because of the complex and dynamic relationship between tax and constitutional law.

Kenya, borrowing heavily from South Africa's constitutional transformation in the early 1990s, underwent a tremendous constitutional change in the last quarter of a century, adopting a radical constitution which has come to be known as a 'transformative constitution'. A core aim of a transformative constitution is to promote greater democracy and participation in governance and, thus, state-building. Citizen or public participation – referred to in this chapter as public deliberation – is at the heart of transformative constitutionalism. Thus, constitutional rules and principles that enable and facilitate public deliberation in government decision-making in tax matters have significant potential to enable and enhance citizen participation in tax state-building.

This chapter does not purport to offer a comprehensive or authoritative account of transformative constitutionalism or the complex literature on public deliberation, which are expansively and ably covered elsewhere. Instead, it focuses on tracing the evolution of the relationship between the Kenyan state and its citizens and how constitutional changes have gradually changed the nature of that relationship and allowed citizens to play a more significant role in state-building through involvement in tax matters, specifically through the mechanism of public deliberation. Finally, it concludes by looking at issues that may threaten progress in this area.

Defining three key terms that will appear repeatedly in this chapter is essential. This chapter uses the term 'public deliberation' interchangeably with the term 'public participation' as it appears in the 2010 Kenya Constitution. It has been argued that the term public deliberation:

[2] See Michael L. Ross, *Does Taxation Lead to Representation?*, 34 Brit. J. Pol. Sci. 229 (2004); Wilson Prichard, Taxation, Responsiveness and Accountability in Sub-Saharan Africa: The Dynamics of Tax Bargaining (2015).

> . . . better encapsulates the process envisioned in the constitution, various statutory provisions on public deliberation and citizens' expectations. The intention . . . was beyond simply widening opportunities for participation but instead was focused on establishing thicker discursive opportunities, which are characteristic of public deliberation.[3]

'Transformative constitutionalism' is used to describe the process by which the enactment, interpretation, and enforcement of a constitution transform a country's social and political institutions, and power relationships, steering them towards democracy, participation, and egalitarianism.[4] This radical social change, described by Klare as more than reform but less than a revolution, is delivered through constitutional interpretation and enforcement by courts and public institutions.[5] Finally, 'tax state-building' describes the creation and strengthening of state institutions by increasing their administrative, fiscal, and institutional capacity to positively shape such institutions' interaction with citizens and enable them to pursue public goals more effectively. This chapter focuses on how legislation-making, policy-making, and administration in taxation enable citizens to play a role in state-building. This potential is referred to as 'tax state-building'.

The rest of this chapter is arranged as follows: The first section explores the role of citizens in tax state-building in colonial Kenya; the next section contains a discussion on the role of citizens in tax state-building in the post-colonial state; the following section focuses on the drastic shift in state–citizen relations following the enactment of the Constitution of Kenya in 2010 and the enhancements in citizens' role in tax state-building; while the final section concludes by looking at some of the issues that threaten the progress made in ensuring citizens play their rightful role in tax state-building.

THE ROLE OF CITIZENS IN (TAX) STATE-BUILDING IN THE COLONIAL STATE

Prior to colonialism, Kenya was a vast geographical space occupied by over forty communities or 'mini nations', also known as tribes. The national geographical boundaries we know today did not exist. Instead, each tribe had its distinct territory, socio-political and economic identity and organisation, and rules or laws developed through consensus that governed only the members of the tribe. Notions of citizenship, state, and belonging to one nation, as we understand them today, did not exist. The tribes existed independently, although there was often inter-tribal trade and

3 Brenda Ogembo, *Deliberative Democracy in Legislative Committees: Interpreting Public Deliberation in Kenya's Subnational Legislatures* (July 19, 2022), https://etheses.bham.ac.uk/id/eprint/11853/ (last visited Jan. 15, 2024), Preface.

4 Karl E. Klare, *Legal Culture and Transformative Constitutionalism*, 14 S. Afr. J. on Hum. Rts. 146, 150 (1998).

5 Id.

marriage, and limited and intermittent conflict.[6] Before colonialism, taxation in the conventional sense did not exist; instead, payments were made to the rulers in exchange for peace and protection, but the amount was never more than what the members of the tribe or clan could afford.[7]

Ndege provides an eloquent description of the economic set-up in pre-colonial societies:

> Production was primarily for collective subsistence rather than individual accumulation. The kinship system was the basis of ownership of factors of production which included land, livestock, and labour. Labour was largely cooperative within the family and the larger kin group … There existed little differences in wealth possession. Classes, if they existed, were largely incipient. Reciprocity and the egalitarian ideal ensured that individuals never slid into abject poverty.[8]

British rule in Kenya left a lasting legacy in the relationships between the tribes comprising Kenya and the country's political, economic, and legal arrangements.

> Traditional local ways of organising and regulating the community were gradually displaced by British regulations, and thus one system of governance was replaced by another, alien and powerful, which has become the basis of modern Kenya.[9]

Initially known as the East Africa Protectorate, the British presence in this region was first established in the late nineteenth century through the Imperial British East Africa Company, a commercial association set up to further Britain's commercial interests by developing African trade in the areas controlled by the British empire. Queen Victoria granted the company a royal charter in 1888. The company administered the dependency for a few years but then began to fail. By 1895 the British government took over, and the Protectorate was then administered by the Foreign Office and, later, by the Colonial Office from 1902. Finally, in 1920, the status of the Protectorate changed; the inland areas of the Protectorate were annexed as British Dominions and became the Kenyan colony.

The colonial government introduced ideas of state, centralised power, individual ownership, poverty, wealth, and, most importantly for our purposes, constitutionalism. However, the applicability of the notions of state, citizenship, and belonging was very narrow, and this limited application played a crucial role in shaping the country and laying a foundation for future state-building. Kenya's early constitutions were not *for* the Kenyan people; they set out how the British colonial government

6 Peter O. Ndege, *Colonialism and Its Legacies in Kenya*, 2 (2009), https://africanphilanthropy.issuelab.org/resources/19699/19699.pdf.

7 Attiya Waris, *Taxation without Principles: A Historical Analysis of the Kenyan Taxation System*, 1 Kenya L. Rev. 272, 278 (2007).

8 Ndege, *supra* note 6.

9 Yash Pal Ghai & Jill Cottrell Ghai, Kenya's Constitution: An Instrument for Change 3 (2nd ed., 2021), https://katibainstitute.org/wp-content/uploads/2021/08/Kenyas-Constitution-Instrument-for-Change.pdf.

ruled over them. The state existed for the control of the indigenous population, and the idea of citizenship and its attendant rights, such as the rights to representation and voting, were inaccessible to them. There was no consent, consultation, or participation by the native communities, and the new state was much more powerful than any institution the members of the different tribes or communities had ever experienced.[10]

Indeed, the primary goal of colonial constitutionalism was not to create a responsible and accountable government such as was, at that time, developing in the United Kingdom. Instead, the government created under the new constitutional order was characterised by armed force, bureaucracy, taxation without representation, lack of accountability, and the extinction of community ownership of factors of production, including land – this was the opposite of responsible government. Control (or authoritarian rule) and lack of accountability by an all-powerful executive are two central ideas, colonial legacies, that would plague the newly independent state at the end of the colonial era.

Apart from control and lack of accountability, the colonial government established a territory with defined boundaries and, with that one act, turned the many tribes who had lived in their lands as independent nations for a long time into one nation.[11] The members of these diverse tribes suddenly became the 'citizens' of Kenya, even though the notion of citizenship was hitherto an alien concept and, arguably, remained so under a colonial constitutional dispensation premised on control and exploitation rather than belonging and participation. Suddenly, there was increased contact and competition between members of previously independent tribes, and these tensions were exacerbated by uneven development opportunities and the government's divide-and-rule tactics.[12] More than any other factor, ethnic distrust, a legacy of colonialism in Kenya, has perhaps had the most significant influence over the shape of politics and constitutionalism in the country. 'Ethnicity and ethnic distrust had long been a product of colonial rule; by 1961 they were firmly embedded in Kenyan politics. The colonial state had done much to foster ethnic distrust – for example, through the propaganda campaigns launched after 1952 that demonized the Kikuyu.'[13] Ethnicity, therefore, significantly inhibited and continues to inhibit the development of a healthy sense of nationhood or national identity or a sense of citizenship that overrides ethnic identity. The political reality remains that pre-colonial societies were 'based strongly on kinship ties and ethnicity, a trait that continues to permeate notions of social and political

[10] Id., at 5.
[11] Id., at 3.
[12] Id., at 5.
[13] Robert M. Maxon, Kenya's Independence Constitution: Constitution-Making and End of Empire 54 (2011).

belongingness, and consequently influences definitions and understandings of nationhood in most African states'.[14]

Who was a citizen in the colonial state per the constitutional set-up, and what did this mean for the role of citizens in tax state-building? To determine the role of citizens in tax state-building in colonial Kenya, it is necessary to determine who the 'citizen' was. As just alluded to, the connection between the indigenous communities and the newly formed states was tenuous; despite being bound together by arbitrary geographic boundaries, their citizenship remained in doubt. The colonial legal framework divided the population into two; 'the elite urban population considered "citizens" who enjoyed a wide array of civil and political rights'[15] and the African populations, legally and economically confined to rural and concentration areas, for whom the notion of citizenship was inapplicable. Instead, the latter was governed by native or customary law, and 'the customary or traditional sense of kinship and common ancestry continued to largely define belongingness to a specific ethnic community'.[16] Indeed, the introduction of the term 'citizen' in British legislation in 1948 made it clear that citizenship was only available to people living in nine select countries (including Canada, Australia, India, South Africa, and Ireland) that had attained independence or self-government but remained inaccessible to persons of African descent born in British colonies.[17]

Against this backdrop, when the colonial government introduced the taxation of the African populations, it was not tied to citizenship or representation. The indigenous communities were taxed without representation, as it was not until 1944 that the first African joined the legislative council (LegCo) to represent African interests, and the position was a nominated one, filled by the colonial governor. Elected representation for Africans in the LegCo would not be introduced until 1954, a decade before independence, and such representatives only had eight seats, a number that did not reflect the composition of the society. Even then, only Africans over 40 years old and with substantial assets and those who were educated and over 21 years old qualified to vote for the representatives.

African participation in state-building was never the objective of colonial taxation of indigenous communities. In the same way that the colonial legal framework divided the population into two, the legal framework for taxation distinguished between the settler and African communities. The main direct tax applicable to the African communities was the inequitable Hut and Poll tax, imposed on all males who had their own huts (a proxy for puberty) from 1901 onwards; the objective was to indirectly coerce the African populations, accustomed to a subsistence economy, to provide poorly remunerated labour for the emerging capitalist economy in order to

[14] Caroline Nalule, *Report on Citizenship Law Kenya*, 2 (2020), https://cadmus.eui.eu/bitstream/handle/1814/66749/RSC_GLOBALCIT_CR_2020_7.pdf?sequence=1.

[15] Id., at 3.

[16] Id.

[17] See the British Nationality Act 1948, section 1(3).

earn the cash required to pay the tax.[18] 'The tax weapon had the desired effect in forcing more Africans into wage employment, the Kikuyu ethnic group in particular responded to its pressure by entering the labour market in large numbers.'[19] However, as the taxation was neither tied to citizenship nor representation, the taxation of Africans failed to result in their participation in state-building; in fact, 'tax revolts were suppressed with bullets, defaulters had their houses burned down and were imprisoned if caught'.[20]

In summary, the colonial constitutional and legal order played a significant role in othering African populations and inhibiting participation and a sense of belonging. As a result, despite the taxation of these populations, the taxation was disconnected from notions of citizenship, representation, and nationhood; thus, the taxation resulted in coercion, the violent suppression of revolt, and disenfranchisement rather than citizen contribution to state-building.

THE ROLE OF CITIZENS IN (TAX) STATE-BUILDING IN THE POST-COLONIAL STATE

After independence, it quickly became evident that it would be exceedingly challenging to shake off the colonial legacy of a nation without a common identity and an authoritarian and all-powerful executive that could not be held accountable by citizens through democratic processes. This single-party autocracy and authoritarian rule were not unique to Kenya; they characterised most African countries after independence. Ghai and Ghai argue that:

> When Britain annexed the territory in eastern Africa, it found numerous self-sufficient communities, leading their lives separately, with their own systems of governance and economy. What it bequeathed to Kenyans was a country with these communities bound together by ties of political structures and economy devised for their subordination, but with the additional problems of finding and creating a common identity and destiny: a state without a nation. We can draw various lessons from this history. Perhaps the most important is that it is very hard to restructure the colonial state to make it democratic and accountable. The primary function of the colonial state was to dominate and exploit the local communities and their resources, not to promote their welfare. Its authority was based on its coercive power, not the consent of the people. It was estranged from the people whom they tried to divide and rule. Democracy and rights were inconsistent with this kind of state and rule.[21]

Both the Kenyatta and Moi administrations were characterised by the centralisation of power in the hands of one person, a powerful president akin to the colonial

[18] Waris, *supra* note 7, at 293.
[19] Id.
[20] Id.
[21] GHAI & GHAI, *supra* note 9, at 10.

governor, the loss of democracy and accountability, patronage politics, and ethnicisation of politics. In addition, the abolition of regional governments led to a highly centralised government at the national level and the gradual removal of administrative and financial powers of local government, which weakened democracy and participation at district and sub-district levels.

After independence, two key constitutional realities meant the relationship between citizenship and tax state-building was less tenuous than during the colonial era. First, even though the young state continued to struggle with finding and forging a common identity and a united nation, the post-independence constitution, for the first time, used the term 'citizen' to refer to Africans, granting them a legal sense of belonging to this new nation. They were no longer 'non-citizen citizens' of Kenya. Since taxation lies at the foundation of the relationship between a government and its citizens, the scope for their participation in tax state-building became possible. Further, despite the persistence of single-party autocracy and authoritarianism, under the post-independence constitution, the citizens had a right to vote and representation (within the limitations of single-party politics).

However, these constitutional advancements were tempered by the fact that the executive control of the civil service and the police force enabled the repression of the people through exclusionary state policies and practices, militarisation of politics, political assassinations, death and displacement of citizens, violation of rights with no redress, distrust in government, tribal suspicion, hatred, and conflict, and finally the death of the rule of law.[22] The result was that, without alternative legal and constitutional channels, citizen engagement in promoting accountability, democracy, and state-building inevitably frequently occurred through popular resistance. Against this backdrop, in the late 1990s and early 2000s, the unpopular Moi administration found itself at the receiving end of popular resistance to taxation by the citizens; this resistance led to a drastic decline in tax revenue that precipitated political changes culminating in the end of Moi's 24 years of dictatorial reign.[23] According to Prichard:

> in Kenya, in the late 1990s, ... public resistance to taxation failed to prompt immediate government concessions. Instead, persistent and politically motivated tax evasion progressively undermined the fiscal position of the increasingly unpopular government. By starving the government of revenue, this tax resistance helped to precipitate a political transition in 2002, as the incumbent government was removed from power.[24]

This popular resistance is evidenced by the revenue collection trends over time, in line with political changes. For example, before 2003, the period referenced by Prichard, the Kenya Revenue Authority would collect very little tax; between

[22] Id., at 8–9.
[23] PRICHARD, *supra* note 2, at 3.
[24] Id.

1998–2002, tax revenue in Kenya fell drastically from 20.5 per cent of GDP in 1995–1996 to 15.7 per cent of GDP in 2001–2002.[25] Prichard explains that this decline was partially a result of the 'declining legitimacy and popularity of the government', with the President's opponents deliberately withholding tax to frustrate and undermine the financial stability of his government.[26] However, following the 2003 elections deemed the first free and fair elections in 24 years, and the election of Mwai Kibaki under an immensely popular coalition government, taxpayer attitudes changed, and citizens were willing to support the new government through taxation.[27] In 2004–2005, tax collection hit a figure of 21.8 per cent of GDP, a remarkable jump from 15.7 per cent, signalling the beginning of a period of public goodwill and faith in government, increased levels of compliance, and little public resistance towards taxes.[28] Subsequent cracks in the coalition, in its third year, were accompanied by declining revenue collections in 2004–2005 and 2005–2006.[29]

TRANSFORMATIVE CONSTITUTIONALISM AND THE ROLE OF CITIZENS IN (TAX) STATE-BUILDING

Despite the reintroduction of multi-party politics in the early 1990s and the election of a new government in 2002, the constitution and public institutions had lost their legitimacy, and the clamour for a new constitution, written by and for the people, persisted. The 2010 constitution, in its preamble, highlights Kenyans' determination to build a united nation of different tribes. It also acknowledges the difficulties that came with colonial geographical boundaries and administrative decisions. The preamble also emphasises that it is a constitution for and by the people and an express move away from British and presidential imperialism.

In this context, public deliberation became a crucial tool for remedying various ills, including state power to pass oppressive legislation and the disunity, mistrust, and marginalisation that persisted between the different ethnic communities and prevented state-building. As Ogembo explains, 'as part of the push for a new constitution before its promulgation in 2010, Kenyans had consistently advocated for mandatory public deliberation in legislative processes. Public deliberation was viewed as obligatory for accountability and ensuring citizens' views were considered in all legislative decisions'.[30]

Thus, when the 2010 Constitution was enacted, one element that stood out was the emphasis on public deliberation (public participation in the actual text) in

[25] Id., at 134.
[26] Id.
[27] Id.
[28] Id.
[29] Id.
[30] Ogembo, *supra* note 3.

government decision-making processes.[31] Ogembo also points out the usefulness of public deliberation in deeply divided societies and its capacity to contribute to consensus and community-building by addressing 'existing challenges of nationhood associated with colonial and post-colonial experiences on the continent'.[32] This section, therefore, focuses on the role of citizens in tax state-building through public deliberation processes mandated by the 2010 Constitution of Kenya.

Public deliberation can be defined as 'reasoned argument, strategic bargaining, experiential testimony, and other kinds of discursive claims that are aimed at ensuring the public affected by a decision are able to engage in substantive, balanced and civil discussion',[33] with decision-makers in government, including legislators, administrators, and policymakers.

There are many potential avenues for citizens to play a role in tax state-building; this chapter focuses on public deliberation as one such avenue under Kenya's transformative constitution. One may argue that there are issues on which it is appropriate to consult the public, and issues on which consultation is not desirable such as appropriate tax rates; a related argument is that tax-related matters are not suitable to public referenda. However, the fundamental justification for focusing on public deliberation is that it can produce 'more considered political decisions ... informed by relevant sources and evidence and reflect public will ... [and] will have greater legitimacy owing to public input, which will in turn increase public faith in democracy and its institutions', a crucial aspect of state-building.[34] The Constitution does not place any limits on the areas of public finance and taxation that ought to be subjected to public deliberation.

Kenya's Constitution recognizes public participation, referred to herein as public deliberation, as a national value and principle of governance.[35] Parliament is therefore required to 'facilitate public participation and involvement in the legislative and other business of Parliament and its committees'.[36] In addition, the Constitution requires 'openness and accountability, including public participation, in financial matters'.[37] Thus, unlike the United Kingdom where, although there is some level of public consultation in tax matters, that process is not constitutionally mandated and the government exercises discretion in determining both the issues on which it considers consultation is helpful and the level at which that consultation is to take place[38], citizen participation in tax affairs in Kenya is constitutionally protected and provides an excellent avenue for citizens to play their role in state-

31 Id., at 21.
32 Id., at 39.
33 Id., at 16.
34 Id., at 41.
35 Constitution of Kenya, (2010) art. 10.
36 Id., art. 118.
37 Id., art. 201.
38 HM Treasury & HM Revenue & Customs, *Tax Consultation Framework* (2011), www.gov.uk/government/publications/tax-consultation-framework (last visited 18 Jan. 2024).

building. These constitutionally protected avenues are explored in greater detail here.

The Legislative Process

In accordance with the Constitution, the Standing Orders require that once a Bill has gone through the First Reading, it shall be submitted to the relevant Departmental Committee and the Committee is required to facilitate public participation on the Bill.[39] The mechanisms for public deliberation mentioned in the Standing Orders include inviting submission of memoranda, holding public hearings, consulting relevant stakeholders in a sector, and consulting experts on technical subjects. Thus, any new tax-related bill, including any bill intended to amend existing tax legislation, would go through this process; in this case, the Finance and National Planning Committee, being the relevant Departmental Committee, would invite the submission of memoranda, hold public hearings, as well as receive input from experts and stakeholders.

In addition, the requirement for public participation under the Standing Orders also extends to treaties submitted to the National Assembly for ratification; thus, any double taxation agreements or other tax treaties that Kenya seeks to enter would also be subject to public deliberation and input.[40] Some recent examples include the request for submission of memoranda on the Double Taxation Agreement between Kenya and Mauritius,[41] the request for submission of memoranda on the Tax Laws Amendment Bill 2020[42], and the request for submission of memoranda on the Tax Appeals Tribunal (Amendment) Bill (No. 19 of 2021).[43]

39 National Assembly Standing Orders order 127(3). Note that a 'money bill' is defined in art. 114 of the Constitution as a Bill that contains provisions dealing with, inter alia, taxes and 'the appropriation, receipt, custody, investment or issue of public money' unless a county has raised the tax or public money. Thus, the legislative process of bills concerning the raising and utilising of taxes at the national level takes place solely in the National Assembly, following the procedural rules set out in the Standing Orders. We will return to the challenges posed by this limitation on the Senate in the last section of this chapter.

40 Id., order 170A(2).

41 Published in print media on 25 September 2020. The National Assembly, *Report on the Consideration of the Agreement on the Avoidance of Double Taxation between the Government of Kenya and the Government of Mauritius on the Avoidance of Double Taxation*, 11, http://parliament.go.ke/index.php/the-national-assembly/committees/12/finance-and-planning (last visited 18 Jan. 2024).

42 Published in print media on 1 April 2020 and 8 April 2020, as well as written invitations to stakeholders for their comments on the Bill on 1 April 2020. The National Assembly, *Report on the Consideration of the Tax Laws (Amendment) Bill 2020*, 14, http://parliament.go.ke/index.php/the-national-assembly/committees/12/finance-and-planning (last visited 18 Jan. 2024).

43 Published in print media on 11 June 2021, as well as written invitations to stakeholders for their comments on the Bill on 21 July 2021. The National Assembly, *Report on the Consideration of the Tax Appeals Tribunal (Amendment) Bill (No. 19 of 2021)*, 10. http://parliament.go.ke/index.php/the-national-assembly/committees/12/finance-and-planning.

The Executive's Role in Legislation

The Executive's role in legislation also provides an avenue for public deliberation in tax affairs. Apart from the ordinary tax amendment bills that come through the National Assembly from time to time, the annual budget process will also usually result in the amendment of tax legislation to facilitate revenue raising to fund government expenditure or the implementation of other tax policies in a given financial year. The management of public finances is governed by the Public Finance Management Act 2012,[44] and, according to this Act, during the budget priority-setting stage, the National Treasury ought to solicit public views which will ultimately feed into its proposals for the Budget Policy Statement. Subsequently, the Finance Cabinet Secretary's proposals for the estimates of the revenue, expenditure, and debt and deficit financing of the national government for the next financial year are, in the first instance, discussed and reviewed by the Budget and Appropriations Committee[45], and, in doing so, the Committee is obligated[46] to once again seek representations from the public through public hearings and requests for written memoranda and take into consideration those views.[47] The Committee, with the technical support of the Parliamentary Budget Office, then drafts the Budget Policy Statement taking into account the views of the Cabinet Secretary and the public on the proposed recommendations.[48]

Once the Budget Policy Statement is tabled before the National Assembly and approved, the National Treasury is required by law to 'consolidate, publish and publicise the budget estimates … in a form that is clear and easily understood by, and readily accessible to, members of the public'.[49] There are several subsequent steps in the budget process and opportunities for public deliberation, including the nationwide public hearings for the Appropriations Bill.

However, of great relevance for this chapter is the Finance Bill, which sets out the revenue-raising measures for the National government for the coming financial year. The Finance Bill, when eventually enacted, authorises the government to implement the tax changes required to finance government expenditure for the

[44] The objective of this Act is to ensure that public finances are managed according to the principles set out in the Constitution and its provisions prevail in any matter concerning revenue raising, making of expenditures, and the preparation and submission of budget estimates. See sections 3 and 6, Public Finance Management Act (2012).

[45] See art. 221 of the Constitution of Kenya, *supra* note 35; section 35 of the Public Finance Management Act 2012; and orders 207 and 232 of the National Assembly Standing Orders, *supra* note 39.

[46] These obligations are pursuant to provisions in the Constitution, the Public Finance Management Act, and the Standing Orders.

[47] Art. 221(5) of the Constitution of Kenya, *supra* note 35; and section 39 of the Public Finance Management Act 2012, *supra* note 45.

[48] Section 39 of the Public Finance Management Act 2012, *supra* note 45.

[49] Id., section 39(6).

coming financial year as set out in the approved Appropriations Bill. Once the Cabinet Secretary responsible for Finance makes a public pronouncement of the budget policy highlights and revenue-raising measures for the national government, he or she 'shall submit to the National Assembly a legislative proposal, setting out the revenue raising measures for the national government, together with a policy statement expounding on those measures'.[50] This legislative proposal, that is, the Finance Bill, is then considered by the Departmental Committee on Finance and National Planning in the first instance, and the Committee will invite public comment on the Bill and take into account those views in preparing its report on the Bill for the National Assembly.

The procedures described here are elaborate and precise. It is evident, from a constitutional and a legislative perspective, that the process for public deliberation on the budget process is standardised for ease of participation, and the public has ample opportunity to participate at various points of the process, both on revenue-raising measures and proposed expenditure before the Finance Bill becomes law. The various Committee reports always contain a section on the public participation process, describing the submissions received and explaining why they were rejected or adopted by the Committee. However, the reasons are not always sufficiently detailed or justified.

Citizen and stakeholder participation through the avenues for public deliberation on tax and budget matters described in the preceding section have immense potential to play a crucial role. In a country like Kenya, with a history of deep ethnic division and unresponsive government, these public deliberation processes in finance matters can provide significant opportunities to empower citizens, enhance sentiments of belonging, unity, and nationhood, provide the National Assembly with diverse and innovative views, and improve the relationship between citizens and the state, and all these benefits contribute to state-building, responsiveness, and accountability.

The Executive's Role in Tax Policy-Making Processes

Public deliberation on tax and budget matters has not been restricted to the legislative process. The Constitution makes it clear that openness, accountability, and public participation should guide *all* aspects of public finance in Kenya; this includes the development of tax policy.[51] Unfortunately, while Kenya's tax system has advanced significantly since the introduction of taxation by the colonial government, the changes made to tax legislation and administration in the last sixty years have generally been haphazard, unpredictable, and uncoordinated. A significant contribution to these problems in the tax system is the lack of a coherent, well-thought-out, and sustainable national tax policy. In 2022, to address these concerns,

[50] National Assembly Standing Orders, *supra* note 39, order 244C.

[51] Constitution of Kenya, *supra* note 35, art. 201.

the National Treasury published a draft National Tax Policy described in these terms:

> This Policy sets out broad parameters on tax policy and other tax related matters. It articulates the principles governing tax administration and revenue collection in Kenya. Thus, it provides a set of guidelines that regulate taxation and forms the basis for tax legislation, review, development and administration. It is a vital tool for revenue mobilization to facilitate social and economic development.[52]

In the preamble to the draft Policy document, the Cabinet and Principal Secretaries in charge of the National Treasury go to great lengths to emphasise that the Draft Policy 'has been developed through stakeholders' participation in line with the Constitution requirement with the aim of building consensus on the polices on each tax head' and 'was developed in a consultative and participatory manner in line with the constitutional requirements of public participation and stakeholder engagement'.[53] Further, via a Public Notice in printed media and online, the National Treasury, citing Article 201 of the Constitution, invited 'the public and private sector institutions as well as individuals to submit inputs/comments on the National Tax Policy, for consideration before finalization of the policy'.[54] The Kenya Revenue Authority similarly regularly publishes public notices inviting the public and stakeholders to submit their comments on proposed subsidiary legislation,[55] tax regulations,[56] and administrative changes such as the implementation of Excise Stamps[57] or the introduction of a new Tax Invoice Management System.[58] It is evident, therefore, that the Constitution's requirement for openness, accountability, and public deliberation in public finance is influencing culture and practice in government, and the executive is aware that it needs to demonstrate that it has taken steps to engage citizens in government decision-making that involves public finance.

[52] The National Treasury and Planning, *National Tax Policy*, 1 (2022), www.treasury.go.ke/wp-content/uploads/2022/07/DRAFT-NATIONAL-TAX-POLICY-16.06.-2022-.pdf.

[53] Id., at ii–iii.

[54] The National Treasury and Planning, *Public Notice: Request for Comments on the Draft National Tax Policy*, (2022), www.treasury.go.ke/wp-content/uploads/2022/07/Draft-National-Tax-Policy-Public-Notice.pdf.

[55] Kenya Revenue Authority, *Public Notice: Extension of the Deadline for Submission of Comments on the Draft Excise Duty (Amendment) Regulations*, 2023, https://kra.go.ke/news-center/public-notices/1919-extension-of-the-deadline-for-submission-of-comments-on-the-draft-excise-duty-amendment-regulations,-2023 (last visited 18 Jan. 2024).

[56] Kenya Revenue Authority, *Public Notice: Public Participation Forums for Proposed Tax Regulations*, (2019), www.kra.go.ke/news-center/public-notices/656-public-participation-forums-for-proposed-tax-regulations (last visited 18 Jan. 2024).

[57] Kenya Revenue Authority, *Public Notice: Invitation to a Stakeholder Engagement on the Rollout of Excise Stamps for Cosmetics and Beauty Products*, https://kra.go.ke/news-center/public-notices/1939-invitation-to-a-stakeholder-engagement-on-the-rollout-of-excise-stamps-for-cosmetics-and-beauty-products (last visited 19 Jan. 2024).

[58] Kenya Revenue Authority (@KRACorporate), Twitter, https://twitter.com/kracorporate/status/1120602745155784704?lang = bn.

The View from the Courts

The judicial position on public deliberation on tax matters and what constitutes adequate public participation in taxation is less than clear. The earliest landmark decision on the issue of public participation in public-finance legislation concerned the enactment of a Finance Act at the county rather than the national level. While this chapter is primarily concerned with tax matters at the national level; the decision in *Robert N. Gakuru & others v Governor Kiambu County & 3 others* is nonetheless of importance and significant influence. The High Court judge was called upon to determine, *inter alia*, whether the Kiambu Finance Act, 2013, was passed with sufficient public participation as required by the Constitution of Kenya, 2010. Acknowledging the central role that public participation plays in the legislative and policy functions of the Government at the National or County level, Justice Odunga, in his judgement, found that no public participation as contemplated under the Constitution and the County Governments Act, 2012 had occurred and articulately stated[59]:

> In my view to huddle a few people in a 5-star hotel on one day cannot by any stretch of imagination be termed as public participation for the purposes of meeting constitutional and legislative threshold. Whereas the magnitude of the publicity required may depend from one action to another, a one day newspaper advertisement in a country such as ours where a majority of the populace survive on less than a dollar per day and to whom newspapers are a luxury leave alone the level of illiteracy in some parts of this country may not suffice for the purposes of seeking public views and public participation.[60]

Although the respondents in that case argued that, since the people of Kiambu County had delegated to the County Assembly the task of legislating and formulating policy, the actions taken by the members of the Assembly ought to be taken to reflect the intentions of the residents of the County, Justice Odunga held that this view could not be correct considering the explicit constitutional and legislative provisions regarding public participation in legislative and policy decisions.

However, in another decision,[61] the petitioner unsuccessfully challenged the constitutionality of a provision of the Value Added Tax Act,[62] on the basis that there had been insufficient public participation. The court held that the National Assembly had sought and received written memoranda from the relevant

[59] Gakuru v. Governor Kiambu County, Constitutional Petition No.532 of 2013 (Consolidated with Petition NOS. 12 of 2014, 35, 36 of 2014, 42 of 2014, & 72 of 2014 and Judicial Review Miscellaneous Application No. 1 of 2014) (2014) eKLR, http://kenyalaw.org/caselaw/cases/view/97000/.

[60] Id., para. 76.

[61] Association of Kenya Insurers (AKI) v. Kenya Revenue Authority; Insurance Regulatory Authority (IRA) & another (Interested Parties), High Court Petition No 201 of 2020 (2021) KEHC 402 (KLR), http://kenyalaw.org/caselaw/cases/view/225727/.

[62] Paragraph 10 of part II of the First Schedule to the Value Added Tax Act as amended by the Tax Laws (Amendment) Act, 2020.

stakeholders before the enactment of the Act and that 'the law was not that all persons had to express their views or that they had to be heard and that the hearing had to be oral . . . that the proposed legislation had to be brought to each and every person wherever the person could be. What was required was that reasonable steps be taken to facilitate the participation.'

In *Matindi v CS, National Treasury & Planning & 4 others*,[63] a petition challenging the tax implications[64] of an inter-country agreement between Kenya and Japan,[65] the petitioner challenged the decision of the National Assembly's Committee on Delegated Legislation to classify the Agreement as not being a statutory instrument[66] and thus not subject to public participation.[67] The government's position, as explained by the respondents, was that the Legal Notice was made pursuant to the Cabinet Secretary's powers in respect of delegation legislation under the Income Tax Act and not a statutory instrument requiring public participation and that public participation was not necessary as the matter involved an understanding between two governments, that is, a matter of foreign policy. Apart from ruling that the Cabinet Secretary had no constitutional power to grant a blanket tax waiver without the matter going through the usual process of legislation, that is, that this was a case of unconstitutionality by virtue of excessive delegation, the judge also held that the Legal Notice ought to have been treated as a statutory instrument and subjected to public participation. Therefore, the National Assembly Committee had erred in its decision to exempt the Legal Notice from the public participation requirement. On that basis, the court declared the Legal Notice unconstitutional, quashed it, and directed that the income tax covered by the Legal Notice was collectable from the date of the judgment.

More recently, two important cases on public participation in the budget process at the national level came up for determination in the High Court, and the seemingly contradictory decisions have introduced some ambiguity in the law and there is now uncertainty regarding the constitutionality of amendments introduced into the Finance Bill at later stages of the legislative process.

Mwaura Kabata

In *Mwaura Kabata & Others v National Assembly & Others*,[68] the petitioners challenged the constitutionality of the Finance Act 2022 and some of its provisions.

[63] Matindi v. CS, National Treasury & Planning, Constitutional Petition No. E280 of 2021 (2023) KEHC 1144 (KLR), http://kenyalaw.org/caselaw/cases/view/252017/.

[64] The effect of the Legal Notice was to exempt from income tax all the income which would accrue or be derived from Kenya by Japanese companies, Japanese consultants, and Japanese employees involved in the project under the financing agreement covered by the Legal Notice.

[65] Legal Notice No. 15 of 2021.

[66] Within the meaning of section 2 of the Statutory Instruments Act, No. 23 of 2013.

[67] As required under sections 5 and 51 of the Statutory Instruments Act.

[68] Kabata v. National Assembly; Law Society of Kenya & 16 others (Interested Parties) (Petition E338, E342, 372, 373 & E407 of 2022 (Consolidated)) (2023) KEHC 481, http://kenyalaw.org/caselaw/cases/view/250224/.

The Act came into force on 8 July 2022, with some of its provisions intended to come into effect on 1 January 2023. The facts of the case and the parties' various arguments are quite complicated as the Petition is a consolidation of five different petitions with similar issues and had five petitioners, four respondents, and seventeen interested parties who filed various pleadings and written submissions. Consequently, various issues were up for determination by the court, but of relevance to this chapter is whether the Finance Act 2022 and the impugned sections set out in the Petition and imposition of excise duty at the rate of 10 per cent on imported cellular mobile phones and imported SIM cards were subjected to public participation and if so whether they were constitutional.

The Petitioners' central argument was that, although they accepted that the Finance Bill had been subjected to extensive public participation, they also contended that, after that public participation process but prior to the enactment of the Finance Act 2022, the first respondent, the National Assembly, introduced new amendments to the Finance Bill which were not subjected to public participation. The Petitioners argued that those amendments had far-reaching consequences and ought to have been subjected to deliberation by the relevant stakeholders and the general public. The Respondents[69] counter-argued that: (a) The Memorandum of objects and reasons for the Finance Bill had made clear the purpose of the Bill, and the legislature was empowered to introduce amendments to the Finance Bill as long as it kept with the object of the law; (b) the National Assembly was mandated by the Constitution through legislation to enact tax laws with an aim of raising the nation's revenue; and (c) the Finance Act 2022 enjoyed the presumption of constitutionality and that the petitioners' prayers were offensive to the principle of separation of powers.

While acknowledging the legislature's obligation to ensure public participation in its legislative functions, the judge rejected the petitioners' argument on the basis that the contentious amendments introduced at the Committee Stage of the legislative process did not change the subject matter of the Bill by introducing a different topic, expand its subject, nor was it inconsistent with any part of the Bill already agreed to. In his view:

> Unquestionably, new amendments can be introduced to a Bill under consideration after the First reading so long as the amendment is in line with the original intent of the purposes and objects of the Bill. In my view the whole purpose and intent of the Finance Bill was to [amendment] tax laws which were specifically listed for avoidance of doubt. All the cited impugned amendments fell within the scope of this bracket and hence cannot be deemed to have been new introductions contrary to the purposes and objects of the Bill.[70]

69 The National Assembly, the Attorney General, the Kenya Revenue Authority, and the Cabinet Secretary National Treasury & Planning Ministry.

70 Kabata v. National Assembly; Law Society of Kenya & 16 others (Interested Parties) (Petition E338, E342, 372, 373 & E407 of 2022 (Consolidated)), *supra* note 68, para. 116.

Concluding that Standing Order 133 (5) and (6) allowed such amendments without the need for further public deliberation, the impugned amendments were in line with what had been subjected to public deliberation and the scope of the Finance Bill, and that the appropriate legislative process as set out under the National Assembly's Standing Orders had therefore been followed, the judge held that the impugned provisions did not violate the principle of public participation and were not unconstitutional.

The Association of Gaming Operators of Kenya

The petitioners in *Judith Kangu Kiragu, Daniel Masi Mogeni and Nickson Mwangi Maina (suing as representatives of The Association of Gaming Operators of Kenya) v The Attorney General & Others*[71] challenged the constitutionality of specific provisions in the Finance Act 2021 on very similar grounds to the Mwaura Kabata case – that the contentious provisions were introduced as amendments to the Finance Bill 2021 – after the conclusion of the public participation process, but before the enactment of the Act. The Petitioners' main argument was that the Finance Bill 2021 had proposed the imposition of Excise Duty on betting at 20 per cent of the amount wagered or staked and that proposal had been submitted to public deliberation; however, the Finance Act, 2021 subsequently not only introduced the proposed tax on betting but extended the tax to gaming and lotteries and the latter had not been subjected to the public deliberation process.

The court held that the impugned provisions were 'constitutionally infirm' because they offended the principles of fair administrative action and public participation in public finance as set out in the Constitution 2010.[72] The court also noted that public participation in policymaking requires that policymakers actively seek and consider the views of those most affected by a policy decision. Unlike the court in the Mwaura Kabata decision, the court held that, given the robust representations made during the public deliberation process for the proposed taxes in the Finance Bill 2021, the subsequent amendments were not minor but were substantive amendments that required the National Assembly to return to the public deliberation process.[73]

These two conflicting decisions from the High Court, on very similar facts and legal arguments, have introduced ambiguity in the law regarding the constitutionality of amendments introduced into the Finance Bill at later stages of the legislative process, after the conclusion of public deliberation processes by the relevant Parliamentary committee. In both cases, the courts faced the onerous tax of balancing between citizens' right to the constitutionally protected principle of public

[71] Kiragu v. The Attorney General, Nairobi High Court Constitutional Petition No. E406 of 2021, Unreported.

[72] Id., para. 140.

[73] Id., para. 129.

participation and the need for the National Assembly to carry out its legislative function without excessive constraint. Unfortunately, the courts reached different conclusions on where the balance lies. Therefore, to protect the sanctity of public deliberation in tax matters, it now falls to either the National Assembly to address the issue through legislation, or for the Court of Appeal or the Supreme Court to issue a clarifying and binding decision on appeal or a future case on similar facts.

BEYOND TRANSFORMATIVE CONSTITUTIONALISM: TAXING CITIZENS IN THE NEXT 100 YEARS

Having demonstrated that the constitutionally protected public deliberation principle enables citizens to play their role in tax state-building, in this concluding section, the focus shifts to potential areas of weakness in the implementation of the public deliberation principle that may limit the extent to which public deliberation mechanisms become and remain transparent and inclusive processes in future decades. It is insufficient to have public deliberations mechanisms merely to avoid offending the Constitution; the mechanisms need to be meaningful and progressively transform state culture. In the words of Mahomed, Ag. JA in the Namibian case of *S v Acheson*:

> The constitution of a nation is not simply a statute which mechanically defines the structures of government and the relations between the government and the governed. It is a mirror reflecting the national soul, the identification of the ideals and aspirations of a nation; the articulation of the values bonding its people and disciplining its government. The spirit and the tenor of the constitution must therefore preside and permeate . . .[74]

In order to set up effective public deliberation initiatives, there is a need to balance the dual objectives of this constitutionally protected process. On the one hand, public deliberation ought to contribute to the building of a tax state and reinforce notions of belonging and citizenship. On the other hand, it also ought to act as an early warning system, through the early identification of effective policy objectives as well as potential loopholes or challenges in implementing tax legislation.

The Danger of Tick-Box Exercises

Public deliberation will only be an effective mechanism for facilitating citizens' role in tax state-building if it is meaningful, genuine, and serves the intended purpose. Justice Odunga rightly states that 'public participation ought to be real and not

[74] S v. Acheson, 1991 (2) South Africa Law Reports 805 (Namibia High Court) 813.

illusory and ought not to be treated as a mere formality for the purposes of fulfilment of the Constitutional dictates'.[75]

Several factors put public deliberation in public finance at risk of becoming a tick-box exercise. First, sometimes it is unclear what the state institutions need the public deliberation process to achieve; is public deliberation intended to provide a way of affecting the legislative agenda or simply to provide an avenue for reactions, however limited, to policy and legislative initiatives? For instance, in May 2022, the National Assembly Committee on Finance and National Planning, while considering the Kenya Revenue Authority (Amendment) Bill,[76] initiated a public participation process by inviting memoranda from the public through advertisements in the print media and written invitations to stakeholders.[77] The Committee's Report describes the objective of the Act:

> To amend the Kenya Revenue Authority Act, 1995 by changing the name 'Kenya Revenue Authority' to 'Kenya Revenue Service' accordingly. The public perception of the use of the word 'Authority' is that the word connotes a commandeering body rather than a friendly service-oriented institution. In this regard, the change of name is intended to rebrand the Authority in transforming its public image and thus enhancing tax compliance ... by maintaining a clear focus on taxpayers needs and rights. The Bill is also intended to delete the words 'Minister' and 'Permanent Secretary' and replace them with 'Cabinet Secretary' and 'Principal Secretary', in line with the terms used in the Constitution.[78]

The Bill, therefore, made no substantive amendments to the Act it sought to amend; all the amendments involved replacing one word with another. The Committee received only two memoranda from two stakeholders: the National Treasury and Planning department, in essence providing further support for the Bill, and a private tax advisory firm proposing significant substantive amendments to the Bill by suggesting new provisions on taxpayer rights, taxpayer education, the use of technology, dispute resolution, public participation, and misconduct. The National Treasury's memorandum required no response or resolution as it proposed nothing new. However, the second and more substantive memorandum was considered and rejected by the Committee as 'the proposal by Ernest and Martin Associates were expanding the Bill beyond its scope, contrary to National Assembly Standing Order No. 133 (5)'.[79]

75 Gakuru v. Governor Kiambu County, Constitutional Petition No.532 of 2013 (Consolidated with Petition NOS. 12 of 2014, 35, 36 of 2014, 42 of 2014, & 72 of 2014 and Judicial Review Miscellaneous Application No. 1 of 2014), *supra* note 59, para. 75.

76 National Assembly Bill No. 24 of 2022.

77 Twelfth Parliament – Sixth Session – 2022 Departmental Committee on Finance and National Planning, *Report on the Kenya Revenue Authority (Amendment) Bill (National Assembly Bill No. 24 of 2022)*, 10 (2022).

78 Id., foreword.

79 Id., at 10.

While the Committee was correct in its observations and decisions, the proposed substantive amendments arguably were not irrelevant; rebranding the Revenue Authority by transforming its public image into an entity concerned with taxpayer rights and needs will likely require much more than a name change. That notwithstanding, it is essential to ask what the Committee intended to achieve with this public deliberation exercise, in light of the very narrow scope of the Bill; was it a good use of parliamentary time and resources or the time and resources of stakeholders or was the Committee simply ticking the constitutional compliance box? The repeated performance of public participation exercises places the principle at risk of becoming meaningless and perfunctory.

Second, in some instances, state institutions fail to consider, either deliberately, for political expediency, or inadvertently, how to maximise the usefulness of the public deliberation process to produce a meaningful outcome. For instance, in September 2020, the National Assembly Committee on Finance and National Planning, while considering the Agreement between the Republic of Kenya and the Republic of Mauritius on the Avoidance of Double Taxation,[80] initiated a public participation process by inviting memoranda from the public by placing an advertisement in the print media.[81] A previous attempt to ratify an earlier version of the Double Taxation Agreement had failed following a High Court decision nullifying the agreement because the State had failed to follow the appropriate legal channels for ratification of the Treaty.[82] The National Treasury, after amending some provisions of the Treaty, made a second attempt at ratification, and it was this revised version that came up for consideration before the Committee.

The Committee received memoranda from three stakeholders: the National Treasury and Planning department who, in essence, provided further support for the Bill; the Tax Justice Network–Africa challenging various Articles of the Treaty and proposing amendments aimed at preventing future treaty abuse; and a private citizen seeking amendments to the provisions dealing with withholding tax rates on interest, royalties, and income not dealt with in the Treaty. The National Treasury's memorandum required no response or resolution as it proposed nothing new. However, the second and third memoranda proposing substantive amendments were considered and rejected by the Committee, which noted that it 'could not make any amendments to the Agreement because it was submitted under the Statutory Instruments Act, 2013 and therefore the Committee recommends that

80 National Assembly Committee on Finance and National Planning, Legal Notice No. 114 of 2020.

81 Twelfth Parliament – Fourth Session – 2020 Departmental Committee on Finance and National Planning, *Report on the Consideration of the Agreement between the Republic of Kenya and the Republic of Mauritius on the Avoidance of Double Taxation (Legal Notice No. 114 of 2020)*, 11 (2020).

82 Daisy Ogembo, *The Tax Justice Network–Africa v Cabinet Secretary for National Treasury & 2 Others: A Big Win for Tax Justice Activism?*, Brit. Tax Rev. 105 (2019).

the law be amended so that future Double Taxation Agreements be considered under the Treaty Making and Ratification Act (No 45 of 2012)'.[83]

The Committee's conclusion and its purported legal inability to make amendments to the Treaty strongly suggest that the entire public deliberation exercise was a mere farce, lacking in meaning or purpose. The National Assembly ought to have been aware, when the Treaty was presented for ratification, that the law prevented it from effectively discharging its obligations and taken the steps required to ensure that it did not participate in a meaningless public participation exercise. In any event, the insistence that a legislative amendment is required to bring Double Taxation Agreements within the purview of the Treaty Making and Ratification Act is debatable and has been questioned.[84]

Third, in other instances, legal loopholes may result in the backdoor reversal of the efficacy of public deliberation exercises. For instance, the two conflicting High Court decisions discussed in The View from the Courts section demonstrate that, while citizens are empowered to participate in the budget process through public deliberation mechanisms at earlier stages of the budget process, legal ambiguities or different interpretations of the parliamentary procedure mean that the Finance Bill can be amended after the conclusion of the public deliberation process but before the enactment of the Finance Act. The result of this scenario is that provisions with far-reaching tax consequences that were not subjected to public participation and stakeholder input may very well find their way into the Finance Act.

If public deliberation is to continue to facilitate citizens' effective role in tax state-building in Kenya, there is a need to address these issues. As the Supreme Court of Kenya has appropriately stated, in setting out the parameters for appropriate public participation as envisaged in the Constitution, public participation is not an abstract notion; it must be purposive and meaningful.[85]

Implications of the Limited Role of the Senate in Public Finance

As previously mentioned, the Kenyan Senate can only entertain a money bill if that bill affects the finances of county governments. Thus, because all bills with provisions dealing with taxes are considered money bills, the Senate lacks the jurisdiction to exercise oversight over the National Assembly's decisions on taxation at the national level. This limited role has significant implications because of the major difference between how voting takes place in the National Assembly and the Senate. To ensure greater equity, voting in the Kenyan Senate is carried out by County

83 Twelfth Parliament – Fourth Session – 2020 Departmental Committee on Finance and National Planning, *supra* note 81, at 15.

84 Ogembo, *supra* note 82, at 114.

85 British American Tobacco Kenya Limited v. Cabinet Secretary for the Ministry of Health; Kenya Tobacco Control Alliance & another (Interested Parties) Supreme Court of Kenya Petition No. 5 of 2017 (2019) eKLR, http://kenyalaw.org/caselaw/cases/view/185959/#.

delegation rather than by majority, ensuring that each County has one vote regardless of population. Thus, the Senate is a House of compromise and negotiation because it is much harder to pass legislation, and communities are forced to compromise with each other. In comparison, the National Assembly is characterised by majoritarian rule where each constituency has one vote; constituency boundaries are demarcated by population, giving populous communities greater voting power. Accordingly, the Senate benefits from vote moderation of majority groups and produces more equitable decisions.

The fact that the Senate has no legislative role in national tax legislation-making is a considerable loss. Such oversight would be beneficial in instances where the National Assembly has failed to engage in meaningful public participation or has erred in its failure to adopt useful memoranda submitted by the public during public deliberation. It would also be useful where the National Assembly's decisions on tax matters are not sufficiently influenced by public deliberation exercises and are, instead, too heavily influenced by the executive or by one or two ethnic communities because the ruling party has an overwhelming majority in the National Assembly. As Ogembo articulately points out:

> The executive has turned public deliberation into a smokescreen to hide its influence over elected legislators, often offering them public goods in exchange for ensuring that public deliberation is derailed, or the interests of the executive dominate final outcomes.[86]

In such instances, a legislative role for the Senate may enhance or better protect citizens' role in tax state-building through public deliberation rather than leaving it all up to the National Assembly.

The Risk of Too Much Litigation

The Constitution of Kenya, 2010 has given citizens an unprecedented opportunity to challenge the decisions made by state institutions, and a cursory search for case law on public participation in the Kenya Law Reports online database produces a plethora of court decisions on this constitutional principle. While active litigation on the principle is incredibly useful to entrench it in jurisprudence, refine its parameters, and provide much-needed guidance for state institutions, too much litigation can limit the effectiveness of public participation if it leads to public participation becoming merely performative in a bid to avoid litigation. Some level of organic development of the principle would allow it to truly become part of the governance culture and promote a sense of ownership and participation over these processes by citizens.

[86] Ogembo, *supra* note 3, at 329.

The Role of Civil Society and Corporations

A cursory look at the reports of the National Assembly's Committee of Finance and National Planning and the Budgets and Appropriations Committee reveals that, by far, most stakeholders responding to calls for memoranda during public participation exercises are civil society groups, corporations, and industry alliances or lobby groups. There are some representations made by members of the public, but these are in the minority. There are many explanations for this phenomenon, both historical and contemporary, including citizen apathy and doubts about the effectiveness of these public deliberation mechanisms.

A significant factor, which Ogembo refers to as 'gatekeeping by interest groups', is that members of the public rarely have the resources, knowledge, technical expertise, and time that these more prominent stakeholders have to:

> sustain continuous engagement with committee staff and legislators but they are also able to critically engage with the complex and large amounts of data often presented by committees for public deliberation. Organised groups often have staff who not only have the time to read and prepare technical submissions for the committee but are also often trained in lobbying and can provide well-articulated memorandums to committee staff using familiar legislative terminology.[87]

Thus, these interest groups will likely dominate public participation exercises over time and either trigger suspicion and disengagement by legislators or displace private citizens who attempt to participate as the voices of these often-powerful interest groups begin to appear louder, more organised, and more convincing.[88] If state institutions do not take deliberate steps to empower, inform, encourage, and facilitate ordinary citizens so that they can effectively and meaningfully engage in public deliberation exercises, the role of citizens in tax state-building will be jeopardised.

CONCLUSION

This chapter has traced the role of citizens in tax state-building from the colonial state, where that role was utterly absent, to the limited role of citizens in tax state-building in the post-colonial state, and, ultimately, the drastic shift in state–citizen relations following the enactment of the Constitution of Kenya in 2010 and the enhancements in citizens' role in tax state-building. The colonial legacy of control (or authoritarian rule) and lack of accountability by an all-powerful executive that carried on into the post-colonial era laid the foundation for the clamour for a constitution that better captured the will of Kenyans and the rules, principles, and values that they desired to see in their governance. Undeniably, Kenya's

87 Id., at 337.
88 Id., at 338.

2010 Constitution has and will continue to shape the taxation of citizens well into the next century; the Constitution also provides a crucial opportunity for citizens to play a role in state-building through their participation in tax policy, administration, and legislative processes through public deliberation processes. While the Constitution has provided an impressive legal framework for public deliberation, the final section of this chapter demonstrates that there are still significant obstacles to overcome in implementing public deliberation in tax matters if progress is to be made in ensuring citizens play their rightful role in tax state-building.

9

A Century of Labor and Taxation

Diane M. Ring

INTRODUCTION

Contemplating the interplay of labor and taxation over the next 100 years asks that we entertain a question whose scope is vast, makes predictions, and forecasts evolving economic, labor, political, and social trends. Despite these challenges, we can already see the potential for labor-related shifts and their importance for society and taxation. Beginning the daunting task – of identifying evolving trends and issues, highlighting trade-offs and risks, and exploring shorter- and longer-term policy changes – should not be delayed. Inevitably some analyses will miss the mark, but the project of taking the intersection of labor and taxation seriously over the coming century should not be postponed.

It is easy to imagine the prospect of shifting work patterns. In the two decades preceding the COVID-19 pandemic, some workers began witnessing shifts in the ways in which their work could be performed. Changes in work location, task execution, and hiring process were evident in: (1) the increased ability to perform work at a location distant from the hiring business, client, or anyone connected to either; (2) the use of technology to collaborate through data management systems, shared technology, and other platforms; and (3) the use of platforms and apps to find, hire, and pay those doing work. Of course, the degree of change varied across fields, jobs, and countries. That said, the phenomenon was notable, and the subject of policy, regulatory, and academic inquiry in many jurisdictions. Although some tax issues affected businesses, many impacted workers themselves. Fast forward through a global pandemic, and these workforce trends have, in many cases, accelerated.[1] This acceleration reflects the forced structuring of where work takes

I would like to thank Judith Freedman for her insightful comments and observations on this chapter. I would also like to thank my research assistants Nina Kim and Kristion Green for providing much valued research into evolving labor and technology practices.

[1] See generally Cevat Giray Aksoy et al., *Working from Home around the World* (NBER Working Paper No. 30446, 1-4, Sep. 2022) (reviewing work-from-home trends across 27 countries during

place – that is, not in the office, but remotely at the worker's own location. The shared pandemic experience demanded a widespread and rapid adoption of technology that simultaneously expanded options for when and where work would take place. Although flexibility was not unlimited, certain workers were no longer confined to performing work at the office during the traditional 9 to 5. Finally, platform and app-based work saw expanded markets for their services.

How many of the trends accelerated during the pandemic will permanently reshape work? What other emerging workforce trends will complicate the picture? The rapid attention given to artificial intelligence starting in 2023 hints at a dramatic, though yet to be established, re-ordering of how and by whom work is accomplished. We may see some tentative answers to these questions in the coming years, but long-term results will likely be fully apparent only after many decades. Regardless of the details, sufficiently strong shifts have taken place and countries will need to take account in their tax systems of these transformations.

This chapter proceeds in four parts: The first part reviews major trends in work that, although present before the pandemic, gained a powerful foothold during the pandemic and remain critical features of the work landscape today. The next section identifies and discusses tax issues posed by these workforce shifts and the resulting implications for governments and society. These include: (1) income-tax design issues, such as needed changes to the treatment of home-office deductions and commuting expenses, (2) classification status for workers as employees or independent contractors, and (3) defining nexus to tax in a world of internationally mobile workers. The following section considers how workforce shifts may introduce collateral effects, raising questions about tax revenues, the stability of the tax base, and changing tax burdens. The final section concludes and considers how changes in work intersect with other important developments, particularly AI and climate change, that are poised to shape the next century.

CONTEMPORARY WORK TRENDS

Over the past 100 years, the contours of work in many industrialized economies have undergone gradual, and in some cases rapid, changes. Looking back a century to 1924 would present some familiar features – employees of large and small businesses, sole proprietors, household labor, and work being performed full and part-time. A notable difference was that the income tax system was not yet a major feature in the lives of most workers; it was less than a decade old in the United States and only beginning to take full form globally. Also absent were social insurance taxes (Social

2021 and 2022), www.nber.org/system/files/working_papers/w30446/w30446.pdf; Kim Parker, About a third of US Workers Who Can Work from Home Now Do So All the Time, Pew Research Center (Mar. 30, 2023), www.pewresearch.org/short-reads/2023/03/30/about-a-third-of-us-workers-who-can-work-from-home-do-so-all-the-time/.

Security and Medicare taxes in the United States) that were soon to be, for those jurisdictions implementing them, a critical component in the taxation of work and the path toward some degree of retirement security.

Pre-Pandemic Work

Almost a century later, just before the COVID-19 pandemic, markedly new features in the shape of work were beginning to appear. The same technological developments in information systems that facilitated globalization and the opening of the world's economies starting in the 1970s and 1980s were now introducing new features into the performance of work itself. Expanding use of computers and related technology in the workplace began to offer the prospect of performing work outside the office. Deregulation of airlines brought a reduction in the cost of air travel that changed how businesses thought about distance.

In countries such as the United States, attention focused on job losses triggered by the above intersecting forces. Some jobs were offshored, not just in manufacturing, but in other service areas, where lower labor costs proved attractive and distance could be shrunk by communications technology. Examples include not only the ubiquitous offshore call centers, but also offshore back-office functions, some of which operated in close collaboration with personnel in the US corporate headquarters.[2]

Technology in the early twenty-first century also enabled the rise of platform-based business activities that allow workers to connect with ease to customers, clients, and businesses. Prominent examples include rideshare and delivery businesses, short-term labor platforms, field-specific platforms,[3] as well as virtual storefronts, such as Etsy, that permit individuals who produce goods to connect with the entire internet of potential customers. The value of these changes for workers and the impact on their lives are debated, not uniform, and subject to further assessment. That these trends had major impacts is not debatable.

Pandemic Shifts

The dramatic arrival of the COVID-19 pandemic in spring 2020 first halted and then quickly and drastically re-shaped the performance of much work. Some key services

[2] See, e.g., Mary Amiti & Shang-Jin Wei, *Service Offshoring and Productivity Evidence from the United States* (NBER Working Paper No. 11926, Jan. 2006), www.nber.org/system/files/working_papers/w15287/w15287.pdf (estimating effects of offshoring "growing in response to new technologies"); Alan S. Blinder & Alan B. Krueger, *Alternative Measures of Offshorability: A Survey Approach* (NBER Working Paper No. 15287, Aug. 2009), www.nber.org/system/files/working_papers/w15287/w15287.pdf (assessing the degree to which various jobs were candidates for offshoring).

[3] See *infra* Commuting Costs section (examining platforms for nursing gig work).

had to be provided in person – including medical, public safety such as policing and fire-fighting, food production and distribution, public transportation, and delivery services – these jobs were labeled essential work functions. For other functions, businesses and employers rolled out plans for continuing operations remotely. Central to this shift was the expectation that workers would have access to technology (computers/laptops/cameras), adequate Wi-Fi connectivity, and be sufficiently computer savvy to use communication applications and programs including Zoom, Microsoft Teams, Slack, and a host of shared document programs at home. In some cases, businesses provided the required equipment; in others, workers provided it entirely or supplemented it to make their home setup more conducive to effective performance of their job. Success in working from home varied greatly both by function and by individual workers. For example, many lawyers quickly transitioned to conducting online research at home rather than at the office, and they met with clients, counterparties, and courts on Zoom. In contrast, kindergarten classes conducted by teachers via Zoom ultimately and unsurprisingly proved unsuccessful, although many teachers worked creatively to draw their remote students into the life of the online classroom. Telemedicine, which in varying degrees had been developing pre-pandemic, became widespread for those medical issues not requiring in-person testing or treatment.

Not only did significant segments of the workforce turn to technology to enable work from home, they similarly turned to technology to continue relationships with those outside their household, including family and friends. This simultaneous, global adoption of technology was the kind of sweeping, immediate, and dramatic shift in the basic structure of work that would have been difficult to replicate exclusively through business-driven efforts at restructuring work and ramping up adoption of new technologies. A crisis on the scale of a global pandemic or war[4] would be an expected predicate for such change.

The fact that this shift occurred during a pandemic meant that workers did not just leave the office to work at home. In many cases, sometimes driven by pandemic health-related concerns, they also moved their home – whether to live with relatives outside of a city, to surrender their apartment and move to a less urban or otherwise more appealing destination, or in the case of wealthier workers – to acquire a second home. Regardless of the precise reason or new location, the effect was the same: many workers were not just at home, they had moved their home base physically farther from work. Daily commuting from these new locations into the office, if and when it would be requested, would typically be impracticable or undesirable for these workers.

[4] For example, the rapid shift in the place of women in the workforce during World War II was pervasive in those countries actively engaged in the war. See, e.g., Claudia D. Goldin, *The Role of World War II in the Rise of Women's Employment*, 81(4) Am. Econ. Rev. 741 (Sept. 1991).

Digital-platform work, particularly in the delivery sector, gained significant traction during the pandemic. Individuals uncomfortable with public exposure or unable to venture out to stores, restaurants, and grocers, turned to delivery services accessed via digital platforms and phone apps as an alternative, even if they had not done so pre-pandemic. Online seller Amazon reported tremendous volume and hired extensively during the pandemic.[5]

Post-Pandemic Work Trends

As we move into 2025 and beyond, we are beginning to see ways in which the features that characterized much work at the height of the pandemic are morphing in the post-pandemic economy.

The Office

In some sectors, workers have almost entirely returned to the office. Examples include courts and education (from kindergarten through university), although the availability of online education options will likely prove an enduring addition to the education landscape. But in most sectors, the results are mixed and vary even by employer. Businesses have taken a range of positions on return to the office: (1) insisting it will be required; (2) relenting and exploring delayed timetables; (3) embracing hybrid work schedules with a certain number of days in office (which may or may not be dictated); and (4) continuing to embrace work-from-home arrangements. The calculus in reaching these determinations incorporates multiple factors: (1) cost savings from reduced office space; (2) loss of informal training and mentoring; (3) ability to collaborate effectively; (4) challenges in integrating new workers; (5) ability to attract desired workforce; and (6) productivity. Notably in the United States, the federal government had been especially slow to require a return to the office for its own employees. In April 2023, the US Office of Management and Budget (within the Executive Office of the President) issued a memorandum to the heads of executive departments and agencies stating that "agencies will develop updated Work Environment Plans ... [and that] [i]t is the expectation that as part of these assessments agencies will continue to substantially increase meaningful in-person work at Federal offices, particularly at headquarters and equivalents, while still using flexible operation policies as an important tool in talent recruitment and retention."[6]

5 See, e.g., Karen Weise, *Pushed by Pandemic, Amazon Goes on a Hiring Spree without Equal*, N.Y. Times (Nov. 27, 2020), www.nytimes.com/2020/11/27/technology/pushed-by-pandemic-amazon-goes-on-a-hiring-spree-without-equal.html.

6 Shalanda D. Young, Memorandum for the Heads of Executives Departments and Agencies (Off. of Mgmt and Budget, Exec. of the President Apr. 13, 2023), www.whitehouse.gov/wp-content/uploads/2023/04/M-23-15.pdf.

No single or uniform approach to location of work will emerge. Although initially some observers projected a complete shift to remote work in many fields, the reality is that determination of the location in which work will be performed has become yet another point of negotiation between businesses and workers. The ability to work remotely in some jobs, which was possible pre-pandemic, became dramatically more realistic during the pandemic. Thus, remote work is an option that will remain on the table as workers and businesses continue to negotiate and navigate the terms and conditions. That said, it seems probable that a baseline in which workers are in the office perhaps three or four days a week, and remote one or two days could be established in some firms or sectors. Where truly remote work is possible, new hires may be found far beyond the metropolitan boundaries of the business, and maybe beyond international borders and across continents.

Platforms

Just as the pandemic drove widespread adoption of technologies such as Zoom, it expanded the pool of users of platforms and related features. Even as individuals may be reducing their use of on-line shopping and platform delivery services post-pandemic,[7] the user base has grown overall compared to pre-pandemic.[8] Implicitly, this trend means that a significant number of workers will be engaged in delivery (at least until that step becomes automated).

WORKFORCE TAXATION ISSUES AND IMPLICATIONS

These workplace trends create a range of primary and secondary tax challenges for national and subnational governments. The challenges are not novel, but the trend accelerations place greater pressure on governments to evaluate: (1) design details within tax systems, (2) coordination with other jurisdictions, and (3) choice of taxing tools.

Income Tax Design

Income tax rules currently operating in most countries reflect a vision of workers and their activities that is increasingly dated. This is particularly true in three contexts: general worker deductions, worker classification, and treatment of commuting.

[7] In spring 2023, Amazon announced two series of layoffs (18,000 employees and then 9,000). During the pandemic, their workforce doubled – to nearly 1.5 million – as consumers stayed home and purchased online, but, by 2023, demand declined as the pandemic receded. See, e.g., Sebastian Herrera & Joseph De Avila, *Amazon to Cut 9,000 More Jobs after Earlier Layoffs*, Wall St. J. (Mar. 20, 2023), www.wsj.com/articles/amazon-to-cut-9-000-more-jobs-after-earlier-layoffs-234c3da7.

[8] See, e.g., Norman Shaw et al., *Online Shopping Continuance after COVID-19: A Comparison of Canada, Germany, and the United States*, 69 J. of Retail. Consum. Serv. 103100 (2022) (consumers' online shopping post-pandemic at levels exceeding pre-pandemic), www.ncbi.nlm.nih.gov/pmc/articles/PMC9379614/pdf/main.pdf.

Employee Expenses to Produce Income

Historically, employees in many jurisdictions have had some ability to deduct expenses they incurred for work when those expenses were not reimbursed by their employer.[9] Such expenses ranged from professional fees and home office expenses[10] to job supplies. To qualify, these expenses had to meet the standards governing the deductibility of business expenses generally,[11] and they would not be deductible if deemed personal expenses.[12] Importantly, expenses that satisfied these standards were *not* automatically deductible. Instead, countries traditionally have limited them in various ways, including through the use of caps and floors tied to employee income, denial of expenses thought to serve personal (in addition) to business needs, and the adoption of administratively simplifying flat deductions.

But such limitations need to be reexamined as working from home becomes more common. For many employees who began working from home during the pandemic, the shift entailed a variety of home-office-related costs, many of which were not reimbursed by employers. Those businesses not requiring worker presence in the office may be reducing or eliminating office space and saving on what would have been tax-deductible payments for rent and office equipment. Effectively, these costs are being passed on to employees, who cannot deduct them. Even in the case of businesses that have re-opened their offices and expect employees on-site several days a week, the businesses may downsize and adopt space-sharing arrangements, again reaping savings in terms of rent. Some countries did amend their tax systems to accommodate an increase in employee business expenses, but other countries – notably including the United States – did not. For example, some countries intentionally relaxed requirements for tax deductions in order to allow workers to qualify regardless of classification as employee or independent contractor/self-employed. Germany, for example, permitted employees who shifted to remote work during 2020, 2021, and 2022 to deduct a flat rate of EUR 5 for each calendar day working at home (capped at EUR 600 per calendar year, i.e., a cap on days claimed at 120).[13] But the United States, which unrelatedly introduced increased restrictions

9 For example, US federal or state law may require reimbursement of employees for certain work expenses. See, e.g., CAL. LAB. CODE § 2802 (businesses must reimburse employees for "all necessary expenditures or losses incurred by the employee in direct consequence of the discharge of his or her duties.")

10 US employees must meet special criteria to deduct expenses associated with their home office maintained for the convenience of their employer. I.R.C. § 280A.

11 In the United States, the test is "ordinary and necessary" expenses incurred in the conduct of a trade or business). I.R.C. § 162.

12 I.R.C. § 262 (personal expenditures are not deductible unless specifically authorized by some other provision of the tax law).

13 See PWC, GERMANY: INDIVIDUAL – DEDUCTIONS, TAX NOTES (Dec. 31, 2022), www.taxnotes.com/worldwide-tax-treaties/worldwide-tax-summaries/germany-individual-deductions?highlight=employee%20deduction%20equipment%20%22remote%20work%22.

on employee deductions in 2017, did not suspend these new limitations in light of the pandemic's expanded burdens on employees.

Pre-pandemic, most countries, including the United States, recognized that employees may in some cases incur significant, unreimbursed expenses related to work and that the logic and design of a net income tax warrants their deductibility. Jurisdictions' pre-pandemic restrictions on employees' meaningful ability to deduct those expenses reflected the tax system's effort to monitor the line between business and personal expenses, and the line was often drawn to minimize deductions and reduce the risk that primarily personal expenses would be deducted. Post-pandemic, the real-life boundaries between work and home have become increasingly blurred. In many sectors, it is anticipated that employees will work from home between 20–100% of the time, and current rules on expense deductions will increasingly and inappropriately burden employees saddled with significant work expenses.

Admittedly, there are risks in allowing employees to deduct a wide variety of costs incurred at home. Deductions for equipment such as computers, printers, and related devices may be supporting and encouraging purchases that have significant personal use and would have been made by the taxpayer regardless of the tax deduction or their remote work. Similarly, deductions related to a home office (including portions of mortgage interest, depreciation, utilities, internet, and more) may in reality be subsidizing personal expenditures. But as workers increasingly perform more and more of their work at home, the line-drawing adopted pre-pandemic may tilt too much toward preventing inappropriate deduction of personal expenses. If prior law led employees to regularly bear some work-related costs without tax deduction, we may have accepted that tradeoff as a necessary and reasonable cost of ensuring the deduction was not abused, given the often-limited scale and scope of employee expenditures for work-related costs. But that tradeoff may cease to be reasonable as the dollar amounts at stake become larger and employee outlays occur more frequently.

One possible reaction to the current mismatch between genuine employee expenses and their deductibility under current law is to observe that the lowest wage workers remain working in-person. So perhaps nondeductibility of genuine employee expenses could be viewed as promoting equality. But this position requires accepting an incoherent rule for expenses incurred in producing income[14] as a means of furthering equality, rather than directly addressing inequality through better targeted mechanisms including tax rate changes, income-bracket changes, and expenditure decisions. Additionally, although the lowest-wage workers do not see relief from a reconsideration of employee deductions, remote work is not exclusively the province of extremely high paid employees. For example, survey

[14] It is incoherent both because it measures the net income of remote workers inaccurately and because it may create horizontal inequities between employees and independent contractors (who are generally able to deduct their legitimate business expenses).

data on work from home covering May 2020 through February 2023, as reported by researcher Nicholas Bloom, reveal that university graduates are more likely to report working from home, *but* that the difference was not overwhelming: college graduates reported approximately 38 percent of paid full work days were work from home, whereas respondents with some college or less reported approximately 24 percent.[15]

Going forward, jurisdictions should evaluate their treatment of employees' post-pandemic work expenditures to determine whether the balancing reflected in the tests for deductibility seems fair and consistent with a net income tax in a world in which many employees may be expected to cover a larger share of such costs. Ireland allows deductions for "e-working"[16] for costs such as heat, electricity, and broadband, but not for costs of purchased equipment including computers, printers, or office equipment.[17] Although such limitations prevent significant abuse, they may impose increasing burdens on a growing number of taxpayers who work partly or exclusively from home. Countries could consider a range of tax and non-tax solutions including: (1) requiring employers to provide certain equipment if employees regularly work from home; (2) permitting deduction of a percentage or dollar amount of certain computer equipment or related costs; (3) offering a flat deduction for employees who work from home a certain number of days; and (4) adjusting any of the above rules depending on whether the employer requires work from home or the employer has a certain percentage of workforce working remotely during the year. Not surprisingly, none of these options is ideal or without risk, but the likelihood that pre-pandemic tax rules on the treatment of employee work expenses still strike the right balance is low, and these rules thus warrant examination.

Commuting Costs

Most workers incur some costs in commuting to work. The longstanding approach in the United States[18] has been to deny a deduction for commuting expenses such as the costs of "taking a bus, trolley, subway, or taxi, or driving a car between [the taxpayer's] home and [their] main or regular place of work."[19] These expenses are considered personal and are not deductible even if the distance between work and home is great, or if the taxpayer works during the commute.[20] (Travel undertaken

[15] Nicholas Bloom, *Does Working from Home Have a Future?* IFS Annual Lecture 2023, Slides 13–14, https://ifs.org.uk/sites/default/files/2023-05/Does-working-from-home-have-a-future.pdf.

[16] A phrase used for working from home, also called remote work. See *Working from Home and Tax Relief*, Citizens Information, www.citizensinformation.ie/en/money-and-tax/tax/income-tax-credits-and-reliefs/eworking-and-tax-relief/#:~:text=You%20can%20only%20claim%20for,from%20home%20during%20the%20year) (last updated Jan. 4, 2023).

[17] Id.; see also *Remote Working Relief*, Tax and Duty Manual, Part 05-02-13 (last updated Mar. 2022), www.revenue.ie/en/tax-professionals/tdm/income-tax-capital-gains-tax-corporation-tax/part-05/05-02-13.pdf.

[18] I.R.C. § 162(a); *Travel, Gift, and Car Expenses*, I.R.S. Pub. No. 463, 14 (Feb. 1, 2023), www.irs.gov/pub/irs-pdf/p463.pdf.

[19] Id.

[20] Id.

once the taxpayer arrives at work, for example to visit clients or other worksites, is deductible, but the commute home at the end of the day is not.) Implicitly, the US tax system envisions that workers will reside fairly close to work and that any greater distances are personal choices. Other countries adopt a variety of positions on the deductibility (or exclusion) of commuting costs. Similar to the United States, Australia denies deductions for travel between "home and [the taxpayer's] regular place of work."[21] Germany offers a deduction for certain commuting expenses (the Pendelerpauschale),[22] and Japan permits a commuting allowance to be paid tax-free to employees (capped at the lesser of a specified threshold or actual transportation costs).[23]

Two features of work in the coming years may prove sufficiently common that tax law should re-evaluate the "no commuting deduction" rule and clarify its application in key scenarios.[24] First, the pandemic work restructuring saw many workers performing their duties remotely at their pre-pandemic home. But soon, some workers relocated – to live with family elsewhere, to an existing or newly acquired second/vacation home, or to a permanent new home not in traditional commuting distance to their work. Post-pandemic, to the extent re-located workers do not return to their pre-pandemic residential areas yet remain employed there, or workers accept new positions with employers outside their metropolitan commuting range, several questions emerge: (1) can these workers deduct "commuting costs" if their employers require a minimum on-site presence (e.g., one day a week, or two days every pay period)?, (2) does it matter whether the employer caps the number of days in the office, offers only limited office space for workers, or otherwise embraces a plan of limited in-office work?; (3) what if the employer approves 100 percent remote work with the caveat that occasional presence in the office may be required as dictated by business needs?;[25] and (4) what minimum expectations will a home office be required to satisfy so that travel from that home office to the employer's office location is deductible? With the increasing availability of remote work, newly hired workers may normally be working at a significant distance from the employer's

21 *Motor Vehicle and Car Expenses*, Australian Tax Office (last updated June 15, 2025), www.ato.gov.au/Individuals/Income-and-deductions/Deductions-you-can-claim/Transport-and-travel-expenses/Motor-vehicle-and-car-expenses/#Whenyoucantclaim.

22 See, e.g., *Increase of Commuting Allowance (Pendlerpauschale) and Commuter Euro (Pendlereuro)*, Deloitte (May 27, 2022), www2.deloitte.com/at/de/blog/deloitte-tax-blog/2022/energy-measures-package-temporary-inflation-compensation-enacted.html.

23 See, e.g., *Taxation of International Executives: Japan*, KPMG at 12 (Apr. 2023), https://assets.kpmg.com/content/dam/kpmg/xx/pdf/2023/01/TIES-Japan.pdf.

24 See, e.g., Hayes R. Holderness, *Changing Lanes: Tax Relief for Commuters*, 40 Va. Tax Rev. 453 (2020–21) (detailing changing patterns and recommending policy adjustments).

25 For example, a USDA memorandum on frequently asked questions regarding telework and remote work provides its own definitions of the terms, expectations for worker attendance, and designation of the workers' real place of work. *See* USDA, *Frequently Asked Questions: Telework and Remote Work* www.usda.gov/sites/default/files/documents/faqs-telework-remote-work.pdf.

office.[26] In some two-earner households, the residence may be dictated by the employment of one of the two earners, with the other worker pursuing a remote option. Even if the dominant work model remains either 60–80 percent (or even 100 percent) work at employer site, the ability for both business and worker to manage fully remote work has been firmly established and will serve as a viable option in many contexts.

Second, the continued increase in platform-based work during the pandemic raises the prospect of taxpayers with employment in one metropolitan area, and self-employment/independent contractor work in another. This scenario is not new, but developments in how work and work relationships are structured may increase both the number and the type of cases in which this occurs. For example, labor shortages in nursing that developed during the pandemic in the United States have not fully receded. Current data suggests that nurse employment declined by 100,000 workers between 2020 and 2021 (the greatest decline in the past forty years).[27] Hospitals have responded to nursing shortages by embracing gig work and using apps to connect with nurses seeking flexible schedules and the ability to demand higher rates for in-demand shifts.[28] In some cases, nurses on these platforms are pursuing an exclusively gig-based work schedule. Others have full-time employment but pick up extra shifts through the apps (either as employees or independent contractors). When the gig work is local, commuting questions likely pose few issues. However, if taxpayers are picking up shifts distant from their residence – perhaps including an overnight stay for a multi-day shift, questions about the deductibility of travel costs (including hotel) arise. Scenarios could become even more complicated if gig work occurs where a vacation/second home is located. These shifts warrant attention from tax policy makers regardless of the precise rules currently in place. Moreover, the tension created by remote and gig work on worker classification regimes (see the following section) may put pressure on rules regarding deductibility of employee expenses and those for commuting costs.

[26] See, e.g., Emma Goldberg & Ben Casselman, *What Young Workers Miss without the "Power of Proximity"*, N. Y. Times (Apr. 24, 2023), www.nytimes.com/2023/04/24/business/remote-work-feedback.html?action = click&algo = bandit-all-surfaces-variants-shadow-lda-unique-diversify-time-cutoff-30&alpha = 0.05&block = trending_recirc&fellback = false&imp_id = 882119049&impression_id = e016ae06-e2c9-11ed-b03a-a952907b2b4a&index = 2&pgtype = Article&pool = published-assets-db-4-ls&region = footer&req_id = 876912244&shadow_vec_sim = 0.6030360900935194&surface = eos-most-popular-story&variant = 0_pers_bandit_diversified (noting the ongoing appeal of working from home for many workers despite possible tradeoffs in advising, mentoring, and career advancement).

[27] David I. Auerbach et al., *A Worrisome Drop in the Number of Young Nurses*, Health Affairs Forefront (Apr. 13, 2022), www.nber.org/papers/w30997https://www.healthaffairs.org/do/10.1377/forefront.20220412.311784.

[28] Melanie Evans, *Nursing Shortage Pushes Hospitals into the Gig Economy*, Wall St. J. (Apr. 18, 2023), www.wsj.com/articles/nurse-shortage-hospitals-hiring-gig-economy-dc94bdb2?mod = hp_lead_pos11.

Worker Classification and Its Consequences

Worker classification (as employee or independent contractor) has been a regular subject of tax policy debate in many jurisdictions, especially as the first decade of the twenty-first century saw the growth of platform-based business and the increased potential for gig work across a number of sectors, including delivery, transportation, and short-term services, such as nursing gigs.[29] Accordingly, many jurisdictions struggle with the distinction between employees and independent contractors, and post-pandemic these concerns have increased.

Worker classification matters because the various legal benefits and protections to which workers may be entitled frequently turn on their classification. For example, in the United States, workers properly classified as employees are entitled to: (1) National Labor Relations Act protections;[30] (2) heightened health and safety regulations; (3) overtime and minimum wage protections; (4) enhanced anti-discrimination protections; (5) and retirement, disability, and medical benefits not available to independent contractors. Worker classification determines who (the worker or the business that hired the worker) bears payroll and retirement/medical insurance taxes (i.e., Social Security/Medicare taxes), who has withholding and reporting obligations, whether the worker is entitled to deductions regarding expenditures made for work, and what fringe benefits received by the worker are tax-free.[31]

Where jurisdictions extend benefits to employees, businesses may view hiring an employee (rather than an independent contractor) as more costly. As a result, businesses frequently seek to classify workers as independent contractors, a common practice that has generated much litigation.[32]

A complicated legal story unfolding in California over recent years captures the intensity of parties' interests, the instability of the legal landscape, and the competing views on platform worker classification – a story not unique to the United States. In a

[29] See, e.g., Katharine G. Abraham et al., *The Independent Contractor Workforce: New Evidence on Its Size and Composition and Ways to Improve Its Measurement in Household Surveys*, NBER Working Paper No. 30997 (Mar. 2023), www.nber.org/papers/w30997 (noting the "rise of online platforms has heightened awareness of [the worker classification issues] and prompted various policy proposals to address them").

[30] Protections include the right to unionize and bargain collectively with employers. 29 U.S.C. §§151–169 (2006).

[31] See, e.g., Shu-Yi Oei & Diane M. Ring, *Tax Law's Workplace Shift?* 100 B. U. L. Rev. 651, 666–678 (2020).

[32] See, e.g., Owusu v. LaserShip Inc., No. 1:23-CV-00074 (M.D. Pa. Jan. 13, 2023); Silva v. DoorDash Inc., No. 6:23-CV-00104 (M.D. Fla. Jan. 20, 2023). Long before platform businesses appeared, the US Supreme Court acknowledged how difficult the worker classification issue has proven for the legal system: "Few problems in the law have given a greater variety of application and conflict in results than the cases arising in the borderland between what is clearly an employer–employee relationship and what is clearly one of independent, entrepreneurial dealing." N. L. R. B. v. Hearst Publ'n, Inc., 322 U.S. 111, 121 (1944).

major 2018 ruling,[33] the Supreme Court of California, the state's highest court, established a three-part test for worker classification under the California wage regulations, a test generally viewed as favoring workers (who typically prefer employee status).[34] In 2019, the test, which impacted workers across a variety of sectors, was codified.[35] The following year, 2020, California voters approved a new law making an exception to the new test for drivers working through digital platforms.[36] The exception would allow a rideshare or delivery business to classify drivers as independent contractors if the platform does not: (1) unilaterally set dates and times of work; (2) require acceptance of specific work assignments; (3) block the driver from driving for other platforms except during the engaged time; or (4) bar the driver from engaging in other lawful occupations or businesses.[37] The constitutionality of the new law introducing the exception was challenged by app-based drivers and a California labor union in 2021, and the trial court concluded that the new law was unconstitutional and unenforceable.[38] On appeal, in 2023, the California Appeals Court partially reversed the lower court, ruling that most of the new law was constitutional (in particular, provisions that facilitated classification of platform drivers as independent contractors).[39]

This California tale mirrors the attention worker classification has garnered in other jurisdictions.[40] In 2021, the European Commission (EC) proposed a platform-work directive seeking to harmonize employment definitions across the European

[33] Dynamex Operations W., Inc. v. Superior Ct., 4 Cal. 5th 903 (2018).

[34] Id., at 957.

[35] Independent contractor versus employee, Labor Comm'r's Office, Cal. Dep't. of Indus. Rel. (updated Jan. 2023), www.dir.ca.gov/dlse/faq_independentcontractor.htm (explaining the history and impact of AB 5).

[36] Codified as Cal. Bus. & Prof. Code, §§7448 *et seq.*(2020).

[37] The text of the new law is available as *Text of Proposed Laws* at 31, available at https://vig.cdn.sos.ca.gov/2020/general/pdf/topl-prop22.pdf.

[38] Specifically, the court concluded that Sections 7451 and 7465(c)(4) were unconstitutional, and because Section 7451 "is not severable from the remainder of the statute" the "entirety of [the new law] is unenforceable." Hector Castellanos et al. v. California, Case No. RG21088725 at 12 (Aug. 20, 2021), https://ca-times.brightspotcdn.com/c5/f5/7bba477c4a839d1edd9f5b5a75e9/prop-22-alameda-superior-ct.%208-20-21.pdf

[39] Castellanos v. California, 89 Cal. App. 5th 131, 305 Cal. Rptr. 3d 717 (2023), as modified (Apr. 12, 2023), www.courts.ca.gov/opinions/documents/A163655.PDF. The only portion of Proposition 22 that was ruled unconstitutional was language defining what constitutes an amendment to Proposition 22. In 2024, the Supreme Court of California upheld the constitutionality of the new law. Castellanos v. California, 16 Cal. 5th 588 (2024).

[40] See, e.g., Christina Hießl, *The Classification of Platform Workers in Case Law: A Cross-European Comparative Analysis*, 42(2) Comp. Lab. L.& Pol'y. J. (2022) (analyzing 173 judgements and administrative decisions across fourteen European countries on the classification of platform workers as employees or independent contractors); see also, Katerina Pantazatou, *Taxation of the Sharing Economy in the European Union*, in The Law of the Sharing Economy 261–273 (2018) (Nestor M. Davidson et al. eds., 2018).

Union.[41] The proposed directive generated significant debate over pivotal worker classification provisions. The European Parliament's Committee on Employment and Social Affairs (EMPL) adopted its own report, differing with the EC on key elements.[42] Ultimately, the Directive entered into force in December 2024.

A confluence of factors will keep worker classification in the spotlight.[43] Not only have platform/app-based delivery businesses continued to thrive, but work force pressures (including those demonstrated in nursing) have prompted businesses to explore non-employee models and more platform-based approaches to finding workers. Additionally, continuing worker interest in remote work, an openness to non-employee arrangements in order to facilitate continued remote working, and the rapid adoption of technology together lay the groundwork for ongoing reconfigurations of work and the workforce. Thus, we should expect continuing calls for a reassessment of worker classification.

Nexus to Tax the Global Worker

The shift toward remote work that contributed to these tax issues also resulted in workers crossing subnational borders (state and provincial) and international borders on a scale not previously experienced. When workers cross borders, they trigger questions regarding residence, source of income, social security contributions, VAT, tax administration obligations, and jurisdiction to tax. Although jurisdictions adopt a range of rules to determine tax residency or domicile, objective factors such as location of employment often play a key role with such determinations. Residence serves as a primary basis for jurisdiction to tax, but source-based taxation is a critical (if more limited) basis for taxation.

One issue that emerged in the cross-border context within the United States concerns a (subnational) state's taxation of out-of-state employees of their own local businesses. Versions of this rule have sometimes been referred to as the "telecommuter rule" or the "convenience of the employer" rule. New York long embraced this rule and sought to impose tax on workers employed by New York-located businesses when they worked from home (outside New York) for their own

41 *Proposal for a Directive of the European Parliament and of the Council on Improving Working Conditions in Platform Work*, COM (2021) 762 final (Dec. 9, 2021), https://ec.europa.eu/social/BlobServlet?docId = 24992&langId = en.

42 *I Report on the Proposal for a Directive of the European Parliament and of the Council on Improving Working Conditions in Platform Work*, PARL. EUR. DOC. (COM 0762) (2021). (Dec. 2, 2022), www.europarl.europa.eu/doceo/document/A-9-2022-0301_EN.pdf.

43 Classification in the United States can be critical because many healthcare and retirement benefits may be closely tied to employment. Although 2010 changes in US law, introducing the Affordable Care Act (colloquially referred to as Obama Care) and other changes have reduced the stakes slightly for classification by de-linking employment and healthcare, worker classification continues to dictate much of worker benefits, protections, and taxation. See, e.g., Shu-Yi Oei & Diane M. Ring, *Can Sharing Be Taxed?*, 93 WASH. U. L. REV. 989, 1042–1045 (2016).

convenience.[44] An ongoing source of conflict with neighboring states, this rule created more tension when the pandemic increased the number of employees of New York businesses working outside New York. Application of the "convenience of the employer" rule now subjects more workers to taxation in both their state of residence and New York, with neither providing tax relief.

In contrast, Massachusetts adopted its telecommuting rule specifically for the period of the pandemic. The Massachusetts regulation stated that special sourcing rules "apply to income earned by a non-resident employee who telecommutes on behalf of an in-state business from a location outside the state due to the COVID-19 pandemic."[45] Under the state's new rule for the pandemic,[46] "all compensation received for services performed by a non-resident who, immediately prior to the Massachusetts COVID-19 state of emergency was an employee engaged in performing such services in Massachusetts, and who is performing services from a location outside Massachusetts due to a Pandemic-Related Circumstance will continue to be treated as Massachusetts source income subject to [Massachusetts] personal income tax."[47] The inconsistency and jurisdictional overlap created by states' taxation during the pandemic generated confusion and in some cases litigation. In 2021, the State of New Hampshire sued the Commonwealth of Massachusetts over the latter's purported over-reaching in taxing New Hampshire residents working from home for Massachusetts's employers. Ultimately, the US Supreme Court declined to hear the case.[48] The tension captured in the dynamic between New Hampshire and Massachusetts reflected not just a standard battle over taxing jurisdiction, but also the pressures created by the sudden and abrupt loss of tax base Massachusetts feared from the exodus of many employees of Massachusetts businesses.

The Massachusetts case, though domestic in the framing of its specific tax questions, parallels international issues. Assuming no constitutional law constraints (a question that a future US Supreme Court may entertain), Massachusetts can be critiqued for abruptly changing its "source" rule. The dominant practice of source taxation of labor income has emphasized "sourcing where '*actually*' performed." That backdrop, combined with Massachusetts' quick rule change, supports New Hampshire's outrage. Yet it fails to account for the role of the employer's state in creating a business environment capable of sustaining commerce. Moreover, the

44 20 CRR-NY 132.18.

45 Massachusetts Source Income of Non-Residents Telecommuting due to the COVID-19 Pandemic, 830 CMR 62.5A.3:(1)(a) (Mar. 3, 2021), www.mass.gov/regulations/830-CMR-625a3-massachusetts-source-income-of-non-residents-telecommuting-due-to-the-covid-19-pandemic.

46 The new rule commenced on March 10, 2020 and ran through "90 days after the date on which the Governor of the Commonwealth gives notice that the Massachusetts COVID-19 state of emergency is no longer in effect." Id., at 830, CMR 62.5A.3:(1)(d).

47 Id., at 830, CMR 62.5A.3:(3)(a).

48 *Order in Pending Cases*, Order List: 594 U.S (June 28, 2021), www.supremecourt.gov/orders/courtorders/062821zor_6j37.pdf.

Massachusetts rule change during the pandemic stabilized existing tax revenue streams.[49]

The pressures of a dramatic exodus have receded with many workers returning to the office, but the Massachusetts rule was neither unique nor the first. Absent Supreme Court intervention, states must develop their own mutual accommodations, and, if not, presumably the market for both businesses and workers will respond. Globally, this question of worker taxation intersects with demands for expanded and reimagined grounds on which countries can assert taxing rights. The BEPS Project, particularly Pillar 1, reflects a growing global chorus calling for a serious re-examination of the foundational principles of international taxation and the current and exclusive formulation of source and residence taxation. Resulting conversations may shape negotiations over the future of worker taxation as well. At a minimum, these trends have weakened any claim that existing rules are inherently correct. The ultimate resolution of these questions will be a function of practicality (for example, treaty provisions historically permitted a certain amount of work to be undertaken in a country before triggering source tax), distributional effects, anticipated work trends, and lobbying.

The tax implications of remote work extend beyond debates over jurisdiction to tax labor income. Collateral tax issues include: (1) the multiplicity of jurisdictions in which business and employee tax compliance and reporting is required; (2) the resolution of conflicts and competing tax definitions and rules; and (3) new tax obligations (such as employment tax, corporate tax liability) for workers and businesses. The last point is likely to have particular significance when workers cross international borders. Worker presence in a country may trigger permanent establishment (PE) status for an employer located in another jurisdiction, along with reporting requirements and potentially tax obligations.[50]

Again, this risk is not new. The question of the appropriate threshold to trigger PE status is longstanding and covered by tax treaties. But the pandemic shift did catch business and governments off guard as more employees began working remotely across international borders. Some jurisdictions enacted temporary protections against taxation, at least in contexts where lockdowns and travel restrictions resulted in employees involuntarily engaging in remote work.[51] The OECD issued

[49] One question is whether a fully remote worker has a different connection to the residence state than one who commutes across borders. In the pandemic, health care could be viewed as a new special residence connection. But that claim is complicated by the fact that the employer typically provides health care coverage, and that even a commuting worker typically seeks health care/hospitalization in the residence state.

[50] See Chapter 10, by Richard Collier.

[51] Ireland issued COVID-19 tax guidance on March 23, 2020 regarding employees and PE-related issues: "Where an individual is present in the State and that presence is shown to result from travel restrictions related to COVID–19, Revenue will be prepared to disregard such presence in the State for corporation tax purposes for a company in relation to which the individual is an employee, director, service provider or agent." Irish Tax and Customs, *COVID-19 Information*

guidelines in April 2020[52] (updated a year later)[53] for interpreting the OECD Model treaty during the pandemic, concluding in part that an employee working temporarily from home outside the employer's country likely would not create a new PE for their employer (in the employee's location). Going forward, the OECD included tax issues (PEs, social security, VAT, and tax administrative obligations) generated by the global mobility of workers on their Program of Work for 2023–2024. Coordinating among jurisdictions and ensuring the suitability of existing tax regimes will be important tasks where employees work not just outside the jurisdiction of the employer, but outside the residence of the employee and perhaps in multiple countries. Maybe jurisdictions will embrace bolder reforms to the taxation of individuals, adopting proposals detailed in other chapters in this volume, such as Avi-Yonah's call to revitalize citizenship taxation, or Brauner's design of individual income taxation divorced from residence.[54]

More recently, remote work across national borders has generated concerns about coordination of social security systems and a race to the bottom in personal taxation. The European Commission, anticipating remote work's continued prevalence, encouraged member states to consider common rules on personal taxation.[55] Commenting on jurisdictions adopting tax incentives to attract "digital nomads"/ high-earning remote workers, European Commissioner Director of Taxation, Benjamin Angel, characterized the trend as a potential "race to the bottom" for personal taxation.[56]

Post-pandemic, as temporary safe harbors expire, businesses and employees will need to establish clear internal reporting rules to ensure that businesses have complete information regarding worker locations. As noted, employees may work

and Advice for Taxpayers and Agents, (Mar. 23, 2020), https://web.archive.org/web/20200329114116/https://revenue.ie/en/corporate/communications/covid19/corporation-tax.aspx. Other jurisdictions adopted similar positions. See *OECD Policy Responses to Coronavirus (COVID-19): Updated Guidance on Tax Treaties and the Impact of the COVID-19 Crisis*, OECD, Box 1 at 3–6 (Jan. 21, 2021), www.oecd.org/coronavirus/policy-responses/updated-guidance-on-tax-treaties-and-the-impact-of-the-covid-19-pandemic-df42be07/ (detailing the guidance from Austria, Canada, Germany, Greece, New Zealand, the United Kingdom, and the United States).

52 OECD Secretariat Analysis of Tax Treaties and the Impact of the Covid-19 Crisis, OECD (Apr. 3, 2020), https://read.oecd-ilibrary.org/view/?ref=127_127237-vsdagpp2t3&title=OECD-Secretariat-analysis-of-tax-treaties-and-the-impact-of-the-COVID-19-Crisis.

53 The OECD updated its initial tax treaty-pandemic guidance as it became apparent that pandemic-related travel and work restrictions would be in place longer than initially anticipated. Id., OECD, *supra* note 52.

54 See Chapter 3, by Reuven Avi-Yonah and Chapter 2, by Yariv Brauner.

55 Pieter Baert, *Tax Policies or a New Generation*, Parl. Eur. Doc. (PE 733.697) (Oct. 2022), www.europarl.europa.eu/RegData/etudes/ATAG/2022/733697/EPRS_ATA(2022)733697_EN.pdf.

56 Matt Thompson & Todd Buell, *EU Accord Gives Bloc More Pull in Pillar 2 Talks, Official Says*, Law360 (Apr. 20, 2023), www.law360.com/tax-authority/articles/1599181/eu-accord-gives-bloc-more-pull-in-pillar-2-talks-official-says.

from a single remote location or may use the opportunity of remote work to travel the globe (although the size of this cohort should not be conflated with remote workers).[57] If employees fail to keep businesses accurately informed about their specific work locations, both businesses and the employees risk noncompliance with a host of immigration, visa, licensing, employment tax, corporate tax, PE, and reporting requirements in the remote work jurisdiction. These cases may easily come to the attention of jurisdictions through flags on the immigration/visa side. Ultimately, taxation need not be a barrier to flexible work arrangements. The same advances in technology that have enabled productive remote work also may enable businesses to effectively monitor the tax implications of a dispersed workforce – as long as they are made aware.

CHOICE OF TAXING TOOLS

As workforce trends result in more limited or even no in-office presence, jurisdictions, especially sub-national jurisdictions such as cities and states, may need to re-evaluate the mix of revenue sources on which they rely.[58] The starkest examples involve major metropolitan cities which saw significant reductions in worker population during the pandemic (reflected in, for example, Massachusetts' decision to adopt a pandemic telecommuter tax). To the extent the post-pandemic return to work has not resulted in a return to pre-pandemic levels of office presence, cities may find that sales tax, hotel taxes, property tax, transit revenues, and potentially employee income tax revenues have not rebounded.[59] Even cities which have seen pandemic related migration and growth may not yet be experiencing a return to prior levels of office occupancy. In some cases the pandemic may have exacerbated existing trends and urban challenges.[60]

57 Mobile workers are distinct from flexible workers. Although some workers may be mobile, many are not, but even the latter group is able to engage in remote work for an employer who is flexible regarding working location.

58 See generally Cevat Giray Aksoy et al., Working from Home around the World 29 (Nat'l Bureau of Econ. Rsch., Sept. 2022), www.nber.org/system/files/working_papers/w30446/w30446.pdf.

59 See generally Tom Doolittle & Arthur Fliegelman, Five Office Sector Metrics to Watch (Off. of Fin. Rsch., U.S. Dep't Treasury, June 1, 2023), www.financialresearch.gov/the-ofr-blog/2023/06/01/five-office-sector-metrics-to-watch/.

60 San Francisco, already facing tourism and commercial business challenges pre-pandemic due to homelessness and addiction among its population, continues to struggle post-pandemic See, e.g., George Hammond & Tabby Kinder, *Hollowing Out of San Francisco Raises Fears over Status as Top Tech Hub*, Fin. Times (Apr. 20, 2023), www.ft.com/content/9b17d4a0-032d-4b42-a989-b54a20ee0064. The city's office vacancy rates are approaching double their peak after the 2008 financial crisis, and declines have dramatically continued from 2021 through 2023. *San Francisco Office Figures*, CBRE (Apr. 2023) https://sprcdn-assets.sprinklr.com/2299/5f79915e-c2b1-4314-acfd-96354699307f-567256770.pdf.

It is too early to reach a conclusion on how city space will be used over the next few decades. Perhaps as current businesses downsize their office footprint in cities, the result may be an increase in affordable office space for new businesses to enter the city. Maybe the next equilibrium will be a world in which there are more businesses operating in a given city, but never with 100 percent of their workforce. As tourism continues to rebound and grow, some jurisdictions may find that this portion of their tax base thrives and can even support declines in other revenues. Still other jurisdictions that continue to be attractive places to live, given their array of amenities, may support their tax base through their own residents. Cities and states will need to monitor how work trends are impacting their mix of revenue sources. Whatever mix provided appropriate revenue streams pre-pandemic may cease to be ideal post-pandemic to the extent commuting workers stay home, residents exit the city, businesses reduce office space, and local businesses see limited foot traffic.

REFLECTIONS, OBSERVATIONS, AND ANTICIPATING THE NEXT WORKPLACE CHANGES

If our line of sight is the next 100 years, it may be difficult to predict with accuracy how the taxation of workers will change. Nevertheless, by building on evidence from workplace shifts over the past fifteen years, we can identify critical trends that have already created seismic and permanent shifts in work. The combination of advances in technology and communication, along with what some have characterized as the "natural experiment"[61] imposed by the pandemic, severed the existing link between worker and office, and worker and employee status, with a speed unlikely to be achieved in the normal course of business. That said, now that the pandemic has receded, we should expect to see variations in the volume of remote work across sectors, countries, businesses, and time. The benefits and burdens of remote work will be weighed differently as circumstances change and parties (workers, businesses, and governments) experience fluctuating levels of negotiating power. But with the underlying shift in the workforce baseline, jurisdictions will need to re-examine their current approaches to the taxation of work.

However, our picture is already incomplete. Two nascent but fast-moving trends will complicate the story of worker taxation: rapid advances in artificial intelligence (AI) and climate change. Each is worthy of extensive analysis, but a few preliminary observations can be offered. First, with respect to AI, though the technology is not new, the release of ChatGPT and the opportunity it provided workers and businesses to glimpse the potential of AI were universally stunning and unnerving. Will future

[61] See, e.g., Longqi Yang et al., *The Effects of Remote Working on Collaboration among Information Workers*, 6 Nature Human Behavior 43, 43 (2022), www.nature.com/articles/s41562-021-01196-4.

versions of AI replace workers who found themselves insulated from prior rounds of automation? Or will AI allow such workers to focus their time on the less routine and repetitive functions of their jobs? Likely the answer will be a mix, with the balance yet to be determined. However, with respect to taxation, one lesson we can learn from the past is the importance of incorporating into fiscal planning sufficient supports for workers on the losing side of technology. Globalization in the last decades of the twentieth century may have provided large economic benefits, at least in some jurisdictions, but those benefits were not evenly dispersed, and workers displaced through automation and offshoring did not share in the upside. The increased income that globalization brought some taxpayers provided jurisdictions an opportunity to use tax revenue to support displaced workers – but the reality of the social safety net fell short. As we envision potential implications of AI for workers, we have the opportunity to plan more comprehensively at the outset. Perhaps ideas that have been percolating for years will find a foothold, including increased attention to imputed income and proposals for universal basic income.

Second, climate change has the potential to accelerate shifts in the workforce. Although climate change details are the subject of extensive debate, it seems likely that within the next 100 years some countries and cities will experience dramatic changes – due to rising sea levels, limited water access, or extreme heat – that may drive workers and businesses from the area. Accordingly, climate change could play a cataclysmic economic and fiscal role. Even if that role is not as universal or instantaneous as the pandemic, it may nonetheless prompt losses that exacerbate the revenue and fiscal stability of governments around the world. What we can say with confidence is that significant changes are forthcoming in the labor force and that the tax system must be poised to respond.

10

The Individual, Mobility, and the Corporate

Richard Collier

INTRODUCTION

The notion of "mobility" may be interpreted in many ways,[1] but this chapter uses the term to refer to different cross-border working patterns adopted by individuals including "remote" and peripatetic working arrangements.[2] These working patterns may involve remote work in a state for very short periods or lengthy periods (such as several months or years) and anything in between. They may also have varying levels of recurrence, whether in the same state or in different states. The mobility of individuals potentially raises many issues (such as legal, regulatory, employment, and security issues) and inevitably various tax issues, such as in connection with individual income taxation, value added tax (VAT), and the corporate income tax. This chapter deals with some specific implications of mobility for the corporate income tax.

It seems to be often assumed or stated – as it is in a recent UK Office of Tax Simplification report on mobility[3] – that the corporate income tax effects from human mobility are limited or negligible in terms of tax due, and that the real

The author would like to express his thanks to Vicky Perry for her detailed comments on an earlier draft of this chapter, as well as thanks to the various suggestions made by Reuven Avi-Yonah, Eduardo Baistrocchi, Yariv Brauner, Steven Dean, Mitchell Kane, Wolfgang Schön, Dan Shaviro, and Miranda Stewart in the discussion of this chapter.

[1] The OECD work on mobility has been concerned with road transport and sustainability. See, e.g., OECD, *Mobility 2030: Meeting the Challenges to Sustainability* (2004), www.oecd.org/sd-roundtable/papersandpublications/39360485.pdf, and inter-generational mobility; see, e.g., Orsetta Causa & Åsa Johansson, *Intergenerational Social Mobility in OECD Countries*, OECD J.: Econ. Stud. (2010), www.oecd.org/social/labour/49849281.pdf and is now turning to consider mobility in the sense of the tax issues from remote working.

[2] References to "remote" working are intended to mean the practice of working in a country which is different to that in which the usual place of work is located. Mobility issues may also be raised in a domestic context, but the issues are quite different – see Office of Tax Simplification, *Hybrid and Distance Working Report: Exploring the Tax Implications of Changing Working Practices*, Dec. 2022.

[3] Id., at 5.

impact of mobility involves simply the relevant compliance obligations. This would suggest the issues are largely administrative in nature. However, what this chapter will seek to show is that the impacts of mobility – and the difficulties created by mobility – for the corporate income tax are more significant than is often appreciated, and, as the trend to greater mobility develops, that trend will very likely lead to some increasingly intractable problems in the operation of the rules dealing with the allocation of corporate income.[4]

The following discussion will argue that corporate income tax difficulties created by human mobility stem largely from two factors. The first factor concerns the nature of the changes that have been introduced into the operation of the income-allocation rules over the last twenty years. As will be shown, the impact of these changes means that the most mobile individuals within a multinational enterprise (MNE) group will create significant difficulties in the application of these rules. The second factor concerns the unsuitability of the nexus rules that determine the point at which a corporate entity is to be treated as being present for tax purposes in a jurisdiction, namely the permanent-establishment threshold rules in Article 5 of the OECD Model.

The combination of these factors, together with the sharply increased and increasing mobility of employees, makes it very likely that there will be many more instances where the mobility of individuals raises difficult corporate income-allocation issues. This will inevitably create more tax disputes between taxpayers and tax authorities, and between different tax authorities as they seek to tax the same income. The challenges to the corporate income tax from increased mobility are therefore highly significant.

The discussion is organized as follows. First, some consideration is given to the nature of mobility within MNEs. The discussion then explores the technical rules that are relevant to the mobility issue, namely the rules on how income is allocated within MNE groups and the threshold or nexus rules that determine whether corporate income taxation may be levied on the activities of nonresident companies. The discussion then explores the implications of these technical issues in the context of mobility, and whether the various problems identified can be addressed with workable solutions. The chapter then concludes.

MOBILITY OF INDIVIDUALS WITHIN AN MNE

Following the global COVID-19 pandemic, increased mobility, including increased cross-border mobility, has become a significant trend at all levels of the workforce.[5]

4 This is not to suggest that the relevant compliance obligations may not also be problematic (especially in the case of partnerships as both the partnership and each partner may need to file separate tax returns in the overseas location, whereas a company would only have a single return filing).

5 Office of Tax Simplification, *supra* note 2, at 2.36–2.38 and see also question 4 at 56. In that report, it is confirmed that *all* the large businesses consulted in the project now permit some form of remote working. The mobility trend has caused the International Monetary Fund

The trend has also given rise to the notion of "digital nomads"[6] for whom tax perks may be a "pull factor" in encouraging mobility.[7]

The trend to greater mobility is of special relevance to those at the top of the income distribution, that is, the more senior people within MNE groups or those with specialist skills. This point has been confirmed in recent research.[8] There may be several reasons for this, for example the more senior people within an MNE may often have a regional or global role or a role that cuts across a number of separate business lines, meaning there is less need for them to be permanently located in a specific location; the arrangement may arise as a consequence of competition in the market for talent, with an MNE group accepting the arrangement as an incident of a new hire;[9] and in some cases the more senior people within the organization may simply have the power to work under whatever working arrangements suit them.

The discussion within The Taxable Presence Threshold Tests section explores two sets of rules – the fixed-place and dependent-agent permanent-establishment tests – that in combination create some acute corporate income tax problems from mobility.[10] These rules are first outlined, and the discussion then explores the implications that arise due to mobility issues.

(IMF) to note the consequential risks to the global personal tax base: "As opportunities expand for cross-border remote work, a bigger segment of the labour income tax base becomes more mobile – estimated currently at 1 1/4 percent of the global personal income tax base. In the future, personal tax coordination will gain importance and raise issues such as those related to corporate taxation." – see IMF, *Fiscal Policy from Pandemic to War*, Fiscal Monitor (Apr. 2022) (imf.org) at the executive summary and ch. 2.

6 The US Chamber of Commerce defines a digital nomad as "someone who performs their occupation entirely over the internet while traveling." See www.uschamber.com/co/grow/thrive/what-is-a-digital-nomad. See, e.g., Akcighit et al., *Taxation and the International Mobility of Inventors*, 106 (10), Am. Econ. Rev. 2930–2981 (2016), www.aeaweb.org/articles?id = 10.1257/aer.20150237.

7 The IMF noted, in Fiscal Monitor (Apr. 2022) (imf.org), that over forty jurisdictions are offering "Digital Nomad visas" with tax breaks to attract individuals and their spending to their country. These visas typically permit an individual to spend up to a year in the country, without personal tax liabilities. See Rita De la Feria & Giorgia Maffini, *The Impact of Digitalisation on Personal Income Taxes*, Brit. Tax Rev. 2, 154–168 (2021).

8 See, e.g., Office of Tax Simplification, *supra* note 2, at 2.9, 2.34, and 4.9; De la Feria & Maffini, *supra* note 7, at 156; KPMG, *Mobility Matters*, Dec. 2021, https://tax.kpmg.us/content/dam/tax/en/pdfs/2021/mobility-matters-121021.pdf. The research is consistent with anecdotal evidence gathered by the author from discussions with the tax directors of several MNEs.

9 The acceptance of increased mobility is clearly a factor in the competition for individuals and a pressure to meet requests for remote or home working; see Office of Tax Simplification, *supra* note 2, at 3 and 5.

10 The discussion here does not deal with all corporate income tax issues from mobility – for example, an issue not addressed here concerns the impact of mobility on effective management or management and control tests that may be relevant to the residence of a company for tax purposes.

INCREASING IMPORTANCE OF DECISION-MAKING

A problem that has beset the transfer-pricing system for many years is the legal "booking" issue, namely the potential for MNE transfer-pricing abuses based on contractual and/or booking arrangements involving capital, intangibles, etc., that are "booked" for legal purposes into companies in low-tax states. The comments that follow are intended to show that the way the income-allocation rules have responded to this issue, especially in the last fifteen years or so, raises some difficult issues in the context of individual mobility. It should be clarified that references here to the "income-allocation rules" are intended to refer to both the transfer-pricing rules (Article 9 of the OECD Model) that deal with pricing transactions and arrangements between related legal entities, together with the rules on the attribution of profits to permanent establishments or PEs (Article 7 of that Model) that determine how profits should be allocated within a legal entity, for example, as between a head office and overseas branch (i.e., PE).

The General Response to the "Booking" Issue

The response of the OECD to concerns about abusive legal "booking" arrangements has been markedly strengthened over the last ten to fifteen years, with the primary OECD response being to moor profits to the location of relevant functional activities, and, in particular, there has been a progressive gravitation to reliance on the location of relevant decision-making.[11] This is based on the broad assumption that, because of the assumed immobility of the relevant decision-makers, reliance on the location of the decision-making of senior people may act as a break or limitation on tax-driven contractual allocations or mere "booking" of assets, risk, and capital within an MNE, for example, by removing or reducing the possibility of booking an intangible asset in a low-tax, low-function company. The approach might alternatively be seen as permitting the "reality" of a transaction or arrangement within an MNE to be identified. Such a position would be on the basis that merely deferring to the contractual documentation and/or booking arrangements alone would not necessarily reflect the substantive reality of the arrangement, a matter better identified by recourse to the location of the relevant substantive functions, and, in particular, the relevant acts of decision-making by individuals.

The OECD's work in the modern era on the "important problems regarding the taxation of corporate profits" stemming from "the development of so-called

[11] It is important to emphasize that, though there is a much-heightened focus on decision-making in OECD rules and guidance, technically transfer-pricing returns should by no means be based exclusively on functional activity under the OECD Transfer Pricing Guidelines – see *OECD Transfer Pricing Guidelines for Multinational Enterprises and Tax Administrations*, para. 1.59, OECD 2022. (For the avoidance of doubt, all references in this chapter are to the 2022 version of the Transfer Pricing Guidelines, unless otherwise expressly stated.)

'multinational enterprises'" started in 1979 with the publication of the first OECD transfer-pricing report, Transfer Pricing and Multinational Enterprises.[12] However, by current standards, the discussion in that early transfer-pricing guidance is rather vague and undeveloped. For example, while it is suggested that it is always useful to begin a transfer-pricing exercise with a functional analysis relating to the contributions of the parties, the guidance on the use of a functional analysis is no more than a single brief paragraph (which may be contrasted with the thirty or so pages of current guidance). Because of concerns about the ease with which contracts could be altered, suspended, extended, or terminated by MNEs, including by retroactive actions, there is in the 1979 Report an invitation to look at what is the "underlying reality" behind a related-party contractual arrangement in considering what an arm's-length price would be, though there is next to nothing on how that might be done and by what tests the "reality" is to be appraised.[13] Also, at this time there remained a general deference to respecting the "actual transactions" entered into, meaning a broad-based acceptance of the relevant legal agreements, with an ability to disregard those legal agreements only in exceptional cases.[14]

The 1984 Report

The general response to the booking issue has been transformed by more recent reforms. The use of functional activity (including especially certain functional actions of individuals) as a more explicit anchor point for the allocation of corporate income and profits (for both transfer pricing and PE profit-attribution purposes) started to take hold with the publication of the short 1984 OECD Report, "The Taxation of Multinational Banking Enterprises."[15] The report recognized that in a banking business the large number and complexity of intra-group or intra-entity transactions create "considerable difficulty" in deciding to which part of the business or the group any particular part of the profit should be allocated for tax purposes. This point had been highlighted by the emergence in the late 1970s of certain "loan parking" practices under which loans negotiated by a bank branch in one jurisdiction were then booked into another (typically low-tax) jurisdiction in which the bank had branch operations, and which advanced the funds under the loan. The

[12] *Transfer Pricing and Multinational Enterprises*, 7, OECD (1979). The Commentary to the earlier OECD 1963 Draft Model Treaty contains only a single brief paragraph which explains the transfer-pricing approach (reflected in art. 9 of the OECD Model) as "evidently appropriate" and as one which "seems to call for very little comment."

[13] See *Transfer Pricing and Multinational Enterprises*, *supra* note 12, at 20. The 1979 report includes some other references to the usefulness of considering the functions of the parties (see e.g., paras. 35, 47, 54, 55, 58, 60, and 159) but there is no real guidance on what that means or involves.

[14] *Transfer Pricing and Multinational Enterprises*, *supra* note 12, at 19.

[15] *The Taxation of Multinational Banking Enterprises* (OECD 1984).

1984 guidance (which concerned the rules on the attribution of profits to PEs) was intended to respond to those difficulties.[16]

On how to test if income and expenses are "properly attributed to the branch," the guidance responds with a test of "whether the income produced by the relevant assets can be regarded as having been *substantially generated* by the activities of the PE." The response is that "this will depend on the extent to which the *negotiation and conclusion* of the transaction has been the work of the PE" (emphasis added).[17] The guidance then goes on to itemize the activities that would normally be involved in the negotiation and conclusion of the transaction in the banking context. This includes obtaining the offer of new business; establishing the potential borrower's credit rating and the risk involved in providing credit; negotiating the terms of the loan with the borrower; deciding on whether to make or extend relevant loan and, if so, on what terms and conditions; concluding the contract and dispersing the proceeds of the loan; and administering the loan and holding and controlling the securities pledged. The 1984 guidance therefore offers a response to the task of "proper" attribution or allocation of profits to PE by reference to the critical business activities in any case – which in a traditional banking context are identified as being the negotiation and conclusion of loan agreements.[18]

The Impact of the AOA

An OECD overhaul of the approach to how profits should be attributed to PEs started in the late 1990s. In 2010, this work ultimately led to the finalization of a new approach, namely the "authorized OECD approach" or AOA. This work led to an emphatic shift in the use of functional activities as anchor points for the attribution of assets, risks, and capital – and therefore in consequence – also for the attribution of profits. The OECD output also went much further in clarifying the individuals and the functional activities that were of particular relevance in this regard.

The new AOA approach placed a sharply increased emphasis on the location of certain decision-making by individuals. This was achieved by the conclusion that the relevant functional analysis would determine the location of assets, risks, and

[16] Id., para. 32.

[17] Id., para. 86.

[18] The approach was also developed in later publications. See, e.g., *The Taxation of Global Trading of Financial Instruments*, paras.15–17, 72, and 116, OECD (1998). From 2005, the OECD work on Business Restructurings increasingly advocated the checking of conduct as a corroboration mechanism, with a particular focus on the functional analysis of the relevant decisions made. The work was ultimately reflected in a new chapter of the Transfer Pricing Guidelines – see the 2010 version of the Transfer Pricing Guidelines, paras. 9.11, 9.13–9.16, 9.20, 9.22–9.28, 9.36–9.38, and 9.85. Much of this thinking on the OECD Business Restructurings project paved the way for the further developments in the BEPS Project which are discussed in the main body of this article.

capital.[19] In the case of assets, the economic ownership of assets would be determined, according to the location of the "significant people functions" relating to the asset concerned, that is, those functional activities concerned with the assumption and management of the asset concerned. Risks would be similarly allocated within the enterprise according to the location of the "significant people functions" relevant to the assumption and management of risk. Capital would then be allocated as necessary to support the assets and risks allocated under this approach. The approach of using the location of the "significant people functions" was developed as a response to the task of needing to identify the location of "economically significant activities." In broad terms, these "significant people functions" are normally reflected in the acts of active decision-making of individuals relating to the assumption and management of assets and risks, for example, through decisions taken on assuming new risks (such as in decisions about new business ventures) or managing existing risks in the business (such as in decisions about deploying or developing existing intellectual property).[20] For example, "The significant people functions relevant to the assumption of risks are those which require active decision-making with regard to the acceptance and/or management . . . of those risks."[21] The appreciable advance in the use of functional activity as the critical anchor point for income and profits could be seen in the shift from the thinking reflected in the OECD's earlier work on global trading. In that earlier work, the OECD guidance had not yet reached the point of concluding that the functional activity relating to managing a risk meant that the risk concerned should be borne in the location where that management activity is conducted.[22] Yet the OECD's work on profit attribution in the AOA project takes a decisive step to that conclusion. An even bigger step in that direction would shortly afterward be taken in relation to the transfer-pricing rules. This occurred in the OECD Base Erosion and Profit Shifting (BEPS) Project.

The Impact of the BEPS Project

The BEPS Project action items form a package of measures that are intended generally to end the artificial diversion of profits to low-tax states, thereby ensuring

[19] See 2010 *Report on the Attribution of Profits to Permanent Establishments*, Part I, paras. 18–31 and 57–182, OECD (2010).

[20] See, e.g., id., paras. 25, 85, and 86. The guidance on the new approach under the AOA is more complex in the case of assets (there is separate guidance on tangible and intangible assets and the place of use of the asset may also be relevant in the case of tangible assets – see id., paras. 72–97. The AOA guidance on the approach to risks is more straightforward, centering on active decision-making relating to the assumption and management of the risk concerned – see id., paras. 68–71).

[21] Id., paras. 22, 23–25, 44, and 45.

[22] See *The Taxation of Global Trading of Financial Instruments*, *supra* note 18, paras. 192–196.

that profits are taxed in the location where value is created.[23] This goal led to several changes being made by the BEPS Project to the transfer-pricing rules. The most fundamental and far-reaching of these transfer-pricing changes are those concerning the treatment of risks.[24] These changes have taken the reliance in the income-allocation exercise on decision-making to new levels.

As a result of the BEPS changes, a new "risk framework" is now a central part of the required approach that must be followed in all transfer-pricing exercises. The central tenet of the approach to risk is that if an entity is to be treated as bearing risk for transfer-pricing purposes, it must both "control" that risk and also have the financial capacity to assume the risk.[25] In consequence, the factual investigation of "control over risk" is now central to the determination of whether the conduct of the parties is consistent with their contractual arrangements. To the extent it is not, the contractual arrangements are ignored.

Fundamentally, and given that the financial capacity requirement is in practice generally less problematic, what is required to demonstrate "control over risk" in any particular location hinges on the relevant decision-making: The test of whether a party "controls risk" in the manner now required is determined by the test of whether the party makes informed decisions relating to taking on, laying off, and declining risk, and whether it makes informed decisions regarding how to respond to risks that arise. In broad terms, this amounts to making the key decisions relating to the assumption and management of risk.[26]

[23] The notion of "value creation" was central to the BEPS Project: "the OECD/G20 BEPS Project consisted of 15 separate action areas targeting the gaps and mismatches in the international corporate tax system that facilitated the shifting of profits by MNEs away from where the underlying economic activity and value creation took place." See *Tax Challenges Arising from Digitalisation: Interim Report 2018: Inclusive Framework on BEPS*, 17–18, OECD (2018). There are sharply divided views on the merits of the value creation approach. A more positive view is offered in Stanley Langbein & Max R. Fuss, *The OECD/G20-BEPS-Project and the Value Creation Paradigm: Economic Reality Disemboguing into the Interpretation of the Arm's Length Standard*, 51 Int'l Law. 259, 259–409 (2018). The author is in the decidedly skeptical camp – see Richard S. Collier, *The Value Creation Mythology*, *in* IBFD, Taxation and Value Creation (Werner Haslehner & Marie Lamensch eds., 2021).

[24] In a transfer-pricing context, the nature of risk is to be regarded as the effect of uncertainty on the objectives of the business under consideration. See *OECD Transfer Pricing Guidelines for Multinational Enterprises and Tax Administrations*, *supra* note 11, para. 1.71.

[25] The new approach to risk is presumably premised on the assumption that a third party would assume risks only where it is able to control them and has the required financial capacity to do so.

[26] Technically, the new rules first define "risk management" as consisting of three activities: (i) having the capability to make, and actually making, decisions regarding whether to take on risk, lay off risk, or to decline a risk-bearing opportunity; (ii) having the capability to make, and actually making, decisions regarding how to respond to the risks arising in connection with a business opportunity; and (iii) having the capability to make, and actually making, decisions to mitigate risk by taking actions that affect risk outcomes. The guidance then states that "control over risk" includes the first two of these aspects of risk management but not the third.

What is significant in relation to this new approach to risk based on functional decision-making is that this designated type of control-over-risk decision-making is now *determinative* of the relevant transfer-pricing result, thereby representing a further material shift from the position established in the OECD Transfer Pricing Guidelines only five years earlier.[27] This boosted focus on risk and the control of risk is reflected in a number of other elements of the BEPS Project work on transfer pricing (such as the work on intangibles, cost sharing, and financing returns) as well as in the more recent transfer-pricing work on financial transactions. All these instances reinforce the notion that the geographical location of the control of risk through the exercise of relevant decision-making by individuals is the decisive factor in the allocation of profit.

These changes have significantly boosted the importance of relevant decision-makers in the transfer-pricing exercise.[28] Not only that, but it has been argued by several authors that the way the rules are being applied in practice by some tax authorities assigns a relevance to the functional acts of decision-making that goes significantly beyond what was intended.[29]

Impact of These Changes

What may be seen from the discussion so far is the marked shift in the way the income-allocation rules have developed to rely on the location of functional activity, and in particular decision-making about risks and assets, as the cardinal anchor point for income and profits.[30]

It may therefore be seen that the practical application of the transfer-pricing and PE-profit-attribution rules now relies significantly on the nature and location of

[27] In the earlier 2010 version of the Transfer Pricing Guidelines, it is expressly clarified that the control of risk is not determinative. See *OECD Transfer Pricing Guidelines for Multinational Enterprises and Tax Administrations*, *supra* note 11, para. 9.20, OECD (2010).

[28] The approach has been criticized as incoherent and a perverse "bourgeois labour theory of value" turning the Marxist labor theory of value (which asserts that the value of a good or service is derived from the labor used in its production or supply) on its head. See Itai Grinberg, *International Taxation in an Era of Digital Disruption: Analyzing the Current Debate*, 45 Int'l Tax J. 39 (Mar.–Apr. 2019).

[29] See, e.g., Andrew Hickman, Arm's length principle mutations: control of risk in the OECD guidelines and variations in practice (MNE Tax Jan. 13, 2021); Eyal Gonen et al., *Control over Risk, DEMPE Functions, and the Remuneration of R&D Service Providers*, 102 Tax Notes Int'l 1615 (June 21, 2021); Richard S. Collier & Ian F. Dykes, *On The Apparent Widespread Misapplication of the OECD Transfer Pricing Guidelines*, 76 Bull. for Int'l Tax'n, IBFD, no. 1 (2022).

[30] This point has been the subject of significant concerns. While recourse in the operation of the income-allocation rules to the location of decision-making might be thought to involve an apparently simple mechanism, the reality is that it gives rise to a raft of significant problems. The scale of these problems has increased as the OECD has over recent years placed ever greater reliance on decision-making in applying arts. 9 and 7 of the OECD Model. These problems are discussed in Collier & Dykes, *supra* note 29.

functional decision-making. As may be readily appreciated, it also leads to some very difficult and often highly subjective issues as to how to determine the appropriate level of allocable income or profits, for example in cases where individuals in different locations participate in the decision-making process.

Before exploring the implications of this point in the context of the mobility of individuals, a second technical matter will be explored. This relates to the PE threshold test of Article 5 of the OECD Model.

THE TAXABLE PRESENCE THRESHOLD TESTS

Article 5 of the OECD Model provides tests for determining whether the business activities of a nonresident entity are taxable in a state. The tests are designed to identify whether a taxable PE exists in the state concerned. These tests are highly relevant in cases of mobile individuals employed by MNEs because they normally operate to determine whether the relevant employing entity – or possibly other group entities – may be subject to corporate income tax in a state where an individual working remotely is located.[31]

For most businesses,[32] there are two alternative threshold tests that apply. If either is satisfied, a taxable PE will be established. The first test is the "fixed place of business test" derived from Article 5(1) of the OECD Model. The test is whether, in the state concerned, the nonresident company has "a fixed place of business through which the business of an enterprise is wholly or partly carried on." Under the second test the nonresident entity will be deemed to have a taxable PE if a person in the state creates a "dependent agent" PE. This would normally require that the person habitually concludes contracts on behalf of the nonresident entity, though the test has recently been expanded (as discussed further in The Dependent-Agent Business PE Test section).[33]

[31] A company undertaking activities across borders may be taxed on its profits by reference to: (1) the territory it is resident in (typically where the company is incorporated or effectively managed); (2) where it has physical activities; or (3) the source territory (where certain types of income arise). The discussion here is focused on (2) relating to physical activities. The current proposals from the BEPS Inclusive Framework on new approaches to profit attribution and taxation (Pillar 1) without physical presence represent a new approach for digital activities.

[32] There are separate rules which apply to a building site or construction or installation project: these rules are not discussed here. It is also true that in the absence of an applicable double tax treaty, local tax rules, which may be different to those discussed here, may apply to determine the circumstances of "taxable presence."

[33] The two tests referred to here may vary in their precise terms when adopted in double tax treaties. In many cases these differences will arise due to differences in the approach adopted by the OECD and UN model double taxation conventions as these two conventions are used extensively as the model for individual double tax treaties entered into by states. The discussion here is, therefore, somewhat generalized, though there is a significant overlap between the OECD and UN versions of these articles.

In recent years, tensions relating to the threshold PE rules have been very common in practice.[34] In many cases, it is very hard to arrive at a conclusive answer on whether a PE is on the relevant facts created. Even for states, such as the United Kingdom, which are not normally known for the vagueness of their tax rules or for variations in the way they are applied or administered, this seems to be a common problem.[35]

Leaving aside variations due to the local "practice" of tax authorities (which may be significant), this problem arises because the core guidance from the OECD on applying the tests is somewhat vague and subjective, relying to a significant extent on the relevant facts and circumstances. The position can be illustrated by reference to the OECD guidance on applying the first test, namely whether there is "a fixed place of business through which the business of an enterprise is wholly or partly carried on."

The Fixed-Place-of-Business PE Test

There seems to be a very low threshold for what is required to "carry on a business." This is because the activities involved in carrying on a business do not need to be "productive," meaning routine back office and administrative functions could satisfy the test. In practice, therefore, this part of the test is easily satisfied and the focus usually shifts to the question of what is a "*fixed* place of business."

The reference to a "fixed" place of business necessitates a specific place or situs of business operations, but the term is also to be interpreted as requiring a degree of permanence.[36] This leads to what is arguably the most commonly encountered problem with this rule, namely the question of what time period is required before a place of business might be regarded as a "fixed" place of business for the purposes of the PE threshold rule. Unfortunately, the answer to this question is far from clear and very often depends upon the relevant facts and circumstances and the practice of the state in which the relevant place or situs is located.

Somewhat tentatively, the relevant OECD guidance (the Commentary to Article 5 of the OECD Model) notes that "experience has shown" that a fixed-place-of-business PE is normally considered to arise where the activities in the relevant place of business are carried on for more than 6 months. However, this is more of a

[34] See, e.g., *Permanent Establishments 2.0, An Overview of Some of the Main Trends which Can be Identified on the Topic of Permanent Establishments*, PwC (2012), www.pwc.com/gx/en/tax/publications/assets/pwc-permanent-establishments-at-the-heart-of-the-matter-final.pdf.

[35] See Office of Tax Simplification, *supra* note 2, at 4.21. However, there are some countries that have published rulings applying the PE tests to individuals choosing to work remotely for an overseas employer from their home office in their jurisdiction. See, e.g., KPMG, *European Union: Remote Working and Corporate Taxation*, GMS Flash Alert 2022-197, https://kpmg.com/xx/en/home/insights/2022/11/flash-alert-2022-197.html.

[36] See, e.g., *Commentaries on the Articles of the Model Tax Convention*, art. 5 para. 28, OECD (2017).

(distanced) observation than a rule, and in any event any assistance it might be taken to give is limited by several exceptions that are also contained in the Commentary. For example, there is an exception for activities that are much shorter than the 6-month period mentioned when those activities are recurrent in nature – meaning that short but repeated activities may be regarded as meeting the "fixed" place of business test.[37] It is also clear that a place of business may constitute a fixed-place-of-business PE even if it only exists for a very short time due to the nature of the business.[38] Further, it is continually emphasized in the Commentary to Article 5 that the issue of whether there is a PE has to be addressed by reference to the circumstances of the case, and the application of the guidance is further weakened by the observation that OECD member states practices vary.[39]

The PE threshold issue is commonly raised in cases of home working (such as where a senior employee works in a second home located in a different state to the one in which his employing company – and its business premises – is located). In such a case, all the issues discussed above will usually need to be addressed – including whether the home might properly be regarded as a "place of business" through the activities of the employee. Such an inquiry would involve questions of whether, say, repeated short visits by the employee to the home could be sufficient to meet the "fixed" requirement, etc. In such cases, reliance is often placed on another element of the fixed-place-of-business test to avoid the conclusion that a fixed place of business has been created. An apparent requirement of the fixed-place-of-business test (or at least one that is widely assumed based on the OECD guidance) is that the place concerned must be "at the disposal of" the nonresident entity concerned. Ordinarily, we might not think of the home of an employee as being "at the disposal of" the nonresident entity, even if an employee of the nonresident entity sometimes (or even regularly) works out of the home. However, it is important to note that: (1) the "at the disposal of" wording does not form part of the formal test in Article 5 but is merely intended as an explanation of that test and (2) the meaning of the wording "at the disposal of" is somewhat elusive and has therefore been further explained in the Commentary. The Commentary states that a place may be "at the disposal" of the nonresident entity even if there is no formal (legal) right to occupy; instead, whether a place is at its disposal depends on its "effective power to use that location," though the Commentary also makes clear that a presence can be "so intermittent or incidental that the location cannot be considered a place of business of the enterprise."[40] The explanation of the term goes on to include some examples that are intended to illustrate its meaning, but these have been somewhat controversial as one of the examples at least may be interpreted as implying that mere factual use of

[37] Id., para. 29.
[38] The Commentary notes this can be a difficult point to apply – see id., para. 28.
[39] See, e.g., id., paras. 8, 18, 28, 59, and 62.
[40] Id., paras. 10–12.

or presence at a location is sufficient to meet the test.[41] If correct, this suggests the "at the disposal of" wording adds little by way of meaningful qualification of the operation of the fixed-place-of-business rule.[42]

Several other technical and practical difficulties with the fixed-place-of-business PE threshold rule may also be identified.[43] These various difficulties, and the significant emphasis in the relevant OECD guidance on the importance of the facts and circumstances, coupled with the different approaches and the variation in practice of tax authorities, means that the fixed-place-of-business test is generally difficult to apply with certainty.[44]

The Dependent-Agent PE Test

The second PE threshold test referred to, the dependent-agent test (which is satisfied by a person's habitual conclusion of contracts on behalf of the nonresident

41 The examples make it difficult to know exactly what standard is imposed by this test and therefore how far it meaningfully qualifies the requirements of art. 5 (1). See, further, JÜRGEN LÜDICKE, *Recent Commentary Changes Concerning the Definition of Permanent Establishment*, Bull. – Tax Treaty Monitor 190, 191 (May 2004); Joel Nitikman, *The Painter and the PE*, 57 no. 2 CAN. TAX J. 213, 220–228 (2009).

42 Guidance issued by the OECD in response to the COVID-19 pandemic does, however, suggest the "at the disposal of" test has a more significant role as a test of whether a PE is created. That guidance was first issued on April 3, 2020 then updated on January 21, 2021, see *Updated Guidance on Tax Treaties and the Impact of the COVID-19 Pandemic*, OECD (Jan. 21, 2021). However, for various reasons, the relevance of that guidance outside its immediate COVID-19 context seems limited. This is because: the guidance is framed as representing the OECD Secretariat's view, not the member states' view, and it notes each jurisdiction can adopt its own guidance; the guidance notes that much of the analysis covers circumstances where factual determinations by tax administrations are required and the guidance does not purport to replace the judgement of tax administrations in those cases; and it is made clear that the guidance applies only to the exceptional circumstances arising during the COVID-19 pandemic while relevant public health measures to restrict the spread of COVID-19 are still in effect and that the position may be different in respect of activities carried on before or after the pandemic.

43 For example, where a PE is created by intermittent activities, it will usually be regarded as existing from the start of those activities, though this may be very hard to assess at the inception of those intermittent activities. As acknowledged by the Commentary (para. 59) there are also various difficult borderlines created by the application of certain exemptions from PE status which are contained in art. 5(4) of the OECD Model. These require potentially very subjective determinations of what can properly be regarded as activity that has a "preparatory or auxiliary" character, namely activities that are "so remote from the earning of profits" that it is difficult to allocate profits to those activities. The guidance notes that it is often difficult to distinguish between activities which have a preparatory or auxiliary character and those which have not, and it suggests the decisive test is whether the activity forms "an essential and significant part of the activity of the enterprise as a whole" and that each case has to be examined on its merits – see para. 59. The Commentary refers to the different views of some states on these matters (para. 79).

44 For examples of the different views of states on questions relating to the fixed-place-of-business test, *see United Nations Model Double Taxation Convention Between Developed and Developing Countries 2021*, Commentary on art. 5, at 183–184, 186, 191, U.N. (2022).

enterprise), also commonly presents similar technical and practical difficulties to the fixed-place-of-business test. This often makes it hard to be certain of the circumstances in which the rule is applicable. For reasons of available space, these difficulties are not discussed in detail here. However, by way of an example, it may be noted that, though the test is expressed in terms of the requirement of "concluding contracts," it is clear that activities that do not include a formal conclusion of a contract may be enough to satisfy the test.[45] Equally, it might be thought that the requirement for "habitual" contracting might lessen the relevance of the test. However, the test of what is habitual is to be assessed based on the commercial realities of the situation and depends on "the nature of the contracts and the business of the principal."[46] It is also evident that a new set of uncertainties have been created by the recent lowering of the dependent-agent threshold as a result of the work done in the BEPS Project. That work has led to an additional limb of the test which, broadly, is satisfied by a person who "habitually plays the principal role leading to the conclusion of contracts that are routinely concluded without material modification by the enterprise." The terms in this new limb of the test – particularly the reference to "principal role" – have been criticized as vague and subjective, opening the door to a variety of possible interpretations.[47]

It is also true that, in the last few years, certain developments relating to this second PE threshold test have in practice made the difficulties with the PE threshold tests discussed here commonly relevant as they have increased the tendency of tax authorities to raise PE points. The earlier discussion noted that the OECD's work on the AOA and its work on the "risk framework" in the BEPS Project have had the most significant impact in boosting the relevance of functional decision-making as providing anchor points in the income-allocation exercise. The output from the work on the AOA in the 2010 OECD Report on Attribution of Profits to Permanent Establishments (2010 PE Report) and the work in the BEPS Project have, for different reasons, also had the effect of expanding the circumstances in which PE points are in practice raised by tax authorities. The 2010 PE Report has had this effect due to comments made in that report: broadly, these comments explain that, in certain circumstances where a dependent-agent PE is created, the AOA approach will expand the taxing rights available to a jurisdiction in comparison to those that would otherwise be available if a transfer-pricing approach were applied to the "dependent agent enterprise" that creates the dependent-agent

[45] See, e.g., *Commentaries on the Articles of the Model Tax Convention*, *supra* note 36, para. 87. Another area that is commonly disputed is the scope of the exclusion for independent agents – see art. 5(6).

[46] Id., para. 98.

[47] See, e.g., for example, Richard S. Collier, *More Guidance Needed on PE Threshold Issues*, Tax Notes Int'l 249 (Oct. 19, 2015); Gary D. Sprague, *Playing the Principal Role in Creating a Permanent Establishment*, Tax Mgmt. Int'l J. 25 (Jan. 8, 2016).

PE.[48] Certain work in the BEPS Project has had a similar effect of encouraging tax authorities to focus on PE nexus arguments, though for more practical reasons. Specifically, the lowering of the dependent-agent threshold by the introduction of the new limb of the test (i.e., the newly introduced "playing the principal role" test) has been interpreted as implying that a more advantageous result is or may be achieved for a jurisdiction that pursues PE arguments rather than transfer-pricing arguments.[49]

Strictly, these two developments concern the dependent-agent PE test but as a matter of practice they seem to have had the effect of encouraging tax authorities to pursue PE threshold points more generally (i.e., including those concerning the fixed-place-of-business test).[50] The overall picture concerning the PE threshold rules is therefore of vague and problematic rules with significant variation in the approach or "practice" that governs their interpretation and application. Additionally, the effect of the OECD's work on the AOA and in BEPS has in practice encouraged the wider use of the PE rules by tax authorities.

Given the nature of the PE threshold difficulties discussed, it should already be evident that they are highly relevant to the position of mobile workers. The following section pursues the implications for mobile workers of the discussion of both the income-allocation rules and the PE threshold rules.

MOBILITY CONCERNS

Concerns about the impact of increased mobility on corporate income tax are not new.[51] However, the nature and scale of individual mobility post-COVID-19 is clearly of a different order to what has been contemplated previously.

48 The basis of this point is explained in 2010 *Report on the Attribution of Profits to Permanent Establishments*, *supra* note 19, paras. 227–247. The essential difference between the transfer-pricing approach and the attribution of profits to a PE under the AOA is explained in para. 235, which contemplates transactions between a nonresident enterprise and a "dependent agent enterprise." The explanation notes that, under a "single taxpayer" transfer-pricing approach between the two enterprises, risks (and potentially assets) of a nonresident enterprise would never be allocated to the jurisdiction of the dependent-agent enterprise. However, where the dependent-agent enterprise does perform the significant people functions relevant to the assumption and/or subsequent management of those risks (and potentially assets) those risks would be attributed to any dependent-agent PE of the nonresident enterprise that is created in the jurisdiction of the dependent-agent enterprise.

49 The implication that a PE approach rather than a transfer-pricing approach may be more advantageous for a tax authority to follow is derived from the lowered PE threshold on the basis of why else would the OECD otherwise seek to lower the dependent-agent PE threshold in BEPS?

50 Though the practical result seems clear, the technical basis for this increased interest in the PE rules is much more debatable. The introduction by the BEPS Project of the "risk framework" approach has delivered a much closer alignment of the transfer pricing and PE attribution rules. See the discussion in *Public Discussion Draft, Additional Guidance on the Attribution of Profits to Permanent Establishments, BEPS Action 7*, OECD (July 4, 2016).

51 Concerns about the impact of increased connectivity through improvements in information and communications technology (such as video conferencing and electronic discussion group

In the context of the increased mobility of employees, the core impacts of the rules discussed here are: (1) a materially increased uncertainty about the circumstances in which taxable presences under the corporate income tax rules may be created and (2) uncertainties in the measure of the relevant allocable income where the income-allocation rules are engaged. The consequence is therefore a significant increase in the potential for dispute, double taxation, and inadvertent (and potentially significant) tax exposures due to increased mobility.

These issues are made more acute due to the tendency for the senior people within an MNE group to be especially mobile. That is relevant of course because senior people within an organization are likely to exercise relevant decision-making for the purposes of the income-allocation rules and so, from the perspective of those rules, make a high-value contribution to the conduct of the MNEs business, increasing the revenues at stake because of these issues. Further, to the extent such mobile staff occupy an operational management role and contribute to the business of several companies in the group, when carried on remotely, the activity has the potential to create taxable presence and income-allocation problems in respect of multiple group companies.

These difficulties are a consequence of the technical rules and guidance. The threshold test is vague, highly facts-and-circumstances specific (and so highly subjective) and governed by significant variations in "practice." This makes it difficult to identify hard and fast rules that can be relied on to determine the point at which an arrangement involving one or more mobile employees will trigger the PE threshold test. As noted, there are also incentives (or at least perceived incentives) for tax authorities to raise the threshold PE point in practice, increasing the practical significance of this point. Issues concerning whether the fixed-place-of-business test is triggered or not may arise in a wide range of circumstances. These may include, for example, working from a second home or holiday house, or in a specially leased office or in a room in the business premises of a local group subsidiary company. In all these cases, the pattern of working may be sporadic or regular, with varying time periods from one case to another. This obviously means that mobility magnifies the uncertainty about the potential application of these rules. The mobility of senior decision-makers also has the potential to create problems under the dependent-agent PE test given that such people may well habitually conclude contracts on behalf of companies in the MNE group.

Where the PE threshold test is met, the relevant PE income-attribution issues will need to be addressed. Similar profit-allocation issues may also need to be addressed under the transfer-pricing rules, for example in cases involving short-term

applications) emerged in the OECD's e-commerce work in the late 1990s – see *Draft for Public Comment, The Impact of the Communications Revolution on the Application of "Place of Effective Management" as a Tiebreaker Rule, a Discussion Paper from the Technical Advisory Group on Monitoring the Application of Existing Treaty Norms for the Taxation of Business Profits*, OECD (Feb. 2001).

secondment of staff arrangements to a local subsidiary. It is also possible that both the PE attribution rules and the transfer-pricing rules may be engaged simultaneously, as in the more troublesome scenario where the activities of one or more senior workers working remotely (perhaps under a secondment arrangement) create multiple PEs of group companies. In any event, determining the allocable return will require account to be taken of the relevant decision-making analysis. This will frequently create some difficult issues relating to the quantum of the return that is allocable to that activity under attribution or transfer-pricing principles given that, in any case, a highly facts-and-circumstances-based analysis will be required to determine the appropriate value of the contribution made in any one case. The contribution of the individuals involved to that decision-making process may also vary over time, or vary from one instance to another, depending on the specialist or management expertise that is required in each case. This obviously raises both practicability and subjectivity concerns. Also, again, individual country practice on these questions of profit allocation will be important.

The overall picture is that mobility issues can create corporate income tax issues that are extremely difficult to deal with, and that can have financially significant impacts. It is also the case that some novel tax problems may be created by these increased mobility issues. For instance, given that significant value may be attributed to the contribution of senior decision-makers, could a remote-working arrangement involving one or more such people trigger an "exit charge" disposal (or part disposal) in the jurisdiction in which they previously worked? At what point might one or more remote workers be said to be exercising "control or risk" or DEMPE[52] functions under the transfer-pricing rules (or "significant people functions" under the PE-attribution rules) with the result that some or all of the return on the assets and risks concerned is redirected to their location? What is the proper characterization of their role (which might be relevant for withholding tax, VAT or customs duty purposes)? For example, are such people merely providing a service or might they be creating or enhancing some sort of asset (e.g., brand value) by their actions?

An irony of the current position is that the increasing tendency of the income-allocation rules to rely on the decision-making of senior individuals has historically assumed the relative *immobility* of such individuals, making them a suitable anchor point to counter abusive "booking" structures. Now, however, those individuals are generally the most mobile group within an MNE. As this point suggests, the existing rules were never built to cope with the level of problems that are now created by this new-found mobility.

[52] The DEMPE tests (Development, Enhancement, Maintenance, Protection and Exploitation) are used to determine whether an entity has economic ownership of an intangible asset. See *OECD Transfer Pricing Guidelines for Multinational Enterprises and Tax Administrations*, *supra* note 11, para. 6.59–6.64.

ADDRESSING THESE PROBLEMS

Is it possible to address these difficulties with clearer, more certain rules that could function in the context of greater mobility? In theory, a range of possible solutions for the difficulties discussed here could be identified. For example, one or more safe harbor approaches, preferably relying on objective tests (rather than tests based on subjective assessments and/or the particular facts and circumstances) could be used. In the case of any taxable presence issues, this could involve factors such as a threshold test based on the number of days spent in the jurisdiction, or an exemption for the use of hotels or holiday homes, or a special regime to deal with temporary visitors, and so on. In the case of any relevant allocable return arising due to remote working arrangements, simplified approaches might include the use of simple cost-plus approaches to the quantum of return, or an exemption where any allocable return would fall under a specified amount, for example.

However, for several reasons, such approaches will likely prove very difficult to implement in practice. Persuading states to limit their actions (or refrain from applying their existing rules) will be difficult, if not impossible, particularly in the current revenues-pressured climate, and especially if states see the opportunity to raise revenues through simply applying the rules that are already available to them.[53]

Alternatively, MNEs could introduce their own measures such as curtailing the mobility of senior employees, or constraining their mobility by reference to per-country time limits or granting freedom for remote working only by reference to certain designated countries, etc. However, tracking individual mobility within an MNE can be very difficult, and, even if it is possible to track mobility, the practical reality may be that it is very hard to enforce tax-related disciplines on the senior executives within the group.

Solutions are unlikely to arrive soon. The OECD is planning to address several worker mobility and tax questions, including the issues discussed in this chapter, though that work is at a very early stage and will not be done quickly.[54]

CONCLUSION AND PROGNOSIS

The shift in worker mobility represents a rapid and major change in working patterns. It is therefore not surprising that the corporate income tax system (which

[53] However, there are some limited cases in which these problems have been addressed by states bilaterally – see, for example, the recent amendment to the Switzerland–France double tax treaty which is discussed at www.taxathand.com/article/28391/France/2022/France-and-Switzerland-agree-to-amicable-tax-agreements-for-cross-border-workers.

[54] See https://news.bloombergtax.com/daily-tax-report-international/oecd-plans-workstream-to-address-worker-mobility-tax-questions. The European Commission has also been encouraged to develop an approach to deal with these issues – see www.eesc.europa.eu/en/news-media/news/taxation-rules-cross-border-teleworking-must-be-updated-and-simplified.

was never designed to accommodate high levels of individual mobility) has not kept pace with these developments. However, the current position is made more difficult by the fact that the tax rules on income allocation have, through their increasing reliance on individual decision-making, developed in a way that means that individual mobility amplifies the difficulties, opening the door to significant problems and uncertainties about the appropriate level of income that is properly allocable in cases involving senior staff working remotely and creating novel problems, as discussed earlier. The rules on taxable nexus are similarly problematic. The problems that previously existed are materially exacerbated by a world of greater mobility, making those rules vague in scope, uncertain in application, and too prone to individual country interpretation and practice. The overall picture is therefore that these corporate income tax rules are inadequate and unsatisfactory in the face of greater individual mobility.

These difficulties, which are a function of the way the rules have been developed and now operate, will not be easy to address in the absence of wholesale reform which would remove the need for the existing rules.[55] The current pressure on states for revenues will make it hard to find workable solutions for these issues, making the immediate prognosis one of a continuing increase in disputes based on a threshold test and income-allocation rules that are already barely fit for purpose.

[55] Such reform would need to involve radical change to the existing international tax system, for example involving a formulary approach or, and more coherently, a shift to a destination-based approach.

11

Time Is, Time Was

Evaluating the Use of the Life-Cycle Model as a Fiscal Tool

Daniel Shaviro

INTRODUCTION

What time periods should we use in tax and other fiscal policy to evaluate people's circumstances, and thus to determine either how they are being treated, or how they ought to be? This question is both fundamental and pervasive. For example, one can neither intelligently evaluate the longstanding debate concerning income versus consumption taxation,[1] nor assess prevailing economic inequality and the degree of progressivity of a given country's fiscal system, without addressing the time period question.

The shortest possible time period would be limited to the present moment, under a 'tax system [that] operates continuously, instantaneously creating taxes or refunds as cash flows occur . . . [with a] zero-length accounting period'.[2] In practice, however, the typical short-term period is one year. While the use of annual systems is widely recognised as administratively necessary, there is little disagreement regarding their essential arbitrariness. Few would dispute, for example, that in principle a receipt on 1 January should not have greatly different tax consequences than one on the immediately preceding 31 December. Likewise, it is surely generally agreed that a taxpayer who earns a million dollars in one year and loses a million dollars in an adjoining year does not greatly differ from one who breaks even in both years.

For helpful comments on earlier drafts, I am grateful to Daniel Hemel, Linda Sugin, and the participants in the 'Taxing People: The Next 100 Years' conference that was held at Worcester College, Oxford, on 2–3 June 2023.

1 On the relevance of the time period question to evaluating income and consumption taxation (as well as on the desirability of 'income averaging' by the tax system), see Daniel Shaviro, *Beyond the Pro-Consumption Tax Consensus*, 60 Stan. L. Rev. 745 (2007).

2 Jeff Strnad, *Deflation and the Income Tax* 21 (John M. Olin Program in L. and Econ., Working Paper 261, August 2003).

On the other end of the spectrum, standard economic reasoning offers grounds for entirely basing one's thinking on lifetime (or longer)[3] models. In particular, the closely related permanent-income[4] and life-cycle[5] hypotheses support employing a purely lifetime perspective in evaluating people's circumstances and treatment. The resulting life-cycle model (as I will call it) posits that people make decisions on a lifetime basis, seeking to optimise lifetime utility in the face of both (1) period-specific declining marginal utility of consumption and (2) whatever preferences they happen to have as between consumption in different periods. Accordingly, in the presence of complete markets (including a lack of borrowing constraints), the question of when one earns a given dollar ostensibly makes no difference regarding when one spends it on consumption. And equivalently, when one pays a given dollar of tax will make no difference regarding how much one spends in any period.[6]

The choice between lifetime and shorter-period approaches can be politically fraught because, in policy debates, the latter are often at least more directly compatible with support for certain progressive positions.[7] Yet there is also what one might call a strong aesthetic element to the choice. As we will see, the common neoclassical assumptions of complete markets and consistent rational choice push insistently in favour of the life-cycle model, especially if one also rejects the pertinence to tax and fiscal policy of intra-lifetime information.[8] With these inputs, the life-cycle model's capacity to draw far-reaching conclusions from very restricted information gives it a degree of at least apparent intellectual power, clarity, and elegance that few adepts in the field (myself included) can entirely resist.

The life-cycle model's importance and influence was recently illustrated by a major new contribution to the US inequality and progressivity debate: the publication, in the *Journal of Political Economy*, of an article by Alan Auerbach, Laurence Kotlikoff, and Darryl Koehler entitled *U.S. Inequality and Fiscal Progressivity: An Intragenerational Accounting* (AKK).[9] This piece extends earlier work on generational accounting – which focuses on the relative lifetime treatment by the fiscal

3 When one is evaluating multigenerational households in which people transfer resources to their heirs, a case might even emerge for treating such households as if they were single long-lived individuals, and thus applying a framework that is longer than any one individual's life.

4 Milton Friedman, A Theory of the Consumption Function 20–37 (1957).

5 Franco Modigliani & Richard Brumberg, *Utility Analysis and the Consumption Function: An Interpretation of Cross-Section Data*, *in* Post Keynesian Econ. 388 (Kenneth K. Kurihara ed., 1954).

6 I ignore here questions of time value that might cause when an item is paid or incurred to affect its present value.

7 For example, a lifetime perspective pushes towards support for consumption taxation, to the exclusion of income or wealth taxation. See Shaviro, *supra* note 1.

8 On the relevance of such intra-lifetime information, see, e.g., Shaviro, *supra* note 1, at 777–778.

9 Alan Auerbach, Laurence Kotlikoff & Darryl Koehler. *U.S. Inequality and Fiscal Progressivity: An Intragenerational Accounting* (Nat'l Bureau of Econ. Rsch., Working Paper No. 22032, 2016), https://ssrn.com/abstract=2747187 [hereinafter AKK].

system of members of different (including future) age cohorts[10] – in order to measure both US economic inequality and the US fiscal system's progressivity. AKK concludes that measures of economic inequality in the prior literature, typically based on income or wealth, 'dramatically overstate'[11] inequality by reason of using those snapshot measures in lieu of a lifetime approach, and that prior work fails to show how 'highly progressive' the US fiscal system is.[12]

AKK relies on the view that '[e]conomic inequality is fundamentally about differences in spending power, that is, the ability to engage in current and future consumption',[13] and that fiscal progressivity depends on the lifetime net tax rates faced by people who differ in their lifetime spending power. AKK cashes out these premises by applying a 'life-cycle, consumption-smoothing program that includes hard borrowing constraints and all major federal and state tax/transfer programs, whether cash or in-kind',[14] to 2016 Survey of Consumer Finances data. AKK applies this model by 'assum[ing] that households engage in life-cycle consumption-smoothing behaviour, captured by an assumed uniform, across households, desired longitudinal age-consumption profile … subject to borrowing constraints'.[15]

AKK appears to view economic inequality as a concern based on the premise that individuals derive utility from their own consumption plus leisure, and experience declining marginal utility as lifetime spending power increases. Hence, higher lifetime spending power implies greater personal welfare than lower lifetime spending power, and progressively redistributing it without affecting incentives would be expected to increase total utility. AKK's use of a life-cycle model reflects an underlying view of people as rationally seeking to optimise lifetime utility, aided by generally complete markets apart from the special case of borrowing constraints.[16]

As we will see, the life-cycle view suggests that people will seek to equalise the marginal utility derived from the last unit of consumption in each period.[17] With period-specific declining marginal utility, consumption in different periods is akin to the consumption of different commodities – like, say, movies and pizza in an introductory microeconomics textbook. This, in turn, under a standard consumer model, yields the result of allocating one's budget (i.e., one's lifetime spending

[10] See, e.g., Laurence Kotlikoff, Generational Accounting (1993), and Daniel Shaviro, Do Deficits Matter (1997).

[11] AKK, *supra* note 9, at 0 (abstract).

[12] Id.

[13] Id., at 1.

[14] Id., at 5.

[15] Id., at 7.

[16] AKK's model does, however, assume that '[l]ife insurance purchases are constrained to be non-negative, i.e., households don't buy annuities at the margin'. Id., at 5.

[17] Since the model allows for bequests, one can think of them as akin to consumption in yet another period, yielding utility (and presumably, declining marginal utility) to the prospective bequester as she contemplates them.

power) in such a way as to equalise the marginal utility derived from the last unit consumed of each commodity.

Equal marginal utility of consumption in all periods (EMU) turns out to be a very important concept. While AKK's reliance on lifetime spending power and lifetime net tax rates does not absolutely rise and fall with it, the case for such reliance is compelling insofar as EMU holds, and subject to significant challenge insofar as EMU does not hold. Evaluating EMU therefore plays a critical, even if not completely decisive, role in evaluating not just AKK's conclusions regarding economic inequality and the US fiscal system's progressivity, but also the broader time period issues regarding how to conceptualise and measure distribution and tax burdens.

I will conclude that the life-cycle model is not entirely correct. Indeed, like other such 'it doesn't matter' theories[18] – for example, the Coase Theorem, the Efficient Markets Hypothesis (EMH), and the Modigliani-Miller Theorem (MMT) – its value lies as much in its showing us where to look for falsifying conditions as in its actual empirical accuracy.

The Basic Consumer Choice Model

Consider the basic two-goods model of consumer choice that introductory microeconomics classes have been using for decades. Under it, suppose that a consumer can use her budget line to purchase two commodities – say, movies and pizza – in whatever relative proportions she likes, given their prices. They are both available continuously – that is, she can always purchase a penny less of one and a penny more of the other.

Suppose further that she has an insatiable appetite for each good, but derives declining marginal utility from each, as the quantity of it that she consumes increases. She will choose between them such that the marginal utility that she derives from the last penny that she spends on movies equals that derived from the last penny that she spends on pizza. After all, if one marginal utility exceeded the other, she could increase her total utility by shifting a penny of consumption from the low to the high marginal utility commodity.

In this set-up, there is no underlying high theory regarding how to define distinct commodities. The crucial characteristic of a distinct commodity is that, in one's utility function, there is declining marginal utility for it in particular (not just for *all* consumption). For example, one gets less hungry with each bite of pizza, and less attentive or enthralled with each additional moment of movie-viewing. This assumption is needed to motivate the consumer's ranking of bundles with different proportions of each commodity.

[18] Scott Sumner, The 'It Doesn't Matter' Theories (EconLog Nov. 4, 2014), https://www.econlib.org/archives/2014/11/the_it_doesnt_m.html.

Applying the Model to Consumption over Time

Applying this simple model to consumer choice over time is straightforward. Consumption in different periods equates to consumption of distinct commodities, so long as there is period-specific declining marginal utility. Suppose, for example, that one is choosing between (a) one dinner plus one place to sleep both tonight and a year from now and (b) two dinners and two places to sleep on one of these occasions, and zero on the other. It would come as no surprise to learn that the typical consumer strongly preferred (a) to (b).

There are, however, a number of considerations that may complicate intertemporal consumption choices. For example:

- With a positive interest rate (r) for saving from Period 1 and Period 2, one may have a choice between spending \$X in Period 1 or \$X(1 + r) in Period 2. An analogous relationship holds for borrowing in order to consume sooner (e.g., in Period 1 rather than Period 2).
- Other preferences may also influence one's choice regarding when to consume. For example, impatience may induce one to prefer consuming sooner, all else equal. Or suppose that, due to habituation to current consumption levels and enjoyment of positive changes, one prefers a rising consumption level over time.
- One predictably experiences physical and mental changes across time. In consequence, one might get more utility out of skiing at age thirty when one is more fit, and/or out of drinking fine wines at age sixty when one has a more experienced palate, than the other way around. While this example pertains only to particular consumption items, it is possible that one would want to consume absolutely more in one period than the other due to one's changing physical or mental state.
- One may need to plan for retirement periods when one can no longer work but still needs to consume. Moreover, a finite life expectancy indicates a (possibly uncertain) endpoint to one's own consumption, although bequest motives may imply deriving utility from the thought that others will consume one's resources in the future.

In a model, such as that in AKK, that attempts to simulate consumer choice across time, such considerations may be assumed to operate in some unknown fashion, without weakening the model's potential validity. For example, it may be immaterial exactly *how* they cause a consumer to choose a particular age-consumption profile. AKK also, by focusing on lifetime spending power that need not be exercised in full during one's lifetime to generate utility, avoids treating people as worse-off simply because they voluntarily decide to leave bequests rather than spending everything that they have on own consumption.

Despite the lifetime model's potential flexibility, a lurking problem may become significant once we more thoroughly interrogate its real-world validity. In a single-period choice like that between movies and pizza, it is (relatively) easy to think of the consumer as having a consistent, unified set of preferences that she applies to different items, all of which are available, and will be enjoyed, right about now. By contrast, the relationship between one's self or selves at very different times is not quite so simple or straightforward. My connection to myself thirty years in the future or the past may be more problematic than my adjudicating between the distinct appetites I feel that may drive me to consume both movies and pizza.

Massive literature in multiple realms examine problems of choice across time – often addressing the difficulty of exercising choice wisely across long time periods. Consider the parable of the Grasshopper and the Ant, the former of whom fails to plan adequately (or at all) for the coming winter. Or the literature discussing addiction, which may involve a failure to weight properly the future cost of one's taking up (say) smoking or heroin today, unless one happens to accept the Becker-Murphy theory of rational addiction.[19] More generally, consider the sociological and economic literatures that examine problems of myopia, or time-inconsistent hyperbolic discounting.[20]

Even if such myopes as the Grasshopper or the beginning teenage smoker are unusual in the magnitude of their failures to exercise rational and consistent intertemporal choice, they help to remind us just how hard a task it is. Choice across time is much more challenging, requiring both self-control and a great deal of predictive knowledge about the future, than (as in the pizza-movies hypothetical) making a one-time budget choice between food and entertainment. Moreover, one only gets one lifetime in which to experience choice across time. It is not as if one can learn from previous failures in quite the same way as with respect to movies and pizza.

EQUAL MARGINAL UTILITY OF CONSUMPTION IN ALL PERIODS AND A PURELY LIFETIME PERSPECTIVE

Despite the difficulty of exercising consistent rational choice over multiple decades, suppose we fully accept the life-cycle model for now. Again, it suggests that people will execute age-consumption profiles that leave them with EMU for each period. While I will question this result in the last section of this chapter, it is worth first briefly reviewing here just how powerfully EMU would drive the analyses of inequality and progressivity in precisely the directions suggested by AKK.

[19] See Gary S. Becker & Kevin M. Murphy, A *Theory of Rational Addiction*, 96 J. POL. ECON. 675, 675–676 (1988) (outlining a theory of rational addiction in which rationality means a consistent plan to maximise utility over time).

[20] See discussion *infra* in text accompanying n. 62.

Direct Consequences of EMU

To see how strongly EMU supports gauging economic inequality based solely on lifetime spending power, and the fiscal system's progressivity based solely on lifetime net tax rates, suppose we look first at a given individual across her lifespan, and then at comparisons between individuals.

Individuals across Time

Suppose that I achieve EMU by exercising consistent rational choice across time in the presence of complete markets, including a lack of borrowing constraints. For example, suppose that I can readily borrow against earnings that I would only accrue in the future, despite the actual real-world possibility that market failures – based, for example, on lenders' reasonable concerns about moral hazard or adverse selection[21] – would stand in the way.

In this scenario, it makes no difference when I pay taxes or receive transfers (assuming that I cannot respond strategically to their timing). For example, suppose we redesigned a pre-existing tax system so that it would impose greater tax liabilities on me during my high-income than my low-income periods, without thereby changing my lifetime spending power or lifetime net tax rate. Relative to the case where it was not doing this, I would simply adjust my saving and/or borrowing as between periods to implement the very same age-consumption profile as I would have in the absence of this tax system design feature.

Different Individuals

Once people have uniform EMUs across their lifespans, it becomes conceptually easy to decide which transfers between individuals would be progressive and (absent other complications, such as adverse incentive effects) increase total utility. For example, suppose that Ann is a career high-earning professional, while Bill is a career low-earning supermarket clerk. Even if Bill, being in mid-career, has higher income in the current period than Ann (e.g., because she is on the front end of her career and still in school, or on the backend and already retired), she is better-off on a current as well as a lifetime basis, if she can and does borrow and lend freely between periods.

Prior literature suggests that this view supports imposing a progressive consumption tax, rather than an income or wealth tax. Moreover, even if this tax is levied annually, it should be structured so that lifetime net tax rates depend purely on lifetime spending power. Insofar as graduated rates are applied annually, they should

[21] Moral hazard arises from the possibility that I might choose to work and earn less if I would have to use future earnings to repay the lender, and, by working and earning less, I could otherwise escape full repayment. Adverse selection arises from the possibility that I know more than the lender about my actual future earnings prospects.

include features (such as multi-year 'income averaging') that minimise the differences in burdens imposed on people with highly variable, as opposed to relatively constant, annual flows.

Lifetime Spending Power and Lifetime Net Tax Rates' Potentially Exclusive Relevance under Restrictive Models

Even if one accepts EMU, it need not follow that lifetime spending power and lifetime net tax rates are the only pertinent inputs.[22] such a view can gain credence, however, if one makes certain additional assumptions. For example, it can follow if one generalises from the famous optimal income tax model that won economist James Mirrlees the Nobel Prize.[23]

Mirrlees' model presumes that the social planner is a welfarist, or one for whom 'social welfare is postulated to be an increasing function of individuals' well-being and to depend on no other factors'.[24] Moreover, his model effectively presumes that individuals' wellbeing depends purely on the utility that they derive from market consumption plus leisure, subject as usual to declining marginal utility.

Since Mirrlees employs a one-period model in which there are no savings or wealth (other than fully formed human capital), market consumption is funded through earnings from work. The model assumes, moreover, that all the people in a given society have identical utility functions, and differ only in ability or wage rate, which is defined as the amount that one can earn per unit of time or effort. The social planner's aim is to maximise social welfare, as defined by her social welfare function (which may be utilitarian, or else weighted in varying degrees towards egalitarianism), via redistribution from higher-ability to lower-ability individuals.

In the model, neither time nor effort are directly observable. Moreover, while ability is innate and unalterable, it, too, cannot directly be observed. By contrast, earnings, which are the joint product of ability and time or effort, can be observed. Earnings therefore offer the only differentiating information about particular individuals that is both observable and relevant to distribution policy. Accordingly, once one has set the optimal policy, which depends both on the planner's normative stance and on certain inputs that relate to the broader society but cannot be observed at the individual level,[25] that policy's application to a particular member of the society depends solely on how much she earned.

22 I leave aside here issues such as household status (e.g., singles versus couples, one-earner versus two-earner couples, and the presence or absence of children) whose relevance to distributional policy is widely accepted.

23 See James A. Mirrlees, *An Exploration in the Theory of Optimum Income Taxation*, 38 REV. ECON. STUD. 175 (1971).

24 LOUIS KAPLOW & STEVEN SHAVELL, FAIRNESS VERSUS WELFARE 24 (2002).

25 Broader societal inputs that may help determine the optimal policy include the distribution of earning ability in the population, the specification of people's (generally applicable) utility

Suppose we change the model to allow for decades-long lifespans, with people borrowing and saving between different periods, and also potentially having heirs to whom they may leave bequests. Moreover, suppose they are behaving in accordance with the life-cycle model, achieving EMU between periods (such as years). Then we can continue to apply the Mirrlees model, if we are so inclined, substituting lifetime spending power for one-period labour income and using lifetime net tax rates to assess the system's progressivity.

However, among the problems posed by doing this, without further modifications, is that it involves positing that there is nothing of interest to be learned from observing people's earning and spending patterns across time. In the more than fifty years since Mirrlees promulgated the original model, the optimal income tax literature has explored various reasons why such patterns might indeed be considered pertinent.

For example, consider evidence suggesting that 'savings decisions are [heterogeneous, and] heavily influenced by psychological elements (such as self-control) or minor transaction costs (like the default effects in employer-sponsored 401(k) plans)'.[26] Then one might not only question the basic framework positing consistent rational choice over time, but also conclude that savings behaviour is evidence of broader ability that is relevant to distribution policy.[27] Or suppose that, when we observe current-period low-earners who were previously high-earners and have accumulated substantial savings, we infer that they may be responding to the incentive effects of the earnings tax. Specifically, they may voluntarily be working less – using their savings to fund current consumption – so that they can in effect misrepresent themselves as having low current-period earning ability.[28]

Both hypotheses straightforwardly support taxing savers more than non-savers with the same lifetime spending power. Yet the use of separate-period information might also conceivably offer grounds for treating savers *more* favourably. Suppose, for example, that we consider them more 'efficient' than non-savers at extracting lifetime utility from a given dollar of lifetime spending power, because their greater self-control or foresight makes them better at deploying it to maximum lifetime advantage. Then there are welfarist grounds for giving them more resources than non-savers, at least relative to the case where they lacked this advantage. Either way, however, evidence about earnings and consumption patterns over time – ruled out

functions, and the degree of labour supply responsiveness to an earnings tax. See Shaviro, *supra* note 1, at 757.

[26] Peter Diamond & Emmanuel Saez, *The Case for a Progressive Tax: From Basic Research to Policy Recommendations*, 25 J. Econ. Persp. 165, 178–179 (2011).

[27] One possible implication is that savers, because they have higher ability, should be taxed more than non-savers. An opposite implication might be that savers should be favoured in distribution policy, because they are more able than non-savers to derive high lifetime utility from their lifetime spending power.

[28] See, e.g., Diamond & Saez, *supra* note 26, at 182; Mikhail Golosov et al., *Optimal Indirect and Capital Taxation*, 70(3) Rev. Econ. Stud. 569 (2003).

by definition in the Mirrlees model, and ignored if one simply relies on lifetime spending power in a life-cycle model – contains relevant information that, at least in principle, ought not to be ignored.

As I have discussed elsewhere,[29] such considerations unmistakably complicate the case, which might otherwise be clear under a Mirrlees-influenced welfarist analysis, for favouring a progressive consumption tax with the equivalent of income averaging. But are they also relevant to AKK's measurement exercise? Here much depends on what one makes of AKK's decision to focus on what it calls 'economic inequality'.

Defining 'Economic Inequality'

Again, AKK sets out to measure not *all* inequality (however defined) but 'economic inequality', which it says is 'fundamentally about differences in spending power, that is, the ability to engage in current and future consumption'.[30] As the word 'fundamentally' suggests, this is no arbitrarily selected metric, but reflects an underlying view, to the effect that 'differences in spending power – the ability to spend now and in the future, either on oneself or on one's descendants – [are] of ultimate economic concern'.[31]

Once again, although AKK does not elaborate on the underlying normative framework here, one can infer it from the economics literature, with its assumptions of complete markets, consistent rational choice, and narrowly defined utility functions. Yet such a framework ignores many things.

For example, consider racial or gender inequality, which can greatly affect both people's experienced welfare and an assessment of social justice that reflected egalitarian or other (such as deontological) concerns. AKK understandably excludes such types of inequality from its analysis, without necessarily thereby positing their unimportance.[32] The full experienced consequences of, say, racial inequality are not directly measurable using AKK's methodology – although the methodology could be deployed to compare the distribution of lifetime spending power between groups.[33]

If such a study were conducted based on lifetime spending power, rather than wealth, it is plausible that AKK's main finding regarding economic inequality would be replicated. That is, as to self-identified members of different racial and ethnic

29 See Shaviro, *supra* note 1.

30 AKK, *supra* note 9, at 0 (abstract).

31 Id., at 1.

32 AKK does, however, also say – without using 'economic' as a modifier – that '[i]nequality, in our view, primarily concerns who gets to spend the economy's resources'. Id., at 11.

33 See Neil Bhutta et al., Disparities in Wealth by Race and Ethnicity in the 2019 Survey of Consumer Finance (FEDS Notes, Sept. 28, 2020), www.federalreserve.gov/econres/notes/feds-notes/disparities-in-wealth-by-race-and-ethnicity-in-the-2019-survey-of-consumer-finances-20200928.html.

groups, 'inequality in … wealth [might once again turn out to] dramatically overstate … inequality in spending power'.[34] It is thus worth briefly asking what we would learn from such a finding, if the data indeed confirmed it.

On its face, it would mean exactly what it said: that racial economic inequality (as defined by AKK) is smaller than many may have thought by reason of their relying on measures that are inferior if one sufficiently accepts the life-cycle hypothesis. One thing it would *not* tell us, however, is whether US racism – or racial inequality in its other-than-'economic' dimensions – is a less serious problem than many have thought.

One point about racism's other dimensions – applicable as well to other types of inequality – concerns its relationship to life expectancy differences. According to one recent estimate, as of 2020 (but pre-pandemic), life expectancies were estimated at 74.9 years for Black Americans, as compared to 78.5 years for white Americans.[35] The COVID pandemic then lowered life expectancies across-the-board, but with a net effect of increasing racial disparities.[36]

AKK incorporates life expectancy estimates into its analysis of the fiscal system's progressivity. Specifically, it assumes uniform life expectancies as between 'resource quintiles' in its baseline analysis, and then conducts a sensitivity analysis under which life expectancies are higher for the top quintile.[37] Life expectancy matters here because, for survival-based old-age transfer payments, 'higher mortality translates into lower lifetime benefits'.[38] Hence, a programme such as Social Security with a progressive benefit formula (relative to covered earnings) becomes less progressive insofar as career high-earners live longer, and thus get more years of benefits.[39] As it happens, however, AKK's sensitivity analysis does *not* find reduced progressivity overall if members of the top quintile live longer.[40]

It is worth noting, however, that life expectancy affects people in more dimensions than just the computation of their lifetime spending power and lifetime net tax rates. While I will need greater lifetime resources if I live longer – making longevity, in effect, a downside risk against which I might want to insure through annuitization – it is presumably a good thing for me overall. So long as my quality of life does not decline too sharply, I would be expected to prefer living longer, and to have greater aggregate lifetime satisfaction if I succeed in doing so. Thus, a full assessment

[34] AKK, *supra* note 9, at 1.

[35] Theresa Andrasfay & Noreen Goldman, Reductions in 2020 US Life Expectancy due to COVID-19 and the Disproportionate Impact on the Black and Latino Populations, PNAS (Jan. 14, 2021), www.pnas.org/doi/full/10.1073/pnas.2014746118.

[36] Id.

[37] See AKK, supra note 9, at 41 and table 3.

[38] Id., at 41.

[39] See id.

[40] See id., at 41 and table 3. Specifically, in the table 3 column denominated 'High Income Mortality', lifetime net tax rates decline for the bottom four quintiles and remain the same for the top quintile (as well as for the top 5% and 1%).

of even purely 'economic' inequality in the United States surely requires assigning some weight to life expectancy differences between better-off and worse-off individuals.

Returning to the topic of race, suppose that racial life expectancy differences were to persist even after the (hypothetical) equalisation of lifetime spending power and lifetime net tax rates by race. Moreover, suppose that these differences result from racially disparate treatment of individuals (for example, by police and medical personnel) along with the stresses associated with living as a Black person in a society still culturally poisoned by racism.

It would then be reasonable to conclude that the United States still suffered from racial inequality. In this regard, the persistent life expectancy differences would both matter for their own sake and be a diagnostic suggesting the importance of factors apart from 'who gets to spend the economy's resources'.[41]

Suppose we now apply these points outside race, and we acknowledge that economic inequality may matter for reasons apart from just what share of the economy's resources one gets to spend. I have elsewhere argued, for example, that humans are 'an intensely social species, and often a rivalrous one, prone to measuring ourselves in terms of others, and often directly against others'.[42] People's subjective welfare does not depend solely on own consumption of market goods plus leisure. Indeed, they may have 'deep-seated psychological responses to inequality and social hierarchy' that create the potential for material differences to 'invoke … feelings of superiority and inferiority, dominance and subordination' that powerfully 'affect … the way we relate to and treat each other'.[43]

If that is so, then AKK's reduction of inequality to 'who gets to spend the economy's resources'[44] may be missing important dimensions of the problem. Suppose, for example, that current period wealth and income differences trigger sentiments of dominance and subordination.[45] Likewise, suppose that two societies with identical economic inequality, as measured by lifetime spending power, had very different felt experiences of hierarchy, by reason of their distinct cultures. A case in point might be differences between the United States sixty years ago and today, if changing cultural norms have prompted a rise in conspicuous consumption at the top, triggering loss of subjective welfare below that leads to 'expenditure cascades'[46]

41 Id., at 11.

42 Daniel Shaviro, *The Mapmaker's Dilemma in Evaluating High-End Inequality*, 71 Univ. Mia. L. Rev. 83, 87–88 (2016).

43 See id., at 88, quoting Richard Wilkinson & Kate Pickett, The Spirit Level: Why Greater Equality Makes Societies Stronger (2010).

44 AKK, *supra* note 9, at 11.

45 This would perhaps be less likely if people actually acted as posited by the life-cycle model, and therefore achieved EMU as between periods. *Infra* the following section discusses reasons for not expecting the achievement of EMU.

46 *See* Robert H. Frank et al., *Expenditure Cascades*, 1 Rev. Behav. Econ. 55, 56–57 (2014).

as others strive to keep up.[47] Then it might be the case that high-end inequality in the United States has grown worse over this time, even if (or insofar as) the distribution of lifetime spending power has remained the same.

A further set of issues pertains to AKK's exclusive focus on lifetime spending power. This effectively presumes people's equal ability to derive lifetime welfare from lifetime spending power. To defend such an assumption, one might argue one or more of the following:

(1) It is actually true, rather than being merely a convenient simplification for purposes of economic analysis.
(2) Even if it is not actually true, departures from uniform optimisation are too random, unsystematic, and unobservable to be used constructively in an economic analysis.
(3) When people fail to optimise the use of their lifetime spending power, despite complete markets, it is their own 'fault' and not the fiscal system's, and this makes it normatively irrelevant to distributional analysis.

Of these three claims, the first appears to be clearly false. An extensive literature describes the types of rational choice errors that it appears millions of Americans systematically make – for example, saving too little for retirement.[48] The third is an ideological claim that might affect one's interest in using the fiscal system to address welfare differences between individuals. However, it does not rebut concluding that rational choice failures, along with lifetime spending power, can affect the lifetime welfare that people achieve, and even that such failures might be remediable through public policy.

By contrast, the second claim, dismissing people's errors as in effect randomly distributed, is crucial. If it were true, rational choice failures, like preference differences, might have no particular implications for AKK's distributional analysis, apart from reminding us that this analysis inevitably greatly simplifies a more complicated (but imperfectly observable) reality. For two reasons, however, it cannot so readily be dismissed. The first is that the ability to extract lifetime utility from lifetime spending power, such as by deploying foresight and self-control, might be positively correlated with the ability to generate high earnings.[49] The second is

[47] While this suggests that high-end inequality in the United States might create greater problems today than it did sixty years ago, even insofar as 'economic inequality', as measured by lifetime spending power, remained constant, it is plausible that the non-material aspects of invidious racial and gender inequality have eased over that time.

[48] *See* Daniel Shaviro, *Multiple Myopias, Multiple Selves, and the Under-Saving Problem*, 47 CONN. L. REV. 1215, 1240–1241 (2015) (citing and discussing evidence regarding the under-saving problem).

[49] See Emmanuel Saez, *The Desirability of Commodity Taxation under Non-Linear Income Taxation and Heterogeneous Tastes*, 83 J. PUB. ECON. 217, 228 (2002). ('[T]here is a strong presumption that higher income individuals save more not only because they have more income to save but also because they might have a better financial education and be more

that rational choice failures may involve failing to equalise the marginal utility of consumption for all periods – which, as we will see in the Conclusion, significantly undermines the case for relying exclusively on the life-cycle model.

To bring out these points more clearly, recall the parable of the Grasshopper and the Ant, both of whom have earnings during the summer ('Period 1'), but who, due to the Grasshopper's myopia, face very different circumstances in the winter ('Period 2'), when they cannot work. If Ants tend to have higher lifetime spending power than Grasshoppers, then the ratio between their lifetime spending power might understate the degree of inequality in their lifetime circumstances. And, if Grasshoppers are making rational choice failures, rather than merely responding to the lesser utility they derive from Period 2 than Period 1 consumption, then redistributing resources to them in Period 2 might have very different lifetime welfare consequences than doing such redistribution in Period 1. Moreover, Period 2 information might help to guide distribution policy, in lieu of one's basing it purely on lifetime spending power.

DO INDIVIDUALS ACTUALLY HAVE THE SAME MARGINAL UTILITY OF CONSUMPTION IN ALL PERIODS?

The previous section discussed how assuming EMU in all periods would powerfully push towards enshrining lifetime spending power and lifetime net tax rates as guides to distribution policy that would not need any supplementation by period-specific information. The push would be more powerful still if (counterfactually) information about people's earning and consumption sequences was not potentially relevant. This section discusses multiple reasons for doubting that people typically achieve EMU. They all rest, one way or another, on the ways in which time matters, causing life-cycle choices to be orders of magnitude more challenging than allocating a given night's budget between movies and pizza.

Borrowing Constraints

As AKK recognises, borrowing constraints can importantly compromise people's ability to equalise consumption between periods. In response to this concern, AKK not only incorporates significant hard borrowing constraints into its model, but analyses current spending power in addition to lifetime spending power, where the two differ due to credit constraints plus several other factors.[50] With respect to

aware of the need to save for retirement.') Note that, while Saez calls this a taste difference, I classify it as involving rational choice failures, on the view that those who save too little may be making a mistake from the standpoint of their own lifetime wellbeing, rather than deriving more utility from sooner and less from later consumption.

50 *See* AKK, *supra* note 9, at 28. Lifetime and current spending power differ due not only to credit constraints, but also by reason of (a) time-varying in-kind benefits, (b) trapped home equity, (c)

lifetime net tax rates, it also conducts a sensitivity analysis in which a credit-constrained household's valuation of currently inaccessible future resource flows and spending are additionally discounted by 50 per cent.[51] This turns out to make surprisingly little difference with regard to lifetime net tax rates, in part because credit-constrained low-income households' remaining lifetime resources and remaining lifetime net taxes are *both* being discounted.[52]

One possible criticism of AKK's approach is that, in order to head off endogeneity problems, it models a uniform hard-borrowing constraint, rather than one depending, say, on information about people's earnings (which itself reflects their choices).[53] By contrast, a study it cites that allowed for varying credit constraints[54] found that they are especially significant for two groups: the 'chronically poor with low initial endowments', and 'initially well-endowed persons with high levels of acquired skills ... who cannot immediately access their future earnings'.[55] Prospective doctors and lawyers, for example, might know by their early twenties that they are likely to have high career earnings, yet be unable to borrow significantly against these expectations for consumption purposes until their full-time work careers have started.

The relevance of such heterogeneity goes less to how adjusting for it might have affected AKK's results (probably, not much) than to how one should think about life-cycle models. The impact of borrowing constraints on the chronically poor suggests that such constraints might reduce their welfare – or more specifically, their capacity to derive lifetime utility from how they use their lifetime spending power – by impeding the use of borrowing to meet current needs. However, suppose that people can be prone to myopically undervaluing future, relative to current, consumption needs. Then such an individual's lifetime welfare might conceivably be improved by borrowing constraints.

Now consider someone in the second group, such as a doctor. Suppose we are comparing her to an individual with the same lifetime spending power but more front-loaded earnings – say, a professional athlete – initially, under the assumption that both of them optimise correctly given available financial markets. It follows straightforwardly that (all else equal) the doctor should have lower lifetime utility. Given the borrowing constraint, she may be stuck with having a higher marginal utility of consumption in her penurious student years than in her plush later years.

certain time-specific cash-flow constraints, (d) forms of wealth, such as annuities, that may affect unintended bequests, and (e) differences in mortality rates, which may affect current-period spending. Id., at 28–29.

51 See id., at 43–44.

52 Id., at 44.

53 Id., at 6.

54 See id., at 6, citing Rong Hai & James J. Heckman, *Inequality in Human Capital and Endogenous Credit Constraints*, 25 Rev. Econ. Dynamics 4 (2017).

55 Hai & Heckman, *supra* note 54, at 34–35.

She would have gained lifetime utility by being able to smooth more, in accordance with her preferred age-consumption profile, as the professional athlete can do.

One immediate implication is that the doctor would gain lifetime welfare if the government acted to ease her borrowing constraints – for example, by subsidising her in her student years, and commensurately taxing her more in her later years.[56] One could describe this, if one liked, as redistributing resources from her older self to her younger self, although it would leave her lifetime spending power and lifetime net tax rate unchanged.

Yet consider as well how we might compare her marginal utilities in different periods to those of the professional athlete. With identical lifetime spending power, complete markets, and an assumption of no other differences between them, they would have had the same marginal utilities as each other in each period (in addition to each achieving such equality as between their own periods). Now, however, by reason of the doctor's inability so to equalise, she has higher marginal utility in her early years and lower in her later years. In effect, she is 'poorer' in the first period and 'richer' in the second period.[57] One might thus want to transfer resources from the athlete to the doctor in the earlier period, and from the doctor to the athlete in the later period.

Now suppose that we allow for decisional failures, such as myopia or else overly basing current-period consumption on current-period income. This might make it plausible that the professional athlete will reduce her lifetime utility, and fail to achieve EMU as between periods, by reason of spending too much in her early high-earnings years and, thus, leaving too little for her subsequent low-earning years. If so, then just as the doctor is first 'poor' and then 'rich', so may the athlete be first 'rich' and then 'poor'.

Recall that, by the rubric of lifetime spending power if one assumes EMU, these individuals are presumed to be equally well-off in all periods. But one can now see the possibility that period-specific information would be informative about their relative welfare and marginal utilities of consumption. We might actually learn something of value by separately observing that (a) the athlete has higher income and wealth in Period 1 and (b) the doctor has higher income, along with a higher sum of wealth plus expected future earnings, in Period 2.

Changes in Information

Suppose that the information on which one has been basing one's consumption choices suddenly changes drastically, either for better or worse. For example, there

[56] However, the policy merits of doing this might depend on the extent to which the government could use its powers to ease the problems of moral hazard and adverse selection that deter private lenders from lending more copiously to future professionals.

[57] The doctor's being 'richer' than the professional in the second period reflects that her over-consuming in that period (relative to the case where she could have smoothed more of it forward) does indeed increase her total utility, while reducing her marginal utility, in that period.

might be a shock to one's expected future earnings, the value of one's assets, one's remaining life expectancy, or one's health condition. This may mean, ex post, that one is worse-off on a lifetime basis than an individual who had (ex post) exactly the same outcomes and preferences, but who knew earlier on what was going to happen, and who thus could better optimise her consumption across periods.

Some of these shocks are expressly or effectively insurable, but others are not. For example, given the market failures caused by moral hazard and adverse selection, it is hard to insure against shocks to the value of one's specialised (and hence under-diversified) human capital. One can engage in precautionary saving to address downside risk, or (via what one might call precautionary dissaving) spend a bit more currently given upside risk, but even those are only partial responses. Even with the optimal use of available risk mitigation techniques, new information potentially changes the choices that would (ex post) have been optimal in *all* periods, looking back as well as forwards.

AKK recognises the potential importance of risk, which it raises in connection with the point that risky investments may have higher expected returns than safe ones, and reserves addressing it for future work.[58] Such work might, for example, explore such issues as (1) how optimal responses to risk might affect people's consumption and investment choices, given the market failures that limit the availability of insurance, (2) how government policy might address such risks (e.g., via social insurance), and (3) how we should think ex ante about a risky career or investment choice that has a probabilistic distribution between favourable and adverse outcomes.

Wholly separate from such important questions, however, is that of how changes in information affect EMU and reliance on life-cycle versus separate-period models. Suppose that I end up with high lifetime spending power, but that this unexpectedly results from my experiencing a lucky break at age forty. Suppose, for example, that I win the lottery, either literally, or metaphorically such as by reason of my experiencing an unexpected sudden jump in my earnings prospects. Because I cannot increase my past consumption to what it would have been had I known for certain that this change in information was coming,[59] I will be worse-off than had I always known. Specifically, my marginal utility will be high pre-shock and low post-shock.

As with the doctor in the borrowing constraint case, I am worse off on a lifetime basis than someone who *does* get to consumption-smooth properly. But I am better-off than that individual, and I have lower marginal utility (all else equal), in the post-shock period. Once again, this suggests that looking at the two periods separately yields pertinent information for distributional purposes that would be ignored if one took a purely lifetime focus.

58 AKK, *supra* note 9, at 7.

59 This is not to deny that, had I known the surge *might* be coming, I could have increased prior consumption a bit – engaging in what one might call precautionary dissaving. But I will still turn out to have consumed too little given that the positive change *did* happen.

People's Actual Decision Methods

Few still defend the complete accuracy of the assumption that people generally act consistently and rationally in furtherance of consistent, well-framed preferences. Instead, behavioural economics has won widespread acceptance.[60] Debate has largely shifted to the question of what to make of the motley array of cognitive frameworks, information-processing heuristics, and shifting context-dependent preferences that we now understand to underlie failures in the exercise of rational choice. If anything, there are now too many, rather than too few, plausible explanations of why actual consumption and savings choices might fail to conform to those assumed by the life-cycle model.

A relatively extreme, but not necessarily uncommon, example of such rational choice failure is hyperbolic discounting, or applying a much higher discount rate between the current time and any future time than between future times.[61] One who is subject to hyperbolic discounting cannot hold consistent preferences. For example, at Time One she will want to apply a normal discount rate in dividing consumption between Times Two and Three. But once Time Two arrives, she will be far more inclined to concentrate consumption in Time Two.[62]

Also, consider evidence that people use 'mental accounts', causing them to classify fungible dollars differently depending on their source. In effect, these are rules of thumb that people use to economise on decision costs. They cause amounts that are coded as 'current income' to be more readily spent than amounts coded as 'current assets', which in turn are more likely to be spent than those coded as 'future income'.[63]

While the use of mental accounts might be viewed as higher-level rational choice, since economising on decision costs is a rational objective, it leads to consumption and savings choices that depart systematically from those predicted by the life-cycle model. In support of its empirical accuracy, a large body of evidence suggests that current consumption is much more closely linked to current income than the life-cycle model would predict.[64]

60 See, e.g., Ryan Bubb & Richard H. Pildes, *How Behavioral Economics Trims Its Sails and Why*, 127 HARV. L. REV. 1593, 1595 (2014).

61 See, e.g., David Laibson, *Golden Eggs and Hyperbolic Discounting*, 112 Q. J. ECON. 443, 445–446 (1997) (defining hyperbolic discounting). An intuitive illustration might be eating too many chocolate chip cookies (in light of one's long-term objectives) when they are passed around at a dinner party.

62 Evidence supporting hyperbolic discounting comes both from self-reporting and from the steps people take in advance to restrict its impact on their behaviour by limiting their choice sets. See, e.g., B. DOUGLAS BERNHEIM & ANTONIO RANGEL, *Behavioral Public Economics: Welfare and Policy Analysis with Non-Standard Decision-Makers* 6–9 (Nat'l Bureau of Econ. Rsch., Working Paper 11518, 2005).

63 See Hersh M. Shefrin & Richard H. Thaler, *The Behavioral Life-Cycle Hypothesis*, 26 ECON. INQUIRY 609, 609–616 (1988) (describing a theory of mental account coding).

64 See, e.g., ANGUS DEATON, UNDERSTANDING CONSUMPTION 218 (1992).

To help show mental accounts' relevance to distributional policy, suppose that – going beyond what the evidence actually supports – people always annually spent all of their current-year income,[65] and nothing else, on current-year consumption. In this scenario, the marginal utility of consumption would depend entirely on current-year income, and not at all on lifetime spending power. There would, thus, be a case for basing distribution policy entirely on such income to correctly identify the taxpayers who have high, as distinct from low, marginal utility.

If people did this, it would still be an open philosophical question, requiring further inquiry, as to what extent such life-cycle measures mattered. There would certainly be grounds for arguing that they remained important. For example, one might view inequality as far less objectionable if, while high on an annual basis (reflecting typical life-cycle earnings profiles), it was low on a lifetime basis. After all, this would imply that people were generally cycling between being 'rich' and 'poor' in different periods, as opposed to being stuck with one status or the other. But the very fact that people were making decisions on an annual (or other short-term) basis, rather than based on their lifetime circumstances, would arguably open the door for deeming more short-term perspectives also normatively relevant.

THE SIGNIFICANCE OF DIFFERENT MARGINAL UTILITIES OF CONSUMPTION AS BETWEEN PERIODS

Beyond Purely Current-Period Judgements?

The most obvious implication of departures from EMU, reflecting consumption's 'stickiness' in a particular period in which it responds to current-period, not just lifetime, resources, is clear. Contrary to the teachings of the life-cycle model, a social planner can increase aggregate utility by transferring resources from better-off to worse-off individuals as defined by their *current*-period circumstances, as distinct from just information about their lifetime spending power.

This leaves open, however, a deeper question as to how lifetime, as distinct from just current-period, considerations should reflect our distributional aims if the latter are *not* just based on aggregate utility but also reflect concern about its distribution as between individuals. In this regard, consider John Rawls' argument that utilitarianism 'does not take seriously the distinction between persons',[66] or 'the plurality and distinctness of individuals'.[67] Or consider Robert Nozick's response to Rawls, to the effect that, not just utilitarians, but also Rawls himself, by reason of his

[65] This assumption raises the question of how people define current-year income when basing the decision on mental accounts. One might be unsurprised to learn that the relevant income definition included a realisation rule, such that, for example, mere stock appreciation was not coded as increasing current income but the receipt of a dividend was.

[66] John Rawls, A Theory of Justice 27 (1971).

[67] Id., at 29.

countenancing redistribution to increase some measure of overall social welfare or justice, 'does not sufficiently respect and take account of the fact that [each individual] is a separate person, that his is the only life he has'.[68]

A belief in individuals' separate and distinct relevance in normative analysis need not commit one to applying a lifetime perspective. Even just within utilitarianism and other welfarism, social welfare functions can operate on either a lifetime or a sub-lifetime basis.[69] Indeed, the timeframe question for applying one's concerns regarding distinct individuals is the subject of a 'vast literature in contemporary philosophy concerning personhood and personal identity'.[70]

However, a lifetime analysis becomes at least plausible if one is interested in individuals' separate moral status. It might be viewed as especially compelling if people so regularly acted on a lifetime basis that EMU generally held. Even insofar as people do not do so, however, it might matter to the social planner, depending on her broader normative framework.

In illustration, recall the earlier example of the professional athlete and the doctor, who have the same lifetime spending power but different earnings patterns. Suppose that they have the same preferences regarding consumption in different periods, but that the athlete consumes more earlier in life, and the doctor consumes more later in life. What is more, suppose that these differences reflect not just the doctor's early-life borrowing constraints, but also the athlete's making bad decisions when she was young. Accordingly, when they are old, the doctor is materially better-off – reflecting her having consumed less when she was young, rather than her having a greater preference than does the athlete for late-in-life consumption.

In these circumstances, how should we think about redistribution from the doctor to the athlete? To what extent should we care about the fact that the athlete had things better when she was young? Should our view about this depend at all on whether she made errors in judgement while she was young, or on how forgivingly we view those errors? This obviously will depend on one's broader normative views. However, taking a lifetime view – even when the individuals whose circumstances (and distributive desert) one is evaluating have not consistently acted on such a basis – presumably reflects considering a given individual relevantly the same person across her entire life. The question of whether and when one should regard an individual as the same person across her entire life has received much attention in the philosophical literature.

Different Times, Same 'Person'?

The ancient Greek philosopher Heraclitus of Ephesus famously remarked: 'No man ever steps in the same river twice, for it's not the same river and he's not the same

68 Robert Nozick, Anarchy, State, and Utopia 33 (1974).
69 Matthew D. Adler, Wellbeing and Fair Distribution 405 (2012).
70 Id., at 409.

man'. The last five words of this quotation, while less well-known than the first half, might be viewed as expressing more than just the point that we continually change as we grow older. It also relies on our unavoidably travelling through time, at its pace (whether we want to or not), stuck always in the present moment, like strapped-in amusement park riders. It thus may help remind us that the question of whether and to what extent we should view a given individual, throughout her entire lifespan, as always normatively the same 'person' cannot just be presumed – it needs to be demonstrated.

Here a question of central interest, as Derek Parfit puts it, is '[w]hat makes a person at two different times one and the same person?'[71] To Parfit himself, '[w]hat matters' is what he calls the Psychological Criterion, rooted in one's degree of 'psychological connectedness and/or continuity'[72] across time with regard to memories, character traits, and the like. Parfit concludes that, in the ordinary case, it is 'clear' that 'I am the same person as myself twenty years ago, [even] though I am not strongly connected to myself then' as 'I have few memories of experiences that I had on any day twenty years ago'.[73] While connectedness therefore fails, the missing gap is supplied by continuity if, on each day during the twenty years, I was closely connected to myself the day before.

Similarly, within welfarism, Matthew Adler argues that 'a normal human being (a human being who possesses the psychological attributes sufficient to make her a person, and who doesn't undergo a brain transplant, suffer profound amnesia as a result of an injury, or otherwise experience a radical rupture in the intertemporal connectedness of her psychological states and physical body) remains one and the same person from birth until death'[74] for purposes of morally ranking alternative outcomes.

However, even if we view an individual as being the same 'person' across many decades – in part because there is no single moment of sufficient discontinuity to break the chain – does this necessarily mean that we must give full weight to the distant past in evaluating how she should be treated today? Must we favour equalising things on a lifetime rather than a current period basis, when people's choices may not (as under EMU) reveal their preferences regarding consumption in different periods? Certainly, the athlete, late in life, might think not – based, perhaps, on viewing her past affluence as distant and irretrievably gone, and herself as having become, moment by moment, a materially different (even if not wholly unrecognisable) person than she was back then.

Similarly, perhaps a social planner might reasonably be able to take a Heraclitean approach when considering periods that lie decades apart, even if there is no one

71 Derek Parfit, Reasons and Persons 202 (1984).

72 Id., at 215.

73 Id., at 206.

74 Adler, supra note 69, at 406.

moment when an individual's personhood discontinuously changes. Perhaps one should not deem oneself irretrievably tied to an all-or-nothing approach. For example, might one increasingly discount the present relevance of past events as one moves further back in time, to reflect the view that they have gradually diminishing current relevance?

CONCLUSION

In applying a life-cycle approach to assess US inequality and fiscal progressivity to recent Survey of Consumer Finances data, AKK performs a huge public service. This is not to say, however, that its central policy conclusions – finding less inequality and more progressivity than did some recent studies that were based on wealth or income – can be definitively either accepted or rejected. Not just more empirical work, but also more reflection and research regarding both why economic (or other) inequality matters, and how people make choices across multiple periods, is still needed.

There is no simple answer to the question of how lifetime, as opposed to shorter periods (themselves requiring further definition) should be used in measuring economic inequality, fiscal progressivity, or the question of why (and how much) inequality matters. Indeed, perhaps more important than any conclusion in particular is the need for continuing methodological humility and agnosticism in how we think about these issues.

12

Living Long and Living Well

Tax Systems and Population Ageing

Miranda Stewart

The economic success of families and nations is defined in terms of their ability to sustainably reproduce themselves.[1]

INTRODUCTION

The prosperity of most OECD member states since the middle of the twentieth century relied on economic growth to lift incomes, and on a tax-and-welfare state to share the wealth. The expansion of the market economy contributed to these countries becoming wealthy,[2] while labour-capital wage negotiations and the regulation of work increased the market return to labour. Public expenditures on security, health, education, and the social safety net did much to equalise disposable incomes of households and contributed to economic growth, so that wealth grew both across the population and within households. Public expenditures were financed by substantial and progressive taxes.

The second half of the twentieth century saw the enrichment of OECD member states, and their citizens, after the massive loss of wealth during the depression and world wars. By the end of the twentieth century, more people in developed countries owned wealth than ever before, so that we can think of developed countries as being asset-owning societies. This democratisation of wealth was achieved by a mix of tax, transfer, and public investment policies that enabled the mass expansion of home ownership and, more recently, of retirement savings, albeit with varying trajectories in different countries. Wealth has increased overall, and much of this wealth

For helpful comments I thank Andrew Hayashi.

1 Nancy Folbre, Greed, Lust & Gender: A History of Economic Ideas 325 (Oxford University Press, 2009).

2 Economic growth and the building of wealth among OECD member states also benefitted from former, or ongoing, empires that embedded inequality in colonial and post-colonial economic relationships, and from exploitation of natural resources, leading to current challenges of climate and environmental degradation.

increase has been in private hands, in particular through home ownership and retirement savings.

The symbiosis between market and government leading to growth in both public and private wealth was envisaged by an early advocate of capitalism and taxes. Adam Smith argued in 1776 that the 'statesman's' science of political economy had the aim 'first, to provide a plentiful revenue or subsistence for the people, or more properly to enable them to provide such a revenue or subsistence for themselves; and, secondly, to supply the state or commonwealth with a revenue sufficient for the public services.'[3] By the middle of the twentieth century, many governments had become successful 'tax states' that were dependent on and defined by their power to tax in a fiscal bargain with their population, and on growing returns in the market economy.[4] Tax states through expanded revenue collection were able to finance welfare systems and public goods, and this shared the increment to economic growth so that these states achieved some approximation of distributive justice, which has been defined as 'the fair distribution of the benefits and burdens of social cooperation'.[5]

The fiscal bargain of successful tax-and-welfare states also relied fundamentally on a gendered and unequal care economy. For most of the last century, the provision of care was primarily focused on children. Care was done mainly by women in the household, or in low paid work in the market. Care in the home was not taxed because it was not monetized; instead of earning an independent income, women responsible for caring relied on an intra-household economic bargain and did not control the economic return to their household work. Women who worked in the market commanded relatively low wages or were dependent on parsimonious governmental support for care labour. Market wage growth, which facilitated the accumulation of savings, accrued largely to men.

Today, economic conditions in OECD member states are increasingly unlike conditions of the mid-twentieth century.[6] Significant demographic change, through increased longevity and declining fertility, is causing rapid population ageing. Since the 1980s, there has been a reversal of earlier equalizing trends in income and wealth. Assets are held more widely than ever before, yet wealth is more unequal. Popular and academic anxiety has been expressed about these shifts in countries around the world.[7] Moreover, despite significant change in the last fifty years, the gender inequality underpinning prosperity remains. Population ageing is a renewed

3 Adam Smith, An Inquiry into the Nature and Causes of the Wealth of Nations (Methuan & Co 1776; 1904 Edwin Cannan compilation of 5th edition of 1789), Book IV, 'Of Systems of Political Economy', Introduction, available at econlib.org/library/Smith/smWN.html.

4 Miranda Stewart, Tax and Government in the 21st Century (Cambridge University Press 2022).

5 Colin Farrelly, *Taxation and Distributive Justice*, 2 Pol. Studies Rev. 185, 185–197 (2004).

6 Thomas Piketty, Capital in the 21st Century (Harvard University Press 2013).

7 Id. Lucas Chancel et al., *World Inequality Report 2022* (2022). https://inequalitylab.world/en/; Gabriel Zucman, The Hidden Wealth of Nations: The Scourge of Tax Havens

focus of policy, with care at the centre, but tax and welfare policies have not adjusted to address the continued gender inequality in care.

The first section of this chapter discusses the impact of demographic trends on dependency in society. The next section explores the implications for work and caretaking and the gender inequality embedded in work and care. The following section discusses the growth in private wealth across the population, in particular home ownership and retirement savings, and gender inequality in wealth linked to inequality in work and care. The final section explains the need to reorient the tax and transfer system to share care to support a more equal and sustainable sharing of work and caretaking in the future.

DEMOGRAPHY AND DEPENDENCY

The Demographic Transition

At the start of the twenty-first century, Nancy Folbre and Julie Nelson observed that the 'sweep of demographic change has transformed the relationship between the family and the economy – and vice versa'.[8] This is because it permanently alters the 'dependency burden' in societies. Today, most countries around the world have experienced a demographic transition from high-mortality, high-fertility societies to low-mortality, below-replacement fertility societies with increased longevity. This slows population growth, while altering the age distribution within countries.[9] The second half of the twentieth century saw a human development success, despite the tragedies of holocaust, war, and disaster. A global population boom was followed by declining fertility and improvements in longevity. This generated the conditions for today's trend of slower population growth and even population decline in some countries.[10]

(University of Chicago Press 2015); ANTONY ATKINSON, INEQUALITY: WHAT CAN BE DONE? (Harvard University Press 2015); ANTONY ATKINSON & THOMAS PIKETTY, TOP INCOMES OVER THE TWENTIETH CENTURY: A CONTRAST BETWEEN CONTINENTAL EUROPEAN AND ENGLISH SPEAKING COUNTRIES (Oxford University Press 2010); JANE RAYNER, GENERATION LESS: HOW AUSTRALIA IS CHEATING THE YOUNG (Black Inc. 2016); MAX RASHBROOKE, TOO MUCH MONEY: HOW WEALTH DISPARITIES ARE UNBALANCING AOTEAROA NEW ZEALAND (Bridget Williams Books 2021); FRANK STILWELL, THE POLITICAL ECONOMY OF INEQUALITY (Cambridge University Press 2019).

8 Nancy Folbre & Julie A. Nelson, *For Love or Money – or Both?* 14 J. OF ECON. PERSPECTIVES 123, 124 (2000).

9 Laura Blue & Thomas J. Espenshade, *Population Momentum across the Demographic Transition*, 37 POPULATION DEV. REV. 721 (2011).

10 These trends are affected by migration, including waves of both 'legal' and 'illegal' migration which are likely to continue in response to economic, climate, and social phenomena. However, in general, inward migration does not reverse fundamental demographic trends, as migrants also age and have fewer children. See, e.g., Peter McDonald & Meimanat Hosseini-Chavoshi, *What Level of Migration Is Required to Achieve Zero Population Growth in The Shortest Possible Time?* ASIAN EXAMPLES' 4 FRONTIERS IN HUMAN DYNAMICS (2022).

Life expectancy at the birth of the twentieth century was below fifty years in most of the world. Today, life expectancy across the globe is seventy-four years, and across the OECD is eighty-one.[11] For example, Australia's life expectancy increased from about fifty in 1900 to sixty-eight in 1950, and is today eighty-four, one of the highest life expectancies globally.[12] Life expectancy is gendered; in most countries, women have a life expectancy of about two years longer than men.

Living longer requires financing consumption for longer and raises the issue of a new and long period of elder dependency. There are many health, housing, and other challenges as we learn how to support those who live into their ninth, tenth, or eleventh decade.[13] Meanwhile, fewer working-age people are available to financially support and carry out care work. On the other hand, living longer permits a longer working life to earn income and to provide support and care for others, and a much longer period in which assets can generate substantial compounding returns. In many countries, the long-lived who accumulated assets since the 1970s (especially the 'baby boomers' born between 1946 and 1964) have benefited from decades of economic growth and rising asset prices, combined with the ability to save in new forms of financial assets and retirement savings vehicles.

The other contributor to demographic change is declining fertility. The standard assumption in the population literature is that a total fertility rate of 2.1 children per woman is 'replacement' fertility, that will generate a stable population, without migration and assuming unchanged mortality.[14] Global fertility rates have declined from 3.2 in 1990 to 2.3 in 2021.[15] In a few African countries, fertility rates remain as high as four or six live births per woman, but fertility rates in the rest of the world, in particular in most developed countries, are below 'replacement', including the most populous countries. In China, fertility is 1.2 and in India it is 2.0. The latest OECD average is 1.58; the range is from low fertility rates, such as those in South Korea (0.81), Japan (1.33), and Italy (1.25), to 1.8 in France and 2.0 in Mexico, while Israel is

[11] The COVID-19 pandemic led to a reduction in life expectancy. See *Life Expectancy and Healthy Life Expectancy*, World Health Organisation, https://ourworldindata.org/grapher/life-expectancy; the WHO estimates that healthy life expectancy is a decade shorter. Id. *Health Indicators 2021, Trends in Life Expectancy*, OECD, www.oecd-ilibrary.org/social-issues-migration-health/health-at-a-glance-2021_ae3016b9-en.

[12] *World Population Prospects 2022*, United Nations, https://population.un.org/wpp/.

[13] Many governments are seeking to upgrade aged care, while seeking new ways to finance this care: e.g. *Ageing and Long-term Care*, OECD, www.oecd.org/els/health-systems/long-term-care.htm; *Final Report of the Aged Care Taskforce*, Australia Government Dep't of Aged Care, www.health.gov.au/resources/publications/final-report-of-the-aged-care-taskforce?language = en.

[14] *Fertility Rates*, OECD, https://data.oecd.org/pop/fertility-rates.htm.

[15] From 1990 to 2019, the global fertility rate fell from 3.2 to 2.5 live births per woman. Ritchie et al., *Five Key Findings from the UN 2022 Population Prospects*, https://ourworldindata.org/world-population-update-2022; *World Population Report 2022*, United Nations https://population.un.org/wpp/. The author does not take a position on the 'right' level of fertility, or population, for any country.

an outlier with fertility of 3.0.[16] In the OECD, fertility rates peaked in the 1960s at between 3.0 and 6.0; the decline is a product of the last fifty years. For example, Australia's fertility rate peaked at 3.3 in 1965 and declined to 1.63 in 2022.[17] The relationship between fertility and population is complex and affected by migration. It has been estimated that even accounting for a continued inward migration policy, the Australian fertility rate must be kept at or above 1.6 to maintain a stable and age-balanced population.[18]

Declining fertility is caused by a range of factors including economic development, reduced child mortality, increased investment in (and cost of) raising children, urbanization and housing costs, and the education and empowerment of women.[19] For our purposes, what is important is that declining fertility, together with ageing, has a direct impact on the care needs of society, and hence on the cost, type, and distribution of caretaking work. Having fewer children reduces childcare obligations on women, a phenomenon that is closely associated with increased gender equality. Nonetheless, gender inequality in work, care, income, and wealth has persisted despite increases in women's workforce participation and access to assets in many countries.[20] This is mainly because of gender-differentiated patterns of work, with unequal wages, and the concentration of women's labour in caring occupations.

The Dependency Ratio

It is common to represent population ageing by reference to the *old-age dependency ratio*, which is the ratio of the population aged sixty-five and older to the working-age population (aged 15–64). A rise in the old-age dependency ratio implies increasing fiscal transfers from working-age to old.[21] The OECD states that 'population ageing

[16] *Fertility Rates*, OECD, https://data.oecd.org/pop/fertility-rates.htm. Without Israel, the OECD average comes down to 1.55.

[17] Population, Australian Bureau of Statistics, www.abs.gov.au/statistics/people/population.

[18] Some countries, including China, Korea, and Japan, face a steeply ageing and ultimately declining population; demographers suggest that these countries cannot achieve a stable and age-balanced population at current fertility and migration rates: McDonald & Hosseini-Chavoshi, *supra* note 10.

[19] There is not the scope to discuss these issues here but there is a wide literature; see, for example, Aboulghasem Pourreza et al., *Contributing Factors to the Total Fertility Rate Declining Trend in the Middle East and North Africa: A Systemic Review*, 40 J. HEALTH POP. NUTR. 11 (2021); Kadir Atalay et al., *Housing Wealth, Fertility Intentions and Fertility*, 54 J. OF HOUSING ECON. 101787 (2021).

[20] *The Pursuit of Gender Equality*, OECD (2017).

[21] *Fiscal Challenges and Inclusive Growth in Ageing Societies*, OECD (2019), www.oecd.org/economy/ageing-inclusive-growth; AGUSTIN REDONDA ET AL., TAXATION IN AGING SOCIETIES: INCREASING THE EFFECTIVENESS AND FAIRNESS OF PENSION SYSTEMS (Asian Development Bank Institute 2020); *Fiscal Costs of Ageing Population*, Australian Parliamentary Budget Office (2019).

will put unprecedented stress on public finances to finance pension, health and long-term care expenditures'.[22] In most OECD member states, the aged pension, care, and health care are the largest social expenditures and often the fastest growing expenditures.[23] For example, in Australia, assistance to the aged is the single largest social welfare function, costing $76 billion in 2021–2022 and projected to exceed $100 billion in 2025–2026.[24] The fiscal challenge of population ageing is a major theme in Australian Intergenerational Reports, which examine a forty-year time horizon.[25]

However, policy anxiety about old-age dependency mischaracterizes the challenge we face. The central issue for fiscal policy is not old age as such, but the society-wide need to fund and provide care, privately or publicly, for those who need it. To examine this issue requires us to think in terms of the *total dependency ratio,* measured as the ratio of dependents (often defined as those below 15 and those aged 65 and over) to the working age population. As Folbre and Nelson explain, this ratio 'is an important indicator of the amount of time, energy, and money the working age population must devote to nonworkers'.[26]

Dependency ratios are blunt indicators and there are valid criticisms to be made for this kind of population ageing analysis.[27] Other factors, such as automation, may also have a significant effect on workforce participation and dependency. Nonetheless, consideration of the total dependency ratio brings into focus the requirement and need to distribute the benefit and burden of care fairly across society, and it also indicates the importance of expanding workforce participation in the paid labour market to expand both private and public resources for care needs.

Figure 12.1 compares the old-age dependency ratio to the total dependency ratio for the whole world. It shows that over the period from 1960 to 2022, the global old-age dependency ratio has almost doubled, from 8.5 per cent to 14 per cent (with an upward trend), but the global total dependency ratio has *declined* by more than 20 per cent. While country experiences are diverse, the explanation for this *downward* trend lies in declining fertility. We can see that this global decline hit bottom in about 2012, and the total dependency ratio has now gradually started to increase but remains far lower in 2022 (55%) than in 1960 (75%).

22 *Old Age Dependency Ratio,* OECD, https://data.oecd.org/pop/old-age-dependency-ratio.htm#indicator-chart.

23 OECD, *supra* n. 21.

24 *Budget Paper 1, State 6, Table 6.9,* Australian Treasury (2022), https://budget.gov.au/2022-23-october/content/bp1/index.htm.

25 *Intergenerational Report 2023, Chart 2.1,* Australian Treasury.

26 Folbre & Nelson, *supra* note 8, at 124.

27 The age range of 15–64 years for dependency is less plausible today for many developed countries where young people are dependent and in education for a longer period and a larger proportion of older people continue to work. However, adjustments do not change the overall trend for Australia, presented in Figure 12.3.

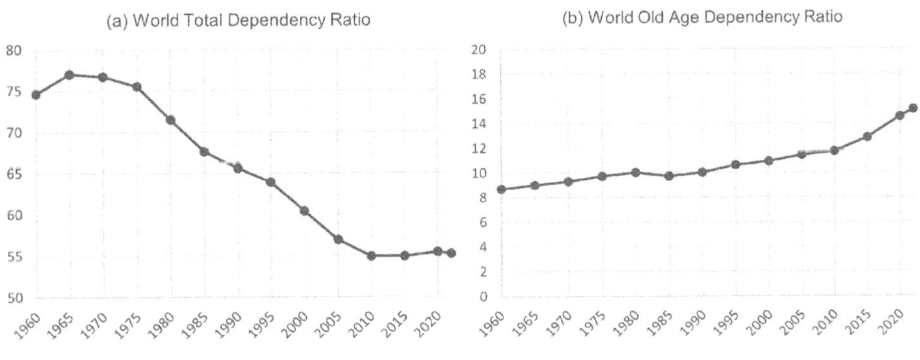

FIGURE 12.1 World total and old-age dependency ratios (% of working age) (1960–2022)
Source: World Bank, https://data.worldbank.org/indicator/SP.POP.DPND

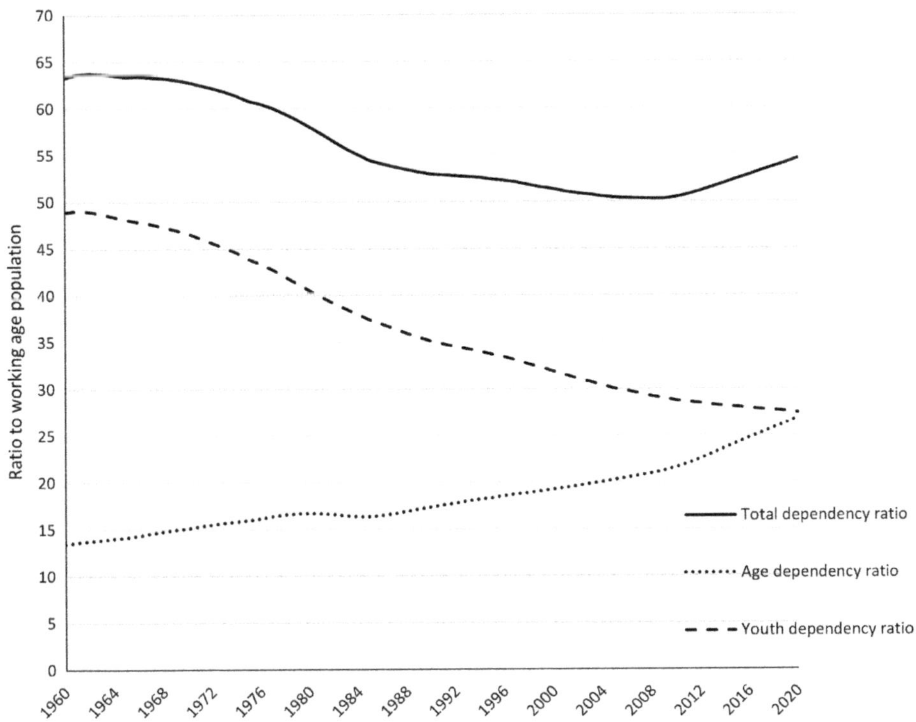

FIGURE 12.2 OECD total, old-age and youth dependency ratios (% of working age) (1960–2021)
Source: UN Population Data, OECD member states

Figure 12.2 presents the total, old-age and youth dependency ratios for OECD countries, where population ageing is most acute. The dotted line is the old-age dependency ratio from 1960 to 2021, compared to the dashed line which is the youth dependency ratio; together, they generate the total dependency ratio (black line).

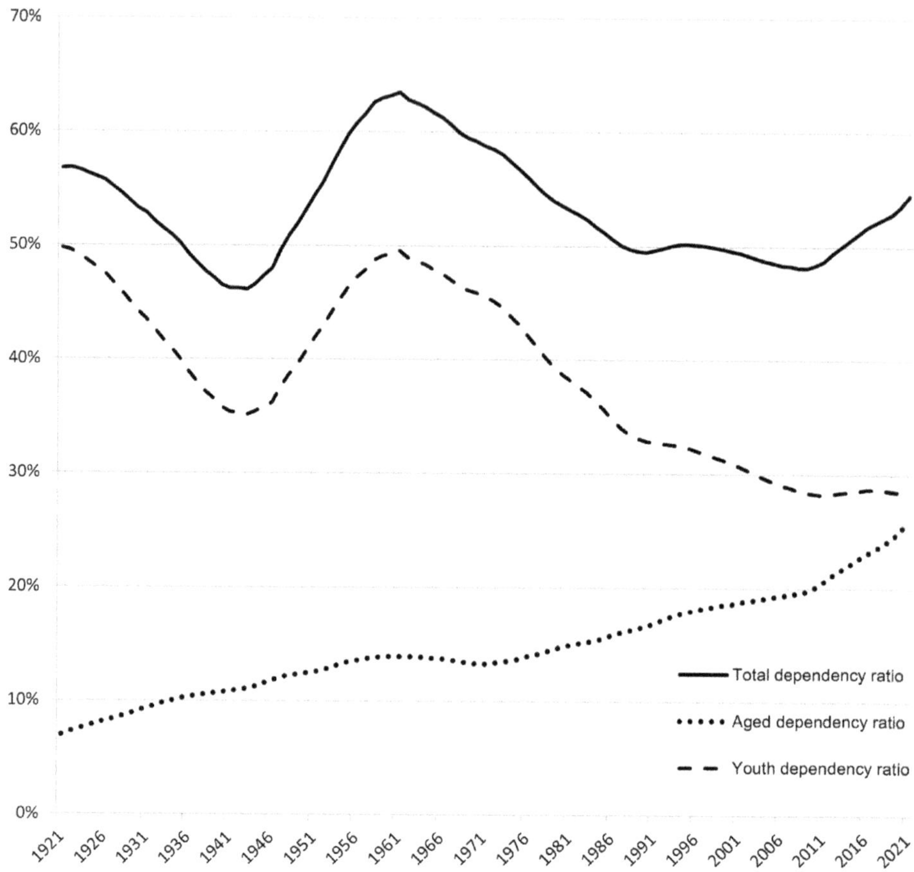

FIGURE 12.3 Dependency ratios (Australia) (%) (1921–2018)
Source: April 2019 release of Australian Historical Population Statistics used for 1921–2016 data, and March 2019 release of Australian Demographic Statistics used for 2017–2018 data – Australian Bureau of Statistics; www.ausstats.abs.gov.au/ausstats/subscriber.nsf/0/ACFD01ECA5FD8A88CA2584880015486 2/$File/31010_mar%202019.pdf; www.abs.gov.au/ausstats/abs@.nsf/0/632CDC28637CF57ECA256F1F0080EBCC?Opendocument

Figure 12.2 reveals that the total dependency ratio remains significantly below the high point of close to 65 per cent in 1960, albeit it is now trending up after a long decline.

Figure 12.3 presents the example of Australia, for which we have long-run data showing the rise and fall of the dependency ratio over the last century, encompassing most of the tax-and-welfare era since federation in 1901. The dotted line is the old-age dependency ratio, compared to the dashed line which is the youth dependency ratio; together, they generate the total dependency ratio (black line). While the old-age dependency ratio has more than doubled from below 10 per cent in 1921 to 23 per cent, the youth dependency ratio has declined significantly since the 1960s, so that the total dependency ratio has also *declined*.

The upward trend in the old-age dependency ratio around the world warrants attention from policymakers, but it is not the crisis sometimes suggested. The total dependency ratio has been above 50 per cent in all countries throughout most of the last century. What has changed is the shape of care needs: who needs care (the old, versus the young), and the distribution of wealth, work, and caretaking resources.

GENDER INEQUALITY, WORK, AND CARE

The primary burden of care in the twentieth century was focused on children and fell largely on women in an unpaid, or under-paid, care economy. The work of women as caretakers (in Martha Fineman's language[28]) underpinned the accumulation of wealth, and its unequal distribution, which persists today. We return to discuss wealth in the next section. Here, we focus on work and care, and relate this to population ageing and gender inequality.

The total dependency ratio discussed in the previous section shows us that the challenge of population ageing is not only, or even mainly, about how to care for the elderly. It is important to ensure continued large investment in children, distributed equitably across society, to support our prosperity and wellbeing in future. The care of children requires resources 'far greater than those required, on average, by a retiree. Every child requires at least a decade of parental and public investment in their education. Most importantly, every infant and preschool child requires full-time care. Time use data reveal that a child is extremely costly in terms of parental time.'[29]

Market (paid) work is recorded in gross domestic product (GDP). An increase in market work contributes to economic growth, measured as the increase in GDP, or GDP per capita, which is an increment to the stock of national wealth. However, GDP fails to observe and measure the stock of human capital, and the value of social and household reproduction required to generate it.[30] Marilyn Waring's groundbreaking book *Counting for Nothing: What Men Value and What Women Are Worth*[31] argued that the value of care comprises a large fraction of the value of

[28] Martha Fineman, *Cracking the Foundational Myths: Independence, Autonomy, and Self-Sufficiency, in* Feminism Confronts Homo Economicus: Gender, Law, and Society 179 (Martha Fineman & Terence Dougherty, eds.) (Cornell University Press 2005).

[29] Patricia Apps, *Gender Equity in the Tax-Transfer System for Fiscal Sustainability*, in Tax, Social Policy and Gender: Rethinking Equality and Efficiency (M. Stewart, ed.) (ANU Press 2017).

[30] *Gross Domestic Product*, International Monetary Fund, www.imf.org/en/Publications/fandd/issues/Series/Back-to-Basics/gross-domestic-product-GDP. GDP also fails to measure environmental assets and degradation. Alternative approaches are being developed but are still in their infancy: e.g. the concept of 'gross ecosystem product': Zhiyun Ouyang et al., *Using Gross Ecosystem Product (GEP) to Value Nature in Decision Making*, 117 Proceedings of the Nat'l Academy of Sci. 14593–14601 (2020).

[31] Marilyn Waring, What Men Value and What Women Are Worth (Allen & Unwin 1988).

'market' exchanges of goods and services. Leaving aside social reproduction through child bearing, the International Labour Organization (ILO) estimates the value of unpaid care work as comprising half of the value of GDP; in Australia, the ILO estimated unpaid care work at the minimum wage as 41.3 per cent of GDP.[32] A more recent market-wage-replacement estimate found that unpaid care of children comprised 24.6 per cent of GDP, while the total value of unpaid work, including volunteer, domestic, and care of adults and children, was estimated at 33.9 per cent of GDP.[33] If we were to measure it as an 'industry' sector, unpaid childcare would be the single largest industry (19.9 per cent of industries).[34]

By the middle of the twentieth century, the tax-and-welfare system of most OECD states had been built on the basis of a paradigmatic waged worker (the male 'breadwinner'), who worked full time for four decades before a short, pensioned retirement (as already noted, life expectancy was much shorter). The breadwinner supported a family, in which his spouse (the female 'homemaker') provided full time care for the breadwinner and children. This gendered breadwinner–homemaker household was represented in many tax systems as a joint tax unit, and the system provided exemptions and deductions to assist in family support. As direct government support through payments to families with children grew, this family unit was also the basis for the welfare system which used joint income to determine eligibility for income support. Today, many families in OECD countries have transitioned towards one-and-a-half or dual earner households and no longer fit the traditional 'breadwinner–homemaker' mould.[35] Declining fertility has significantly reduced the care burden, helping to drive this transition, but private investment of time and money in each child has grown dramatically.

Australia provides an example of the incomplete sharing of care and the impact on women's work and income. As in most OECD countries, women's workforce participation has risen in Australia since the 1970s but it remains significantly lower than men's, in particular where there are care obligations. Women do about two-thirds of unpaid caretaking work and three-quarters of paid caretaking work.[36] Just over half of women's labour contribution is unpaid, while the lower pay in

32 *Care Work and Care Jobs for the Future of Decent Work*, International Labor Organisation (ILO), www.ilo.org/global/publications/books/WCMS_633135/lang–en/index.htm, figure 2.4, 50.

33 PricewaterhouseCoopers, *Understanding the Unpaid Economy*, PwC Economics and Policy, Economic Views Australia, www.pwc.com.au/australia-in-transition/publications/understanding-the-unpaid-economy-mar17.pdf.

34 Id.

35 Felix Bierbrauer et al., *The Taxation of Couples*, CEPR Discussion Paper 18138 (2023). In Australia, about 70 per cent of families with children have both parents employed: *Labour Force Status of Families*, Australian Bureau of Statistics (ABS), www.abs.gov.au/statistics/labour/employment-and-unemployment/labour-force-status-families/latest-release.

36 ILO, *supra* note 32.

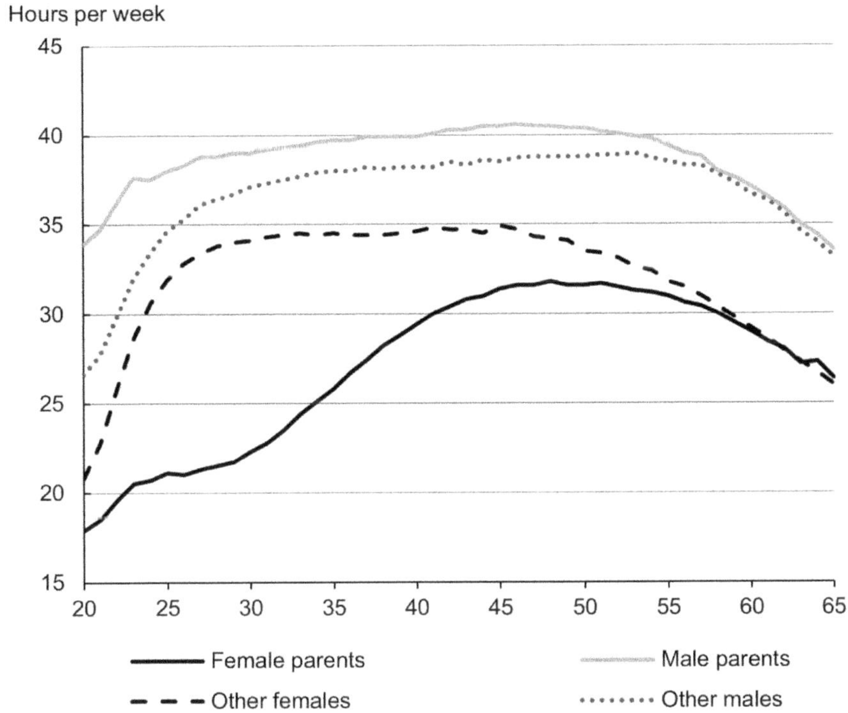

FIGURE 12.4 Average paid work hours, age 20 to 65, Australia (2021)
Source: Adapted from Treasury, *Advice on Amending Tax Cuts to Deliver Broader Cost-of-Living Relief*, Chart A3, available https://treasury.gov.au/tax-cuts/treasury-advice; Australian Bureau of Statistics Census of Population and Housing, 2021.

female-concentrated sectors adds 4.5 percentage points to the gender wage gap.[37] Twenty per cent of households with children are sole-headed, predominantly by women, and these households face particularly acute challenges with low income and a high care burden.[38]

Figure 12.4 shows that female hours of paid work per week in Australia are significantly lower than male hours over the life course, and dip dramatically when women become parents (black line). In contrast, male parents work more hours than other men throughout child rearing years (grey line). One important reason, addressed in the final section of this chapter, is that tax-and-welfare systems create economic disincentives for paid work by mothers and inhibit full sharing of care between male and female parents.[39]

A recent study of social policy in ten European countries presented the distribution of public and private resource transfers between generations and revealed the

[37] Leonora Risse, *By How Much Is 'Women's Work' Undervalued in the Economy? And Why Does It Matter?* AUSTRALIAN CONFERENCE OF ECONOMISTS (2023).

[38] ABS, *supra* note 35.

[39] Apps, *supra* note 29.

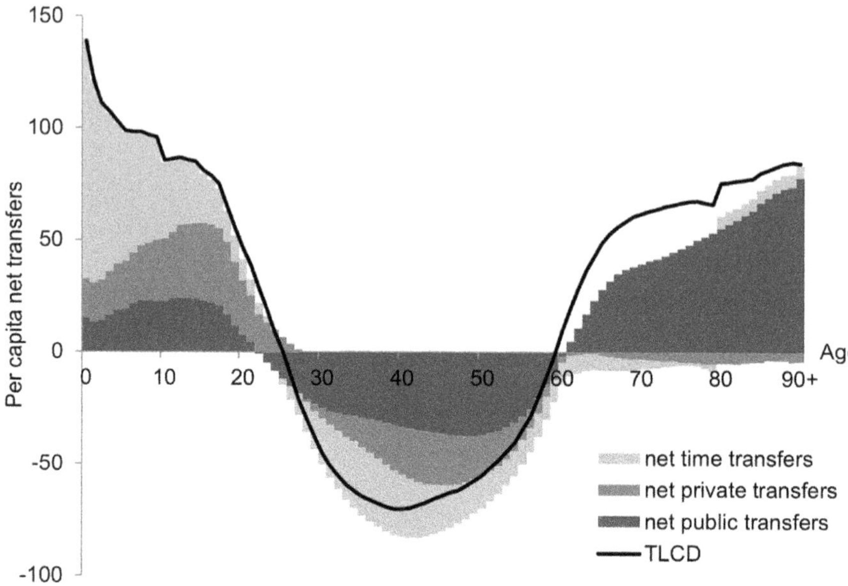

FIGURE 12.5 Per capita public, private, and time transfers and the total lifecycle deficit by age in Europe

Note: The gap between the black line and the grey or black transfers is the transfer life course deficit in public and private transfers of money and time at different ages through the life course. *Source*: Róbert Iván Gál et al., *Pro-Elderly Welfare States within Child-Oriented Societies* 25(6) JOURNAL OF EUROPEAN PUBLIC POLICY 944–958 (2018), figure 2.

scale of private resources in money and time dedicated to care of children.[40] Figure 12.5 shows that infants and children in these societies receive large positive private transfers of money and time and some public transfers. Not surprisingly, working-age people are net contributors of public taxes and private transfers of time and money. The elderly mainly receives public transfers and small private transfers of time in very old age. Overall, children receive more than twice in net transfers than do the elderly.

WEALTH INEQUALITY

The Growth of Private Wealth

Globally, privately held wealth is highly unequal. In 2021, the top 10 per cent of the global population owned 52 per cent of total income and 76 per cent of total

[40] Róbert Iván Gál et al., *Pro-Elderly Welfare States within Child-Oriented Societies* 25 J. OF EUR. PUB. POL. 944–958 (2018). The transfer of time for care was quantified through time use survey data.

wealth.[41] The wealth owned by the top 1 per cent of wealth holders is growing significantly faster than that held by the bottom 50 per cent. The top 1 per cent captured 38 per cent of the global increment in wealth between 1995 and 2021, while the bottom 50 per cent saw a 2 per cent increase in their wealth. Data on long-run trends in wealth in specific countries is difficult to come by, but an analysis of available studies for ten OECD member states indicates that wealth concentration declined through the twentieth century but this trend has now flattened out and may be reversing.[42] Thomas Piketty has suggested that both income and wealth inequality has returned as a core characteristic of twenty-first century capitalism.[43] Developed countries may be becoming increasingly like European countries during the nineteenth century, where individual prosperity depends more on the ability to harness wealth handed down by gifts or inheritance, than by earnings in the market. The building of private wealth has combined with privatization or running down of publicly owned assets, creating a phenomenon that the World Inequality Database calls 'rich societies and poor governments'.[44] Poorer governments have less capacity to respond to fiscal challenges including that posed by population ageing.

In OECD member states , there has been in the same period an expansion of private wealth holdings to create an asset-owning middle class. Most private wealth is held in housing (especially home ownership) and retirement savings, except for the very rich who hold their wealth in business equity. In OECD member states, more than two thirds of households own their own home.[45] This was achieved through the expansion of mortgage debt markets enabling the purchase of housing by wage-earners. This changed the nature of both work and wealth, 'securitizing' human labour in a new way.[46] Tax systems also helped – home ownership is exempt from tax, or even subsidized (through mortgage interest deductibility) in most countries. However, this trend has reversed in the twenty-first century, as home ownership seems increasingly out of reach for young people in many countries.[47] Meanwhile, the wealth of older generations who already own a home has increased relative to younger generations.

[41] Chancel et al., *supra* note 7.

[42] Jesper Roine & Daniel Waldenstrom, *Long-run Trends in the Distribution of Income and Wealth, in* Handbook of Income Distribution (Anthony B. Atkinson & Francois Bourguignon, eds.) (2015).

[43] Piketty, *supra* note 6, at 518.

[44] Chancel et al., *supra* note 7.

[45] *Housing Tenures*, OECD (2022), www.oecd.org/housing/data/affordable-housing-database/housing-market.htm.

[46] Lisa Adkins, The Time of Money (Stanford University Press 2018); Jeffrey Chwieroth & Andrew Walter, The Wealth Effect: How the Great Expectations of the Middle Class Have Changed the Politics of Banking Crises (Cambridge University Press 2019).

[47] Boris Cournede & Marissa Plouin, No Home for the Young? Stylised Facts and Policy Challenges (OECD 2022), www.oecd.org/housing/topics/affordable-housing/.

The extent of public or private ownership of financial assets, especially retirement savings, differs across countries. Public retirement systems have achieved redistribution and prevented poverty in old age for the mass of the population in OECD member states, but population ageing has generated concern that this is fiscally unsustainable and sharpened the political debate around provision for old age. In France, where 37 per cent of the population are older than sixty-five years, riots followed proposals to raise the age for pension eligibility, a change that was widely perceived as a real cut in people's wealth held in the public pension fund.[48] In the United States, there is ongoing debate about the social security fund because benefits will need to be cut by 23 per cent in 2033 unless more tax revenue is applied; this is a political choice, not an actuarial constraint.[49] Yet, as illustrated in Figure 12.5, the total transfer of public and private resources to support the elderly is lower than to the young.

Late in the twentieth century, OECD member states began to 'provide tax advantages and other financial incentives (e.g., subsidies) to encourage savings for retirement'.[50] The OECD recommends policies to support private 'asset-backed' pensions to ensure adequacy of income in retirement. In Australia, a need-based public age pension established a century ago remains the basis of old-age support but it is supplemented by a mandatory private retirement savings system (superannuation) that commenced in 1992. While the mandatory nature of this scheme ensures wide application across workers, the lion's share of benefits from the scheme has accrued to the top of the income distribution. The top 20 per cent received nearly 70 per cent of the benefits of low-taxed superannuation in 2023.[51] In the United States, tax concessions increase inequality in retirement saving while their substantial fiscal cost reduces the availability of revenues to fund public pensions.[52]

The theory of lifecycle saving argues that individuals can accumulate these savings while of working age and will consume them when old.[53] Developed by Franco Modigliani and others during the middle of the twentieth century, the theory supports a 'consumption tax' approach in which savings are exempt from

48 Peter Whiteford, *Why the French Are Rebelling and Australians Aren't, Austaxpolicy: Tax and Transfer Policy Blog* (2023), www.austaxpolicy.com/why-the-french-are-rebelling-and-australians-arent/.

49 Alicia Munnell, *Congressional Republicans Want Big Cuts to Social Security,* Center for Retirement Research, https://crr.bc.edu/congressional-republicans-want-big-cuts-to-social-security/.

50 Annual Survey on Financial Incentives for Retirement Savings (OECD, 2022), www.oecd.org/daf/fin/private-pensions/financial-incentives-retirement-savings-country-profiles-2022.pdf.

51 *Tax Expenditures and Insights Statement*, Australian Treasury, https://treasury.gov.au/publication/p2024-489823.

52 Michael Doran, *The Great American Retirement Fraud,* 30 Elder L.J. 265 (2023).

53 Franco Modigliani, *Life-Cycle, Individual Thrift, and the Wealth of Nations* 76 Am. Econ. Rev. 297–313 (1986). Franco Modigliani, *The Role of Intergenerational Transfers and Life-Cycle Saving in the Accumulation of Wealth* 2 J. of Econ. Perspectives 15–20 (1998).

income tax, and then taxed when dissaved, or consumed, in retirement. The theory assumes that people would save to consume in retirement, rather than seeking to leave bequests (although a bequest motive may be built into this lifecycle savings model). The theory does not take account of windfall gains, such as increasing house prices, nor does it predict the significant unequal impact of tax concessions for saving that go to the rich. Fifty years later, we can observe that private retirement savings systems have expanded wealth holdings, but at the same time have increased wealth concentration. They have delivered much better retirement living standards for the top third of the population, while failing to solve the challenge of elder support for society as a whole.

An ageing population with fewer working-age people may also be a contributing factor in slower economic growth and this in itself may produce greater wealth concentration. Piketty and Saez predict an increase in wealth inequality as an inevitable consequence of a growth rate (g) that is lower than the rate of return to capital (r), generating the famous $r > g$ equation.[54] They identify reduced tax rates since the 1980s as a key contributor to this trend. Top income tax rates exceeded 60 per cent in the 1960s but in most OECD countries are now below 50 per cent.

Gender Inequality in Wealth

Twentieth century capitalism legitimated the 'pursuit of wealth ... for everyone'; but in reality, this was not possible for most women.[55] The work of women as caretakers was fundamental to economic prosperity in tax-and-welfare states but the private economic returns to market labour and capital investment accrued mostly to men. The link between gender inequality in caretaking work and the wealth of women and men is exhaustively demonstrated in *The Gender of Capital* by Céline Bessière and Sibylle Gollac.[56] This requires examination of the intrahousehold distribution of care and wealth, which is not immediately visible in wealth statistics which utilize household-level data. Most wealth statistics incorporate a basic assumption that net assets of a household are equally distributed between adults in the household (usually, male and female spouses). Reliance on this household unit for assessing wealth has the effect of 'masking the reality of individual ownership and control of assets'.[57]

Women could not accumulate wealth while carrying out caretaking responsibilities, as they did not earn, save, consume, or dissave like the paradigmatic male worker. The data reveals a substantial gender wealth gap. One estimate for the United Kingdom reveals a gender wealth gap of 35 per cent on average,

[54] Thomas Piketty & Emmanuel Saez, *Inequality in the Long Run* 344 SCIENCE 838, 841 (2014).

[55] Folbre & Nelson, *supra* note 8, at 324 (quoting Robert Heilbroner).

[56] CÉLINE BESSIÈRE & SIBYLLE GOLLAC, THE GENDER OF CAPITAL (Juliette Rogers, trans.) (Harvard University Press 2023).

[57] Id., at 9.

accumulating over the life course.[58] Gender inequality in caretaking responsibilities over the life course is the main reason. Both private and public retirement systems that rely on contributions from labour income entrench the gender gap arising from care responsibilities, while older women rely more heavily than men on public pensions. The gender gap in retirement savings is caused mainly by women's lower participation in the workforce, as well as the gender wage gap.[59] For example, in Australia, the average gender gap in superannuation saving at ages 20–24 years is minimal, but it grows to more than 30 per cent over working life until retirement. Women have as a result been denied fair access to a share of the economic increment to growth of the last few decades.

Women accumulate wealth in home ownership, more than any other kind of asset, especially through joint ownership in a couple. However, a gender wealth gap is also apparent in ownership of housing. One Australian study has examined wealth by gender of single-adult households.[60] In 2010, single-male-headed households had average wealth that was 23 per cent larger, and median wealth that was 70 per cent larger, than single-female-headed households. The wealth gap between separated or divorced single-male-headed and single-female-headed households was 21 per cent and that between never-married single male and female headed households was 48 per cent. The gender wealth gap is driven by the large differentials between the net worth of single male- and female-headed households in housing wealth when younger. Single men may be better able to borrow and invest in higher value housing than single women because higher wages enable men to service a larger mortgage, or because of discrimination in credit markets. The study indicates that lower earnings of young single female-headed households sets up a lifelong gender wealth gap, and their reduced ability to borrow and invest in higher value housing means that young women benefit less from growth in house prices.

REORIENTING THE TAX SYSTEM TO SHARE CARE, REDUCE INEQUALITY, AND ENSURE SUSTAINABILITY

Individual Progressive Taxation of Labour Income

Progressive income taxation on an individual unit is a highly effective policy to raise revenues and fund income support, paid parental leave, public childcare, and other

[58] *Why Taxation of Wealth Is a Feminist Issue: A Gendered Analysis of Wealth in Great Britain*, Women's Budget Group (UK) (2023), https://wbg.org.uk/analysis/reports/why-taxation-of-wealth-is-a-feminist-issue-a-gendered-analysis-of-wealth-in-great-britain/.

[59] Id. Guyonne Kalb, Taxes, Transfers, Family Policies And Paid Work over The Female Life Cycle in Tax, Social Policy and Gender: Rethinking Equality and Efficiency (M. Stewart, ed., ANU Press 2017).

[60] Siobhan Austen et al., *Exploring Recent Increases in The Gender Wealth Gap among Australia's Single Households* 26 Econ. and Labour Relations Rev. 3 (2015).

policies to support individuals doing caretaking. Without taking a position on how many children are needed in society, a reasonably age-balanced population will be more fiscally sustainable. It should not be controversial to say that children are socially valuable. Nonetheless, it is commonly argued that the taxes of paid workers are used to subsidize caretakers and that workers who fund taxes cannot afford the fiscal cost of public support for care. As suggested by Martha Fineman, we need to turn the argument around, to reveal that it is the caretakers of people (including children and others) who support the state and the economy.[61]

In the last thirty years, tax-and-welfare systems have changed in response to changing work and family patterns, including through funding expanded public childcare and parental leave subsidies and a shift in many countries from joint to individual tax units; these policies have reduced effective tax rates on women's work.[62] However, most tax-and-welfare states still provide relatively little in public support for caretaking of children. The outcome is that market work, income, and caretaking remain unequal by gender.

Support for caretaking does not imply returning to a breadwinner–homemaker model of privatized care and dependency of caretakers. Rather, to achieve a gender-equal distribution of work and care while supporting caretaking in an ageing population requires a reallocation of the resources that women have historically provided privately into the public sphere. This will enable women to earn more market income because the cost and delivery of care is shared, and also contribute to fiscal sustainability.

To achieve this requires detaching tax rates and means testing for transfers from joint 'spousal' or 'family' units and recognizing each of us as individuals in fiscal systems. Far from undermining the family, this would support our familial relationships and caretaking responsibilities, and would enable the tax and welfare systems to respond better to the changing forms and nature of these relationships. There is substantial evidence that an individual unit removes the economic bias against market work by women, who are usually secondary earners, by applying an equal tax rate to each individual's earnings.[63] This step is needed to generate the social and economic transition that is needed. We are only part-way there, as indicated by the continuing lower participation of women (see the Gender Inequality, Work, and Care section).

The full individualisation of the tax-transfer system goes hand in hand with strengthening the taxation of labour income of individuals and protecting progressive tax rates, including maintaining or increasing top tax rates. The wage tax base

[61] Fineman, *supra* note 28.

[62] Tax Policy and Gender Equality: A Stocktake of Country Approaches (OECD 2022).

[63] See a detailed discussion of both work disincentive and equity effects in Stewart, *supra* note 4, pp. 123–130; *see also* Bierbrauer et al., *supra* note 35; Margherita Borella et al., *Are Marriage-related Taxes and Social Security Benefits Are Holding Back Women's Labour Supply?*, CEPR Discussion Paper No. 14196 (2019).

remains essential for sustainability of the tax-and-welfare state; for example, in Europe (including the United Kingdom), half of all taxation is collected from labour income.[64] To ensure sustainability, the base for progressive income tax on labour income and payroll tax needs to be shored up by greater enforcement and closing of loopholes.

Progressive taxation on an individual unit would also contribute over time to reduce wealth inequality, and to support gender equality in income and wealth. Those who earn less income – often women – will pay less tax, while those who can save more – higher earning men – will have less capacity to save to excess. A recent study confirmed that 'the marked decrease in tax progressivity is by far the most powerful force for the cumulative increase in wealth inequality' in the United States.[65] The level and progressivity of income taxation on both earned and investment income over the life course, 'increases the returns on savings, leading to higher wealth accumulation, especially among the rich for whom wages (earnings) are a smaller part of wealth' (ibid.). Higher income tax rates on higher earnings from work are both equitable and efficient, as labour supply elasticity is generally low for high wage earners and there is, therefore, little warrant for reducing tax rates on high earnings.

It is important to carry through this logic to redesign the welfare system for workers and caretakers. Most OECD member states deliver social support through cash transfers to support individuals who are unemployed or receive low wages. There is significant diversity in the design of payments, but many systems are means tested on joint family income to target them to the lowest income individuals. Most 'work credits', for example the Earned Income Tax Credit (EITC) in the United States, are tested on joint income. The EITC is one of the largest US welfare programs in its federal system and is delivered through the tax code.[66] The UK has in the last few years carried out an extensive reorganisation of welfare payments, aiming to replace working credit and other benefits with a Universal Credit, which is also tested on joint income.[67] The withdrawal rates and conditions of all these types of targeted income support payment also generate high effective marginal tax rates on labour income, creating poverty traps in the system for low-income workers, or those who engage in insecure, seasonal, or casual work.

Public support for caretaking encompasses a social contribution to the care of children, caretaker support during time out of the paid workforce, and support for

64 European Commission Directorate-General for Taxation and Customs Union, Taxation Trends in the European Union (Pub. Office of the Eur. Union 2019).

65 Joachim Hubmer et al., *Sources of US Wealth Inequality: Past, Present and Future*, in National Bureau Of Economic Research Macroeconomics Annual 391–455 (Martin Eichenbaum et al., eds., University of Chicago Press 2020).

66 Center for Budget and Policy Priorities, *Policy Basics: The Earned Income Tax Credit*, www.cbpp.org/research/policy-basics-the-earned-income-tax-credit.

67 UK Government, www.gov.uk/universal-credit.

the elderly to continue to work without losing economic security. The fiscal response of many governments to the COVID-19 pandemic brought the idea of universal income support for individuals to the forefront, as economic shutdowns prevented people from working and many people relied on government payments of unprecedented universality and size. It is worth societies considering the potential of a broadly applicable 'negative' income tax or basic income, that could be utilized to support both caretaking and the renewal of creativity and productivity through human capital development that will be needed to increase economic growth.[68]

These changes would reshape the tax-and-welfare state to support a combination of public contributions and private earnings for different cohorts of workers, caretakers, and dependents. This would facilitate paid work by a diverse workforce, no longer the single paradigmatic 'breadwinner' worker, over a longer life course and in multiple and diverse family, social, and care contexts. More universal income support would smooth high effective marginal tax rates that create poverty traps at lower incomes.

Comprehensive Taxation of Savings and Wealth

The second element of sustainable fiscal policy requires more comprehensive taxation of savings and wealth. This would address inequality and increase revenues for public support of caretaking in an ageing population.

The largest impact will be achieved if we reorient our systems to increase taxation of wealth across the population. This is linked to the taxation of savings over the life course. Gál et al. (Figure 12.5) show that children and young people are net recipients of benefits in care and time in private and public provision. When children become adults, they work and derive market income during the middle years of life and contribute taxes, mostly on this labour income, to finance government and redistribution. During this time, individuals enjoy growing private income for consumption and saving, which is frequently concessionally taxed; and they purchase assets. As individuals age and retire from the workforce, they pay less tax, draw down on private savings, and depend on substantial public support. However, the lifecycle savings theory that proposes exemption or low taxation of retirement savings – essentially consumption-tax treatment – contributes to significant wealth and gender inequality, and it cannot solve the problem of fiscal sustainability for supporting the elderly across the population.

[68] See, e.g., Amitai Etzioni & Alex Platt, Basic Income: The Social Contract Revisited (The Foundation for Law, Justice and Society 2008); Daniel Hemel & Miranda Fleischer, *Atlas Nods: The Libertarian Case for a Basic Income* 2017 Wisc. L. Rev. 1189 (2017).

It is less clear whether high and progressive tax rates on capital income and gains are the answer. At the turn of the last century, personal income taxes in many countries including the United Kingdom, Australia, and New Zealand applied higher tax rates to 'unearned income' from property than to labour income. It was strongly felt as a matter of policy and politics that the higher tax rate on 'unearned' income was 'desirable and just'.[69] Today, most countries apply the reverse policy, as tax rates for capital returns are usually lower than for earned income. The income tax base of many countries does not capture the appreciation in value of many of the assets of the middle class who accumulate wealth in the home or retirement savings.

Lower tax rates on capital are a consequence of policy responses to economic globalization, which facilitates mobility of capital, and more generally to the ability of taxpayers to plan around taxes on capital income. However, it is important to recall that the significant reduction in tax rates on capital was also driven by an economic policy orientation since the 1980s that is no longer the consensus. It is clear that low taxes on retirement savings and other assets have encouraged excessive accumulation far beyond retirement needs, generating increased wealth concentration that is about to generate a wave of bequests. In this context, it is clear that we need to wind back, or cap, the tax concessions for retirement savings. More effective taxation of other components of wealth, including land, financial assets, and bequests, is achievable in many countries. Some governments are beginning to expand taxes on immobile assets, including land. These tax reforms are unlikely to collect as much as broad-based income and consumption taxes but are still necessary to address inequality.

Even if the base and rates of the progressive income tax were consolidated and enhanced for labour and capital income, such a reform could not address wealth of the top 0.1 per cent who derive economic return in capital gains, corporate entities, or by holding assets for the long-term. The very rich do not 'realise' most of their wealth, which accrues in corporate equity and other entities, as income; to capture this requires a net wealth tax and improved taxation of bequests.[70] A consumption tax can be effective to capture some return from this cohort, but the share of wealth consumed by the top 0.1 per cent is very small. As countries expand international tax cooperation to enforce taxation, it may be possible to put a floor on tax competition and collect more tax on mobile capital.[71]

[69] Martin Daunton, Just Taxes: The Politics of Taxation in Britain, 1914–1979 (Cambridge University Press 2002).

[70] See, e.g., Martin-Brehm Christensen et al., Survival of the Richest: How We Must Tax The Super-Rich Now To Fight Inequality (Oxfam International 2023); Emmanuel Saez & Gabriel Zucman, The Triumph of Injustice: How the Rich Dodge Taxes and How to Make Them Pay (New York: W. W. Norton & Company 2019).

[71] While acknowledging that this may require no less than a revisioning of the social contract. See, e.g., Tsilly Dagan, *Tax and Globalization: Toward a New Social Contract*, 44 Oxford J. Leg. St. 487 (2024).

CONCLUSION

In a capitalist economy, 'the economic success of individuals can be defined in terms of their income or wealth', but the same parameters cannot apply to states. Rather, 'the economic success of families and nations is defined in terms of their ability to sustainably reproduce themselves'.[72] Achieving success in social reproduction so that we can live long and live well in today's era of population ageing requires us to place the goal of sharing the cost of care at the centre of policy-making, without exploiting women.[73] Many states today face challenges, including an ageing population, slowing economic growth, and increasing inequality. These are interdependent with current patterns of work and care in these states. Resourcing care is not a new problem, as revealed by the total dependency ratio (see the Demography and Dependency section). The existence of approximately one third of the population being dependent on those of working age is a consistent feature of our social and economic structures. While most concern is expressed about caring for the elderly, our bigger challenge is how to solve the problem of sharing care for children. We have an opportunity in an era of declining fertility to reconfigure our tax-and-welfare systems to recognize that all of us are workers and caretakers, dependants and providers, through the life course.

To achieve a fiscally and socially sustainable society calls for 'substantial social and economic transformations' that invest in care.[74] These include: 'reducing the opportunity costs of having children, family-friendly working conditions, employment security for young people, housing costs, and gender equity'.[75] This can be achieved, in part, by modifications to the tax-and-welfare system because this is a powerful tool available for states to achieve the distribution of benefits and burdens and the delivery of public benefit. It is now acknowledged by policy-makers in the OECD and around the world (albeit reluctant in some quarters) that increasing women's paid workforce participation is important to manage this demographic transition. However, the other side of the coin – managing the provision of caretaking – has not been so well developed. The investment in children that we need can only be achieved if caretaking is more fully socialised. This chapter proposes reorienting tax-and-welfare systems to strengthen the progressive individual income tax on labour income and apply more comprehensive taxation of capital and wealth, to support expanded public investment in care of children utilizing universal systems of income and care support. For us to be living long, and living well in the next 100 years, we need to manage the demographic transition to a society that supports caretaking and shares the economic increment fairly across society.

72 Folbre & Nelson, *supra* note 1, at 325.

73 Martha Nussbaum, *Capabilities and Social Justice* 4 INT'L STUDIES REV. 123, 134 (2002).

74 McDonald & Hosseini-Chavoshi, *supra* note 10, at 15.

75 Id.

For EU product safety concerns, contact us at Calle de José Abascal, 56–1°, 28003 Madrid, Spain or eugpsr@cambridge.org.

www.ingramcontent.com/pod-product-compliance
Ingram Content Group UK Ltd.
Pitfield, Milton Keynes, MK11 3LW, UK
UKHW022059290626
472647UK00010B/433

* 9 7 8 1 0 0 9 6 6 9 3 2 0 *

TAXING PEOPLE

The modern international tax system is a complex framework of national laws, bilateral treaties, and multilateral agreements aimed at coordinating state tax entitlements. Historically, taxation has been based on political allegiance, but globalization and increased mobility pose new challenges. As more people and businesses operate across borders, it becomes harder to determine which states have the right to tax them. Fragmentation of individuals' economic and political lives has complicated states' abilities to balance liberty, justice, and collective decision-making. *Taxing People* addresses taxes on individuals, which are crucial for providing public goods, promoting justice, and legitimizing state power. Exploring the future of individual taxation, the book focuses on global tax governance, social changes including remote work, and the evolving relationship between people and states in a globalized economy. This title is part of the Flip it Open Programme and may also be available with open access. Check our website Cambridge Core for details.

Tsilly Dagan is Professor of Taxation Law at the University of Oxford and a Fellow of Worcester College.

Ruth Mason is the Edwin S. Cohen Distinguished Professor of Law and Taxation at the University of Virginia School of Law and Max Planck Law Fellow.

Taxing People

THE NEXT ONE HUNDRED YEARS

Edited by

TSILLY DAGAN
University of Oxford

RUTH MASON
University of Virginia

CAMBRIDGE
UNIVERSITY PRESS

CAMBRIDGE
UNIVERSITY PRESS

Shaftesbury Road, Cambridge CB2 8EA, United Kingdom

One Liberty Plaza, 20th Floor, New York, NY 10006, USA

477 Williamstown Road, Port Melbourne, VIC 3207, Australia

314–321, 3rd Floor, Plot 3, Splendor Forum, Jasola District Centre, New Delhi – 110025, India

103 Penang Road, #05-06/07, Visioncrest Commercial, Singapore 238467

Cambridge University Press is part of Cambridge University Press & Assessment,
a department of the University of Cambridge.

We share the University's mission to contribute to society through the pursuit of
education, learning and research at the highest international levels of excellence.

www.cambridge.org
Information on this title: www.cambridge.org/9781009669344

DOI: 10.1017/9781009669313

First published 2026

Cover image: Wiley Mason and W. Craghead.

A catalogue record for this publication is available from the British Library

A Cataloging-in-Publication data record for this book is available from the Library of Congress

ISBN 978-1-009-66934-4 Hardback
ISBN 978-1-009-66932-0 Paperback